MAX CHAFKIN is a features editor and tech reporter at *Bloomberg Businessweek*, and has spent fifteen years covering technology and start-ups for publications including *Fast Company, Vanity Fair, Inc.* and the *New York Times Magazine*. His work has been included in the anthologies *Best American Magazine Writing* and *Best Business Writing*, and he has been the recipient of awards from the New York Press Club and the Society for Advancing Business Editing and Writing, among others. A graduate of Yale University, he lives in Queens, New York with his wife and their three children.

The Contrarian

Peter Thiel and Silicon Valley's Pursuit of Power

MAX
CHAFKIN

BLOOMSBURY PUBLISHING
LONDON · OXFORD · NEW YORK · NEW DELHI · SYDNEY

BLOOMSBURY PUBLISHING
Bloomsbury Publishing Plc
50 Bedford Square, London, WC1B 3DP, UK
29 Earlsfort Terrace, Dublin 2, Ireland

BLOOMSBURY, BLOOMSBURY PUBLISHING and the Diana logo
are trademarks of Bloomsbury Publishing Plc

First published in 2021 in the United States by Penguin Press,
an imprint of Penguin Random House LLC
First published in Great Britain 2021
This edition published 2022

A catalogue record for this book is available from the British Library

ISBN: HB: 978-1-5266-1955-6; TPB: 978-1-5266-1956-3; PB: 978-1-5266-1957-0;
eBook: 978-1-5266-1958-7; EPDF: 9781526645548

2 4 6 8 10 9 7 5 3 1

Designed by Meighan Cavanaugh
Printed and bound in Great Britain by CPI Group (UK) Ltd, Croydon CR0 4YY

MIX
Paper from
responsible sources
FSC® C171272

To find out more about our authors and books visit
www.bloomsbury.com and sign up for our newsletters

CONTENTS

INTRODUCTION

t may seem hard to remember, but there was a time when the world seemed ready to put Silicon Valley in charge of everything. This was 2016—the "Age of Unicorns," as business magazines called it, referring to tech companies that were growing so quickly, and had become so valuable, that they seemed almost mythical. Jeff Bezos had saved one of America's great newspapers, Mark Zuckerberg was romancing San Francisco politicos, who'd just named a hospital after him, and transportation activists were showing up in major cities to protest *in favor* of the disruptions brought on by Uber. President Barack Obama, his term winding down, was musing about relocating to California and becoming a tech investor as his next act. Venture capital, he told to reporters that spring, sounded like it could be "very satisfying."

But even as the zeitgeist—all the way up to ambitions of the leader of the free world—celebrated the promise and potential of Silicon Valley, one of Silicon Valley's pioneers had already turned his attention well beyond it. Over the prior two decades, Peter Thiel had accumulated billions of dollars in wealth, backing some of the biggest and most successful tech companies, including Facebook, PayPal, and SpaceX. He'd built a network that gave him access to the best entrepreneurs and the wealthiest investors in the world, and he was idolized by a generation of aspiring startup founders. But Thiel wanted more than sway in Silicon Valley—he wanted real power, political power. He was about to be handed an opportunity to seize it.

It came in the form of what appeared at first to be a minor scandal at Facebook, where Thiel had been an early investor. That May, the tech blog Gizmodo published a report claiming that the opinions of conservatives were being systematically suppressed by the social network. A small team of editors working on a new feature called Trending Topics said they'd been instructed to include stories from mainstream outlets such as CNN and *The New York Times,* but to leave out stories from right-wing media as well as those about fringe topics popular among conservatives, such as the unverified claim that the IRS had been targeting Tea Party–affiliated nonprofits.

The scoop was modest—Trending Topics had nothing to do with the regular news feed, which was curated by algorithm and was full of right-wing content—but it enraged conservatives, who saw it as proof that Facebook was biased in a broader way. The *Drudge Report*, which had been among the banned outlets, led with a giant and unflattering picture of Zuckerberg's deputy Sheryl Sandberg, the author of the book *Lean In*. NOT LEANING IN . . . LEANING LEFT! the headline screamed. FACEBOOK UNDER FIRE was the Fox News chyron.

Facebook denied the allegations, but Zuckerberg sensed that this was a crisis to be managed, and he turned to Thiel to help him. On Wednesday, May 18, a group of sixteen prominent right-wing media personalities were summoned to Menlo Park for a meeting. They included talk show hosts Tucker Carlson, Glenn Beck, and Dana Perino; the presidents of the Tea Party Patriots, the American Enterprise Institute, and the Heritage Foundation; and a handful of others. Officially, they were there to see Zuckerberg and Sandberg, but Thiel was the reason many of them had made the trip.

At forty-eight, he was more than a decade older than the Facebook founder, but the two men had much in common. Like Zuckerberg, Thiel was ruthlessly competitive and awkward in social situations. They'd been close—Thiel had been Zuckerberg's mentor and his patron, the first outside investor in his company and the first person in authority to grasp that Zuckerberg actually knew what he was doing.

Years earlier, Thiel had seen in the Facebook founder—an abrasive, socially inept young man whose chief business qualification at the time was that he'd hacked together a way to rate the attractiveness of his female classmates at Harvard—something huge. After investing in Facebook, Thiel had set up Zuckerberg with absolute control over it, helping to transform the kid with the words "I'm CEO . . . Bitch" on his business cards into the fairly polished capitalist he would become. The relationship had made both men spectacularly rich, and though Thiel no longer owned much Facebook stock, he remained on the company's board and was still very much invested in its influence.

Zuckerberg and Thiel had drifted apart over the previous few years, as Thiel had become more entrenched in the world of conservative politics and Zuckerberg had embraced the spirit of the Obama era, starting a lobbying group aimed at promoting business-friendly immigration reform and pledging billions to the causes of "advancing human potential and promoting equality."

But even as he cultivated Obama and others on the left, Zuckerberg had continued to rely on Thiel as a liaison to the American right. Thiel, according to Zuckerberg's allies, was the company's conservative conscience. "Mark wants to have a balance at Facebook between left and right," said a former Facebook executive. "He doesn't think he can have a healthy debate if everyone's a bleeding-heart Democrat." Zuckerberg's critics saw Thiel's influence on the company as more profound—and more pernicious. He was, in this view, the puppet master: pushing a younger, ideologically uncertain founder toward an alliance with an extremist wing of the Republican party.

As the group of conservative leaders arrived at Facebook's sprawling Frank Gehry–designed headquarters, Thiel and Zuckerberg were a study in shifting generational attitudes toward the concept of business casual. The Facebook founder wore his usual uniform, a gray T-shirt and jeans. Thiel wore a dress shirt with the sleeves rolled up and a pair of hemp-soled shoes. As usual, he carried himself as if braced for a collision—his shoulders hunched forward, his head tucked ever so slightly.

The group sat down at a large table, and Zuckerberg and Sandberg led them through a dense, technical presentation designed to explain that Facebook's software, not editors, selected the vast majority of articles that appeared on Facebook. Zuckerberg asked if there were any questions—which the pundits took as an invitation to light into Facebook, the company's left-leaning employees, and the general sense that Silicon Valley favored liberal causes.

"They were letting him have it," recalled Glenn Beck, the talk radio personality and former Fox News host known for his histrionic conspiracy theories and goofy on-camera antics. "He deserved some of it."

Beck was one of a handful of the attendees whom Thiel had been quietly cultivating. After he'd left Fox News under tense circumstances—rumor had it that Wendi Deng, Rupert Murdoch's wife, had demanded his ouster amid his show's conspiratorial turn during the Obama administration—it was Thiel who'd convinced him to focus on streaming videos and podcasts. "You just have to decide if you are in the future or are you in the past," Thiel had told him.

Beck was fond of Thiel and, in the meeting, assumed the role of Zuckerberg's defender. "You've got thirty people who have spent decades defending freedom of speech," he said, addressing Zuckerberg and gesturing to his colleagues. "And you have this platform that has given hundreds of millions of people the freedom of speech."

Zuckerberg seemed moved by Beck's show of empathy. "We built

Facebook to be a platform for all ideas," he wrote on his Facebook page after the group departed. "Our community's success depends on everyone feeling comfortable sharing anything they want."

The message to employees, and the outside world, was clear: Facebook intended to allow supporters of Donald Trump, who was by then the de facto Republican nominee, to say more or less whatever they wanted on its platform. Over the next several months, misinformation on Facebook—much of it in Trump's favor—outperformed real news. The most popular election headline on Facebook during that period, according to one study, was POPE FRANCIS SHOCKS THE WORLD, ENDORSES DONALD TRUMP FOR PRESIDENT, which, of course, never happened. Another claimed falsely that Wikileaks emails revealed that Hillary Clinton had sold weapons to Islamic State terrorists.

Zuckerberg would eventually apologize—sort of. "We didn't take a broad enough view of our responsibility, and that was a big mistake," he'd later tell Congress when called to answer questions about the ways that Facebook had been used to manipulate the election campaign. But in the moment, the company denied that it was helping to spread misinformation, while downplaying the extent of the Russian government's involvement.

Two months after the meeting in Menlo Park, Thiel formally endorsed Trump, becoming the star of the Republican National Convention in Cleveland. Then, in mid-October, just days after the release of the *Access Hollywood* tape, in which Trump bragged about sexual assault, Thiel donated $1 million to Trump's campaign. The move helped turn a tide of negative press and added to the coffers of a campaign that would buy a barrage of targeted Facebook advertisements as part of a voter suppression strategy designed to discourage potential Clinton supporters.

After the election, Thiel was feted by Trump's inner circle and given an office in Trump Tower, along with the latitude to install his allies in the new administration. "He was something unique," recalled Steve Bannon, who became CEO of the campaign in August. He praised Thiel for bringing intellectual credibility and seriousness to a campaign that struggled at times to convey either. To Bannon and others on the Trumpist right, Thiel was a hero, a key enabler of Trump's unexpected win.

To the left, Thiel was uniquely villainous—a Silicon Valley power broker who'd helped hook Americans on a collection of tech services, then used his influence over those services to elect a candidate who promised to ban Muslims from entering the United States and to deport millions of undocumented immigrants. For years, activist groups had been warning of exactly this kind of thing—of the power that Silicon Valley had been accumulating and of the nationalist undercurrents swelling just below a sheen of left-of-center idealism. The far-right ideas had been there for as long as the tech industry had existed—all the way back to the founding of Stanford University. But it had taken Peter Thiel to bring those ideas above the surface, and then to weaponize them.

THIEL IS SOMETIMES PORTRAYED as the tech industry's token conservative—a view that wildly understates his influence. More than any other Silicon Valley investor or entrepreneur—more so even than Jeff Bezos, or Google founders Larry Page and Sergey Brin, or Zuckerberg himself—he has been responsible for creating the ideology that has come to define Silicon Valley: that technological progress should be pursued relentlessly—with little, if any, regard for potential costs or dangers to society.

Thiel isn't the richest tech mogul—though he's almost certainly better at shielding his assets than the average Valley billionaire, having arranged to pay little in taxes on an investment portfolio worth something like $10 billion—but he has been, in many ways, the most influential. His first company, PayPal, pioneered ecommerce and—after being spun out of the company to which Thiel sold it, eBay—was worth nearly $300 billion, as of early 2021. Palantir, his second company, popularized the concept of data mining after 9/11 and paved the way for what critics of the technology industry call surveillance capitalism. More recently, it became a key player in the Trump administration's immigration and defense projects. The company was worth around $50 billion; Thiel controls it and is its biggest shareholder.

As impressive as this entrepreneurial resume might be, Thiel has been even more influential as an investor and backroom deal maker. He leads the so-called PayPal Mafia, an informal network of interlocking financial and personal relationships that dates back to the late 1990s. This group includes Elon Musk, plus the founders of YouTube, Yelp, and LinkedIn. They would provide the capital to Airbnb, Lyft, Spotify, Stripe, DeepMind—now better known as Google's world-leading artificial intelligence project—and, of course, to Facebook.

In doing so, Thiel and his friends helped transform what was once a regional business hub—on par with Boston and a few other midsized American metro areas—into the undisputed engine of America's economy and culture. In 1996, there were no tech companies among the five most valuable traded on U.S. exchanges; in 2021 the entire top five consisted of U.S. tech companies. Today, the most prolific Hollywood studio is Netflix. More Americans get their news from social media, primarily Facebook, than from cable television.

This growth hasn't been entirely benign. The tech industry, which is still seen by many as a cultural backwater full of socially clumsy but well-meaning nerds, is now an acquisitive and seemingly amoral force, one capable of producing new forms of entertainment, new mediums of communication, and a better way to hail a taxi, but one that is also indifferent to the addiction, radicalization, and economic privation that have come with these advances. The Ubers and Airbnbs America embraced in 2016 had costs. They replaced salaried jobs of taxi drivers and hotel workers with lower-wage, lower-security gigs, and then aggressively thwarted efforts by governments to rein them in.

This shift was part and parcel with Thiel's other project: an attempt to impose a brand of extreme libertarianism that shifts power from traditional institutions toward startup companies and the billionaires who control them. The Thiel ideology is complicated and, in parts, self-contradictory, and will take many of the pages that follow to explore, but it combines an obsession with technological progress with nationalist politics—a politics that at times has seemingly flirted with white supremacy. Sweetening what might otherwise be a rather sour concoction is Thiel's personal story—a journey from washout corporate lawyer to dot-com billionaire that he has recounted many times in college lectures, speeches, and in his book, *Zero to One*. The libertarian success manual also argues that monopolies are good, that monarchies are the most efficient form of government, and that tech founders are godlike. It has sold more than 1.25 million copies worldwide.

For the young people who admire him, watch and rewatch his talks, write social media odes to his genius, and buy his books, Thiel is like Ayn Rand crossed with one of her fictional characters. He is both libertarian philosopher *and* a builder—Howard Roark with a YouTube following. The most avid acolytes among these fanboys and fangirls become Thiel Fellows; his foundation pays them $100,000 each to drop out of college and start companies. Others have taken jobs within his coterie of advisers, whom he supports financially and who promote and defend him, his friends, and his ideas. These people sometimes talk about a "Thiel-verse," a world with its own laws, its own morality, and, always, a gravitational pull toward the patron. As Thiel has become more powerful, those laws have become the laws of Silicon Valley itself. They increasingly seem to have purchase well beyond it.

Thiel's worldview has become so influential that it shows up even among his adversaries. Google's former chair, Eric Schmidt, whom Thiel has skewered as a monopolist and a "minister of propaganda," proclaimed himself "a big fan" of Thiel, praising in particular his campaign of revenge against Gawker Media. That campaign, in which Thiel secretly financed a lawsuit brought by the wrestler Hulk Hogan against the company, drove Gawker out of business in 2016. Thiel's efforts combined financial pressure and deception—an approach that free-speech advocates have criticized sharply but that Schmidt said left him "very impressed." "We need people who can challenge orthodoxy, and he is willing and delighted to do so," he said. Schmidt, a liberal who served as an adviser to Hillary Clinton's campaign, told me he considers Thiel's support of Trump admirable and "part of his contrarian view of the world."

This has been the consensus view on Thiel—that he is a consummate freethinker, a man constitutionally incapable of following the herd. It's one that Thiel himself has endorsed at times. "Maybe I do always have this background program running where I'm trying to think of, 'O.K., what's the opposite of what you're saying?' and then I'll try that," he said shortly after the 2016 election. "It works surprisingly often."

Even so, Thiel's role in Trump's rise to power stunned members of the tech press, as well as some of Thiel's friends. How, they wondered, could a bookish, gay immigrant from the most liberal part of California, who'd gotten rich in the world's most globalized industry, who seemed so profoundly committed to the promise of a better future, come to support a reactionary would-be authoritarian? I was transfixed by another question: How had Thiel, who'd arrived in Silicon Valley in the mid-'90s as an unknown, failed financier, come to wield so much power? He was a contrarian, yes, but contrarianism is a methodology, not an ideology. What exactly, I wondered, did Thiel actually believe? And how deeply embedded were those beliefs in Silicon Valley itself?

IN 2007, when I was a junior reporter with *Inc.*, a small business magazine, I'd sat in Elon Musk's cubicle at what was then the very modest headquarters of SpaceX, his rocket company. Musk was on the phone, half-listening to a conference call and checking his email at the same time. While I waited for him, I stared at a poster for the movie *Thank*

You for Smoking, based on the novel by Christopher Buckley, son of William F. Buckley and a former speechwriter for George H. W. Bush.

The credits listed on the poster included Musk's name, along with those of several other PayPal Mafiosi: Mark Woolway, a PayPal vice president, and David Sacks, the company's COO. Thiel's name was there, too. By then, he already had a reputation as a bomb thrower, which made the movie, a satire in which the hero is a tobacco industry lobbyist, seem appropriate. Peter Thiel *would* be a fan of Big Tobacco—or, at least, he'd be totally fine being seen that way.

Later that day, Musk told me the story of his firing from PayPal. He'd been the victim of a secret boardroom plot, masterminded by Thiel while he was on his honeymoon. Musk forgave Thiel eventually. "I buried their hatchet," he said, referring to Thiel and his coconspirators. He reached behind his back, miming the removal of a blade from his left scapula. During the interview—and in another much more recent one for this book—Musk managed to affect grace while also making it clear that he does not entirely trust Silicon Valley's most important venture capitalist.

From that point on, Thiel seemed to hang behind or above or somewhere in the middle of almost every story I reported about the tech industry, and increasingly, many stories beyond it. In 2011, years before progressives started talking about free college, Thiel was warning about rising tuition prices, calling the higher education industry a bubble more troubling than the one in real estate. He helped to jumpstart the backlash against big tech in 2014 when he called Google a monopoly—years before Elizabeth Warren or Bernie Sanders would. And then, of course, came his destruction of Gawker and the election of Trump.

In 2018, I started interviewing former employees, business partners, and other associates—in Silicon Valley, Washington, D.C., and elsewhere—to try to understand how this had happened. Thiel had come to the tech industry with little in the way of money and no engineering ability to speak of. He had no special social graces, and rarely seems to enjoy himself. He speaks haltingly. He is not charismatic, at least not in any traditional sense.

What I learned was eye-opening: Thiel, according to his friends, is brilliant—capable of visionary insights and with an uncanny ability to know exactly how to win. He has the special ability to see life like a chess game—using his friends, his business partners, and his portfolio companies as means to an end. There was a less appealing side to this, of course. The Machiavellian tendencies could make him coldly transactional, to the point, sometimes, of cruelty.

I'd expected Thiel's close friends to blandly sing his praises. Some did. But the more common reaction to my questions, from Thiel's friends— people in positions of political power; businesspeople worth many, many millions of dollars; investors able to command the attention of billionaires— was not admiration, exactly. It was fear. They told me they were scared of him. He was that powerful, and he was that vindictive.

During one of these early interviews, a person who has known Thiel for many years, with a successful career in Silicon Valley built in part thanks to associations with Thiel's network, told me to stop my digital audio recorder. "I'm paranoid," he said. Then he proceeded to share a series of anecdotes that portrayed his patron as an incredible investor, with a knack for identifying and nurturing young talent, but who had a ruthlessness that made him uncomfortable.

Then he got personal. "Why do you want to write this book?" he asked. "I mean, aren't you worried he'll, like, come after you?"

As I write this, a cohort of the Valley's investors and entrepreneurs— nearly all of them with strong financial and social ties to Thiel—have decided that even the act of reporting critically on Thiel and his friends is no longer acceptable. Balaji Srinivasan, an investor who was one of Thiel's picks to lead the FDA under Trump—has argued that the media deserves to be destroyed and replaced by something he calls "full stack narrative"—public relations, in other words. "Builders must critique the critiques," he tweeted, using the Randian word for *entrepreneur* that is favored by Thiel and his friends. "Stop the people standing athwart the future yelling stop. It's your duty."

In certain circles, Thiel's name itself is a verb. To "Peter Thiel" a media outlet or a journalist is to bankrupt them, à la Gawker. The suit, which led to a $140 million verdict against a media company that had published a series of unflattering posts that suggested that Thiel was a "so-called visionary" and disclosed that he is gay, sent an unmistakable message to critics: those who publicly criticize Thiel, or any of his friends, do so at their peril.

Because of his track record for trying to hurt those who've attempted to uncover his secrets, many of the more than 150 former employees, business partners, friends, and others with whom I spoke over the course of hundreds of hours of interviews for this book insisted on anonymity. Thiel's most powerful allies fear him and so, naturally, do some of his former middle-school classmates. I was in communication with Thiel throughout all this—mostly through intermediaries. I'd met him once in 2011, and we met again, in person, in 2019. He insisted that the meeting be off the record. He declined to respond to a lengthy list of fact-checking questions.

My goal, in the pages that follow, is to try to understand a man who has made billions of dollars in part by being inscrutable. I wanted to understand how he'd managed to build such a devoted following and how he'd been able to so consistently make the right bets, even when they seemed crazy. I wanted to understand how somebody so respected and beloved could have gotten that way while also acting ruthlessly. Was Thiel a genius worthy of admiration and study, or a sociopathic nihilist? Could he be both?

These questions matter because they are the same ones we are asking of the big tech companies that the Thielverse gave us. In part because he was instrumental in building it, and in part because so many powerful people came to admire and copy him, much of Silicon Valley is today a reflection of Thiel's worldview, for better or worse. If we want to understand Zuckerberg or the new monopoly capitalism—or for that matter the Trumpian far-right, which Thiel nurtured secretly too—we need to understand him.

1

FUCK YOU, WORLD

n Foster City, California, in 1980, Peter Thiel and a small group of eighth-grade boys were crammed around a table in a tiny box of a kitchen, their faces hidden behind three-ring binders that had been stood on end for privacy. Their eyes were trained on a map and a set of many-sided dice.

The homes in the San Francisco suburb were modest, packed close together under the hulking San Mateo–Hayward Bridge. The span connected Silicon Valley—the name for the military research parks and corporate campuses clustered up and down the 101 freeway on the San Francisco Peninsula—to Oakland and the industrial East Bay. Foster City, which had been built in the 1960s after real estate developers drained a marsh by digging a series of narrow lagoons, felt close to neither of these places. It was Levittown-by-the-Sea, full of mostly white, working-class families who'd been drawn to the promise of decent schools, safety, and bayfront property. The children of Foster City, the kids at the kitchen table, weren't the children of the geniuses who'd built Intel or Hewlett-Packard; their parents were firefighters and schoolteachers and, in the case of Peter Thiel, a mining engineer who went to work in boots and a hard hat.

Thiel's friends were the nerds, and, being nerds in 1980, they played Dungeons & Dragons on weekend nights. Though commonly understood as a board game, D&D is less about winning and losing than it is about fantasy storytelling. The game called for each boy to create an imaginary character for himself. Wizards, barbarians, druids, and monks were among the many options, each with different skills. Wizards cast spells, barbarians are ferocious in combat, and so on. A final player took on the role of narrator and referee; he was in charge of coming up with an adventure for these characters.

This narrator was known as the dungeon master, and although the role was supposed to rotate, Peter—skinny, brilliant, and painfully, painfully serious—would always try to claim the job for himself. "You get to determine the reality," said a man who used to play with him. "He liked that quiet control."

Besides being an escape, D&D carried a hint of danger, at least for the boys' parents. After a seventeen-year-old gamer from Michigan killed himself in 1980, there had been a moral panic among Christian conservatives who worried about the mind-warping potential of a game that encouraged teenagers to playact magic, witchcraft, and other blasphemies. The kids in Foster City laughed this off, but it may have explained why Thiel, whose parents were deeply religious, never once invited them to play at his house.

He told people he was from Cleveland, and he spoke English without an accent, but he was also clearly foreign. He was smart and self-possessed, but he also seemed joyless. "I can't remember him laughing. I never saw him smile," said a friend who knew him back then. "You could tell there was something . . . a nice way of saying it would be *structured*—about his family."

HIS PARENTS, Klaus and Susanne Thiel, had come to the United States in 1968 from Frankfurt, Germany, where the year before, in October, Peter Andreas Thiel was born. Klaus, then in his early thirties, worked for Arthur G. McKee & Co., an American engineering consultancy, which specialized in the construction of oil refineries, steel plants, and other heavy industries. He'd graduated with the equivalent of a bachelor's degree from Staatliche Ingenieurschule Dortmund—a forerunner of the modern TU Dortmund University. The following year, 1968, McKee moved the little family to the United States, where Klaus enrolled in a graduate engineering program at Case Western Reserve University.

The move would have been jarring. West Germany, consumed with rebuilding from the war and suspicious of mass social movements, had been late to the counterculture, which had barely hit West Berlin, let alone the country's financial capital. Frankfurt in the late 1950s and early '60s was a boomtown, and full of pious white Christians like the Thiels.

Cleveland, by contrast, was pulsing with the currents of free love, Black power, and, worst of all to any good West German, communism. Two years earlier, in 1966, a white-owned bar in Hough, about a mile and a half from the Case Western engineering school, refused to serve a Black man and then posted a sign: "No water for n——." A mob formed and attacked the bar, and then moved on to other businesses, looting and setting fires. In the summer of 1968, there was a riot near campus after police and a radical group, the Black Nationalists of New Libya, engaged in a four-hour gun battle and standoff, resulting in seven deaths and days of looting, fires, and militaristic police operations. As if racial tensions could have been further inflamed, reporters later learned that the New Libyans had received a $6,000 redevelopment grant—part of a program created by the city's newly elected Black mayor, Carl Stokes—which they used to buy their weapons.

Several weeks later, in August, Richard Nixon, then running as a uni-
fying candidate, but who'd implicitly promised to stop Black people, hippies, and sexual nonconformists from overrunning America, accepted the
Republican nomination for president. "We see cities enveloped in smoke
and flame," Nixon said, praising the "great majority of Americans, the
forgotten Americans, the non-shouters, the non-demonstrators." Thiel's
parents would be fanatical Republicans, and their son would absorb the
sentiment, too, coming to identify with these non-shouters, venerating the
Nixon era as well as Nixon's political successor, Ronald Reagan.

The Thiel family, which added a fourth member, Peter's younger
brother, Patrick, in 1971, was stern. Not long after his brother had been
born, Peter's father would explain death to him in terms that—as Thiel
relayed them years later—would seem cold, bordering on cruel. Peter, in
an existential mode for perhaps the first time, had asked Klaus about a
rug in their apartment, which Klaus explained was made out of the hide
of a dead cow.

"Death happens to all animals. All people," Klaus said. "It will happen to me one day. It will happen to you one day."

This moment would be deeply upsetting to the three-year-old boy,
and to the man, decades later. Most children—either through the love of
their parents or through a happy sort of cognitive dissonance—recover
from these early encounters with their own mortality. Thiel never did
and would return to the cow—and the brutal, finality of the thing—
again and again, even in middle age.

Klaus earned his master's degree over the next six years, becoming a
project manager who oversaw a team of engineers on mine projects. His
specialty was the construction of open-pit mines, which involves exca-
vating huge mounds of dirt and rock and then treating them chemically
to extract minerals. The family moved frequently, and Klaus traveled
even more, often spending weeks at a time on job sites far from home.

After Cleveland, the family chose for their new home a place that
couldn't have been more different than the relatively diverse city where

Thiel had spent his early years: apartheid South Africa. Klaus was assigned to work on the construction of a uranium mine in the Namib desert, not far from the town of Swakopmund, in modern-day Namibia.

For Peter, there was a stop at Pridwin, an elite whites-only English prep school in Johannesburg, followed by two years at the Deutsche Grundschule—the public German-language school—in Swakopmund. It was a lonely time. A picture from that era shows a sullen boy in shorts, knickers, and a tie, carrying an adult-sized briefcase. A grade-school classmate in Namibia, Georg Erb, recalled Thiel as smart but withdrawn. He had "that distinct, striking, smart look about him, almost like he seemed bored," Erb said. "We didn't really mingle a lot with Peter in school though. We always knew the miners' kids would not stay long in town."

The work that Klaus had been hired to do was sensitive. South Africa, which administered Namibia as a client state called South West Africa, was already coming under pressure over the apartheid system and had been attempting to create a clandestine nuclear weapons program. The Rössing Mine, which Klaus was building, was a crucial part of that plan—a way for South Africa to survive U.S. attempts to cut it off economically and to defend itself in the event of a Soviet attack. Mineworkers had no illusions about this. "Rössing mined Uranium in direct contravention of the United Nations," said Pierre Massyn, a public relations executive who worked there in the early 1980s. "It was my job to tell the world that our presence was justified."

To mine uranium in South West Africa was not just to be complicit in the preservation of the apartheid system, it was to exploit that system. Rössing was said to be better than some of the forced labor operations in South Africa itself, but was still known for conditions not far removed from indentured servitude. Migrant workers served under yearlong contracts before being forced to return to their "homeland"—as the apartheid regime described the semiautonomous Black-only areas. White managers, like the Thiels, had access to a brand-new medical and dental center in

Swakopmund and membership in the company country club. Black laborers, including some with families, lived in a dorm in a work-camp near the mine and did not have access to the medical facilities provided to whites. Walking off the job was a criminal offense, and workers who failed to carry their ID card into the mine were routinely thrown in jail for the day.

Uranium mining is, by nature, risky. A report published after the end of apartheid by the Namibia Support Committee, a pro-independence group, described conditions at the mine in grim terms, including an account of a contract laborer on the construction project—the project Klaus's company was helping to oversee—who said workers had not been told they were building a uranium mine and were thus unaware of the risks of radiation. The only clue had been that white employees would hand out wages from behind glass, seemingly trying to avoid contamination themselves. The report mentioned workers "dying like flies," in 1976, while the mine was under construction.

Thiel experienced his two-and-a-half years in southern Africa much differently. He would recall hours spent reading or playing alone in a dusty riverbed behind the family's house, or playing chess if either Klaus or Susanne was willing.

The Thiels returned to Cleveland the year the mine opened, but they only stayed a year. Their next stop was California, where Klaus had been detailed to the construction of a new gold mine, in Knoxville, a desolate corner of high desert, west of Sacramento. Perhaps having learned their lesson from their time in Cleveland, the Thiels settled down in the kind of idyllic suburb befitting the Reagan revolution: Foster City. They paid $120,000 for a three-bedroom house on Whalers' Island, which stuck out into an artificial lake like a fist; each of its four small peninsulas had a single road ending with a cul-de-sac.

At Foster City's Bowditch Middle School, Thiel was placed on a gifted and talented track and told, over and over again, that he was destined for greatness. "We were so bought into this sense that you had to get good grades to get into a good college and that your entire happiness depends on that," said Nishanga Bliss, a classmate of Thiel's. One spring, as a joke, Thiel's history teacher told the class that no one would be getting an A, then waited a beat while the class recoiled in shocked silence before dropping the punch line. "April Fools'!"

Among the academically chosen, Peter was widely understood to be the best—the one with the top grades and the highest test scores. And unlike the rest of his social circle, who knew they were nerds and were vaguely ashamed about that fact, Peter didn't seem to really care. In his friends' yearbooks, along with the see-you-this-summers and the nice-knowing-yous, Thiel taunted: "Maybe you'll come within one point of me."

"In our generation being smart was not cool," said a friend. "I remember working hard to hide that I was intelligent. Peter never tried to hide the fact that he was the smartest guy in the room." Everybody, even the nerds, played soccer or baseball and pretended to like it—except Peter.

Chess was his game of choice. In 1972, just before Thiel turned five, Bobby Fischer, the reclusive and combative onetime prodigy, had become the first American to win the World Chess Championship. As Americans watched—the "Match of the Century" was the first to be televised in prime time in the United States—Fischer beat the Soviet champion Boris Spassky. The win, which marked the first time a non-Soviet had held the title since 1948, was presented as a testament to the achievements of American capitalism. The new champion was welcomed home with a Bobby Fischer Day and appeared on the cover of *Sports Illustrated*. The ranks of high school and middle school chess teams ballooned accordingly.

At San Mateo, which Thiel entered in 1981, the chess club had dozens of members and attracted crowds when it met for lunchtime matches. They played speed chess—a variation in which players have a limited amount of time, generally between five or ten minutes each for the entire game—or bughouse, a team sport where players can capture pieces and then pass them to a partner to play. The club maintained a leaderboard with slots for thirty spots; Thiel, who kept a sticker on his chess set that boasted "born to win," always had his card in the first spot. He was the best in the school and, at least for a time, among the best chess players in the United States under the age of thirteen.

If he did suffer a defeat, the normally stoic young man would lose his cool. Once, at a tournament, he was playing a scrimmage match for fun in between games and seemed to be only half paying attention. His opponent was inexperienced and, not really aware of what was happening, put Peter in check. Then he realized, to both of their surprise, that it was actually checkmate. Peter became visibly distraught and was unable to regain his composure for the rest of the tournament and lost the rest of the matches he played. A defeat, even a meaningless one, was too much to handle.

When he wasn't busy being the best at chess, Thiel immersed himself in worlds of fantasy and science fiction. There was Dungeons & Dragons, of course, plus J. R. R. Tolkien, whom he read and reread obsessively—so much that he'd later brag he'd memorized the entire *Lord of the Rings* trilogy. He also played video games, including Zork, a crude, choose-your-own-adventure game that he played on a Tandy TRS 80 that Klaus brought home.

The computer revolution was happening just miles to the south, where Apple Computer, a company founded by another American prodigy, Steve Jobs, now had more than $100 million in sales. Klaus had been an early adopter, urging his coworkers at the California gold mine to use computers, and his son picked up his interest in technology. Peter programmed a little, but what really grabbed him were visions of the future. He read Isaac Asimov and Arthur C. Clarke, writers who conjured humanoid robots, space travel, moon settlements, petroleum-based foods to cure hunger, cars that floated on the air instead of rolling on wheels, and immortality.

He was not a popular boy. A classmate—and fellow geek—said that he and others were "in awe" of Peter, but found him inscrutable, distant, and haughty. "I don't know that he had any close friends," he said. Thiel's smarts and his physique—he was small and very slender as a high schooler—made him a target for bullies. A friend, Kevin Wacknov, recalled that Thiel had been pushed around early on in high school.

All of this—and, though it was never remarked upon, the fact that his mannerisms could be subtly effeminate—made him a target of mockery, even among people who considered themselves Thiel's friends. One of his classmates' favorite tricks was to drive around the neighborhood at night looking for houses with for sale signs in the front yard. They'd grab as many signs as they could—sometimes twelve or more—and then drive straight to Whalers' Island and set them up on the front yard of Peter's house.

"Peter, I hear you're moving," they would say the next day. It seemed funny the first time they did it. "It's obvious in retrospect that what we were doing was bullying," said one of the pranksters. "I've always thought he might have a list of people he's going to kill somewhere and that I'm on it."

As he matured physically, Thiel's confidence grew. By his junior year, he was good looking, with a defined jaw, an angular nose, and a sweep of light brown hair that he wore parted to the side. His academic accomplishments proceeded on schedule: He was the best at chess, the best on the math team, and a National Merit Scholar with a near-perfect score on his SAT. He was not confident so much as disdainful, walking around with an expression that, according to a friend, said "Fuck you, world."

THE 1984-85 EDITION of the *Elm*, San Mateo High School's yearbook, is dedicated to memories of dances, football games, lunches on the school's green, and surfing at the beaches on the other side of the Peninsula. Peter Thiel makes no appearances in any of these social pages, but he showed up on nearly all of the pages dedicated to San Mateo's clubs and academic societies. This was a departure from previous years, and probably, classmates assumed, an effort by the least well-rounded guy anyone knew to present himself as appropriately well-rounded to college admissions officers.

He stands, confidently, in the front of the aerospace club, wearing a blue Members Only–style windbreaker and a Casio digital watch; he poses, in deep contemplation, over a chessboard; he looms over members of the German and Latin clubs. He also appears with the science club, the Model U.N., the executive council, and, posing with a pen and a pile of documents, as if he were about to file a legal brief, on the superlatives page. He'd been voted Most Likely to Succeed.

Thiel's senior quote was from *The Hobbit*: "The greatest adventure is what lies ahead / Today and tomorrow are yet to be said." Years later he'd say that he'd memorized the entire passage, which continues: "The chances, the changes are all yours to make / The mold of your life is in your hands to break." It would become, in a way, the motto of his life— though it was still, at this point, a confused life. The passage is not, in fact, from Tolkien, who wrote *The Hobbit,* as well as the *Lord of the Rings* trilogy, books Thiel obsessed over. It is from a theme song, written by Jules Bass, creative genius behind the 1980s cartoon *ThunderCats*, for the animated version of *The Hobbit*, which had come out in 1977. That spring, Thiel got into Stanford, his dream school. Among his classmates, legend had it that on the application, Peter had been asked to pick a word that best describes himself, and Thiel chose "intelligent."

From then on, friends noticed Peter becoming more distant, as if he'd already moved on from Foster City. He never tried to settle scores, never confronted his old tormentors. In their yearbooks, in addition to the usual taunts about his scores being better than theirs, he indicated that he had little desire to see them again. "Have a good summer and a good life," he told Bliss, noting, at once somehow cold-blooded and sweet, "I could never (even hypothetically) have aborted you." Bliss thinks she must have shared the fact that her mother's pregnancy had been un-planned, and thinks Thiel was trying to be nice, in a profoundly strange way. He signed the note, "Love, Peter Thiel."

Thiel had always been aloof but now he seemed indifferent to everything—high school, his friends, his teachers—and he started push-ing the boundaries. According to a classmate, Thiel put out the word to younger students that he would take their SAT for them for $500 per test. At Stanford that fall, two classmates recall Thiel talking about the side business. One said he asked for ways to "arrange untraceable pay-ments."

It would be the first instance in a long career of using his intelligence and irrepressible disregard for norms to profit. It was also, given Thiel's ambitions and the possibility of losing his spot at Stanford, unbelievably risky. But Thiel didn't seem to care. He had no more fealty to the aca-demic rules than he did to the other social niceties he ignored. Maybe that's what made him different, what it meant when he said he was "born to win."

2

A STRANGE, STRANGE BOY

The annual commencement, at what was then known as the Leland Stanford Junior University, featured two hundred or so young men and a few women who'd gathered inside Assembly Hall on a Wednesday in May 1907 to hear from the Bay Area's original right-wing bomb thrower.

After a quick lesson on the history of the word *maverick*, which had once referred to free-roaming cows that had not been branded by a ranch, Stanford's president, David Starr Jordan, suggested that the college's sixteenth graduating class should follow the lead of those liberty-loving bovines. "My plea this morning, is for the human maverick—for the man who is born free, with no man's brand or tag upon him—as the hope of free institutions in America," Jordan said in a speech that appeared in the *Stanford Daily*.

By academic training, he was an ichthyologist—a fish biologist—but Jordan had won fame as a wunderkind college president, first of Indiana University, which he took over at age thirty-four, and then, six years later, as the first president of California's answer to the Ivy League. Jordan would become infamous as a eugenicist; in October 2020, Stanford announced it would remove his name from its buildings. But the commencement speech was less concerned with his racist theories than it was with a very specific notion of freedom—that is, for Stanford graduates to operate free from government interference or regulation.

A year earlier, Upton Sinclair had published *The Jungle*, an exposé about working conditions in the Chicago meatpacking industry. Jordan held that the "true moral" of the book was not that workers were being exploited by factory owners and other capitalists, as Sinclair intended, but that the problem was the workers themselves. "The moral is found in the danger to free institutions of the presence of hordes of people who are not and cannot be free, who crowd the slums of great cities, who cannot take care of their own rights," Jordan said. The true victims in other words were factory *owners*, who were being unfairly maligned for treating workers as they ought to be treated. "Whole races of men were born to be exploited," he said, "but woe unto the nation that exploits them."

There was no doubt in Jordan's mind—and likely in the minds of his audience—that the new graduates were destined to be exploiters, and it was their rights he was interested in defending. They were, Jordan said, members of a new "aristocracy of brains," which he called "the final purpose of democracy." He urged these newly minted aristocrats to preserve America as a redoubt for individual freedom, especially the freedom from paying high taxes. They would be "standing together as watchdogs of the treasury, as guardians of the rights of the taxpayers of California."

This ultraconservative worldview—albeit with Jordan's white supremacy omitted from official histories, though perhaps never entirely absent from the psyche—would embed itself thoroughly into the character of the university. Stanford would later attract Herbert Hoover's conservative think tank and its commitment, according to a mission statement, "to demonstrate the evils of the doctrines of Karl Marx, whether Communism, Socialism, economic materialism, or atheism."

The Hoover Institution had been founded in 1919 as a library for archives from World War I by the future president and adamant opponent of the New Deal. But it expanded its ambitions in the 1940s and '50s, becoming increasingly political and looming, literally and figuratively, over student life for the rest of the twentieth century. Its 285-foot tower was the campus's tallest building and its defining landmark. The institution's executive director, W. Glenn Campbell, would serve as a senior adviser to Barry Goldwater's 1964 presidential run. Ten years later, he named Goldwater's ideological successor, California governor Ronald Reagan, an honorary fellow.

By the time Thiel showed up on campus, in September 1985, Reagan was into his second term as president, and the White House was full of Hoover Institution alumni and fellows, including Martin Anderson, the economist credited with writing a policy memo that led to Reaganomics. Reagan had appointed at least thirty of Anderson's Stanford colleagues to prominent positions, crediting the university with having "built the knowledge base that made the changes now taking place in Washington possible," as Reagan put it at a White House reception for the group. Stanford became the presumed future home of the Reagan presidential library and the place where many of the brightest conservatives were coming to be groomed for positions of power.

Importantly to Thiel, Stanford was also the best of the best. *U.S. News & World Report* had ranked it ahead of Harvard, Yale, and Princeton over the previous two years. The place should have been perfect for him.

INSTEAD, THIEL FOUND STANFORD wildly disappointing, and he was unhappy from his first day on campus. He was assigned to Branner Hall, a Mission-style building that housed 147 first-year students a few blocks from the main quad. He shared suite 240 with two other students: Greg Louden, a marching band geek, and Chris Adamson, an aspiring comedy writer who that spring ran for a student government seat on a platform that called for a campus-wide hide-and-seek game in which the college president would have to find every registered student. They seemed to regard Thiel with a mixture of derision and wonder.

Thiel had expected great books and scholarly quietude. What he got, in dorm life anyway, was silliness. The university's residence halls had sundecks, which were typically filled with shirtless men and bikini-clad women, and music blasted from speakers during what should have been study hours. They drank; they smoked pot; they hooked up. Needless to say, Thiel did not partake in any of it. He didn't really seem interested in making friends. "So many (myself included) were deeply unserious from his point of view," said someone who lived in Branner that year.

Each morning, Peter would emerge from suite 240, walk to the water fountain, and make a big show of taking his vitamins, one by one, always at the same time, in the same order, always taking a sip in between pills, as if intent on showing his classmates that he was, in every way, superior to his hungover peers. "It was like a ritual," said classmate Megan Maxwell. "He was a strange, strange boy."

Thiel approached his schoolwork with the same intensity. He wanted to learn, but more than that he wanted to excel, to dominate his peers. He was out of the dorm by 8 a.m., and generally stayed away until the library closed. In early 1986, after Christmas break, Thiel opened an envelope containing his grades, and learned he'd earned a 4.0 GPA—an achievement that would help him receive a President's Award that year as one of the top first-year students. He celebrated by finding the only other student he knew who also got a 4.0 GPA and arguing for ten minutes about why his 4.0 was "better" because it included more classes in which he'd gotten an A+. "That's freshman Peter in a nutshell," a classmate recalled.

Outside of competing over the best grades, Peter had only two interests, at least as far as his classmates could perceive: chess and politics. He was conservative, for Reagan and against Alan Cranston, California's three-term senator, who won a fourth term in 1986—though those views made him a rather conventional type at Stanford. Reagan had just won in the biggest landslide since the unopposed election of James Monroe in 1820, and the undergraduate class had quite a few aspiring William F. Buckleys.

Not that Thiel spent much time mixing with them, either—at least not at first. Each Friday afternoon during his first year, he would get in his old Volkswagen Rabbit and make the twenty-mile drive back to Foster City to spend the weekend in the little house on Whalers' Island with Klaus, Susanne, and Patrick, by now a junior in high school. Thiel's lack of interest in socializing, combined with his affected superiority and his general squareness, all made him a target for mockery among his peers. When a group of his fellow students made an audiotape featuring comedy skits about Branner hijinks, the only mention of Thiel was several seconds during which someone said "Good-bye" in a haughty tone, slammed a car door, turned the engine, and drove off. "God," said one of the tape's creators, "we were such dicks to him."

Another time, Thiel swore while quoting one of his roommates. The roommate responded by printing up a mock commemorative sign and taping it to the ceiling. It had the date—January 1986—and declared, "Under this spot, Peter Thiel first said the word fuck." It stayed there for the rest of the semester, like the FOR SALE signs his high school friends had put on display in front of his parent's house. This elicited laughs from the rest of the hall—from everybody but Thiel, who didn't notice it and wasn't told. In May, he was all packed up and preparing to leave the dorm for the final time when someone directed his attention to the sign.

"Dude," one of his roommates said. "Look up." He looked up and then, wordless, moved his desk under the marker, stepped up, tore it down, and left for the summer.

His vanity left him open to further mockery, as well as subtle manipulation. At one point, his classmates hatched a plan to trick Peter into getting drunk by challenging him to a made-up game called "beer chess." The rule was you had to chug every time you lost a piece—but the real concept was to see if Peter Thiel was capable of relaxing for an hour or two. Peter was the superior chess player, of course, but Greg, the marching band guy, was half-decent, and they figured he might be able to get enough of Peter's pieces early enough in the game to make it a fun night. Peter couldn't resist the challenge, chugging a few beers and easily winning the game. He never stopped scowling.

THE MOCKERY WASN'T about politics, at least not initially, but that was how Thiel processed it. "He viewed liberals through a lens as people who were not nice to him," said a classmate. "The way people treated him at Stanford had a huge impact. That's still with him." He hadn't been aggressively political in high school, but at Stanford he began to embrace a new identity—that of the right-wing provocateur.

He joked about starting a fake charity, Liberals for Peace, that would simply raise money based on a vague agenda of lefty causes and then do absolutely nothing with the money except pay him. And on at least two occasions, he told peers that he thought their concern about apartheid was overblown.

"It works," he told Megan Maxwell during a conversation about the push to get colleges and companies to stop doing business with the apartheid state. At the time, Black student associations around the country, including at Stanford, had been conducting sit-ins to encourage divestment from South Africa—protests that would have felt at least a little bit personal to Thiel, who often spoke fondly of his childhood in South Africa. Maxwell said she was taken aback as he explained matter-of-factly that the country should not be held to the moral standards of American students, without at any point acknowledging that Maxwell, as a Black woman, might find this offensive. "He said it with no affect," recalled Maxwell. "That was possibly the creepiest thing about it."

Another African American student, Julie Lythcott-Haims, confronted Thiel about his pro-apartheid stance, knocking on the door of suite 240 one night and asking him to clarify. Thiel looked at her blankly and, according to Lythcott-Haims's account, told her that South Africa's systematic denial of civil rights to Black people was economically sound. Any moral issues were irrelevant. The point—a common one made by apologists of the apartheid state at the time—seemed to be that South Africa was much more developed than its neighbors and that life there, even for those who were systematically denied their rights, was better than it was in, say, Ethiopia or Burundi.

In the years that followed, Lythcott-Haims would attend Harvard Law School, practice law at the big corporate firm Cooley LLP, and serve as a dean at Stanford Law School, before becoming a bestselling author. (Her book *How to Raise an Adult* is a critique of so-called helicopter parenting.) Even so, she would write in 2016 that the exchange "stuck like a lump in my throat for 30 years." Thiel's spokesman responded that Thiel had "no recollection of a stranger demanding his views on apartheid" and that he had "never supported it."

Thiel eventually joined the College Republicans and discovered Ayn Rand. He also became friendly with Robert Hamerton-Kelly, a South African academic and theologian who was dean of the chapel at Stanford and minister of the big nondenominational church on campus, whose growing membership he'd ascribed to "the same forces that elected Ronald Reagan." Hamerton-Kelly was a moderate on South Africa; he was against apartheid but confessed feeling "ambivalence" and favored partial, rather than a full, divestment.

Thiel and the minister had something else in common besides South African roots: a shared admiration and fascination with another iconoclast on campus, René Girard, who frequently lectured at events organized by student religious groups. A professor of French literature, Girard was an intellectual celebrity in France, if not at Stanford. He was unusual on campus in that he was openly devout, and he made his Christianity central to his worldview.

Girard's big idea—which Thiel would internalize and adopt as a guiding principle, both in investing and in life—was that people are motivated, at their core, by a desire to imitate one another. We don't want the things we want, Girard argued, because we judge them to be good; we want them because other people want them. This "mimetic desire" was universal, leading to envy and, in turn, violence. Societies had historically used scapegoating—turning the violent impulse on a single, innocent member of the community—to channel and control these feelings, providing an outlet that staved off wars and mass killings. Oedipus, Joan of Arc, and Marie Antoinette had all been scapegoats, according to Girard, but the most important scapegoat was Jesus, whose sacrifice promised to lead humanity beyond the envious violence of the past. These ideas were mostly grounded in literature, but they had an undeniable resonance for anyone who'd felt outnumbered, for anyone with a victim complex, and for anyone who knew his Gospel—all qualities that described an undergraduate Thiel.

Though Thiel has described his upbringing as evangelical, he seems to have kept his beliefs bottled up. Friends from this era don't recall him talking about religion at all or seeing him at campus Bible study groups. His cold rationality created the impression more of an atheist than someone of faith. But the discovery of Girard seems to have awakened something new in him—if not a profound sense of personal zeal, then an awareness of the role that religion could play in his public identity. Being a conservative Christian could be an act of defiance against the campus culture he was coming to despise. And that was very attractive to Peter Thiel. He would later describe Girard as "this very interesting professor with a different account of the world. It was very much out of tempo with the times, so it had a natural appeal to a somewhat rebellious undergrad."

—————

THIS WAS HOW he was starting to see himself: not as the polite, skinny nerd, but as the rebel. At Stanford, he became a gym rat, putting on a weight-lifting belt and sweats, holding forth on Plato while pumping iron. When he wasn't at the gym, he was hanging out at Coffee House, as the university's student union was known, where there was a room full of chessboards. Each evening, Thiel would walk over and post up at a table.

The game was blitz, or speed chess, and Thiel would sit there for hours, playing dozens of consecutive five-minute games, absorbing the lessons of the intense, cerebral sport. In blitz, the trick is to move as quickly as possible, not only to conserve your own time, but also to limit your opponent's ability to think in between turns, forcing them to sweat as they burn clock. Because of this dynamic, a game that appears close at first can quickly turn into a rout. If you fall behind, your only hope is, essentially, to fake certainty and decisiveness. Move quickly and with purpose—*as if* you have a strategy, even if you really don't. Make them think you know where you're going, and hope they make a mistake.

During the first semester of his sophomore year, he and several other students formed a team, organized a club game on Tuesday nights, and began trying to promote the group. The team would never attract more than a handful of players, but it would put Thiel at the center of the college's chess scene.

Elite chess required a combination of cerebral planning and intuition. Not only did you have to memorize every common opening, along with a portfolio of possible defenses, but you had to be able to quickly adapt as the game shifted. Thiel was stronger at the former than the latter and could be easily thrown off if an opponent did something unexpected. He played, as another student, Adam Lief, put it, "by the book," using prepared openings, especially the Ruy Lopez, also called the Spanish Opening, which started with the king's pawn, the maneuver favored by

Bobby Fischer. "It seemed to me that he'd learned by himself," said Grisha Kotlyar, a teammate who'd come to Stanford as a graduate student after attending Moscow's State Academy of Oil and Gas and training in a state chess academy. "He was very competitive. He liked to attack."

During Thiel's junior year, he and Lief—the only undergraduate with a higher ranking than Thiel—would sometimes set up a board in a dorm room, which would become the evening's entertainment for the hall. "It was like a spectacle," Lief said. Once, Lief recalled, he had a Howard Jones record playing in the background. At some point the British crooner's 1985 hit, "No One Is to Blame," came on. "You can see the summit but you can't reach it / It's the last piece of the puzzle but you just can't make it fit," Jones sang balefully. Then came the hook: "No one, no one, no one ever is to blame."

Thiel looked up from the board. "That's ridiculous," he said. "There's always someone to blame." It was the only time in the several thousand games they played that Lief could remember Thiel ever breaking concentration.

Another former chess player shared his own fond memory of Thiel from this era. Around the spring of 1988, the team was driving to Monterey for a tournament, with Thiel behind the wheel of the Rabbit. They took California's Route 17, a four-lane highway that crosses the Santa Cruz Mountains and is regarded as one of the state's most dangerous.

The team was in no particular hurry, but Thiel drove as if he were a man possessed. He navigated the turns like Michael Andretti, weaving in and out of lanes, nearly rear-ending cars as he slipped past them, and seemed to be flooring the accelerator for large portions of the trip. Somewhat predictably, the lights of a California Highway Patrol cruiser eventually appeared in his rearview. Thiel was pulled over, and the trooper asked if he knew how fast he was going. The young men in the rest of the car, simultaneously relieved to have been stopped and scared of the trooper, looked at each other nervously.

"Well," Thiel responded, in his calmest, most measured baritone. "I'm not sure if the concept of a speed limit makes sense."

The officer said nothing. Thiel continued: "It may be unconstitutional. And it's definitely an infringement on liberty."

The officer looked at Thiel and the geeks in the beater car and decided the whole thing wasn't worth his time. He told Thiel to slow down and have a nice day. "I don't remember any of the games we played," said the man, now in his fifties, who'd been in the passenger seat. "But I will never forget that drive."

What made the encounter truly memorable was that after he'd successfully made the argument, and miraculously been let off with a warning, Thiel hit the accelerator just as hard as before. It was as if he not only believed that the laws of the State of California did not apply to him—but believed the laws of physics didn't either.

WHEN HE WASN'T PLAYING CHESS, Thiel gravitated to fellow intellectual rebels. Sophomore year, he befriended a geeky computer scientist and chess player, Barney Pell, who exposed him to extropianism: the idea that advances in technology would allow humans to live forever and that cryonics should be used to freeze people's brains postmortem so they could eventually be reanimated or have their minds uploaded to computers.

Around the same time, he became close with Reid Hoffman. They were in the same class, but didn't become friends until the second quarter of their sophomore year when they started talking during an introductory philosophy lecture, Mind, Matter, and Meaning. After class, they walked out together and talked for another hour on the quad, "arguing about life, the universe, and everything," Thiel would later recall.

Hoffman, who'd also been bullied in high school, had grown up in a family of radical activists in Berkeley and had attended a progressive

New England prep school. He'd heard of Thiel's dorm room extremism and thought of him, as he'd later put it, as a "libertarian wacko." But what made Hoffman different from Thiel's dormmates was that he took Thiel's conservatism seriously.

The two men spent many hours together over the next few years and were so taken with each other that they decided to form a sort of ticket to run for student senate. Their platform was anti-bureaucratic: Stanford's student government, known as the Associated Students of Stanford University, or ASSU, had spent about $80,000 on office renovations, they learned. Hoffman, playing the progressive, used this fact to argue that the ASSU was failing to spend its budget on bettering student life. Thiel, sounding like a proto–Tea Partier, proclaimed himself "disgusted," that students were "helping friends pack their resumes with positions in the ASSU bureaucracy."

They both won, but Thiel would be an odd fit in the lefty body. During the same election, students voted overwhelmingly for resolutions calling for South African divestment and a rejection of the plan to locate the Reagan library on campus. Thiel embraced his oppositional role, but was often frustrated. After the Reagan Presidential Foundation announced it was scrapping plans to locate the library at Stanford in favor of a site in Southern California, Thiel gave a speech arguing that the university's liberal leaders had made a huge mistake and was shouted down, he would later tell a friend. With the same frustration he'd sometimes displayed in high school after losing a chess match, Thiel walked out. The incident, the person said, was formative. Thiel came to see Stanford as a fundamentally hostile place. "He was treated badly by a lot of students," the friend said.

He poured his grievances into the *Stanford Review*, a monthly tabloid-style newspaper aimed at conservative readers that he founded that spring with a high school friend (and soon-to-be Stanford student), Norman Book. It was his first entrepreneurial venture and would include the first nodes of a network that would come to dominate Silicon Valley.

The masthead of the inaugural issue, published on June 9, 1987, listed twelve names, with Thiel as editor in chief. All twelve were men—a pattern that would play out throughout Thiel's career.

That issue included a mix of political opinion and campus news, including a front-page story on a class trip to El Salvador that, the writer argued, had presented students with an "unbalanced" view of Latin American politics. Another front-page story presented liberal faculty members as closet Marxists. There was a satirical sex column, "Confessions of a Sexual Deviant," about a young heterosexual man who'd chosen to be celibate, and a list of "alternative" summer reading books. (Strangely, perhaps, given the *Review*'s prudishness about sex, Bret Easton Ellis's debut novel of carnal exploration, *Less Than Zero*, made the cut alongside Tolkien, T. H. White, and Edmund Burke.) "A vocal few have succeeded in dominating the discussion, often with views very different from those of the Stanford mainstream," Thiel wrote in an editor's note. "Many of the more moderate students in the Stanford community remain silent, believing that it makes little difference whether they speak out or not."

Thiel's primary innovation with the *Review* was to connect parochial concerns of a small, elite group—conservative Stanford undergraduates—to mainstream national politics. Hence the dues charged by the left-leaning student senate became a microcosm of tax-and-spend liberalism—even if the amounts of money in question were minuscule, an optional fee of $29 per student per year. And a faculty plan to add non-white authors, like Zora Neale Hurston, to Stanford's Western Culture course became Stanford's own War on Christmas. "Western Culture in the Balance," read the *Review*'s cover story on the topic, with an illustration of a scale. On one side were the Bible, Plato, and Shakespeare. On the other was a looming question mark.

The *Review* would pay for all of this in part with grants from the Intercollegiate Studies Institute, which backed campus conservatives, and with donations from older alumni solicited using warnings of Stanford's creeping liberalism. One particularly successful fundraising letter a few years later would alert alumni that a Stanford professor was teaching a course on Black hairstyles, implying that Stanford had effectively replaced the traditional Western Culture curriculum with discourses on kinky hair. This was false on any number of levels, but it would lead to a flood of new donations anyway.

The debate over Stanford's core curriculum eventually caught the attention of education secretary Bill Bennett, who agreed in the spring of 1988 to appear at a *Review*-sponsored event. Afterward, Bennett told PBS's *MacNeil/Lehrer NewsHour* that his audience had indicated, with a show of hands, that they'd been "intimidated" into changing Stanford's curriculum. When Stanford's president, Donald Kennedy, tried to dispute this—pointing out, correctly, that the audience was full of rightwing students who'd been primed by Thiel's newspaper to respond in such a way—Thiel defended Bennett in interviews with UPI, *The Washington Post*, and the *Los Angeles Times*. "There was quite a bit of pressure from one side," he told the *Post*. That summer he was accepted into an internship at Bennett's Department of Education.

Thiel graduated in 1989, but he didn't leave campus, earning a place at Stanford Law School. He would later confess to not having thought particularly deeply about this decision to apply. He was "still very much that undergraduate—how do you get straight A's, how do you ace the LSATs" mode, he said. "Maybe I was attracted to law school because it was somehow very precisely rank-ordered."

But it was about more than just overachieving. Thiel had an adversary now, and he wanted to continue the fight. The Western Culture changes were slated to go into effect in the fall of 1989; those Zora Neale Hurston books weren't going to indict themselves. Over his four years at Stanford, he had come to see the university's multicultural liberalism as uniquely despicable, maybe even dangerous.

A section of the 1989 yearbook celebrating Stanford's first one hundred years included an archival picture of Dean of Student Affairs

Michael Jackson, a Black man who'd been an undergraduate in the 1960s and who had eventually returned to campus as a university administrator. Thiel would write about the picture a few years later, paying special attention to the way that Jackson's personal style had evolved. "In a Centennial yearbook photograph of Dean Jackson, taken in 1969, he is the picture of radical chic, sporting an unkempt Afro and wearing brightly colored bell-bottoms," Thiel wrote. "Now, some 20 years later, the well-groomed dean could be seen strolling the campus, chatting with students, his hair coiffured, his double-breasted suit neatly pressed. Having never left campus, many of 1960s activists now are the professors and teachers."

Thiel's point seemed to be that Dean Jackson, who holds a doctorate in education administration from the University of Massachusetts at Amherst in addition to his Stanford undergraduate degree, was part of some sort of 1960s sleeper cell intent on multiculturalizing Stanford. The liberals might look respectable, Thiel was saying, but they were dangerous. Defining that danger would consume him for decades. He would come to see Stanford and other elite universities not as nurturing institutions, but as essential elements of a stifling and dangerous power structure, a priesthood "as corrupt as the Catholic Church 500 years ago," he would say. Thiel would eventually discover the allure of technology and money, but the desire to destroy that priesthood—or, perhaps, to replace it— would only grow stronger once he found his way into the real world.

3

HOPE YOU DIE

n January 1992, the *Stanford Review* published a special issue, "The Real World," devoted to a topic of particular interest to Thiel: getting a job. He was halfway through his seventh year on campus but seemed frozen in time. He was a third-year law student, still fighting the campus culture wars alongside teenage prepsters who layered their polo shirts. He was also still writing editor's letters for the *Review*, even though he technically hadn't been the editor for two-and-a-half years and even if it was technically an undergraduate publication.

"It can be very liberating to be politically incorrect, since one will be far less inhibited from doing things that might disappoint the campus thought police," Thiel wrote in an editor's note. His column, titled "PC to Employment," was an occasion for extended mockery of the nonconformist conformity of his politically correct peers. According to Thiel, the acceptable job choices for a good liberal were pursuing graduate studies in anthropology, counting spotted owls, and "educating people about how to use condoms."

That Thiel—the Reagan-loving conservative attending a Reagan-loving university—would come to see Stanford, of all places, as the epicenter of a pernicious liberal plot dedicated to attacking people like him must have been at least partly the result of his own insecurity. He was still, even as he began law school at age twenty-one, closeted, seemingly uncomfortable in his own skin. He didn't date, and although he could be vocal about legal and political matters, he wasn't warm. It was as if, classmates would say years later, he was holding all of himself back from the world. It wasn't just his sexuality; it seemed to be much of the normal register of emotions and intimacies—joy, friendship, silliness, anger, hatred.

But Thiel must have also seen this perception of persecution at Stanford as useful—and seems to have deliberately cultivated it. Conservative grievance, especially grievance as expressed by anyone on a college campus, was especially marketable in the late '80s and early '90s, with Allan Bloom's 1987 book, *The Closing of the American Mind*, leading the way. Bloom, a University of Chicago professor and protégé of the neoconservative pioneer Leo Strauss, complained in the book that students had been rendered doltish by their obsession with rock and roll, comparing campus leftists with the Hitler Youth in the 1930s.

At the time, the idea that hippies were as close-minded as Nazis seemed clever to reviewers—and was unexpectedly appealing to an American public that was sick of the counterculture. Bloom's book received glowing praise from critics and spent months on the top of *The New York Times* bestseller list, helping to create a generation of devotees who were vociferously complaining that their voices had been taken away by the leftist thought police.

This was a contradiction, obviously, but one that didn't seem to bother Thiel or his conservative peers. "It was a huge generalized conversation," said Dawn Chirwa, who was in Thiel's law school section and who now consults to nonprofits. "The conservatives in our class were pretty outspoken. I sort of thought they were whiny crybabies." On the other hand, for someone like Thiel, complaining about one's liberal class-mates was probably the straightest line into elite Republican circles. "He was mugging," said Jon Reider, then a Stanford admissions officer and lecturer, who once faced Thiel in a public debate on campus on diversity issues. "There was sometimes intelligent conservatism in the *Review*. But Peter wasn't that. He wanted to throw stones at the administration."

The model for all of this was a young conservative named Dinesh D'Souza, who was six years older than Thiel and who'd played an almost identical role to Thiel on the East Coast in the early '80s as a founding editor of the *Dartmouth Review*. The paper would serve as the template for the *Stanford Review* and many similar campus publications founded in the same era. It was unapologetically reactionary and relentlessly pro-vocative, often to the point of cruelty. During D'Souza's tenure it had published, among other things, an anti–affirmative action column writ-ten by a white student entirely in mock-Ebonics, an interview with for-mer Ku Klux Klan leader David Duke, and a confidential list of members of the gay student group, some of whom weren't out.

By the time Thiel hit Stanford in 1985, D'Souza had parlayed his tal-ent for grabbing attention into a job editing *The Prospect*, a right-wing magazine for Princeton University alumni backed by wealthy conserva-tives. In 1987, he became a White House policy adviser, joining fellow *Dartmouth Review* alumni (and future conservative television commen-tators) Laura Ingraham and Peter Robinson, who'd also served in the White House as speechwriters.

D'Souza had visited Stanford's campus while researching his book on left-wing intolerance on campus, *Illiberal Education*, which came out in early 1991, during Thiel's second year of law school. It received main-stream acclaim and landed on bestseller lists—successes that undoubt-edly influenced Thiel and may help explain why the Stanford described in the *Review* differs so dramatically from the real university as remem-bered by others who attended.

In early 1987, Jesse Jackson, the civil rights activist, had appeared at a rally just before the vote to replace the old curriculum with a new one that included some non-white authors alongside the Bible, Plato, and Shakespeare. "Hey hey, ho ho," students chanted. "Western Culture's got to go." They meant the Western Culture curriculum, but in his own book about the era, Thiel would claim the student protesters were referring "to the West itself—to its history and achievements, to its institutions of free-market capitalism and constitutional democracy, to Christianity and Judaism."

His account of the Jesse Jackson protest wasn't the only way he sensationalized his time on campus for the benefit of conservative readers. In reality, Stanford was not an especially sexed-up place; the joke among undergraduates, a common one at elite colleges, was that these strivers were too awkward or nerdy to actually get laid. But the *Stanford Review* presented undergraduate sex lives as positively debauched, leaving the impression that it was impossible to visit a men's restroom without witnessing a gay sex act or to cross the quad without having a fistful of free condoms pressed into your hand.

Stanford was giving out condoms for good reason. AIDS was raging in the Bay Area, where an estimated 4 percent of the city's population were already infected. Among gay men, the rate was thought to be closer to 50 percent. By 1988, more San Franciscans had died of the virus than had died in all twentieth-century wars combined, and experts were warning of possible labor shortages and civil unrest. The *Review*'s reaction to all of this was a chortle and a finger wag. "If the disease's spread is so alarming, why doesn't someone in the mainstream media urge that we practice sexual abstinence," one columnist asked, presenting homosexuality as a sort of addiction. Gay men, the columnist wrote, had engaged in "unnatural forms of sex," and "yielded to temptation so many times that the fires of lust burn within them, making it indeed difficult for them to control themselves."

"There was a general atmosphere of homophobia," said Megan Maxwell. "But the *Review* was virulent about it." To the *Review*, homophobia was not a bias to overcome, but rather a liberal conspiracy. The real scourge, Thiel's paper had it, was homophobia-*phobia*, that is, fear of being labeled a homophobe. In a 1992 column, editor in chief Nathan Linn, who would later work at several Thiel companies, proposed that anti-gay bias should be rebranded "miso-sodomy"—that is, a hatred of anal sex—to focus on the "deviant sexual practices."

IN THE EARLY 1990s, none of this was incompatible with a career—at least not the kind of career Thiel was envisioning. He saw himself as a Buckley-like figure, or perhaps a future Supreme Court Justice, according to friends who knew him during this era.

He also wanted money. In "PC to Employment" he'd complained that only one in four Stanford alumni were millionaires, a class he praised—in the great tradition of Stanford conservatism going back to David Starr Jordan and Herbert Hoover—as morally superior to the liberal hordes. "These are the people who pay for the bulk of this country's government transfer programs, and who have helped endow universities like our own," he wrote. Greed wasn't exactly good, as Michael Douglas's Gordon Gekko had boasted in *Wall Street*, Thiel said, but it was "preferable to envy," the prevailing sentiment of the liberals he knew. It was greed, rather than envy, he said, that had allowed the United States to defeat the USSR in the Cold War. "Like the Soviet Union, PC will eventually self-destruct," he predicted.

He figured his future would begin with a prestigious clerkship, a job at a white-shoe law firm, millions of dollars, and whatever glories came after that. In law school, he befriended Gregory Kennedy, son of Supreme Court Justice Anthony Kennedy, became an editor of the *Law Review*, and joined the Federalist Society. He also continued to cultivate the most reactionary undergraduates he could find—especially Keith Rabois, who was two years younger and in many ways his miniature.

Rabois was also an aspiring lawyer—like Thiel, he would enroll at

Stanford Law School immediately after graduating. He was also closeted. The *Review* in these years was "so gay," said a friend of Thiel's, which is both strange and entirely predictable given the protest-too-much quality of the paper's coverage of gay issues. Temperamentally, though, Thiel and Rabois were polar opposites. Rabois was more outgoing than his mentor—he even belonged to a fraternity—and he had none of Thiel's sangfroid. He was the *Review*'s resident jock, and his columns generally consisted of a series of insulting quips aimed at various campus groups—minorities, liberal arts majors, gays, feminists, *Stanford Daily* staffers, Stanford administrators—with a few sports references mixed in.

In March 1992, a month after Thiel had published his editor's note about career prospects, Rabois, who was then a first-year law student, decided to take his trolling beyond the pages of the *Review*. Several years earlier, a sibling of one of his frat brothers had been thrown out of university housing for using a homophobic slur to describe a gay resident assistant. Now, while walking through the same dorm, Otero House, after a night of socializing, Rabois decided to make a point. He stood outside of the home where Otero's resident fellow, Dennis Matthies, lived and repeated the same word.

"Faggot!" Rabois screamed, at the top of his lungs. "You are going to die of AIDS. You're going to get what's coming to you! You're going to get what's coming to you! Damn faggot!" At some point during this tirade, he added another taunt: "See if you can kick me out of housing."

Matthies, a lecturer who taught great books classes and who was not, as far as anyone knew, gay, had not been home. But students reported the incident, and the *Stanford Daily* covered it as a possible violation of the university rules prohibiting hate speech. Rabois maintained he'd done nothing wrong—and said that he had calibrated his insults specifically to avoid running afoul of the rules. He told the *Daily* that his comments were permissible because they were "mostly about faggots being bad in general," rather than being specific to Matthies. He said he'd intended his outburst as a protest against the campus regulation of speech. "I'm a first-year law student," he boasted. "I know exactly what you can say and what you can't." In a follow-up letter, Rabois wrote, "I don't necessarily hate homosexuals," but went on to say that he thought they shouldn't be schoolteachers.

The reaction on campus was predictably harsh. Rabois had been correct that yelling anti-gay slurs wasn't a violation of Stanford policy, but that didn't stop the Stanford administrators from publicly condemning what he'd done. There was a press release that included an account of his comments, along with a rebuttal from Michael Jackson, the dean of students, describing Rabois's outburst as "juvenile and brutal." His fraternity apologized, and students at the law school shunned him socially. "He was persona non grata," said one.

The stunt and its aftermath were an echo of an affair described in D'Souza's book, which had been published the previous year, at the University of Michigan. In *Illiberal Education*, the student who'd made homophobic comments had been forced, tragically in D'Souza's view, to make a public apology. Rabois would do no such thing. He left Stanford and landed, comfortably, at Harvard Law School, followed by a federal clerkship and a job at a prestigious law firm. But in the years that followed, Thiel would portray this as a persecution, using the incident in a way almost identical to the way D'Souza had used the Michigan case.

The *Review* didn't directly defend Rabois's comments, but it treated the outcry against them as a case of political correctness run amok, attacking Jackson for issuing the press release. When a former *Review* staff writer wrote a letter critical of Rabois, a columnist published a response accusing the letter writer of promoting "a lifestyle that frequently includes multiple partners, anonymous bathroom sex, ingestion of bodily excrement, sadomasochism, pederasty, and cruelty to gerbils."

Two days after Rabois screamed his slurs, the *Review* published "The Rape Issue." In it, David Sacks, another undergraduate conservative close to Thiel, wrote an impassioned defense of Stuart Thomas. He was a Stanford senior who'd recently pled no contest to the statutory rape of a first-year student and whose graduation was in doubt. Sacks argued that Thomas was deserving of sympathy and his diploma because statutory rape was a B.S. crime—"a moral directive left on the books by pre-sexual revolution crustaceans"—and also because, at least according to his account, the victim had not resisted. To make the point, Sacks included a graphic description of the encounter, noting that the seventeen-year-old victim "still had the physical coordination to perform oral sex," and "presumably could have uttered the word, 'no.'"

On an ostensibly lighter note, the editors included a guide for men hoping to avoid getting entangled in a feminist witch hunt, illustrated by a symbol for femininity that had been fused onto a swastika. "Feminazis have enlarged the definition so that now all men are rapists," Mike Newman complained. He recommended that *Review* readers stay away from Stanford women, many of whom were "ugly" anyway. Instead they should direct their amorous intentions toward women at local junior colleges who were "far too busy training for secretarial careers to bother with the collected works of Betty Friedan." Rabois contributed a column in which he and a coauthor joked that Zapata House, the residence hall where Thomas had taken advantage of the younger student, might contain "the solution to asexually frustrated freshmen."

TODAY, THERE IS not a complete record of the Thiel-era *Stanford Review*. Unlike the *Daily*, which offers an online archive that includes scans of every issuing going back to 1892, anything that appeared in the *Review* prior to 1999 can only be read by making a trek to a special section of the university library where Stanford stores university records and rare books. To read them, you have to request access ahead of time, sign a wordy agreement warning you not to make copies of any material, and then sift through a stack of well-worn cardboard boxes, in which the old newspapers are stored, out of order, with a few missing. For years, there have been rumors on campus that the missing editions had been deliberately removed from the archives to protect Thiel's reputation. But those rumors seem almost irrelevant given all that's still there to be found.

To flip through the pages, as I did on a long day at the end of 2019, is to be continually flabbergasted that the authors managed to amass so much power in the decades that followed without suffering any apparent blowback. The exception that proves the rule: Ryan Bounds, a federal prosecutor who was nominated to be a federal judge in 2018. The Trump administration withdrew his name from consideration after a 1995 *Review* column surfaced in which Bounds complained that campus diversity initiatives "contribute more to restricting consciousness, aggravating intolerance, and pigeonholing cultural identities than many a Nazi book burning." It was objectionable by the standards of the Trump White House but hardly any more extreme than what Rabois had been up to.

Did Thiel condone this? Sort of. He seemed embarrassed by some of Rabois's antics—and would never have been able to act them out himself—but he also found them useful. He'd been telling friends that one problem with conservatives was that they were, well, too conservative about their associations. In Thiel's mind, according to a classmate and former *Review* staffer, mainstream liberals had accepted communists, but conservatives were unable to bring themselves to associate with members of the far-right. "He really wished the right would become more like the left," this person said. "They'd say, I don't agree with this further-off person, but we can all work together." This line of thinking, this former staffer believes, was the "kernel" that would produce Thiel's support of Trump twenty-five years later.

Thiel himself stayed out of the fray, grinding toward his professional goals. He socialized from time to time, but the subject matter was almost always serious—case law, politics, political philosophy. From law school it was straight to a clerkship, with Judge James Larry Edmondson at the Eleventh Circuit appeals court in Atlanta, where he lived in an apartment in the northern suburb of Brookhaven from 1992 to 1993. Edmondson, like Thiel, had been an ambitious conservative—a young lawyer who'd run Reagan's campaign operation in suburban Atlanta before Reagan nominated him for the bench.

Federal law clerks don't generally work as hard as ambitious law students or first-year corporate lawyers, so Thiel created a little extra intensity for himself. A fellow clerk told me that when he visited Thiel, there was a stack of books on his kitchen table. "He said he needed to round himself out," this person said. "So he was rereading *Ulysses*."

Thiel's experience in the real world, which started the following fall when he moved to New York to begin as a first-year associate at the elite corporate law firm Sullivan & Cromwell, was less glorious than the PC-free zone he'd fantasized about on campus. He'd imagined corporate law as a profession full of righteous anti-communist greed; in fact, it was a grind. Law, as practiced in the real world, had all the naked, humbling ambition of Stanford, but with none of that pleasant self-righteousness. There were no liberals to fight, just an endless supply of young men and women, spread out across a familiar selection of white-shoe firms, with the same near-perfect grades, the same near-perfect LSAT scores, the same willingness to work eighty hours a week, no matter how inane the task. He had no discernible edge; it was almost as if he didn't matter.

He told a friend that being a corporate lawyer made him feel like a cog, a functionary, with no hope of having any impact on anything. To succeed—to make partner—was exciting in a sense, but that goal, too, felt empty of any real meaning. If he was being honest with himself, he was becoming depressed. "I thought that a lot of the conventional ways people competed resulted in too many people [doing] conventional things," he would say years later. "Then you end up in very competitive dynamics, and then even when you win it's not quite worth it. You might get a slightly better paying job than you otherwise would, but you sort of have to sell your soul. That doesn't sound like a very good economic or moral tradeoff."

After his clerkship had ended, Thiel had assumed he'd be in line for the logical next step for a world-beating young lawyer: a Supreme Court clerkship. He'd landed interviews with Justice Anthony Kennedy (his friend Greg's dad) and Antonin Scalia, and felt he'd done well. But in the spring of 1994, while he was struggling at the law firm, he received rejection letters. "I was devastated," he would later say, describing the period that followed as a "quarter-life crisis." He was done with being a lawyer, he suddenly realized. After seven months and three days—he'd been counting, a bad sign in itself—he walked out of Sullivan & Cromwell.

He stayed in New York for another year or so, getting a job as a derivatives trader at Credit Suisse Financial Products, but he was unhappy and frustrated there, too, and was mostly going through the motions at work. Former colleagues remember him as polite and unimpressive—if they remember him at all. "He was a nobody," said one.

Thiel spent his brief tenure at Credit Suisse learning the business—at least that's what his colleagues figured. In fact, he was already scheming: He was planning on moving back to the Bay Area. He wanted to publish a book about his experiences at Stanford. He missed the dorm room debates terribly and wanted to be back arguing with his friends. He also wanted money. He was making $100,000 a year and somehow feeling poor. If he stayed—even with his pedigree and brilliance—it might be a decade before he could conceivably be in charge of anything, maybe longer. So he quit again, this time telling his colleagues that he was moving back to California to start a hedge fund. They nodded politely. "The traders above him were kind of laughing behind his back," said the former coworker at the bank. "Like, 'What an idiot.'"

He'd had trouble making friends in New York—Thiel would later complain that nobody at Sullivan & Cromwell seemed to like one another, or even have much to talk about when they weren't writing memos or marking up contracts. He'd had a roommate in New York, Jack Reynan, the son of a real estate entrepreneur, who'd been a few years ahead of him at Stanford, and there had once been a miserable weekend in the Hamptons, but that was pretty much it. He doesn't seem to have had a dating life of any kind, which must have felt painful—but also, perhaps, like the responsible choice at the time. New York's gay community was bigger and more vibrant than anywhere else in the world, but was of course also an HIV hotspot.

While Thiel was depriving himself of socialization, he'd been writing, working on a manuscript that portrayed Rabois's homophobic outburst as a martyrdom, even though Rabois had not been punished by Stanford and had been as conventionally successful as Thiel. No matter: In Thiel's telling, Stanford's decision to comment on Rabois's remarks was unconscionable, even though those remarks had been made in public as part of a free speech stunt. Rabois had been, to use the current term, canceled. The chapter discussing his case was titled "Welcome to Salem," and Rabois was given special thanks in the acknowledgments as one of the "victims of multiculturalism interviewed for this book, who selflessly shared their special insights."

Though *The Diversity Myth: Multiculturalism and Politics Intolerance on Campus* would make only a limited attempt to defend the substance of comments, it would leave no doubt what Thiel and his coauthor, David Sacks, believed about gay rights:

> There is a vague uneasiness, a sense of foreboding that "tolerance" and "acceptance" (conventionally understood as you leave me alone and I'll leave you alone) would not be quite enough to satisfy some of the more militant homosexual activists. Much of the gay rights movement seems to go beyond what would be needed for public education or awareness and appears more designed to shock the general public. If homosexuals merely wanted to be tolerated like everyone else, many Americans wonder, then

why do they have to go out of their way to define themselves
not just as individuals seeking to live freely but as a special class
of victims demanding reparations.

Of course, Thiel considered himself oppressed, not as a gay man, but
as a white, conservative, non-PC man. "He had this kernel of a victim
mentality," said a former *Review* colleague. Decades before the emergence of online communities of self-identified "incels"—generally right-
wing men who blame shifting mores for their poor dating prospects—the
Diversity Myth would identify an "open hostility to the dating scene" on
college campuses that Thiel and Sacks said was ruining young people's
romantic prospects.

In particular, Thiel and Sacks blamed liberal overreach on sexual assault, which, they said, had redefined seduction as rape and therefore
made what they deemed normal sex impossible. "When verbal pressure
means coercion, and coercion means rape, then the number of rapes will
become as large as the number of seductions that are later regretted,"
they wrote. In 2016, shortly after Thiel donated to Trump's presidential
campaign and the passage appeared in columns, pointing out that he
seemed to share the candidate's indifference to rape, Thiel apologized, as
did David Sacks. "I wish I'd never written those things," Thiel said in a
statement. However, the following year at a *Stanford Review* event, he
reportedly told a student editor that the apology had been for show. "Sometimes you have to tell them what they want to hear," he said.

Meanwhile, according to *The Diversity Myth*, gays were having all the
fun. The book complained that Stanford had "failed to reseal 'glory
holes' in a number of the campus's public bathrooms, despite the dis-
comforting effect on people seeking to use toilets for more prosaic purposes." It's tempting to psychologize this, of course. And some who know
him speculate, convincingly, that Thiel's mid-'90s homophobia was an
expression of self-hatred. But the book's incendiary qualities might just
have easily been a product of Thiel's single-minded desire to achieve

something. Thiel wanted to make his mark, and he surely knew that the prospect of recent graduates defending the guy who'd shouted "Die, faggot!" on the quad of an elite university would get noticed. The conservative press would eat that up.

The book would be published in 1995 by the Independent Institute, a conservative Bay Area think tank that made Thiel a fellow, giving him a bit of income and a platform to promote his ideas. Starting that fall, he and Sacks wrote a series of columns in *The Wall Street Journal*, starting with "Happy Indigenous People's Day," a contemptuous survey of the new multiculturalism on college campuses pegged to the "anti-Western" holiday. Stanford's president Gerhard Casper and provost Condoleezza Rice wrote a letter to the editor calling their writing "demagoguery." With that, the fight was on.

The John M. Olin Foundation, the conservative nonprofit dedicated to nurturing a "counter-intelligentsia" and a financial supporter of D'Souza's book, had given the Independent Institute a $40,000 grant to help publicize *The Diversity Myth*. Thiel made the most of it. The book was endorsed by D'Souza, of course, plus René Girard, *The Weekly Standard*'s William Kristol, *The American Spectator*'s Emmett Tyrrell, and then-congressman Christopher Cox. (Cox would later serve as SEC chair under George W. Bush.) There were op-eds in the *National Review*, *The Washington Times*, and a dozen local newspapers, as well as appearances on Pat Robertson's *700 Club* and right-wing talk radio networks. The book was promoted by the Intercollegiate Studies Institute, the Young America's Foundation, and by Thiel himself, standing in front of the student union with a giant stack of books that he handed out to anyone who passed by. It wasn't celebrity, exactly, but Thiel enjoyed the response so much that he attempted to leverage it into his own political talk show with his old liberal college buddy Reid Hoffman, which aired briefly on Bay Area public access channels in 1996. (Think: *Crossfire*, but way, way more pretentious.)

Of course, Thiel didn't just want to be an intellectual celebrity. He wanted to be rich—a goal that seemed exceedingly far off. Thiel had lived with his parents, briefly, after returning to the Bay Area in 1995, and was now living with a roommate in a dumpy apartment near the freeway in San Mateo, eating a lot of Chinese takeout and, when he needed to blow off steam, playing chess in downtown Palo Alto.

And so, one day in 1996, he and another former law clerk went into the Stanford Law Library and began researching how to start a hedge fund. He hired the *Stanford Review*'s editor in chief, an ambitious conservative named Jeff Giesea, as an assistant and rented a closet-sized office on Sand Hill Road that could serve as the fund's mailing address.

For the next year, Thiel would be consumed by trying to scrape together enough money for the fund from friends, the families of his friends, and really anyone he could find. On paper, perhaps, it didn't look great—and it certainly wouldn't have looked like much to his former colleagues at Credit Suisse, or the ambitious junior associates at Sullivan & Cromwell. But Thiel didn't care. He'd chosen to reject those who'd rejected him, resolving to see his failure to win the Supreme Court clerkship not as a failure, but rather a stroke of luck. The highbrow East Coast establishment might not want him. Fine. "He wasn't humbled by the experience in New York," said a friend who was close to him at the time. "He was ready to take things over."

In this, Thiel was hardly unique. Silicon Valley was, at this moment, brimming with overachieving young men convinced of their own genius and relentless in their determination to get rich, and the Valley just beginning to reward them for it. Thiel didn't know it yet, but there had never been a better time or place for unearned confidence.

4

WORLD DOMINATION INDEX

The Golden Geeks," as *Time* magazine called them in a February 1996 cover story, were the heralds of a new era in American business. These young technology entrepreneurs were enriching themselves on a scale that surpassed even that of the railroad and steel barons. "Certainly there were many people who rose from modest wealth to vast riches over a lifetime at the turn of the century," historian Alan Brinkley told *Time*. "But it was nothing like the people today, who are worth a few hundred thousand dollars one day and take their companies public the next and become billionaires."

Extreme wealth wasn't the only thing that impressed the editors of America's most influential weekly. Not only did they have more money than the robber barons; the young techies were cooler. "Rather than build huge houses of questionable taste in Newport or Palm Beach or Aspen, the brand-new millionaires may live in two-bedroom apartments and wear T shirts and jeans," the magazine said. "This modesty appears genuine. Today's newly superrich are models of free enterprise, except for one thing: they don't seem all that interested in money." It was a new Gilded Age, we were told, with none of the guilt.

In the past, according to *Time,* initial public offerings—IPOs—had been sketchy attempts by rapacious bankers to pawn off shoddy securities on regular Joes. But now the IPO had become an egalitarian institution, enriching not just executives and bankers, but lowly employees who held stock options. The excitement was so profound that it threatened to break down traditional partisan rivalries, *Time* said. Conservatives and liberals both agreed: The Silicon Valley entrepreneur was "the ideal economic agent."

The prototypical Golden Geek was Marc Andreessen. At just twenty-four he appeared on the magazine's cover seated on a red-velvet throne. He was barefoot with a wild, open-mouthed expression that seemed like some mix of wonder and aggression. Andreessen, readers learned, had created the Netscape Navigator, the first commercial web browser, which had brought the internet to the mainstream.

He'd been a college student in 1993 at the University of Illinois at Urbana-Champaign, where while being paid $6.85 an hour at a university-affiliated lab, he'd helped create Mosaic, an early browser. Since there was no money to be made on the web at that point, the lab had made Mosaic available for free to the academics, who were pretty much the only people using the internet anyway. Andreessen understood that the internet could actually be a huge business and created a more user-friendly browser, Netscape, which he sold for $50 a copy.

He'd been on the money. Amid a sudden surge in computer ownership, the web was embraced by nearly every big company and lots of small ones. Newspapers and magazines started posting articles online, restaurants started digitizing their menus, and catalog retailers started taking orders electronically. By 1994, Netscape was ubiquitous, and the following year, the company went public, with bankers planning to sell its shares for $28 each. Instead, the stock opened at more than double that price. In a matter of hours, Andreessen's net worth had spiked to $58 million.

Thiel, meanwhile, had been struggling to stay relevant. He was, it seemed, the only person in Palo Alto who wasn't trying to make his fortune in tech, and his old shtick was wearing a little thin. The culture warriors had done well in the 1980s and early '90s. Bill Clinton had broken with Jesse Jackson in 1992 by criticizing a divestment activist and rapper, Sister Souljah, and easily won the presidency. Then in 1993 he had urged Americans that "the time has come to stop worrying about what you feel is politically correct." Thiel and his peers had won the argument, but that meant that by the time *The Diversity Myth* came out in 1996, it no longer seemed quite as provocative. After a brief burst of attention, interest in the book faded quickly, even at Thiel's alma mater. As a *Daily* columnist put it, Thiel's complaints were a product of "a cultural moment which passed Stanford by nearly a decade ago."

Thiel's plan had been to use his political notoriety to establish himself as a serious macro investor—a category of fund manager that places bets on big global economic swings, which are often connected to politics. He'd published an op-ed with Sacks in *The Wall Street Journal* that tied the Democrats' budgetary profligacy with the recent failures of Asian economies and another in the *San Francisco Chronicle* that used the Monica Lewinsky scandal to talk up the disruptive power of the internet. But the columns generated little attention, and, with no track record as an investor, he strained to raise the initial capital for his fund, scraping together just $1 million or so at first from friends and family. As enticement, he offered investors a share of the performance bonuses that fund managers normally kept for themselves.

His performance as an investor, at least at first, wasn't encouraging. During a year when the NASDAQ was up 40 percent and the restaurants and bars of the San Francisco Peninsula were floating almost exclusively on corporate credit cards from bankers, Thiel lost investors' money betting on currencies.

And so, in 1998, with the dot-com boom in full swing, Thiel decided to pivot away from hedge fund investing and into the hot field of the moment. He would find his own Golden Geek.

TECH INVESTORS, it turned out, were doing better than people like Mark Andreessen. Though *Time* had mostly ignored him, Andreessen's Netscape cofounder, Jim Clark, was even more successful. He'd recruited Andreessen to start the company, had provided the initial capital, and had arranged to raise money from venture capitalists. For this, Clark wound up with around $600 million in Netscape stock at the time of the IPO, ten times what Andreessen made.

Clark did not fit the cultural archetype of the moment. He was not in his twenties, no longer wrote code, and was not a two-bedroom-apartment kind of guy. He would use his Netscape earnings to buy a 150-foot yacht that he could drive by remote control, and, eventually, a $125 million divorce from his third wife. It would be Clark, not Andreessen, on whom Thiel would model the next phase of his career, and, in some respects, his life. Thiel would not be an idealistic techie—not the *Time* magazine version of a Silicon Valley entrepreneur with torn jeans who just wanted to make cool stuff—but the investor behind those guys. And so, on a sweltering summer day in 1998, he found himself in a classroom at Stanford's Frederick E. Terman Engineering Center attempting to chat up an awkward but brilliant coder.

Max Levchin was twenty-three years old and fresh out of the University of Illinois, where he'd graduated with a degree in computer science just a few years behind Andreessen. He was, in some ways, much more impressive than the Netscape founder. Levchin had been born in Ukraine to a Jewish family during the last years of Soviet power. His parents hadn't had enough money for a computer, so Levchin had learned to code using a pen and paper. Then, after his parents moved to the United States in 1991, he'd taught himself enough English to get into college in part by watching *Diff'rent Strokes.*

At Urbana-Champaign, he'd gotten interested in cryptography, the science of making and breaking codes. It was an arcane field that proved to be essential to anyone hoping to build services that would operate securely on the internet. Levchin had also become convinced that he was destined to start a company, which meant relocating to the Bay Area as soon as possible. "When I was graduating, basically if you were a good student in computer science you were figuring out the cheapest apartments in Palo Alto," Levchin later recalled.

The cheapest apartment had been the floor in a friend's apartment. But the friend, Scott Banister, who by this point had sold a small company and had become an investor, didn't have air conditioning, so Levchin had been coping that summer by spending a lot of time in random guest lectures on Stanford's campus. He'd often just find his way to the back of some classroom, feign interest for a few minutes, and then settle into a nap, enjoying the cool air. That had been his plan, more or less, when he'd sat down for a talk about currency trading by a recent Stanford graduate, whose name he vaguely recognized. He was one of roughly six people in the room.

He stayed awake out of a sense of obligation—it seemed weird to nod off in such a small room—and when Thiel finished his talk, Levchin introduced himself. He told Thiel they knew someone in common—another entrepreneur, Luke Nosek, who'd started a company that Thiel had recently funded—and said he was trying to start something of his own. Thiel seemed relieved at the change of topic and walked with Levchin out to the parking lot. "We should meet for breakfast," Thiel said, before they parted.

Sure, Levchin responded.

"How about tomorrow?" Thiel asked.

They met the following morning at a diner just south of the Stanford campus. As Thiel sipped a berry-and-banana smoothie, Levchin spoke about his fascination with PalmPilots, the handheld computers that had a certain cache among geeks. He'd taught himself to program on the digital planners, which, like proto-iPhones, had apps that let users write memos, keep track of appointments, and—wonder of wonders—send messages remotely. The process was clumsy: You had to buy a special modem that snapped onto the end of the device, plug the entire waffle-iron-sized appliance into a phone jack, and then suffer through the noisy, slow process of transferring data by dial-up modem. But Levchin thought it was awesome.

"One day," he told Thiel, "everyone is going to use these at work."

The one problem, Levchin said, was that PalmPilots didn't have any security built in, making them effectively useless for businesses. As a cryptographer, he figured the answer was to build an encrypted network that would allow the handheld computers to communicate with the mainframe systems run by big companies. Thiel looked at Levchin intensely.

"Great," he said. "I want to invest."

Within twenty-four hours, Thiel had agreed to put around $250,000 into Levchin's idea, making the kind of quick bet on an inexperienced founder that he would become known for. Levchin called the company Fieldlink, since the plan was to link PalmPilots at worksites—in the field, as it were—to corporate systems. The idea was far ahead of its time: Handheld computers wouldn't take off in corporate settings for another ten years, and the problem of secure communications between corporate systems and personal devices wouldn't be widely recognized until the mid-2010s. But the partnership between Levchin and Thiel was auspicious for other reasons.

After meeting with the two men in late 1998, Martin Hellman, a Stanford computer science professor famous for inventing the encryption technology that underlies online banking and ecommerce, signed on as an adviser to Fieldlink in exchange for a small equity stake. "It was clear to me in five minutes that Max knew more about cryptography than most people with PhDs in the subject," said Hellman. "And he was hungry."

Thiel and Levchin had figured they needed somebody with Hellman's credibility in order to convince the big providers of business software, like Microsoft, to partner with them. But the big software companies pretty much ignored their inquiries, and within a few months, they'd moved on to a new use for Levchin's encryption—one that wouldn't require the permission of any big software companies, or for that matter any intermediaries at all.

Earlier that year, Palm had announced that its latest device, the Palm III, would not only come packed with memory—2 megabytes, huge for the time—but also include an infrared transmitter, like the one found in garage door openers. This feature could be used to send data, such as contact information, between devices without dialing up. Starting at the end of 1998, Levchin and Thiel began experimenting with the idea of using the same technology to send an IOU, which could then be linked to a bank account once the PalmPilots were connected to a dock. They renamed the PalmPilot software company Confinity, a neologism Levchin came up with for "infinite confidence," and made Thiel CEO.

Levchin's technology was almost absurdly narrow—only super-nerds owned PalmPilots at the time—but Thiel continued to see the basic idea as potentially disruptive. Levchin hadn't invented a new kind of IOU; he'd invented a new currency. Once you had Confinity's payments app on your PalmPilot, which could be downloaded by zapping it from your friend's handheld, you could then use digital IOUs instead of dollars to buy stuff.

They called the money transfer service PayPal, but from its earliest days Thiel understood that it could be a lot more than just a clever way to split checks. During the Asian, Russian, and Latin American financial crises, citizens worried about hyperinflation hadn't been able to move their money into dollars and put it into foreign bank accounts; with

PayPal, all they'd needed to do was ask to be paid on their PalmPilots, which could be turned into a pocket-sized Swiss bank account. If it took off, it would make it impossible for governments to regulate their economies, leading to, he boasted to a reporter, "the erosion of the nation-state."

The implication, to anyone paying attention to what he was saying, would be profound—and, of course, destabilizing. Anonymous foreign bank accounts, which Thiel wanted to make available to all, were used by tax cheats, money launderers, weapons dealers, and other international criminals. If you followed his logic, all manner of gray- and black-market transactions would be impossible for governments to stop, and the fees for those transactions would be revenue to PayPal. It was a real-world version of the wild arguments he'd published in his *Stanford Review* days. Forget bringing down morally bankrupt university administrators—PayPal had the potential to bring down governments. Two decades later, bitcoin enthusiasts would use a similar logic to pursue the same goal.

Thiel made no secret of his revolutionary ambitions, communicating them freely to early employees, as well as investors, who put $3 million into the company using a PalmPilot to send Thiel the money at a press event in July 1999. "Paper money is an ancient technology," he explained in a meeting later that year. He suggested that PayPal could be the "Microsoft of payments." But that was just the beginning—because paper money was also a means of government control. "Of course, what we're calling 'convenient' for American users will be revolutionary for the developing world," he continued. Governments "use inflation and sometimes wholesale currency devaluation . . . to take wealth away from their citizens." PayPal would make that impossible.

Thiel imposed this libertarian ethos in ways large and small. At PayPal, employees were free to show up late to all-hands meetings as long as they paid $1 for every minute they were late, and Neal Stephenson's new cyberpunk thriller *Cryptonomicon* became something close to required reading, alongside *Atlas Shrugged*. Stephenson's book focuses on a group of entrepreneurs, descendants of World War II codebreakers, who build a secret offshore "data haven" to protect an encrypted online banking system from the reach of authoritarian governments.

Most—but not all—of the early hires considered themselves libertarians, including Levchin, whose Soviet upbringing made him skeptical of most forms of authority. Eventually Thiel would hire many of the former *Stanford Review* editors from his college and law school days—Keith Rabois, David Sacks, Nathan Linn, Norman Book, David Wallace—plus a half dozen young former *Review* staffers, including Paul Martin, Ken Howery, and Eric Jackson. Levchin brought along a few of his former Champaign-Urbana classmates, including Nosek, Yu Pan, and Russell Simmons.

The company leased its first office above a stationery store and a French bakery in downtown Palo Alto. Before long, twenty or so young men were packed in with grease-soiled pizza boxes stacked to waist height alongside pyramids of empty Coke cans. "It looked like a tech fraternity house," said Martin, who visited the company his junior year of college, while working at the *Stanford Review*, before dropping out of school to join full time. Nobody at PayPal was over thirty-five, and most were in their early twenties. "Experience was seen as a black mark," said Todd Pearson, another early hire. "If they found out you had an MBA, they'd probably fire you."

Besides youth, PayPal's other defining quality was its male whiteness. The author of *The Diversity Myth* made good on his aversion to multi-culturalism. In its earliest days, PayPal employed no women, and there were no Black employees. Years later, Levchin would boast about rejecting a candidate who'd used the word *hoops*, instead of saying *basketball*: "No PayPal people would ever have used the world *hoops*," he said. "Probably no one even knew how to play '*hoops*.' Basketball would be bad enough. But '*hoops*'? That guy clearly wouldn't have fit in."

Levchin would later say that his feelings about diversity were myopic, but, at the time, the only people uncomfortable with PayPal's hiring practices were those who worried Thiel was hiring flunkies. "I used to think it was a mistake, because what does a guy who worked on a weekly newspaper know about tech support?" said Hellman. "But Peter was brilliant in hiring people who recognized him as the leader and would not fight with him."

Silicon Valley prides itself on meritocracy—on hiring super-smart weirdos and nerds, whatever their personality types. This included catering to the needs of difficult employees, so long as those people were productive. "As long as people can figure out any way to work with the divas, and the divas' achievements outweigh the collateral damage caused by their diva ways, you should fight for them," Eric Schmidt put it in *How Google Works*. But Thiel prized loyalty and homogeneity in addition to competence. He would later write, perhaps unaware that this might read as biased, "We were all the same kind of nerd."

Besides seemingly arbitrary cultural tests—for instance, do you play Ping-Pong?—Thiel also subjected new hires to the sorts of brainteasers that were common on Wall Street at the time. He would stare intently at a young man and say, "You have a round table, and a limitless supply of quarters. You and a competitor take turns placing a quarter on the table, and the quarters cannot overlap. The last person to place a quarter without knocking any coins off is the winner. Do you go first or go second?" Solution: Go first and place the coin at the precise center of the table, and then just mirror whatever your competitor does. Those who answered correctly would be asked to turn their attention to destroying PayPal's many competitors.

TO SPEND A FEW DAYS in Silicon Valley at any point over the past two decades has been to feel as if you've been airdropped into a secret revolution. On the outside, Palo Alto and the rest of the Peninsula between San Jose and San Francisco could just as well be in suburban Tucson or Tulsa—full of small houses, strip malls, and office parks. But then you'll wander into a Panera or the breakfast buffet at a Courtyard by Marriott and see, glancing at a presentation on somebody's laptop, plans for 3D-printed houses that are so cheap they'll end homelessness or molecular structures for lab-grown meat.

These entrepreneurs and financiers, preparing or receiving the presentation, will talk gleefully about overturning the old order—"the paper belt," they call it. They mean New York, Los Angeles, and Washington, D.C., which they believe will one day go the way of Flint, Erie, and Youngstown. And it's hard, as you imagine a thousand years of your life stretching ahead of you with total freedom from ignorance, disease, and inconvenience, not to think, *Good riddance*—even if you're from one of those dying places.

But hang around a little longer and you'll notice two things: First, most of the startups that actually get off the ground are not quite so ambitious—they're mostly attempts to take some small, and hopefully lucrative, part of the old economy and sell it on the internet (for instance: books, with Amazon, in the mid-'90s; advertising, with Google, in the 2000s; and taxis, with Uber, in the 2010s). Second, these freethinkers tend to not be especially original. They're almost all graduates of the same five colleges (Stanford, Berkeley, CalTech, Harvard, and MIT) and they're all backed by the same group of venture capital firms. The VCs, as they're known, like to talk about disruption and invention, but they're often backing whatever happens to be the fad of the moment.

In the Valley, at the height of the tech boom in the 1990s and early 2000s, payments were the next obvious corner of the market to be conquered. The internet had grown to reach hundreds of millions of people, who were reading news, sending messages, and accessing pornography, but not, as yet, using the new medium to move money around. The Valley's entrepreneurs were developing lots of different options, including pure payments companies such as PayMe, Ecount, and eMoneyMail, online gift card companies like Flooz, and point-based digital currency companies like Beenz. (All the brightest minds in the country were, for inexplicable reasons, really into the letter Z at the time.) Every big retail and finance company had a digital payment arm. Amazon had a payments service, Accept.com, Yahoo! had one called PayDirect, and eBay had its own nascent PayPal competitor, Billpoint.

The market was so packed with competitors offering nearly identical services that PayPal wasn't even the only company of its type in its building. In early 1999, a visitor to Thiel's office at 394 University Avenue would have entered through a doorway next to the small stationery shop. Inside was a staircase, and up those stairs was a second-floor landing. On one side was the company Thiel and Levchin were building; on the other side was a second one called X.com, which was founded by an entrepreneur who was in every way as ambitious as Peter Thiel: Elon Musk.

Musk had come to Silicon Valley, by way of Canada, after running away from his home in Pretoria, South Africa, at age seventeen. Like Thiel, he'd also passed through Stanford, arriving as a graduate student in 1995, the year Thiel came back to California. He'd planned to pursue a PhD in physics there, but dropped out to start Zip2, a business directory on the web that functioned as an online version of the Yellow Pages. Musk quarreled with his investors almost from the jump. He'd wanted to turn Zip2 into a destination website, like Yahoo!; the VCs wanted to partner with media companies. They replaced Musk with a professional CEO in 1996 and eventually fired him as chair. Musk was hurt, but he did all right financially, taking home $22 million when the company was sold to Compaq for around $300 million in early 1999.

Despite their similarities, Musk was Thiel's temperamental opposite. Musk was instinctively combative and a bit goofy, with an ebullient and adolescent sense of humor. Whereas Thiel could be comically secretive, even among close friends, Musk was incapable of censoring himself. Whereas Thiel tended to think in terms of limiting risk, Musk was perpetually going for broke. After selling Zip2, he spent $1 million on a

McLaren F1, and he put most of the rest of what he'd made into X, which offered not just electronic payments but also checking accounts, stock trades, and a line of X.com mutual funds.

Musk's hope was that users who received money from friends would simply leave it in their account and slowly transfer all of their money to his online bank. HIGH TECH'S NEW "IT GUY": ELON MUSK IS POISED TO BECOME SILICON VALLEY'S NEXT BIG THING one headline declared. In mid-1999, on the strength of a demo website, Musk raised $25 million from a group of investors led by Michael Moritz of Sequoia Capital. This was bad news for Thiel and PayPal. Moritz was among the most re-spected VCs in Silicon Valley, after having invested in both Yahoo! and an upstart search engine called Google.

True to form, Musk spent X's money liberally. New users who signed up got $20, for free, just by opening an account. The service then en-couraged them to add their friends' email addresses and invite them to use the platform as well, rewarding them with another $10 per referral. Musk chose to ignore most of the established banking conventions. Fi-nancial institutions are required to verify that customers are who they say they are by checking identifications—a practice called "know your customer," or KYC for short—and they can be held liable for their cus-tomers' wrongdoing if they fail to report it to the authorities. If someone walks into a bank, plunks $600 on the counter, and demands to open a checking account under the name Mick E. Mouse, the teller isn't sup-posed to just smile and take the money. Musk was unfamiliar with nor-mal banking conventions and built a company that allowed exactly this kind of thing to happen. In late 1999, he bragged to CBS News that it was easier to get a line of credit at X than it was to sign up for an email account. "You can fill out the whole thing, be done in two minutes, be in your account and have funded it already," Musk said.

Of course, there was nothing stopping X's customers from lying about who they were and where they lived when they signed up for an account, which they did all the time. Every day, the mail carrier would stop at

394 University and deliver a giant bag of letters that X had sent to its customers that, having arrived at fake addresses, had been returned to sender. Not knowing what to do about this, an X employee bought a safe and just stuffed all the letters in there.

X gave most of its customers checking accounts, and so those customers who were able to get their mail would sometimes immediately take advantage by writing a series of bad checks. "I was thinking, 'What the hell did I step into,'" said an early hire who was tasked with handling fraud. "There was no sort of risk mitigation in place." When employees told Musk that the bank that X had partnered with to handle the checking accounts was complaining about bounced checks, Musk seemed confused by the concept. "I don't understand," Musk said. "If you don't have money in your account, why would you write a check?"

Musk and his employees didn't know that the engineers across the landing at 394 University were also working on digital money transfers—albeit using PalmPilots. All they knew was that the company had a sign on its door that said CONFINITY. "We didn't know what they were doing and they didn't know what we were doing," said a former X employee. "Until they found a business plan out back in a dumpster."

X and Confinity shared a trash bin in the alley behind the building. Confinity engineers later bragged to a group of X employees that they found documents that described X's web-based payments and its referral scheme, which they incorporated into PayPal's strategy after it outgrew its space at 394 University and moved down the street later in 1999. Some X employees I spoke with took the boast literally—"I'm 99.9 percent sure it's true," said one—though Musk cast doubt on the story. "It's possible I suppose," Musk said, "But it's a bit like saying 'You stole my idea for going to the moon.'"

In any case, that fall Thiel and Levchin started moving toward X's business model. In November they also built a crude web interface that mimicked the functions of the PalmPilot money transfer service. The following month, while raising another $23 million in venture capital from Goldman Sachs and the tech incubator Idealab, they hired James Doohan, the actor who played Scotty on *Star Trek*, to show up at a launch event to send money to a group of lucky customers. "I've been beaming people up my whole career, but this is the first time I've ever been able to beam up money!" Scotty said in the press release.

The joke fell flat as Thiel's old Liberals for Peace crack, but PayPal eventually stumbled into a winning audience: eBay sellers. At the time, the main way to pay for something you'd bought in an online auction was to go to the post office, purchase a money order, and then mail it to the seller, who'd have to take it to a bank to turn it into cash. "It was absurd," said a senior eBay executive. "It took weeks to sell something."

To speed things along, Levchin wrote a software bot that automatically messaged eBay sellers offering to buy their items—but only if they accepted PayPal. If PayPal won an auction it would donate the item to the Red Cross, which was good because the plan was a little devious (not to mention a violation of eBay's terms of service). Levchin wasn't trying to win the auctions; he was trying to get sellers to sign up for a PayPal account.

PayPal further juiced its growth by appropriating X's aggressive tactics, giving $10 to every new user and another $10 for every user they referred. To sweeten the deal even further, PayPal allowed users to immediately withdraw any money they earned, which they could have sent to them as a check or applied to their credit card as a refund credit. It was an expensive feature, costing PayPal on average $20 for every new user it added.

Soon, there were a lot of users. Luke Nosek, Levchin and Thiel's mutual friend and now PayPal's head of marketing, created a little software app that the company used to track how many people had signed up for new accounts. It appeared on employees' computer monitors as a little box titled "World Domination Index." Every time a new user joined and the counter climbed, the app played the sound of a bell being struck.

In November PayPal's user count was a few thousand. By January, the World Domination Index had risen to 100,000, and just three months later, it was up to 1 million. That was a more or less unprecedented rate of growth, even in Silicon Valley, but it meant that PayPal had spent something like $20 million on referral fees out of the $28 million raised so far. Early employees tell stories of walking in and seeing that thousands of users had signed up overnight—and feeling a sense of awe and terror.

PayPal accelerated its growth through an even more extreme form of regulatory arbitrage than the one X was pursuing. X, at least, was registered as a bank; PayPal hadn't bothered. The company made little obvious effort to collect information from consumers or to stop them from using the money for illicit purposes, and, at least in the eyes of some employees, was blatantly flouting the rules of the banking industry. The credit card refund mechanism that PayPal used to return customers' cash, in fact, was technically banned by the credit card companies. When those companies complained the following year, PayPal simply apologized. "They were like, 'What the fuck are you doing?'" recalled Pearson. "We were like, 'We're trying to take advantage of your incredible system to facilitate payments.' Then we'd negotiate. We did this dozens of times."

There was, of course, a world where this kind of aggression was seen as legitimate and even worthy of celebration—and it was one with which Thiel and many of the senior PayPal executives were intimately familiar: activist conservative politics. The *Review*'s fundraising mailing about the dangers of Black hair had been ripped straight from the playbook of Richard Viguerie, a prominent fundraiser for the insurgent conservatism of Goldwater and Reagan. Viguerie had run Young Americans for Freedom, part of the network that had provided grants to the *Review* and other conservative campus publications and famously built its fundraising list by copying records from the office of the clerk of the House of Representatives. He wanted names and addresses of anyone who had donated to Goldwater, and, because it was illegal to photocopy the records, he went to the office with an army of secretaries and handwrote the records, which then became a mailing list that he sold to right-wing activist groups as well as Alabama segregationist George Wallace.

Viguerie and his admirers in Washington political circles rehashed the incident for decades as an example of conservative pluck—in fact, Dinesh D'Souza was said to have pulled off a similar caper at the *Dartmouth Review*—but of course any Silicon Valley entrepreneur would now recognize the tactics by a different name: growth hacking. Today, the use of unsustainable or ethically dubious tricks to get a startup off the ground is widely accepted—even celebrated in some circles of tech— and has been widely credited to the growth hacks that Thiel and his peers developed at PayPal.

But at the time, Thiel's competitors complained about his company's tactics. PayPal was spending money recklessly, allowing transactions to pass through its system that would never have passed muster at a normal bank, and signing up customers without following many of the basic rules. Thiel's message to them, essentially, was to point at the World Domination Index as if it were a scoreboard.

When a reporter noted that many other online payment companies had chosen to comply with federal banking regulations—by, for instance, asking for social security numbers and verifying customers' addresses before allowing them to make payments—Thiel called them "insane" and suggested that was why they were growing so slowly. When the reporter suggested that PayPal might have to do the same, he shrugged. "No one knows what defines a bank," he said. "There's no clear standard." If PayPal was breaking the law, now was not the time to apologize—and especially not the time to fall in line. The boom was on.

5

HEINOUS ACTIVITY

B y early 2000, the outlook among Silicon Valley's entrepreneurs, investors, and engineers was one of limitless opportunity. The stock market was on fire—the NASDAQ had tripled over the previous two years—billion-dollar companies were appearing from the ether. "It's hard to describe how crazy it was," said Mike Moritz, the X.com investor and venture capitalist. "Everybody was very young, working twenty-four hours a day on these businesses, eating poorly. All of that collided and made an ungodly emotional stew. You had some people who were supremely confident they would prevail, and others who thought they were going to lose everything."

It was a new millennium, but it didn't feel like it. Al Gore seemed poised for a third term of the Clinton presidency, and Y2K—the fear that a glitch in the way that computers coded dates would crash networks around the world and bring on an apocalypse—had been proven alarmist. The ball dropped—and nothing bad happened.

PayPal, which raised another $23 million in January of that year, was hot. Nine thousand or so users, mostly eBay buyers and sellers, were joining every day, claiming their free $10, and then referring a few more new users to take advantage of the $10 per new user referral bonus. The result was a level of customer growth that was unprecedented in the history of Silicon Valley—and possibly in the history of the world. "It's easier than catching a cold," Thiel bragged to *The Wall Street Journal*. "And it's spreading as fast as a virus." The paper noted that investors valued online financial services companies based on the number of users, which meant that PayPal might be worth anywhere from $100 million to a staggering $1 billion, mere months after it had opened up the service—though this assumed that at some point PayPal would be able to make at least some money.

It was typical for tech companies to seek rapidly accelerating revenue growth—the famed hockey-stick-shaped pattern—while incurring some losses. This could work out in the long run; as the money-losing company grew, it would take advantage of economies of scale and its losses would narrow. As long as it kept growing, it would eventually be profitable. But PayPal didn't follow the playbook because unlike most other fast-growing startups before it, it had no revenue whatsoever. The PayPal service was free. Officially Thiel had told investors and the public that the company planned to make money by collecting interest on the cash that users kept in the system, which banks call the float. Unfortunately, almost nobody was keeping money inside of PayPal.

Even worse, what little money there *was* in the system had come from PayPal itself. In February 2000, it was paying out $100,000 per day in incentives alone—and that was just to get people to open new accounts. Once users started using PayPal to buy stuff, the company lost even more. Credit card processors charged as much as 3 percent in so-called interchange fees, meaning a "free" $100 transaction cost the company $3. The more money people moved, the more PayPal lost. And if a PayPal user committed fraud by stealing someone's credit card and using it in a PayPal transaction—something that seemed to be happening with increasing regularity, though no one was sure just how often—the card issuers could force PayPal to pay back the stolen sum as a chargeback, deepening the losses.

THE RESULT OF ALL of this was that the closer PayPal got to taking over the financial system, the less financially successful it became. Top managers at eBay, who were tracking the company's growth closely, found this strategy mystifying. They'd limited the use of Billpoint to only the most prolific sellers to keep shady characters off their system and stop fraud. PayPal, on the other hand seemed to be doing nothing to ensure it operated profitably or that it complied with banking rules and regulations. "They were going through a shitload of money," an eBay executive told me.

There was a way out of this: namely, PayPal could get so big that it'd be impossible for competitors stay open. Nobody would want to send money with Billpoint if PayPal was only the game in town; if that happened PayPal would have a monopoly, and it would be easy to find ways to charge money for its service. The tactic would become common enough among internet companies that an entire philosophy would crystallize around it, but at the time Thiel wasn't even sure it would work. He figured it'd be better to cash out and make PayPal's losses somebody else's problem.

He seemed "terrified of losing the business," one colleague said. The idea of selling PayPal to a larger acquirer would consume him through much of PayPal's history—and would become a source of tension between Thiel and his investors. For now, he asked Reid Hoffman, his college friend and now one of his deputies, to try to shop it to potential acquirers. Lots of companies answered Hoffman's calls. Verisign, which processed credit card transactions online and had just started its own PayPal competitor, seemed open to a deal, as did Yahoo!. But before talks could progress, Elon Musk swooped in. He'd heard about the possible sale and worried that if PayPal were part of Yahoo!, X would be pushed out of the market. He approached Thiel, arranging a meeting at a restaurant on University Avenue in February 2000.

The logic of a merger was undeniable. PayPal and X had user bases that were about the same size—about 200,000 people each—and approximately equal market shares, comprising about 50 percent of eBay payments each. They were both losing money—the combined companies would have losses of roughly $25 million in the first quarter of 2000. Together, Musk argued, they would have a better shot of surviving, and they would have an easier time dealing with federal regulators if and when the government got around to cracking down on the new digital payment technologies.

The deal Musk and Thiel struck called for a fifty-fifty merger. But X, which had better-known investors and a famous founder, was, formally, the acquirer. The name Confinity was retired, and PayPal became a part of X.com's financial services lineup. Musk, who'd started X by himself and therefore had more equity, became the chair and the largest shareholder. Two months later, he appointed himself CEO.

The partnership had been compelling to investors, who put another $100 million in venture capital into the combined operation that spring, but it proved to be awkward interpersonally. Perhaps unsurprisingly, Elon Musk and Peter Thiel had trouble relating to each other. One day, while Peter was riding in Elon's $1 million McLaren to a meeting with Mike Moritz at Sequoia, Elon, attempting to show off the car's acceleration, crashed the car into an embankment on Sand Hill Road, sending the McLaren flying into the air. The car was totaled. As they walked away from the wreck, Elon told Peter, "You know, I had read all these stories about people who made money and bought sports cars and crashed them. But I knew it would never happen to me, so I didn't get any insurance."

The experience shook Thiel, who came to see Musk as reckless; Musk saw Thiel as a money guy who cared about technology primarily as a means to profit. "I wouldn't say we're oil and water, but there are some

pretty big differences," Musk told me years later, offering a more circumspect assessment that was nonetheless withering. "Peter likes the games-
manship of investing—like we're all playing chess. I don't mind that, but
I'm fundamentally into doing engineering and design. I'm not an investor. I feel like using other people's money is not cool." A person who has
talked to each man about the other put it more succinctly: "Musk thinks
Peter is a sociopath, and Peter thinks Musk is a fraud and a braggart."

These feelings trickled down: some former Confinity employees saw
Musk, like their boss, as pompous and grandstanding. They resented
that they'd been forced to give up their company name. PayPal was now
called "PayPal by X.com," a mouthful that seemed to serve little other
than Musk's ego. They missed Thiel's low-key affect. "Elon was exactly
wrong for the organization," said Paul Martin, an ex-*Review* editor who
became a PayPal marketing manager. "The impression Elon gave was
that he knew best and you better do what he said. The impression Peter
gave was that you knew best."

But Thiel had laid a sort of trap for Musk. Though Musk got to be
CEO, most of Thiel's deputies—including Hoffman, Levchin, and
Sacks—filled the executive ranks. X's former executives were marginal-
ized, and Musk was surrounded by a team that was more loyal to Thiel
than to him.

THE CRASH CAME so quickly that most of Silicon Valley didn't realize it had happened. The NASDAQ peaked in March, right as Thiel and
Musk were closing PayPal's merger and $100 million investment. A few
weeks later, in early April, a federal judge ruled that Microsoft had violated U.S. antitrust law, raising the possibility that it could be broken up
by the government. Microsoft's stock fell 15 percent, and the NASDAQ
dropped 350 points, which was 8 percent of its value—the biggest decline in its history.

At the time, it was easy to write it all off as an aberration—a market correction that was more about Bill Gates than it was about the dumb money that had been pumped into half-baked dot-coms. But eleven days later, on Friday, April 14, the NASDAQ fell another 350 points. It was down 25 percent on the week, making the sudden correction worse than the 1987 Black Monday crash. And yet even then, tech optimists were able to dismiss the losses as mere profit taking, or tax planning, or a sign that the market had already hit bottom. "Now is the time for optimism," a Cantor Fitzgerald analyst told CNN. Startups like PayPal still had money in the bank, and there was a widespread sense, however unrealistic, that there was no cause for alarm and that the information revolution would march on. Beenz, the virtual currency startup, raised an additional $51 million from Larry Ellison and others to remake the financial system. In August 2000, *The Guardian* wrote that Flooz had a chance of realizing "Hayek's dream of companies challenging governments for the right to issue money," referring to Friedrich Hayek, the great libertarian economist. Those two companies wouldn't run into serious trouble until the end of the year.

Few noticed the crash, in fact, until the fall, when the first dot-coms started running out of money. Pets.com announced, suddenly, that it was insolvent, the launch parties grew scarcer, and tech workers began nervously checking a new parody news site, FuckedCompany.com.

But Thiel had noticed. In fact, almost as soon as he'd raised the $100 million and just before the bubble began to burst, he disappeared. He stopped coming to the office and cut off regular contact with his staff and the board. He told a few coworkers he was in Brazil, others heard he was playing chess. At one point that spring, Moritz called to plead with him to come back. Thiel waved him off, and then, in May, he emailed a pro-forma memo with a bloodless subject line: "Resignation as Executive Vice President."

Thiel told employees that he was "exhausted" and that he considered himself "more of a visionary and less of a manager." He said the time was right to give Musk the reins to continue "implementing our plans for world domination." Thiel's former employees and investors found his sudden departure inexplicable. That sense wouldn't last long. But, for now, navigating the downturn—and all the fallout that might entail—would be entirely Musk's problem.

To Musk, a born optimist who'd always wanted to be CEO, this seemed only natural, and at first, things went well enough. PayPal developed an innovative, if pesky, system to verify that customers weren't providing stolen bank information. It involved making two small deposits of a few cents each into a bank account and then asking the new customer for the exact amount. The company also cut back on payments to new customers, giving them $5 per new account instead of $10.

Unfortunately, this didn't entirely address PayPal's real vulnerability: fraud. Thiel hadn't worried much about fraud at Confinity, and Musk shared his laissez-faire attitude. In fact, no one at PayPal really knew how much fraud there was.

During the summer of 2000, the company's finance department, now led by Roelof Botha, a young South African straight out of Stanford's business school, began comparing chargeback rates that PayPal had forecast with the actual money the company was losing. Chargebacks happened when a card number was reported stolen after it had been used to fund a PayPal account. According to the credit card industry's protocols, if that happened, the credit card provider would simply withhold payment, which was a problem for PayPal since by that point the customer, who had likely given a fake name, had already spent the money (along with their new account bonus).

At first, the situation looked bad, but not devastating—in a given week, PayPal would lose something like 1 percent of its revenue to chargebacks. That was not great, but it was close to the industry standard. But then Botha realized that these calculations had been made under a flawed premise: that the fraud reporting was instantaneous. This was an assumption that no one from the banking industry would have made, had they been consulted. That's because customers have as many as 120 days to dispute a credit charge, which meant that PayPal would continue to record losses for months after a given period had ended. Instead of taking this into account, the company had been simply dividing the amount of chargebacks in a given month by the total revenue for that period—a faulty approach since the company was growing so quickly. As it turned out, the fraud rate was at least twice as high as Botha had guessed and climbing. "Holy cow," Botha thought, "we're about to go bankrupt."

With Thiel gone, all this fell on Musk, who focused instead on expanding PayPal's ambitions. Since Musk had always seen X as much more than just a payments company, he asked the company's marketing department to rework the PayPal logo to include X—renaming the service X-PayPal and beginning to phase out the PayPal name altogether.

To the group Thiel had hired, this was insanity. Sellers on eBay were already routinely saying things like, "PayPal me the money," using the company's name as a verb—a linguist's nightmare, but a landmark achievement for any startup. Meanwhile, X had conducted a series of focus groups showing that customers disliked the brand name, because it reminded them of porn. Musk was unmoved, possibly, employees gossiped, because of sunk costs. He'd paid at least $1 million to acquire the X.com domain name, legend within the company had it. "Nothing would convince him," said Martin, the PayPal marketer.

Thiel by this point had an office on Sand Hill Road for his hedge fund, but he stayed in touch with the loyalist group, which included the former *Stanford Review* editors, who resented Musk's rebranding, and Levchin, who resented the attempts to rewrite PayPal's software. These battles paralyzed the company, and losses from fraud continued to grow. What had been a $100 million nest egg was gone. "It was like a waterbed," said a former executive. "You'd push down on a leak, and boom— they'd find some other vulnerability. We needed to rally, and Elon wasn't paying attention to this at all."

Musk had married his college sweetheart, Justine, in January, but had been consumed by PayPal almost immediately and skipped taking a honeymoon. Now, he and Justine were planning a two-week vacation that would include a trip to the 2000 Olympics in Sydney along with meetings in Singapore and London with investors who, Musk hoped, would help keep PayPal solvent.

In retrospect, Musk would grant, the whole thing was ill-conceived. He'd known that employees were unhappy and should have stuck around. "I probably should not have been away from the office during that time," he said. "We'd made a bunch of risky moves. It just got too scary." Thiel and Levchin's old friend Luke Nosek secretly commissioned a new survey intended to show Musk that he was wrong to deemphasize the PayPal brand. Musk found out and lost it, ordering a product manager to remove the PayPal name from the company's website. Then he went to the airport.

While Musk was traveling, the group gathered at Botha's girlfriend's house. She lived about five miles south of downtown Palo Alto, meaning they were unlikely to be spotted by any Musk partisans. Besides Botha, whom Musk had hired just before the merger, the rest were Thiel's confidants, including Hoffman, Sacks, and Levchin. They went around the table airing their grievances as they saw them—the misguided rebranding, the code rewrite, the failure to take fraud seriously, the dwindling cash reserves. At some point somebody called Thiel and asked him what he thought. Would he join as CEO if the board fired Musk? Thiel said he would.

The plan was straightforward: They would threaten to resign unless the board went along with the plan. "As a team we felt, why don't we get Peter back as the leader of the band," said Botha. "Yes, he didn't have phenomenal CEO experience"—he'd only led a tiny startup, and only for the year before it merged with X—"but we thought it could work."

The following day they began canvassing other employees, asking them to sign a petition urging the board to replace Musk as CEO.

Musk's presence would have made this difficult under normal circumstances, but he'd be out of the office for two weeks. Former X employees, who were mostly still loyal to Musk, were kept in the dark.

While Musk was on a flight, a group of conspirators that included Botha and Levchin drove to Sequoia's office on Sand Hill Road just outside of town to confront Moritz. They presented him with a folder containing letters of resignation and the petition. Moritz looked at the folder and took it in. The case made by Thiel's allies was strong. PayPal was running out of cash and, if it continued on its current course, it would go the way of Flooz and Beenz. Plus, it wouldn't have a chance of survival if Levchin, the company's cofounder and its most talented engineer, walked out with the top coders and half the business development team.

A negotiation ensued, during which Moritz told the conspirators that he'd agree to a leadership change but would only install Thiel on a temporary basis. The company would need to interview other candidates. That was enough for Thiel, who accepted. He'd figure out how to make it permanent later. The group celebrated at Antonio's Nut House, a local dive bar.

Musk didn't go quietly. "This activity is heinous," he raged. He defended his decisions to the board and expressed dismay that Thiel's gang hadn't had the decency to confront him. Not only had the conspirators waited until he was incommunicado, they'd done it on his honeymoon.

He announced he was flying back to Palo Alto, and, upon landing, gathered his own group to plot a return to power. Moritz was unmoved, and within days the board had voted Musk out. Thiel was temporary CEO.

He spent the next few days trying to keep those whom Musk had hired from quitting. Thiel sat, passively, as employee after employee let him have it. They complained about the secrecy of the coup and defended the wisdom of Musk's strategy.

"Thank you," Thiel would say calmly, then urge the person to stay.

His plan was to jettison Musk's idea of a super-bank, and instead focus exclusively on PayPal, which, he pointed out, was already a huge success, with 4 million customers and (despite Musk's efforts to undermine it) one of the best-known brands on the internet. The approach worked; almost nobody left. "I came away with a lot of respect for him," said a former X staffer. "It was a formative experience."

But retaining the company's engineers was the least of Thiel's challenges. The company needed to address fraud and it needed even more cash. Luckily Thiel had a plan in mind. At a board meeting shortly after being named permanent CEO, he suggested that PayPal turn over all its cash to Thiel Capital, his hedge fund, so that he could take advantage of the economic upheaval of the post–dot-com bubble.

Moritz assumed Thiel was joking, but Thiel calmly explained that his plan was to increase the company's runway—a startup term referring to the number of months it could survive without raising additional capital or achieving profitability—by betting on interest rates falling, which seemed like a near certainty to Thiel given that the U.S. economy seemed to be heading into a recession.

The board shot it down, and Moritz was furious, according to people familiar with the board's deliberations. The idea that the CEO of a company with such enormous opportunity would consider risking its limited cash on speculation—particularly speculation that had the potential to enrich the CEO personally—was something no Valley VC, nor any self-respecting tech entrepreneur, had ever attempted. The fact that Thiel would propose it mere weeks after being handed the CEO job—a job he'd taken in a manner that was not exactly honorable—was doubly galling. "From a governance point of view, it was outlandish," said one of these sources. "Even the idea of suggesting it irked Mike." It suggested, to Moritz and others on the board sympathetic to his point of view, a lack of a moral compass.

Over the next year, George W. Bush would be elected president in a contested vote that went all the way to the Supreme Court, and Thiel would win the permanent CEO job by default. Even after being named CEO, he and Moritz continued to clash. Their disagreement was partly personal—Moritz had originally invested in Musk's company, not Thiel's. But it also reflected the ways in which Thiel was different from Moritz, and Musk, and pretty much every important figure in Silicon Valley who'd come before him.

Years later in an interview, Moritz said, "At heart, Peter is a hedge fund man," rather than an entrepreneur. Entrepreneurs were expected to pour all of themselves into their companies, to risk it all—financially and even personally—in order to grow as big as possible, and, if you were being idealistic about it, to change the world for the better. That is how Musk saw it. It's why he has nearly bankrupted himself several times in his career, and why he would tell me that he regards taking money from investors as "not cool."

By this logic Thiel should've been bleeding for the business, not scheming to grow his investment portfolio on the side. But Thiel didn't care about Moritz's feelings or Silicon Valley's sense of propriety. He conceived of the relationship between investors and entrepreneurs in terms of power, and he saw building a company in less romantic terms.

PayPal had gotten as far as it had by being thoughtful about inefficiencies, by taking advantage of regulatory loopholes, and by doing things that normal, self-respecting companies were too proper to try. Good manners had nothing to do with it. From that point on, Thiel was going to do what he wanted, and no VC—no matter how respected or experienced—was ever going to be able to control him.

6

GRAY AREAS

Around the time of Thiel's coup at PayPal, Silicon Valley's mythology was defined, more or less, by a single person: Steve Jobs, who'd created the personal computer in the early 1980s, built Pixar in exile, and came back to introduce the iMac and iPod, transforming Apple into the greatest consumer products company of all time. Jobs, the story went, had succeeded thanks to his countercultural bona fides—he was a proud hippie, a Zen Buddhist, a phone phreaker—and his willingness to train all of that weirdness on a profit-making enterprise.

Jobs wasn't a liberal, but his idealism helped transform Silicon Valley from the pocket-protector conservatism of the old research parks into a place full of New Age zeal. Pre-Jobs, the highest calling for a tech company might have been a big military contract; post-Jobs, it was something close to enlightenment. Apple—and then every tech company—started telling customers that their products could transform their lives and the world.

This was the "bicycle-for-the-mind value system," explained Roger

McNamee, the venture capitalist who, with U2 frontman Bono, co-founded Elevation Partners. "Bicycle for the mind" had been Jobs's term to describe machines that expanded human potential, and he'd used "Bicycle" as the original name for the Mac because he believed that computers would make people's brains more efficient in the same way that bikes allow them to travel faster and farther.

Thiel, according to McNamee, represented a hard tack away from this kind of thinking. He wasn't interested in human potential, but rather in market power. After the eBay acquisition, almost every Silicon Valley company with any ambition would have its own version of PayPal's World Domination Index. Mark Zuckerberg, the ultimate Thiel acolyte, would take this to the extreme, styling himself as the Roman emperor Augustus. He adopted an Augustan haircut and even used the ancient Roman war slogan—"Carthage delenda est" ("Carthage must be destroyed")—to pump up his employees to battle with Google.

There was a business rationale for this imperial style of technocapitalism. The internet was allowing new products to spread so quickly—"virally," as the emerging term went—that a single company tended to dominate a given category. Once PayPal had reached a certain scale, once all your friends had PayPal accounts, then there was no sense in trying competing products. Even if you liked Billpoint, your preference would become irrelevant if nobody else had a Billpoint account. This applied to payments, and really to everything else on the internet—social networks, food delivery, ride-hailing—and meant that any tech entrepreneur who wanted to succeed would have to grow as quickly and ruthlessly as possible.

There would be a term of art for this, "blitzscaling," coined, naturally, by Reid Hoffman, Thiel's good friend and PayPal deputy. Many companies interpreted it to mean spending huge sums of money to try to take over a market, and then, once they'd achieved market dominance, trying to raise prices. But quite a few entrepreneurs—people like Zuckerberg and Uber's former CEO Travis Kalanick—seemed to see a moral philosophy in blitzscaling as well. Whereas Jobs viewed business as a form of cultural expression, even art, for Thiel and his peers it was a mode of transgression, even activism—a version of what he'd been trying to do at the *Stanford Review*.

To start a company was no longer to help people reach their true potential; it was to flout norms, then change them, and, in changing them, set yourself up to get rich off the new order. Facebook would develop a monopoly on social media and use that monopoly to crush competitors, charging progressively higher fees to advertisers—while telling the world that this predatory behavior was a social good.

Tech would "move fast and break things," as the Facebook motto put it, and entrepreneurs would be told it was better to ask for forgiveness than permission. The industry would be defined by these clichés, convincing itself that "disruption"—that favored TED talker buzzword—wasn't just an unfortunate consequence of innovation but an end in itself. It would show up at Juul, the e-cigarette company that shamelessly marketed to children, at Robinhood, which tempted novice investors with questionable financial products, and especially at Uber, which violated municipal statutes with apparent glee, underpaid drivers, and ignored common safety standards, celebrating these transgressions at every turn. When cities complained that Uber was breaking the law, Kalanick replaced his Twitter avatar with a picture of an Ayn Rand cover, and, as I reported in *Businessweek*, employees at the company's driverless car division distributed stickers that proudly proclaimed, "Safety Third." This was all, in a way, an extension of PayPal. "The PayPal Mafia philosophy became the founding principle for an entire generation of tech companies," said McNamee.

EVEN SO, IN LATE 2000, Thiel wasn't thinking about moving fast and breaking things. The tech crash was well underway, and he was thinking about surviving. If Thiel wanted to avoid the fate of companies like Pets.com, he desperately needed to reduce PayPal's losses, which meant dealing with fraud. Criminals had begun to notice that the company's growth hacks—one of which was its decision not to verify users' identities when they opened an account—had made it an ideal place to launder money stolen from victims of identity theft. They would get their hands on a batch of stolen credit card numbers, then use a software bot to open PayPal accounts for each one. The shell accounts would attempt to make payments to other PayPal accounts, also controlled by the fraudsters. Of course, charges would sometimes be declined by the providers of the stolen credit cards, if for instance a theft had already been reported, but often the charges would go through before the victim realized what had happened. When the victim did realize, they'd call their bank, which would then demand repayment. PayPal, as the merchant of record, was on the hook for the damages.

Thiel could have drastically cracked down—forcing all users to send pictures of their driver's licenses, for instance—but he also recognized that part of PayPal's appeal was that it was more permissive than its competitors. And so Levchin focused on making large-scale fraud harder to pull off, without penalizing anonymous users. Working with another engineer, David Gausebeck, he wrote a piece of software that forced new users to copy a series of letters that appeared onscreen over a crisscrossed background. The Gausebeck-Levchin Test, as PayPal called it, was nearly impossible for computers to pass, but easy for humans. It would be widely adopted by the rest of the tech industry, and would come to be known as a captcha. It's the reason why you have to click on pictures of fire hydrants before you can log into your bank account—a bit annoying, but a tremendous innovation in combating cyber fraud.

Still, this effort didn't address the most prolific crime rings, which were stealing millions of dollars from the company. But in late 2000, PayPal's lead security investigator, John Kothanek, made a discovery. Kothanek, a former military intelligence officer who'd joined the company earlier that year, had been working in a conference room for weeks, sifting through thousands of transactions by suspected fraudsters. The process was manual and maddening.

Kothanek had gotten the idea to try to create a visual representation of the suspected fraud, drawing spiderweb diagrams on a whiteboard to map out connections between accounts. What he'd found was startling. All the accounts led back to a single feeder—a mastermind, apparently, based in Russia. He went by the handle Igor and had managed to siphon between $15 and $20 million out of PayPal on his own, according to a source familiar with the fraud.

This was a breakthrough, and not only because it allowed PayPal's security team to cut off this user. One of the challenges of the Russian operation was that thieves would often mix in real transactions with established merchants to throw investigators off the scent and to make it harder for PayPal to figure out what was legitimate. You could cut off the Igors of the world, but only if you also cut off thousands of legitimate merchants as well, potentially sending them to Billpoint or one of the competing payments systems. Kothanek's visual approach allowed an analyst to shut down bad accounts while leaving real merchants online.

Levchin and a team of engineers began writing software to automate this. It would identify accounts from suspicious locations, like Russia. Then it would create the equivalent of Kothanek's spiderweb diagram on a screen for each one, so that PayPal's security team—which came to include seventy-five analysts by 2001—could quickly suspend the criminals and leave the legitimate customers alone. They called the system Igor, and it was novel enough that the FBI began using it as a way to find money launderers. A small team of agents was given its own conference room at the company's headquarters to access it.

Igor caused fraud to drop to half of what it had been and led to several criminal investigations. There was one against a Los Angeles–based user who had taken $1.2 million worth of orders for Sony PlayStation 2 video game consoles on PayPal but hadn't delivered anything, and another against a pair of Russians who appeared to be stealing credit card numbers en masse and using them to fund PayPal accounts. No charges were brought in the PlayStation case, but the two Russians, Alexey Ivanov and Vasiliy Gorshkov, were indicted based in part on the information provided by PayPal. They were then lured to the United States in an FBI sting and were eventually convicted on conspiracy, hacking, and fraud charges. Gorshkov, who was twenty-five at the time of the indictment, was sentenced to three years in prison; Ivanov, twenty, got four years. From a certain perspective, PayPal had enabled these crimes as part of Thiel's ultra-libertarian vision of a financial system free from the control of any authority. But now he publicized the company's work *with* the authorities in order to market PayPal as safe and to deter fraudsters. "We have been able to stop an enormous amount of crime in its tracks and prosecute those who temporarily succeed," he said.

At this point, the scope of the data that tech companies were collecting was not widely appreciated, and PayPal's willingness to share that data with law enforcement was treated not as a potential violation of privacy but as a classic Silicon Valley innovation story. *Newsweek*'s write-up, "Busting the Web Bandits," had the tone of a *Cops* episode, presenting Thiel and Levchin as geeks who'd chosen to get tough on crooks. "Perhaps PayPal isn't such a great site to victimize after all," the article concluded. *The Wall Street Journal* quoted a privacy expert who conceded that such information sharing was a "gray area," but noted that "PayPal says it takes pains to protect customers' privacy." Assurances like this would go unquestioned for more than a decade, until a related Thiel venture—one with much broader (and, to some, much more terrifying) privacy implications—would cause people to begin to question them.

THE DOT-COM BOOM had been all about freebies, but the venture capital funding to pay for those freebies was drying up. And so, starting in late 2000, PayPal began forcing eBay sellers to sign up for business accounts, where they would pay fees of around 2 percent of every sale, thus allowing the company to begin turning a modest profit on at least some transactions. eBay sellers complained, but almost all of them went along with it because PayPal already had something close to a monopoly for payments on the auction site. "Here's a neat free thing. Use it, come to love it, let it become an integral part of your life (i.e., become addicted)," an eBay seller complained, comparing PayPal's management to drug dealers. "And then we'll start slowly bleeding you dry with fees."

It sounded melodramatic, but it was exactly right—and became a standard part of the Silicon Valley blitzscale playbook. But this wasn't the only way that PayPal tried to goose revenue. Porn and gambling were booming on the internet at the time, but some banks and credit card processors were refusing to approve online purchases that were identified as either category. That is, unless the porn and gambling purveyors chose to take payments with PayPal, which coded every transaction simply "eCommerce," even if that commerce involved placing a bet on a box score or downloading a video of a sex act.

This wasn't necessarily deliberate. PayPal was growing so quickly that nobody bothered to pay attention to compliance. "We would just massively miscode things," said Todd Pearson, the executive whose job it was to bring PayPal up to normal banking standards. Even after PayPal cleaned up and starting coding the transactions appropriately, there was a workaround. If a customer loaded up their PayPal account with a bank transfer and then bought porn or made a bet, the bank couldn't stop the transaction—and, because no credit card had been involved, the cost to PayPal was essentially zero. That made these purchases profitable, unlike almost everything else that happened on PayPal.

This was a boon to the company, which began marketing directly to gambling and adult entertainment business. Gambling customers were charged a higher fee—around 4 percent of every transaction, compared with 2 percent for typical sellers, and PayPal held an additional 10 to 15 percent to cover chargebacks that would result from potential fraud. This structure, along with the growth of online gambling, meant that the category alone would come to account for around 30 percent of Pay-Pal's profits, according to one former employee. It was the one part of the company's business that wasn't squeezed by credit card fees and fraud.

This led to some awkwardness at PayPal's offices. Online gambling was illegal in many states, and although many PayPal employees were staunch libertarians and not necessarily inclined to care about strict adherence to statutes governing internet poker and sex, there was also a group of Christians who conducted a regular prayer group in a company conference room. At times, when talking to the more religious members, Thiel and others would be careful not to mention that gambling and porn accounted for a substantial chunk of the company's sales and growth.

Internet porn, if not universally legal, was universally tolerated by federal and state authorities, but PayPal would receive subpoenas related to its gambling business from Eliot Spitzer, New York's attorney general, and Raymond Gruender, the U.S. Attorney for the Eastern District of Missouri. The company would pay settlements in both those cases. It also attracted scrutiny from New York, Louisiana, California, and Idaho for allowing users to hold funds in their accounts, which it needed to do to facilitate the gambling business but which, according to those states, meant that it was operating as an unlicensed bank.

Thiel pushed back, lobbying members of Congress to keep online gambling legal and to keep PayPal from being classified as a bank by federal regulators. Thiel had Washington connections, through the Independent Institute, as did Keith Rabois, who'd joined the company after stints at Sullivan & Cromwell, where he'd specialized as an antitrust litigator, and as the policy director of Dan Quayle's brief presidential campaign. PayPal executives also made contact with the office of Representative Ron Paul, the extreme libertarian from Texas who'd dabbled in a number of fringe causes, including an end to the primacy of the Federal Reserve and a return to the gold standard. Paul was a marginal figure in the Republican Party, but the PayPal policy team saw him as a possible advocate for the legalization of online gambling. Several other ex–*Stanford Review*ers had worked for influential representatives, including Sacks, who'd interned for Chris Cox, the California representative and future Securities and Exchange Commission chair. Vince Sollitto, who joined in 2000 as head of communications and public affairs, had worked for Cox and Jon Kyl, who served on both the Senate Judiciary and Finance committees.

According to Pearson, members of the House Finance Committee wrote letters to the CEOs of Visa and MasterCard at PayPal's urging, threatening antitrust hearings if the credit card companies blocked PayPal transactions. These representatives received campaign contributions from a PayPal political action committee.

This politicking was unusual at the time. Silicon Valley entrepreneurs tended to pride themselves on being apolitical, and it was almost unheard of for startups as small as PayPal to be actively lobbying Congress. It was also, some employees felt, hypocritical given Thiel's ideology. Should libertarians really be spending money lobbying for antitrust scrutiny of their rivals? Wasn't that the definition of the kind of regulatory capture that libertarians like Thiel supposedly opposed?

Pearson remembered politics coming up on a trip with Thiel to interview a board member. Pearson, who was generally liberal, mentioned voting for a Democrat and then braced himself for Thiel's reaction. To his surprise Thiel didn't criticize the choice to support the ostensibly wrong party; he criticized the choice to support any party at all. He said there was no point in voting. "You're supporting this corrupt system," he said.

Pearson was taken aback. He knew being liberal at PayPal put him in the minority, but the idea that Thiel considered politics of any kind to be immoral was a new one—especially since the company had been playing politics enthusiastically since he'd joined. The company formed a political action committee in 2001, gathering about $40,000, which it dispersed to influential politicians in the House and Senate. Nobody was required to donate—that would have been against the law—but executives were strongly encouraged to do so, in a way that made some at the company uncomfortable. "We'd really pushed employees to contribute," recalled Pearson in an interview years later. He'd personally given $500 to the cause. "We were participating in government while having this really cynical view," he said.

On the other hand, it was never clear whether Thiel's political riffs were meant to be taken literally. At another point, he suggested—possibly in jest—that perhaps political conservatives should simply throw the next few elections, allowing liberals to overreach. Then, he hoped, would come a military coup. "Maybe," Thiel offered, "the U.S. military can run the country better" than the politicians.

IF THE DOT-COM CRASH—and the attendant need to generate cash—was never far from Thiel's mind, neither was eBay, which was where almost all of PayPal's aboveboard customers (as in, paying for things other than porn and betting) were using the service, and which had the power to throw PayPal off at any time.

The auction giant was run by Meg Whitman, a celebrity CEO with degrees from Princeton and Harvard who'd held jobs at Disney, Procter & Gamble, and the toymaker Hasbro, where she'd turned *Teletubbies*, a British children's show that featured the surreal adventures of four large creatures with television sets implanted in their bodies, into an unlikely global hit. She'd never worked in tech before coming to eBay and she'd surrounded herself with people like her—middle-aged MBAs who wore khakis and generally avoided internet casinos. She was, as many at PayPal saw it, a typical Ivy League conformist—exactly the kind of person that Thiel and the *Stanford Review* alums had made it their mission to fight. "Meg was the embodiment of the enemy," said Bill Onderdonk, the company's vice president of marketing. "Her face was on dartboards."

Worse than her by-the-book persona was the fact that Whitman clearly wasn't happy about having an outside company serve as eBay's de facto payments platform. When the auction giant gave sellers a personal ecommerce website as part of its "eBay Stores" offering, it mandated that the sellers sign up for Billpoint. PayPal took this as a sign of aggression, and Reid Hoffman, who was in regular touch with eBay executives, made clear to them that the move could lead to antitrust scrutiny through PayPal's contacts in Washington. "Reid did a wonderful job of always raising the antitrust specter," said a then-senior eBay staffer.

Whitman not only backed down—she indicated that she would happily buy PayPal rather than fight with it. In late 2000, she offered Thiel around $300 million for the company. This was below PayPal's valuation, but Whitman justified it with a threat. "We are teaming up with Wells Fargo and we're going to kick the shit out of you," Whitman conveyed to Thiel, according to a source familiar with the negotiation. "You haven't got a prayer."

Thiel was nearly persuaded. "We felt like we were lurching from one near-death moment to the next," said a former senior executive. "It was unclear if we'd ever get to profitability." Moritz, on the other hand, was adamantly opposed. The dot-com bust had been devastating to Sequoia. Nearly all of the investments that the firm had made around 1999 had failed or were close to failure; all except for the investment in X.com, which had gotten the firm shares in PayPal. PayPal still presented a real opportunity to produce a big return, and Moritz spent hours trying to convince Thiel and Levchin that their company had such potential.

"Max, Max, Max," Moritz said during one argument after Levchin suggested that he could just start a new PayPal after he sold the first one. "Please trust me. An opportunity like PayPal doesn't come along every day. You could live another ten lifetimes and you're not going to have another PayPal–sized opportunity."

In 2001, Thiel continued shopping the company. There were meetings with Sandy Weill, then chair and CEO of Citigroup, and representatives from AOL—though nothing came to fruition. That summer, Thiel also began talking to bankers about an initial public offering. The company's prospectus would show PayPal's finances improving: The company lost $28 million in the second quarter of 2001, against revenue of $20 million. As required by SEC rules, the prospectus also included a lengthy discussion of the legal and regulatory risks the company faced, which noted that PayPal was, in all likelihood, being used to enable drug dealing, software piracy, money laundering, bank fraud, securities fraud, and child porn. Even so, the bankers believed that the company had enough promise to pull it off for more than eBay was offering.

Thiel was persuaded, but before agreeing to the IPO, he asked the board to dramatically increase his pay. At the time, Thiel and Levchin each owned around 3 percent of the company. By contrast, Musk, who'd paid X.com's early expenses out of his own pocket—and thus had kept more of the equity for himself—had 14 percent. This disparity, Thiel argued, was ridiculous, according to three sources familiar with the negotiation. The board was pushing him to reject acquisition deals that would have brought him and Levchin millions of dollars—life-changing money for him and PayPal's employees, even if it didn't mean much to Sequoia. If Moritz wanted him to continue as CEO, he'd need more equity. If not, he said, he would quit that day.

The threat shocked board members, some of whom regarded Thiel with suspicion ever since he'd attempted to invest PayPal cash in his own hedge fund. The sudden departure of the founder and CEO of the company would be viewed as disastrous by investors, which could imperil PayPal's ability to raise more money, and, given its losses and the perilous state of the tech industry, might even send it into bankruptcy. "It was pay me or I'm going to shoot myself, but you'll lose too," recalled one of the board sources.

The board, naturally, chose to pay, and PayPal awarded its CEO nearly 4.5 million more shares at a huge discount, increasing his stake in the company to 5.6 percent. PayPal charged Thiel $1.35 million for a block of shares that would be worth $21 million after the IPO and loaned him the money. Somewhat curiously, Thiel used only about $850,000 of the loan. For the rest, $500,000, he used the proceeds that he had inside a Roth IRA, a retirement account that likely dated to his time in New York. That meant that the $20 million profit from his last-minute hostage negotiation—and any future appreciation—would be entirely tax free.

Leaving aside the eleventh-hour threat, Thiel's use of the IRA put him in a legal gray area. It was illegal to use a Roth IRA to buy stock in a company that you controlled. Thiel didn't have legal control of PayPal, but a strong argument could have been made that he had de facto control. Fortunately for Thiel it would be more than a decade before anyone would notice; by that time his tax-free earnings were in the billions of dollars.

AS PAYPAL WAS PREPARING to file to go public, Thiel traveled to New York with chief financial officer Roelof Botha for a meeting with bankers from Morgan Stanley. It was September 10, 2001. The meeting that afternoon was a total failure. PayPal confused the bankers—was it a technology company or an unlicensed bank, they wanted to know—and neither man cut an especially impressive figure. Thiel was a thirty-three-year-old conservative political wannabe; Botha was, at twenty-seven, absurdly young and inexperienced for a public company CFO.

The Morgan Stanley bankers indicated they weren't interested, and Thiel and Botha took a car to John F. Kennedy International Airport in the rain, feeling dejected. Their sense of misery grew when their plane, the last United flight of the day, was delayed for hours on the tarmac. Eventually, the crew offered passengers the option to disembark and take a morning flight, but Thiel and Botha opted to sit, grimly, and wait while several passengers elected to get off.

They eventually made it home to San Francisco very early the next morning. Hours later, Thiel learned that a San Francisco–bound United aircraft from Newark airport—flight number UA 93—had been hijacked and had crashed in a field in Pennsylvania. It seemed possible that at least some of the people they'd been with the night before were now dead.

The attack—and the sense that he could have been among its victims—made the idea of an IPO even more daunting. But Thiel pressed on, and on September 28, PayPal filed its prospectus with the CEC. The company, which was now represented by Salomon Smith Barney and was looking to raise up to $80.5 million, impressed no one. The stock market was terrible, there had been no IPOs since 9/11, and PayPal had never shown a profit. EARTH TO PALO ALTO, read one headline that suggested the IPO represented a return to dot-com excess.

Whitman made things even more agonizing, tempting the company with yet another offer—this time for around $900 million. Thiel wanted to accept but was overruled by the board. During PayPal's IPO road show, Whitman tried another tactic, preempting PayPal's sales calls to major investors with a trip of her own during which she mentioned her view that the company, which depended on eBay for much of its business, was doomed as an independent entity. "Meg was here the week before," bankers would confess, "pissing all over your shoes."

None of it worked, and on February 14, 2002, PayPal's stock began trading, surging from $13 per share to around $20. The mood at the office in Palo Alto was ebullient: Employees drank beer and smoked cigars in the parking lot. Thiel wore a crown and challenged a group of employees to ten simultaneous chess games. At Stanford he'd watched with a mix of awe and envy as superior chess players pulled off this feat, but at PayPal Thiel was the grandmaster. He won all but one of the games.

The IPO was freeing in one other way. Although he still wasn't legally allowed to unilaterally sell his stock—executives were subject to a six-month lockup period—all Thiel needed was an offer above the company's share price from eBay and he could sell the entire thing. He wouldn't even need Moritz's blessing. He had one within weeks, when Whitman agreed to pay around $1.2 billion, slightly more than the company's market value at the time. Thiel agreed but then reneged and demanded more money after news of the deal leaked in mid-April and PayPal's stock started to climb. Whitman was furious, blaming Thiel for the leak and for failing to honor his agreement. She decided she was done doing business with Thiel and ordered her deputies to cut off all contact.

Still, Whitman allowed PayPal to keep the ten-foot-by-ten-foot booth it had rented for eBay Live, the company's annual meeting for sellers. PayPal made the most of the opportunity, renting a hotel ballroom across from the Anaheim Convention Center, where the conference was taking place. The plan was to embarrass eBay on its home turf. "People should come away from eBay Live liking PayPal better than eBay," David Sacks, the onetime architect of the *Stanford Review* rape issue and now the company's COO, told employees at the time.

The first night of the conference, June 21, PayPal invited 1,000 attendees to a cocktail party, featuring not only free drinks but also, for each guest, a T-shirt with PayPal's logo and the phrase "New World Currency" printed on the back. The actual crowd was much larger, perhaps 2,500. The booze flowed and attendees were told that PayPal would be drawing names out of a hat the following day, with a $250 prize. To be eligible though, they'd have to be wearing the shirt in the morning.

The idea, said Bill Onderdonk, was to "make a visual case for: this is what the community wants." The following day, when Whitman took the stage for her own keynote, she was staring at hundreds of PayPal logos— roughly a quarter of the crowd was wearing the freebie. It was as if "the users were asking Meg, why don't you just buy PayPal," said April Kelly, the company's head of customer service.

That's exactly what happened. The day after Whitman's speech Sacks found his eBay counterpart, Jeff Jordan.

"Should we try this one more time?" he asked.

The two men met again on July 2 and agreed on a price—roughly

$1.5 billion, which would be paid in eBay stock. Sacks and Jordan negotiated through the end of the following weekend. They chose the time frame strategically: Markets would be closed on July 4, and trading would be light on Friday, July 5, with most of Wall Street taking the day off. That would minimize the chance of a leak. More importantly, perhaps, Thiel would be in Hawaii, and therefore unable to antagonize Whitman, who conveniently would be at an ashram in Los Angeles and would be unreachable.

With relations between the two CEOs poisonous, Whitman also kept her distance, allowing Jordan to negotiate on her behalf. Both boards approved the deal over the weekend, and by Sunday, it was done: Peter Thiel was going to be very rich. He'd owned 4 percent of the company after the IPO, which meant he was due stock worth more than $50 million.

OFFICIALLY, THIEL WAS staying put—at least that's what he and Whitman said when they addressed PayPal's staff the following Monday. The audience was skeptical: The engineers showed up in blue oxford shirts and khakis as a jab at the auction site's essential squareness. But Thiel brought them around by promising there would be no layoffs— "except for Billpoint," which, he gleefully told them, would be shutting down.

When Whitman appeared, she played nice, ignoring the engineers' outfits, happily putting on a PayPal baseball hat, and heaping praise on Thiel, Sacks, and their employees. "You should be very proud of the company that you've built, in spite of us sometimes putting up some roadblocks," she said.

After they'd made their remarks, Whitman and Thiel went to Thiel's office. As Whitman sat down, she noticed that there was something sticking out of an open briefcase sitting on the floor. It looked, she remarked, like a plane ticket.

"Are you going anywhere?" Whitman asked.

Thiel responded coolly: Yes. He wasn't planning on staying at eBay after the acquisition and with war looking increasingly likely in the Middle East, Thiel explained that he wanted to squeeze in a trip to meet with investors in the region.

"I've decided I'm going to start a hedge fund," he said.

Whitman took this in. "Peter," she asked. "Do you want to tell the PayPal team?"

He looked at her quizzically. "Good point, Meg," he said. "Good point."

Whitman left the meeting assuming that Thiel would follow her advice. He did not, continuing to leave the impression with senior employees that he planned to stay, even as he negotiated an exit from eBay.

On October 3, the day that eBay was set to announce that its deal had closed, senior managers gathered in a conference room, waiting for the press release. They believed it would explain the new structure, which would have PayPal joining eBay as a wholly owned subsidiary with Peter Thiel as CEO.

When it hit, the release said something else: "Peter Thiel announced today that he has resigned as PayPal's CEO." His replacement would be an eBay vice president who'd previously worked as a consultant at McKinsey—in other words, the exact kind of manager that Thiel had trained his followers to despise.

Thiel's reasoning for negotiating his exit, he explained to a PayPal employee, had been financial. He believed that eBay—the company to which he'd sold PayPal, and one that he'd publicly praised as an ideal fit—was overvalued. He planned to hedge his eBay position, using put options—derivatives that allow investors to make money if the price of a stock falls. Put another way: He wanted to bet against his new colleagues, to "optimize for his hedge fund," as this staffer put it. Some saw this as reasonable, if a little cold. Others saw it in starker terms. Their idealistic CEO wasn't just giving up on PayPal; he was giving up on a value system that saw creativity and innovation as the highest ends. Anyone worth his salt in Silicon Valley knew what it meant to choose hedge funds over technology. Greed.

"Our hearts sank," said the staffer. Even Levchin, cofounder and one of his best friends, looked shocked. "None of us knew."

But Thiel wasn't just protecting his own financial interest. He sensed correctly that his success at PayPal had given him license to operate on a plane beyond Silicon Valley, and he wanted to take advantage. At the time—and even to this day in some corners of the tech industry—Thiel is still seen as a technologist. But of course, tech was a field that he'd stumbled into as an investment opportunity, not one for which he had much real passion. That boom was over—but there were new ones on the horizon.

7

HEDGING

The East Room of the White House was packed by the time George W. Bush walked out, wearing a dark suit, a baby blue tie, and his trademark smirk. Thiel had waited half the day for this, one of two hundred or so tech executives who'd been invited by the White House to meet the new president. Bush, a Harvard MBA who'd styled himself as a businessman even after becoming governor of Texas, had aggressively courted Silicon Valley during and after his campaign, tapping Floyd Kvamme, a venture capitalist with the firm Kleiner Perkins, as his technical and scientific adviser. This had been a departure from tradition since Kvamme was not—like past chairs of the President's Council of Advisors on Science and Technology—a scientist.

Bush opened with a reference to the dot-com bust, noting that "this administration has great confidence in the future of our technology industry" even though "the stock market may be sending a little different message right now." During the speech, which came just two months after his inauguration, in March 2001, Bush promised to expand production of fossil fuels, lower taxes for businesses, and pursue unfettered free trade. He warned that if the economy continued to falter, "the protectionist sentiments around America might start bubbling to the surface." The businessman-president promised to resist them. "We should not try to build walls around our nation and encourage others to do so," he drawled from the modest stage. "We ought to be tearing them down."

There were a handful of prominent Silicon Valley leaders interested in politics at the time, but most of them had been affiliated with Bush's opponent, Al Gore, and his centrist, technocratic vision of Democratic Party politics. The rest of Silicon Valley had tended to evince a brand of libertarianism that, at least publicly, expressed no politics at all. This was the techno-futurism of *Wired* magazine—a fusion of the personal freedom of Summer of Love–era Haight-Ashbury and the don't-tread-on-me spirit that had defined Californian politics since the days of David Starr Jordan.

Thiel, then, was an outlier, in both his renewed vigor for politics and his separation from the squishy "Atari Democrats" like Gore. He'd been immersing himself in neoconservative thinking, reading Carl Schmitt, the conservative philosopher (and Nazi legal scholar) who is sometimes credited with inspiring the expansion of executive powers under George W. Bush, and Leo Strauss, the German Jewish University of Chicago political science professor who'd argued that the West had lost its way as it had embraced liberal values.

Thiel had been happy to be invited to the Bush event—even if it was no more than a photo op—and in the year that followed he became consumed by the prospect of a preemptive war in Iraq, which Bush had been pushing for and which Thiel made clear to employees that he favored. This seemed profoundly strange to PayPal's libertarian staff, who wondered why an ideological fellow traveler was arguing for military expansion. "It was weird," said one. "I was like, 'What the fuck are you talking about, Peter? You're defending big government.'"

This was one of the many ideological compromises that Thiel made starting around 2002 to suit the various projects he was attempting simultaneously. The efforts were related but also distinct—each requiring a slightly different set of beliefs and forcing him to project a slightly different image depending on whom his audience was at the time. They were: a money project, the goal of which was to grow Thiel's wealth, requiring him, at times, to adopt the tastes and manners of a Wall Street mogul; a tech project, which was about establishing himself as a power broker in Silicon Valley after the dot-com bust; and a political project, which involved using those two things—his money and his tech credibility—to establish himself as a thought leader and to accumulate influence in Washington. The three efforts would often be in tension—as he embraced his identity as a hedge fund manager, Thiel would tack away from Silicon Valley, embracing the accoutrements of wealth, acquiring fabulous homes, fancy cars, and vanity businesses. But they were tied together in that they all involved, in one way or another, the elevation of Thiel's contrarianism as a virtue to be celebrated in itself.

WALL STREET HAD BATTERED Silicon Valley after the dot-com crash. An estimated 80 percent of companies created in the few years prior were expected to fail; the gold rush that brought MBAs and others west to get internet rich were headed home, and even established tech companies such as Oracle were struggling. And yet, as PayPal emerged as one of the lucky survivors, Thiel began to embrace Wall Street's fratty aesthetic. When the company had gone public in February 2002, Thiel had celebrated the IPO in nerdy fashion, playing a simultaneous chess exhibition in the company parking lot. By that summer, though, he was hosting a company offsite at a winery in the Santa Cruz mountains and the senior staff, including Thiel, put on fat suits, got into a ring, and sumo-wrestled while employees cheered.

A year earlier, he'd played the tech maverick in an interview with

Wired, promising to dye his hair blue if PayPal got to profitability. (It didn't happen.) "Peter Thiel doesn't often hedge," the magazine had written approvingly about a man who was about to start a literal hedge fund. *Wired* had found Thiel, when he was CEO of PayPal, dressed down, wearing an untucked T-shirt and faded Levi's, and mostly hanging around Palo Alto, where he lived in a modest one-bedroom apartment. Now Thiel had a wardrobe full of suits, and a silver Ferrari Spider 360. "Red," he told *The New York Times Magazine* in 2005, "would've been over the top."

At the PayPal retreat, he brought up the media putdown that had followed his IPO filing the previous year—"Earth to Palo Alto"—and inverted it. "I'd like to send a message back to planet Earth from Palo Alto," Thiel said, according to *The PayPal Wars*. "Life is good here in Palo Alto. We've been able to improve on many of the ways you do things. Come to Palo Alto for a visit sometime and learn something. I think you'll find it's a much better place than Earth."

Not too long after his comments, Thiel would move north to San Francisco, where he'd set himself up in a three-bedroom condo in the Four Seasons and start Clarium Capital.

Thiel would eventually trade the condo for a 10,000-square-foot, Marina-style mansion overlooking the Palace of Fine Arts—a Beaux-Arts monument from the 1916 World's Fair—and with views of the Golden Gate Bridge looming high above the fog. The location, just on the edge of San Francisco's fort-turned-park, the Presidio, evoked, as Thiel would sometimes remind people, a sense of the frontier, which was appropriate since San Francisco, in the wake of the bust, had become a frontier again.

He filled the house with contemporary art and modernist furniture—Parzinger armchairs, Niedermaier dining sets—and renovated it to include a boardroom for meetings, a living room designed for guest lecturers, a dining room configured for buffet-style service, and a "day-to-night lounge" on the roof for parties. One thing that was missing, visitors noted, were any items of sentimental significance. There were no keepsakes, no magazines, and no family photos. "Thiel's homes," as one visitor remarked, referring to the Presidio mansion and a grand apartment that Thiel acquired in New York City, "look like stage sets, and it's hard to tell someone actually lives in them."

Almost everything Thiel owned was now chosen for him by a young assistant, Andrew McCormack, one of a half dozen former PayPal employees who left eBay almost immediately to work for him. "Andrew helped him pick his furniture; he picked the color of his Ferrari," said Scott Kester, a New York restaurant designer Thiel hired to work on another property—a lounge-style nightclub called Frisson—that Thiel would use to project this new identity.

When McCormack approached Kester about Frisson, he'd effused about Lotus, a nightclub in New York's Meatpacking District—infamous for its coed bathrooms, which he said were ideal for late-night trysts. McCormack asked Kester to build something similar for Thiel in San Francisco. The whole thing seemed surreal to the designer, so he told McCormack he'd only design the lounge if Thiel furnished him with an apartment in San Francisco and a brand-new Ducati motorcycle. To his surprise, Thiel agreed. "I can't believe this guy is for real," Kester thought. To plan the menu at Frisson, Thiel hired Daniel Patterson, the city's hottest young chef, and spared no expense on furnishings. There was an enormous light-up mural, a famous landscape designer, and a $1 million sound system. "This was an obscene amount of money for a restaurant," recalled an early server.

When Frisson opened in 2004, reviewers were impressed and only slightly horrified by the excess. "Not since Ian Schrager and Phillippe Starck opened Asia de Cuba has there been such a clear-sighted fusion of design, art, lighting, sound, and interior architecture," one wrote, noting that Kester's bathrooms seemed designed "expressly for couples looking for a quickie," with mirrors, racy art, and an attractive bathroom attendant.

The decision to pile fine dining on top of what was clearly a place for partying ultimately doomed Frisson as a business, but it served its purpose. For several years it regularly attracted celebrities—Lars Ulrich, Robert Redford, Kevin Spacey—and tech millionaires, and it was Thiel's go-to meeting location. If he wanted to convince someone to take a job at one of his other ventures, he'd invite them to Frisson, order a beverage and a bunch of Patterson's weird small plates. He'd then take out his checkbook and theatrically begin filling it out. "I'm going to write you a check right now," he said to one recent graduate. Think about the job, he offered, but either way, keep the money. "This," he explained, "is a zero-risk opportunity."

The mansion, the nightclub, the suits—it was all befitting a master of the universe, as well as someone who had no interest in letting anyone, even his closest friends, inside his head. Thiel was nominally straight, and sometimes was seen with women, including one particular attractive young woman that most of the world assumed was Thiel's girlfriend. Kester figured Andrew McCormack had picked her out, too.

Most of his friends, though, knew that he simply preferred to steer clear of the subject of sex altogether. In 2006, Max Levchin would confess that he couldn't recall Thiel ever mentioning his personal life. Once—once!—Thiel asked about Levchin's girlfriend. "I was shocked," Levchin said.

ANOTHER CASUALTY OF the dot-com era was print journalism, as two of the survivors of the tech boom—Craigslist and Google—were beginning to capture advertising revenue that the media moguls in the 1990s had thought would last forever. So perhaps even more curious than Thiel opening a nightclub was his launching a magazine, *American Thunder*. It was aimed at NASCAR fans, which he funded with a $10 million investment. The launch prompted some snickers: Thiel, wrote *New York Times* media reporter David Carr, "probably would not know

Richard Petty if he ran over him." To run the venture, Thiel hired Aman Verjee, a former *Stanford Review* editor in chief who'd joined PayPal shortly before the sale to eBay, and Lucas Mast, a twenty-nine-year-old Cato Institute analyst who'd also worked at the *Review*. Channeling his inner Dinesh D'Souza, Mast, the new magazine's editor, promised that the publication would "not embody any sense of political correctness."

As it turned out, racing fans were more interested in racing than they were in dorm-room rants about the importance of saying the unsayable. The magazine's "Real Guys" column was written not by an auto journalist but by the online editor for the *Weekly Standard*, who devoted his first column to the idea that ESPN had been "emasculated" by "namby-pamby political correctness." The "Grub" page, where a normal magazine would have stuck the barbecue recipes, included, in its inaugural column, a possibly tongue-in-cheek anthropological discussion of why household cooking should be considered "woman's work." "Everyday cooking is a chore few men ever get around to, or even care to get around to," the article noted. "We're grateful this is how things have worked out. So grateful, we'll even help with the dishes from time to time." Not even a page full of racetrack creep shots of scantily-clad spectators—"Trackside Distractions"—was enough to convince readers or advertisers to stick around.

The magazine was out of money by the end of the year, and Thiel pulled the plug. Daniel Patterson would only last a few months longer at Frisson, leaving in early 2005. The restaurant itself would make it until 2008. But if these were failures, they were strategic failures, setting up Thiel's actual moneymaking plans, which required him to start acting like the hedge-fund manager he hoped to become.

The information age had arrived in the investment-fund world by this point, led by the Renaissance Technologies Medallion fund, which used computers to make thousands of trades a day, but Thiel styled himself as a throwback—a "global macro" investor, which meant predicting major economic and political shifts, for instance a recession in Brazil or a war in the Arabian Peninsula, and then betting based on those predictions. Macro investors might only try to make a trade a week—an approach that fit perfectly with Thiel's unusual combination of indecisiveness and high tolerance for risk. "His worldview is that if you get one big thing right, and move hard with conviction, then nothing else matters," said an early Clarium employee.

It also fit with his appetite for power: Quantitative trading's effects on the market are in most cases hard to parse; macro investors, because their bets tend to be large, involving entire economies, can move—and in rare cases, destroy—those economies. If you bet enough money on a recession as a macro investor, you may end up causing one.

Thiel's choice of strategy was contrarian in another way. At the time, the most famous macro investor was the uber-liberal George Soros. In 2003, Soros, whose lefty activism had been focused outside the United States, would emerge as the most important financial supporter of the effort to unseat George W. Bush. He was also known as the financier who'd correctly predicted—and then hastened—the devaluation of the British pound, by borrowing billions of pounds and using that money to buy other European currencies. "The man who broke the Bank of England" would later anticipate (and also be blamed for) crashes in Southeast Asia, but he took big losses by shorting tech stocks during the late 1990s and buying biotech stocks just as the market was peaking.

Thiel's pessimism had led to tension with Moritz at PayPal; now it was his secret weapon. Clarium's investment thesis held that the tech bubble collapse should have led to a depression, which had only been thwarted by low interest rates and high levels of borrowing by American consumers. Meanwhile, oil prices were bound to rise, driven by growing demand from the developing world and instability in the Middle East, which would further damage America's long-term economic prospects. Soros had bet against England and Asia; Thiel would bet against the United States.

Like Soros, Thiel styled himself as an intellectual—Clarium was "a combination of a startup, think tank, and hedge fund," as chief operating officer Ralph Ho put it. Ho had been a vice president at PayPal since 1999 and was part of a group of loyalists Thiel brought with him. They included Ken Howery, who'd been the original CFO of PayPal, Nathan Linn, author of the column that warned about the "deviant sexual practices" among gays in the *Stanford Review* (and later a PayPal lawyer), and Joe Lonsdale, another *Review* alumnus who'd been a PayPal intern. Thiel also hired Kevin Harrington, a Stanford physics grad student who'd written for the *Review*, as his deputy.

In theory Thiel's employees were supposed to help him come up with ideas for trades and other investments; in practice all the big decisions were his. Clarium employees read, played chess, and debated (sample topic: If you were going to design a country from scratch, what would it look like?). Everyone spent a lot of time talking politics, though it was important that those politics always be of the right-wing variety. An employee told me that it was common to hear talk about climate change denial and to see web browsers open to VDARE, a far-right website with a long record of publishing white nationalist writing. There were liberals at Clarium, but they understood that it was best to keep those views quiet. If Thiel asked you—as he often did, over dinner—what was an opinion of yours that had changed, you knew it was always best to try to think of an issue where you'd drifted right, no matter how obscure. If you believed that the decline of organized labor was bad for America, and Thiel somehow maneuvered the conversation in that direction, you knew enough to change the subject to an area of potential common ground—life extension, for instance. Thiel had begun donating to the Methuselah Foundation, a nonprofit dedicated to the idea of curing aging, which it claimed mainstream science was ignoring; some Clarium staffers, including Thiel, were customers of Alcor Life Extension Foundation, the cryonics center.

In terms of work that would be recognizable as such, well, there wasn't much. Most days they would clear out a little around 3 p.m. Actual investing, if not discouraged, was seen as a relatively small part of the job. "Every two years, I'd do one investment," said Ajay Royan, who joined the firm in 2003. "Then I'd just watch."

Royan, then in his early twenties, was a typical Clarium hire, in that he had impressive academic credentials and the right politics, if not any traditional qualifications. He met Thiel to pitch him on the idea of investing in a startup that would ship vegan meal kits by mail. Royan didn't cook, but he had been active in conservative circles at Yale and had done some investing in high school. That shared affinity was enough. "Why don't you come to Clarium and do your startup," Thiel said. His company, Yoga Food, flamed out—no surprise—but Royan stuck around.

This kind of indulgence was typical at the time for Thiel, who spent just as freely on his company as he did in his personal life, and for employees the perks were magnificent: Partners' assistants were expected not just to schedule meetings, but also manage their homes. Everyone got free food, free vacations, and free sessions with Thiel's extremely handsome personal trainer. "He treated his workers better than any boss I'd ever had," a former employee told me.

BY EARLY 2004, Thiel was getting noticed by the financial press. Clarium now had $260 million under management, returns were up 125 percent, and Thiel featured in a glowing *Barron's* column, accompanied by a photo of him wearing white trousers and a white shirt. Given his worldview, he should have been wearing black, the columnist joked, presenting him as an intellectual who just so happened to also be a dot-com millionaire. "There are an awful lot of funds pursuing disturbingly similar strategies," Thiel was quoted as saying. "Not many people are asking the big questions."

PayPal had thrived under a decentralized approach, and at Clarium, he gave employees even more leeway, setting up little skunkworks groups, asking one or two people to look into an idea for a trade or manage a small pool of capital. Anyone who did well got more; anyone who did poorly got ignored (though rarely fired, for Thiel seemed to abhor conflict).

It was an unconventional approach that may have stemmed as much from Thiel's lack of confidence as a manager as from any grand strategy, but by 2005 it was working beautifully. Thiel had wanted to bet on rising oil prices, and his traders found a perfect way to do it in Canada's barren far north. The region had never produced much conventional crude oil, but it had enormous deposits of a very heavy form of petroleum called bitumen that was mixed into the sandy soil. These tar sands were known to contain lots of oil, but for most of the twentieth century, no one knew how to separate it from the dirt cheaply enough. In the 1950s, the Canadian government had considered detonating a 9-kiloton nuclear warhead in Alberta—the first of as many as one hundred nuclear explosions envisioned—which, in theory at least, would melt the soil and make it easy to drill. There were, as one might imagine, skeptics, and the plan was scrapped before any nukes were deployed.

But as the price of oil neared $100 per barrel in the mid-2000s, the expensive process of mining the sands, trucking them to a plant where they would be mixed with hot water to separate out the oil, and sending that oil to a refinery—so environmentally unfriendly that *National Geographic* would call it "the world's most destructive oil operation"—started to look profitable. Clarium bought stock in a handful of newly public Canadian minerals companies—including Western Oil Sands, which owned a stake in a major Alberta mining operation, and OPTI Canada, an Israeli-Canadian company that had developed a new process for extracting bitumen. Both companies doubled in value that year—and Thiel looked like a genius with returns of nearly 60 percent.

He embraced his identity as a freethinking renegade, relocating Clarium out of the financial district and into an airy office in the Presidio, not far from the headquarters of Lucasfilm, the *Star Wars* production company. He sold the Four Seasons condo and moved to a house near the new office, encouraging the entire firm to follow suit. He paid any Clarium employee who lived within a half mile from the new location an extra $1,000 per month on top of whatever they were already making. He described the change of setting as part of a grand strategy. The idea was "to keep his team away from other money managers and investment bankers who might cloud their thinking," as *Bloomberg* explained it in 2006. By then the fund was managing more than $2 billion, and Thiel was being hailed as the next Soros.

As the firm grew and Thiel's celebrity increased, so did his own comfort. He began telling close friends and then coworkers that he was gay, socializing at bars or on the roof of his new house often with the handsome young men he was hiring, many of whom were out. "It was the best familial experience I've ever had," said one. "Many of us really clicked."

Thiel's self-actualization would pay off. In August 2007—four months before the recession began, and close to a year before most Americans realized the economy was collapsing—he sent a letter to investors declaring that the economic expansion was officially over. "We have begun a post–Long Boom phase that can be called the Long Goodbye," the letter said. Unfortunately, regular Americans didn't seem to realize this and were still borrowing frantically, which meant that there would be a "painful de-leveraging and a reduction in liquidity"—wonk-speak for a financial crisis.

The idea had been Thiel's, and it was brilliant—even by his standards. The firm began shorting the dollar and betting against any company that was borrowing a lot of money. Returns went crazy, almost immediately, jumping from 5 percent in November to 13 percent in December, and then to an eye-popping 24 percent in January. Thiel's return for the first half of 2008, when most hedge funds lost money, was almost 60 percent; by now, Clarium had $6.4 billion under management. "It was amazing," said an analyst. "He was trading like a demigod."

To celebrate, Thiel rented the private plane normally used by the

Dallas Mavericks to fly the entire firm—roughly eighty people by this point—to Maui for a long weekend. When the group arrived at the Four Seasons, they were told that everything was on the company—get massages, go surfing, drink as much as you wanted. In the evenings, executives threw around money like it was candy. At one point, Joe Lonsdale offered $10,000 to anyone who could beat him in arm wrestling. Another partner wrote a $10,000 check to an employee for a particularly good round of karaoke.

BACK AT PAYPAL, Thiel had frantically tried to sell the company, even as it grew with unbelievable speed, and then sought to bet against his position after the eBay sale. Now he started to do so again, even as his investing attracted acclaim. This would become a pattern: When Thiel was in the money, he'd look to sell—or to somehow hedge his bets.

And so, even as Thiel's achievements as a bearish hedge funder were celebrated—"Everything Silicon Valley venture capitalist Peter Thiel touches seems to turn to gold," the *New York Post* observed—he was beginning to get more serious about investing in startups.

Thiel did this quietly, and initially gave the impression that he thought buying stock in tech companies was a fool's game. "It's the worst time ever to be a venture capitalist," he'd said in 2004. He declined to invest in Tesla Motors, Elon Musk's electric car company, and in YouTube, an online video startup cofounded by two lower-level ex-PayPal employees, Steve Chen and Chad Hurley.

Thiel did make some exceptions though, especially for a new and much-hyped category of tech startup that seemed promising, even in the gloomy, post-bubble tech industry: social networks. He made small investments in LinkedIn, the business-focused website that allowed people to post their resumes online, and Friendster, which allowed friends to digitally keep tabs on one another. But Thiel's most important move involved a social network aimed at college students.

Facebook had come to his attention because of a young entrepreneur named Sean Parker. As a nineteen-year-old, Parker had cofounded Napster, the music service that turned every high school and college student into an intellectual property thief by allowing them to download and share digital music with anyone in the world, for free. He was widely seen among venture capitalists as dangerous because of his penchant for rule-breaking and was also exactly the kind of person—young and aggressive, with no apparent regard for following norms, or even laws—that Peter Thiel would be taken with.

After Napster had been sued into oblivion by the recording industry, Parker started Plaxo—another proto-social network. It purported to help people manage their contacts, but in fact worked more like an enormous spam machine. Once you signed up and gave it your contacts, the service would begin emailing your friends relentlessly until they signed up too—resulting in PayPal-like growth.

Mike Moritz, who was also aggressively funding social media companies, introduced Thiel to Parker shortly after Plaxo was founded in 2002, hoping Thiel would invest. Thiel passed—he was in no mood, it seemed, to reconcile with Moritz—but he became friendly with Parker anyway, and their friendship deepened after Thiel learned that Parker didn't especially care for the famous Silicon Valley VC either. Moritz might have hoped Parker would be humbled by his experience at Napster; instead, according to some accounts, Parker acted like the celebrity CEO he believed himself to be. In early 2004, Plaxo fired Parker, amid allegations that he wasn't showing up to the office and had been distributing cocaine to employees. Parker denied the allegations, claiming that they'd been cooked up to force him out. The board fired him anyway.

Parker bonded with Thiel over the experience of tangling with Moritz and asked what he should do. Don't sue, Thiel told him. Start a company. A few months later, Parker got back in touch with a proposal. He'd met a Harvard undergraduate named Mark Zuckerberg who had a website that was going absolutely bonkers on Ivy League campuses. Would Thiel be interested in investing?

"YOU KNOW THIS is where they filmed *Towering Inferno*?" Parker's character, played by the pop star Justin Timberlake, cracks to the Zuckerberg character, played by Jesse Eisenberg, as the two men enter Thiel's office in *The Social Network*, David Fincher's Facebook movie. This was true—*Towering Inferno* was shot at the Bank of America building—though the rest of the meeting itself played out somewhat differently than in the film. Reid Hoffman, who was closer to Parker, came along as a sort of broker, as did Matt Cohler, an early LinkedIn employee.

Zuckerberg—wearing a gray T-shirt, jeans, and Adidas shower shoes—shuffled in and spent most of the meeting looking at the table, though he did pipe up at one point to tell Thiel about another idea he was working on: a file-sharing site, Wirehog.

"No—not interested," Thiel said. He wanted to talk about Facebook.

Parker made the case. Facebook had required users to have an email address from a small group of colleges, starting with Harvard, Columbia, Stanford, and Yale. Now Facebook was set up on dozens of campuses, and each time it added a new one it would sign up 80 percent of the undergraduates in a matter of days. Even more impressive: These users were coming back every day.

Zuckerberg's reticence and awkwardness impressed Thiel, who saw in the young man's indifference a sign of intelligence. They were kindred spirits, really: Zuckerberg, like Thiel, had stuck it in the eye of his politically correct peers when he'd hacked Harvard's online directory to create FaceMash. The website would randomly show users two headshots of first-year Harvard women, eighteen- and nineteen-year-olds, and ask the user to vote for who was hotter. "Were we let in for our looks? No." a banner on the website declared. "Will we be judged on them? Yes."

(Zuckerberg apologized shortly after the 2003 incident, claiming he hadn't meant for the site to be circulated beyond a small group of his friends. "I definitely see how my intentions could be seen in the wrong light," he told the *Harvard Crimson*.)

"Don't fuck it up," Thiel told Zuckerberg at the end of their meeting. He agreed to invest $500,000, using proceeds from the Roth IRA, which had grown substantially thanks to PayPal's sale to eBay. Hoffman kicked in $40,000.

A few months later, in December, Thiel threw a party at Frisson to celebrate Facebook's one-millionth college student signup (and Parker's twenty-fifth birthday). Not long after, Roelof Botha, whom Moritz had hired at Sequoia, suggested that Zuckerberg come pitch the firm. Zuckerberg agreed to meet, but then didn't show up for the appointment. After Botha called him, he arrived at Sequoia's office wearing pajama pants, claiming to have overslept, and then delivered a PowerPoint presentation that listed reasons for the firm *not* to invest. One of the last slides: "Sean Parker is involved." It was an insult aimed at Moritz; Sequoia was being blackballed by what would be by far the most successful startup of the decade.

Though Thiel's investment in Facebook would eventually translate to a 10 percent stake in the company, it was initially structured as a loan. Zuckerberg would have to pay back the money unless he was able to hit 1.5 million users by the end of the year and reincorporate the company so that it would be based in business-friendly Delaware and so that it owned the underlying intellectual property behind the service. Facebook had a messy cap table, as it's known in Silicon Valley, which meant that its founder had given away too much equity. Zuckerberg owned the technology behind Facebook, but the company, which had been set up as a Florida LLC, was jointly owned by Zuckerberg, his roommate Dustin Moskovitz, and Eduardo Saverin, a classmate who had initially been responsible for the company's business affairs but who had taken an internship at an investment bank that summer instead of moving to Palo Alto to work on Facebook.

Zuckerberg, sensing his partner's lack of commitment, wanted to force Saverin out. So he and Parker reincorporated, giving Zuckerberg 51 percent of the new company. Saverin wound up with 30 percent—and would see his share diluted as Facebook made additional grants to Zuckerberg, Parker, Moskovitz, and other early employees. Meanwhile, Zuckerberg would wind up with the right to name three of the four seats on the company's board of directors. Thiel was the only outside director.

The dispute between Saverin and Zuckerberg—with Parker egging Zuckerberg on—became the central conflict of *The Social Network*. But what the movie left out is that the equity play resembled Thiel's high-stakes negotiations with Moritz during the days before PayPal's IPO and that Zuckerberg was self-consciously following Thiel's lead. He acknowledged this in an instant-message exchange with Sean Parker in June 2004. Parker mentioned Thiel's predilection for "dirty tricks" during negotiations and then described these tricks as "classic Moritz shit."

"I bet [Thiel] learned that from Mike," Parker said.

"Well," Zuckerberg responded. "Now I learned it from him, and I'll do it to Eduardo."

It would be the first of many instances in which Thiel used a kind of soft power, setting in motion events that ultimately took place beyond his control, but which would enrich him and further his influence. He hadn't *forced* Zuckerberg to cut out Saverin, but in making the loan, he'd put Zuckerberg in a position where he would have to reincorporate Facebook—or be faced with the prospect of paying back the $500,000 loan. More importantly, perhaps, he'd created a moral justification for these actions by his example—the way he'd ruthlessly guarded his own interests at PayPal at the expense of Musk, Moritz, and others. Founders who followed the Thiel model weren't just allowed to bend the normal rules of decency to protect their creations—they were expected to do so.

8

INCEPTION

The immediate period after 9/11 had been experienced by most Americans as a national trauma—there was a recession, an unpopular war, a rolling sense of doom. The mail wasn't safe—somebody had managed to kill five people by sending letters contaminated with anthrax—nor were the streets around the nation's capital, where a sniper was picking off housewives and schoolchildren at random. Although neither of these attacks would be linked to terrorist groups, the public saw them as connected to the rise of religious extremism, which seemed to be everywhere.

For his part, Thiel was finding himself increasingly consumed by the threat posed by Islamic terrorism—and Islam itself—as well as ways that he might be able to capitalize on the moment. In July 2004, he and Robert Hamerton-Kelly, the conservative Stanford chaplain, organized a six-day seminar with René Girard, during which Thiel criticized Bush for not being tough enough on Islam and complained of "the fundamentalist civil rights mania of the American Civil Liberties Union."

The comments come from an essay Thiel wrote and published based on the conference, in which he also argued that the United States should try to use extrajudicial and extralegal methods—finding, as he put it, "political framework that operates outside the checks and balances of representative democracy as described in high school textbooks"—to deal with terrorism. "Instead of the United Nations," he wrote, "we should consider Echelon, the secret coordination of the world's intelligence services, as the decisive path to a truly global *pax Americana*."

The reference was to a Cold War–era intelligence network in which the United States—with Australia, Canada, New Zealand, and the U.K.—used satellites to spy on Soviet communications, but it also called to mind the Patriot Act, the anti-terrorism law hastily passed by Congress and signed into law by Bush after 9/11. Among other things, the law allowed government agencies to amass enormous troves of data—phone and electronic records from suspected terrorists and, as it would turn out, U.S. citizens.

PayPal had been a libertarian company—in Thiel's most extreme imaginings, it had been a way to unilaterally strip governments of the power to control their own money supplies. But Thiel was, after 9/11 anyway, no longer much of a libertarian, if he'd ever been one in the first place. He was growing skeptical of democracy, of immigration, and of all other forms of globalization—and he was, just then, working on a new company to suit his new politics.

While Mark Zuckerberg and Sean Parker had been pitching Thiel their new social network for college students, another group of young men were sitting at a bank of desks just a few feet away from the forty-third-floor conference room, and right next to the vegan-meal-kit guy. Thiel had given them a specific mission: to see if Igor, the software Levchin had created to thwart the Russian cybercriminals who had threatened PayPal's business, could also catch terrorists.

The initial team, which at times also worked out of an office in Palo Alto, consisted of a mix of Stanford conservatives and a genius coder.

Stephen Cohen was an undergraduate, who'd been editor of the *Review* the previous spring, and Joe Lonsdale was a former PayPal intern and who had been two years ahead of Cohen as editor in chief of the *Review*. The team's senior member, Nathan Gettings, was in his late twenties and had worked for Levchin on the anti-fraud effort at PayPal, which he'd joined from the University of Illinois.

Thiel called the project Palantir, after the mythical Elvish "seeing stone" in *Lord of the Rings* that allows characters to observe faraway events or to look into the future. It was a curious choice: While Tolkien's *palantiri* are powerful, they're not unambiguously virtuous. In the books, the stones are chiefly used by Sauron, the Satanic character who aspires to subjugate Middle Earth, to spy, communicate with conspirators, or manipulate other characters who don't realize that the stones are dangerous to handle.

Thiel's idea—as he explained it to early employees and potential partners—was to mine the government's near-endless trove of data, including financial and cell phone records, and use network analysis to find terrorists. The obvious ways that this practice was problematic from a civil rights perspective were not mentioned; in fact, it was assumed that this would violate pre-9/11 privacy norms, but that would be totally fine in a post-9/11 world. "There's all this information about people and we want to know it," is how one person who heard Thiel summarized it.

By 2004, the *9/11 Commission Report* had made clear that in the years before the attacks, U.S. law enforcement and intelligence agencies could have caught some of the hijackers, or even disrupted the plot, if agents had only paid closer attention to the information the government had already gathered on those involved. Shortly before the attacks, the United States had arrested Zacarias Moussaoui—an apparent Islamic extremist who'd tried to learn how to fly a Boeing 747—but then failed to connect him to Al Qaeda or to the developing plot. Thiel's idea was to adapt the old Igor system and sell it to now overzealous spy agencies. The FBI had used Igor during the late 1990s to find money launderers. Why not sell it to the CIA and see if they could find terrorists?

Gettings built an early prototype and began showing it to potential investors and customers. The response was unequivocal: Interesting idea, but it will never work. As complicated as PayPal's databases had seemed—encompassing buyers and sellers from all over the world, some with credit cards, others with bank accounts—they were straightforward compared with the labyrinthine databases maintained by the CIA, NSA, and the Department of Defense.

Unlike financial fraud prevention, intelligence work was messy. It consisted of reports written by human analysts, who had their own ideas and stylistic foibles. At PayPal a user was either a credit card fraudster or a regular eBay user; in the intelligence world, analysts routinely disagreed about whether a person represented a threat or whether two people were connected to each other. What's more, intelligence data was stored in dozens of different software and hardware setups, many of which were basically incompatible. An analyst might be accessing data from an IBM mainframe, an Oracle database, or an Excel spreadsheet on a laptop—all at the same time. That meant that what Thiel envisioned would require lots of employees to clean up and process whatever went into the system—hardly an efficient upgrade. And even then, the data would be ambiguous.

That might have been it—at least as far as Gettings, Lonsdale, and Cohen were concerned—but Thiel was undeterred. While various employees worked away, he drove to the University Club in Palo Alto one morning to go see Alex Karp, whom he knew from Stanford Law School. Karp was unusual in the Thielverse—which consisted almost entirely of committed conservatives and libertarians. Karp had some libertarian beliefs, but he thought of himself as a liberal, not a conservative, and he would have looked out of place among a group of aspiring Buckleyites. Before law school, he'd had attended Haverford College, the tiny liberal arts school outside of Philadelphia that was basically the antithesis of careerist Stanford, and he'd been miserable in law school almost from the beginning. That made him an outsider, like Thiel. This—their shared misanthropy, not their politics—became a source of friendship.

Karp and Thiel had lost touch after law school—Karp went to Germany to study at the Goethe University in Frankfurt. (He would later tell people he'd studied under the great Frankfurt School philosopher Jürgen Habermas, though he received his PhD from a different part of the university.) After inheriting a modest sum from his grandfather, he used the money as seed capital to reinvent himself as an investor. Karp may have been a failure as a philosopher, but he was a dynamo as a fundraiser, with wild hair and an innate knack for playing to an audience. He raised funds from a handful of outsiders for something called the Caedmon Group, named after the Old English poet. (It's also Karp's middle name.)

Karp lived a bohemian life for a while in Berlin, and then moved home. He kept investing, but took a job as a development officer at a nonprofit. He also got back in touch with Thiel, who asked if he could help raise money for another fund—this one to invest in technology startups. It wasn't easy at first. Thiel was a successful entrepreneur, but he had no track record as a venture capitalist. So Karp leaned into his weird genius quality, presenting Thiel as a fellow traveler—quirky but brilliant—and turning his boss's relative inexperience into a selling point. His pitch was that Thiel was weird but smart; it would serve him well for the rest of his career. But Thiel wanted more than help raising money now. He wanted Karp to run the thing, and Karp accepted on the spot.

For all of Karp's prowess as a salesman, his early efforts to raise money for Palantir were mostly a failure. Moritz naturally passed, as did Kleiner Perkins, the other top Silicon Valley firm. The company had more luck in Washington, where Thiel relied on the connections he'd made at PayPal and courted many of the key architects of the Bush administration's surveillance-heavy approach to the War on Terror. These included John Poindexter, the Reagan White House adviser who had been convicted of lying to Congress about secret arms sales to Iran. Poindexter had appealed the conviction, won, and resurrected his career when Vice President Dick Cheney recruited him to the anti-terror effort. Poindexter was the mastermind of the Bush administration effort known as Total Information Awareness, or TIA, which involved gathering huge amounts of data and trying to find patterns that might suggest terrorism. It was, to civil liberties advocates, a privacy nightmare, since it would amount to surveillance of all Americans, and it was officially shut down in 2003.

Poindexter found Thiel and Karp arrogant, but he liked their idea and was impressed with the visualizations they showed him. Poindexter's involvement as an informal adviser helped Palantir make more contacts in Washington. Thiel and Karp befriended George Tenet, the recently departed Bush administration CIA director, and recruited investors at In-Q-Tel, the CIA's venture capital firm, which put in $2 million based on a rough prototype in 2005. The only other major investor was Thiel himself—once again, he put some of the capital up through the Roth IRA.

Palantir eventually set up an office in Facebook's old headquarters on University Avenue in Palo Alto and rebranded itself with a privacy focus. The company would still help the government mine data—potentially violating the privacy of ordinary Americans—but it added software to keep track of which information was being accessed and by whom. The system, which came to be known as Gotham, would create a record each time an analyst looked something up, theoretically discouraging the government from using it to look up details on a private person and, if abuses did occur, making audits possible. This was Karp's strategy for addressing the mounting civil liberties backlash against the Patriot Act. He was adamant that Palantir would not succeed without a strategy to protect civil liberties.

In later years, Thiel would strongly imply that he'd been in favor of the privacy approach from the start, but, in fact, he was skeptical at first, arguing that no one would believe that a product that claimed to preserve privacy would actually work. Karp won him over, and Palantir's privacy paper trail would become central to the company's pitch to the public. Karp seemed sincere but it was never clear how seriously clients took the idea. One of Palantir's former engineers recalled meetings during which government clients would suggest trying to use the database to look up an ex-girlfriend immediately after hearing the whole privacy spiel. Palantir employees would never object to these requests, this person said. Instead, they would remind the clients that searches were logged—and then allow them to look up whoever they wanted, no matter how flimsy the pretext.

Palantir executives pushed ethical boundaries in other ways. In 2006, Shyam Sankar, a Palantir business development executive, posed as the founder of a security firm to buy software from a more established competitor, i2, according to a lawsuit the company filed. Palantir said that nothing improper had occurred but ultimately paid a $10 million settlement.

Around this time, Thiel was involved in another effort to get sales moving. He asked Joe Lonsdale to work on a version of Palantir that could be used by hedge funds to analyze their portfolios, with Clarium as a test customer. Even though Palantir Finance didn't really work—"a disaster," as a senior executive described it—it helped Karp make the case to government agencies that Palantir was worth buying.

"You can't sell to the government if you're only selling to the government," said someone familiar with the project. "The government never wants to be the only thing that's keeping your company alive. I hesitate to say it was a ruse, but it was a thought-out play."

The characterization describes much of Palantir's work in its early days. For years, its intelligence software was effectively useless—more a demo than a real product—but the U.S. government was desperate to avoid another 9/11 and was willing to nurture a promising idea with some obviously brilliant minds behind it. Slowly, the company won a few contracts: The CIA, which had funded Palantir, began trying out its software, as did a few other intelligence agencies. In the mid-2000s, when much of Silicon Valley was still scarred by the dot-com bust and when the only successful companies were a set of small social media apps known as Web 2.0, this was enough. "Why work on a photo sharing app or a site that helps keep track of your bookmarks"—Flickr and Digg were then two of the hottest companies in the Bay Area—"when you could work on something that keeps people safe?" Palantir recruiters would ask promising students.

The NYPD, which had been operating more like an intelligence agency in the wake of 9/11, also bought a Palantir license. That deal would be a bust, and the NYPD would eventually drop Palantir, but it was enough to catch the attention of JPMorgan Chase's Jamie Dimon, who invited Karp to pitch the bank on its services in 2009.

Over drinks with bank executives, Karp managed to sell the firm not just Palantir's main security product but also Lonsdale's failing Palantir Finance. Staffers had known that Karp, who was disarming in person and often showed up to meetings in his cross-country skiing gear, was a good salesman. But the feat, which resulted in a $10 million per year contract, was seen as gravity defying. Palantir's commercial team, which was in charge of selling the company's software to the private sector, would eventually get a new code name: Inception, after the Christopher Nolan film about corporate spies who implant ideas in the subconscious of their targets to manipulate them.

Palantir was cool, and maybe even a little dangerous—a sense that was summed up in T-shirts that began to circulate around the office that referenced the TV thriller *24*. In each episode of the show, Jack Bauer, an impossibly tough intelligence officer who can waterboard like nobody's business, has twenty-four hours to save America from a calamitous terrorist attack. "If Jack Bauer had Palantir," the shirts proclaimed, "they would have had to call the show *1*."

For all this swagger, it's not clear whether Palantir was doing what it claimed. The original Inception deal didn't go especially well for

JPMorgan, which cut back on its use of the software after it learned that a member of the company's security team had been using Palantir to gain access to the private data of employees and even as a pretext to surveil them. As *Bloomberg Businessweek* reported, Palantir hadn't made an effort to stop this kind of abuse. What the company's clients did with the software, after all, was their business.

IF PALANTIR HAD BEEN an effort to repackage the security technology behind PayPal and offer it to the Bush administration for the War on Terror, then Thiel's venture capital firm, Founders Fund, would be an effort to adapt what he'd seen as the key management lesson from PayPal and turn it into an investment philosophy.

The firm started as a sort of offshoot from Clarium and operated, initially, in the office directly across the hall from Thiel's hedge fund. It was staffed by former PayPal employees Luke Nosek and Ken Howery—as well as Sean Parker, freshly departed from Facebook. Parker had left under contentious circumstances—in mid-2005, he'd been arrested on suspicion of cocaine possession while renting a beach house he'd been sharing with his assistant at Facebook. He resigned, though he denied criminal wrongdoing, and was never charged.

If the allegations of drug abuse—after he'd been pushed out of Plaxo by Moritz, amid similarly tawdry circumstances—hurt his standing in some corners of the Valley, Thiel chose to see Parker's reputation as an asset, and would use Parker's bad-boy persona as a way to differentiate Founders Fund from Sequoia, which was seen as the Valley's top firm. He boasted that Parker had kept Sequoia from investing in Facebook "because of the way they mistreated him," and suggested that Parker's detractors disliked him "because he's been so successful." All of this chafed Moritz. "The narrative got purposely and severely twisted," he said when I asked about Thiel's framing of Parker's relationship with Sequoia. "Sean had huge drug issues at the time and rarely showed up for work. His cofounders wanted him out and Sean left us with no choice. It's the last thing any investor wants to have to do." Parker has said that this portrayal was part of a "smear campaign." He did not respond to requests for comment.

In contrast to his portrayal of Sequoia, Thiel's firm pledged never to fire a founder, and he boasted that Founders Fund was looking for "riskier, more out-of-the-box companies that really have the potential to change the world." This was good branding—and the press began writing about Thiel as a brash risk taker who was pioneering a new industry, "venture capital 2.0," as the *San Francisco Chronicle* put it.

In private, however, Thiel could be conservative and, at times, coldly Machiavellian. One of his first deals was with Barney Pell, his old chess buddy from Stanford who'd started a new search engine, Powerset. It was an audacious bet—a "Google killer" that fit perfectly with the Founders Fund brand for risk taking, especially since Sequoia had been an early investor in Google. In publicizing the deal, Thiel and Parker touted their founder-friendly approach, and Pell was quoted praising Founders Fund as more sensitive to the interests of entrepreneurs. But within a year, the company was struggling, Pell was demoted from CEO to CTO, and Thiel resigned from the board.

There would be a similar gulf between the Founders Fund's marketing and reality in Thiel's dealings with Elon Musk. While Thiel had been setting up his investment firms, Musk had set out to create an electric car that could compete head-to-head with the fastest gas-powered vehicles. Improbably, Tesla Motors succeeded, and by 2006, it was giving out test drives in a prototype of its Roadster that could go from 0 to 60 mph in less than 4 seconds.

Until that point the company had subsisted, almost entirely, on Musk's PayPal earnings. But with the car nearing production, Musk needed capital and asked Thiel if he'd be interested in investing. Thiel said no—indicating that he was passing in part because, according to Musk, "he doesn't fully buy into the climate change thing." In doing so, and in choosing his own political bias over the audacity of Musk's bet (not to mention the overwhelming evidence offered by mainstream climate science), Thiel lost out on a chance to own a substantial chunk of a company that would be worth $800 billion by the end of 2020. Instead of Founders Fund, Musk took the deal to VantagePoint Venture Partners, a little-known firm with a reputation for investing in green energy companies. Vantage-Point wound up with 9 percent of Tesla when it eventually went public.

Musk tends to take any rebuke personally, and Thiel's rejection appears to have strained an already slightly uncomfortable relationship. Musk had invested in Clarium and in *Thank You for Smoking* in part as a way to bury any bad feelings about the coup—"There's a saying: friends come and go, but enemies accumulate," he said—but in 2007 he began complaining about having been written out of PayPal's history. A few years earlier, Thiel had funded the publication of a history of the company, *The PayPal Wars*, by former *Stanford Review* editor and marketer, Eric Jackson. In a letter to *Valleywag*, a tech gossip blog that had recently arrived in Silicon Valley and had been critical of Thiel, Musk called Jackson "a sycophantic jackass" and complained that in the book "Peter sounds like Mel Gibson in Braveheart and my role is somewhere between negligible and a bad seed."

When *Fortune* gathered the PayPal Mafia for a *Godfather*-themed photo shoot—with Thiel styled to resemble Marlon Brando's Don Corleone—Musk skipped the shoot, citing a prior commitment. "Peter's philosophy is pretty odd," Musk said at the time. "It's not normal. He's a contrarian from an investing standpoint and thinks a lot about the singularity. I'm much less excited about that. I'm pro-human."

But as the global economy faltered, Musk needed Thiel's help. SpaceX, his rocket company, had attempted launches in 2006 and 2007, but both prototype rockets had exploded before reaching orbit. Now he was running out of cash and began feeling out Thiel and Founders Fund's Luke Nosek. Thiel was cold to the idea, leading to a blow-up between the two men that became legendary within the Thielverse. "Luke really stuck his neck out for this," Musk said. Nosek won the argument, and Thiel relented, putting $20 million into Musk's space venture.

Musk used the funding to keep the lights on after a third SpaceX rocket exploded in August 2008. "There should be absolutely zero question that SpaceX will prevail in reaching orbit and demonstrating reliable space transport," he said, shortly after the failed launch. "For my part, I will never give up and I mean never." A month later, he succeeded, and SpaceX became the first privately funded company to reach orbit.

The launch was a turning point for both men—setting Musk on a path that would turn his startup into a major aerospace player and giving Thiel his first clear win as an investor. He had investments in two fast-growing defense contractors and a story that was even better than the one he'd been telling about his work as a hedge fund manager. He wasn't just a contrarian investor with a bankroll in the billions; he was a risk taker, betting on the wildest technologies and most audacious founders, with growing clout in Washington, D.C.

This persona would define his career for the next decade, even if it contained obvious inconsistencies: How exactly could a hedge fund guy who was effectively shorting the American economy *also* be a wide-eyed futurist? What kind of a libertarian sold spy technology to the CIA? What kind of gonzo risk taker says no to an early investment in Tesla? These contradictions, along with Thiel's vanity, made him vulnerable to anyone determined to expose them, and at that very moment, an upstart gossip publisher, Gawker, was trying to do just that.

9

R.I.P. GOOD TIMES

Marissa Mayer used to date Larry Page. There, we said it."

This was how, in 2006, Gawker Media came to Silicon Valley, screaming about power, sex, and hypocrisy. In the article about a romantic relationship between Page (Google's cofounder) and Mayer (the company's top executive), the site couched a tawdry gossip item in an argument about the media's fawning coverage of the tech industry. "The real embarrassment is that of Silicon Valley's toothless press corps," Gawker's new Silicon Valley blog, *Valleywag*, continued. "Raised on a diet of pre-packaged anecdotes—ooh, did you know Google hired a chef who traveled with the Grateful Dead—it's incapable of chewing on a real story." A few days later *Valleywag* wrote about another alleged affair, this one involving the married CEO Eric Schmidt, once again framed as media criticism.

This had been Gawker founder Nick Denton's formula since starting the company, which also operated transgressive web publications covering, among other things, politics, media, and Hollywood. Gawker, as

Denton liked to say, published the stories that everyone knew were true but were too afraid to write. Its blogs, including the eponymous flagship, which covered New York media, as well as *Gizmodo* (tech), *Deadspin* (sports), *Wonkette* (politics), and *Fleshbot* (porn), were routinely exploitative and tawdry, in the vein of the *New York Post*'s Page Six gossip column or *The Sun*.

But Gawker was different from those gossip publications because it didn't focus exclusively on politicians and celebrities. The media blog, *Gawker*, published gossip about journalists themselves, writing acidly about the industry's biggest names. It pronounced *The New Yorker*'s Adam Gopnik guilty of "intellectual douchebaggery," accused the *Times*'s David Carr of being "a primate on caffeine," and prompted another one of its targets, *New York*'s Vanessa Grigoriadis, to produce a lengthy takedown titled "Everybody Sucks." The site's jabs were mean, but they were often hilarious, and the mainstream press's handwringing about excessive snark only served to attract ever more attention from readers. By mid-2006 *Gawker* alone was attracting 9 million page views per month.

Valleywag was small compared to *Gawker*, but it was important to Denton, an Oxford-educated journalist who'd covered Silicon Valley for the *Financial Times*. In November 2006 he personally took over the blogging duties at *Valleywag*. Silicon Valley, he said, was "the center of the new world, for better and for worse."

Valleywag under Denton was characteristically vicious and cynical, but it was right about one thing: Silicon Valley journalists had done little to scrutinize the rising class of tech power players. Some of this was natural—technology journalism had traditionally been about gadgets, and to get gadgets you needed access, which meant constant supplication. Reporters guilty of negative coverage of Apple would routinely be banned from launch events, taken off lists for review units, and, worst of all, shunned by Steve Jobs, who maintained close personal relationships with the very reporters who were supposed to be holding his company accountable to investors and the public. The trade journalists covering the emerging internet startups often considered themselves participants in Silicon Valley's technology landscape rather than observers—dabbling in startup investing themselves or raising funds for their media companies from the VCs that they were ostensibly covering.

This had worked out nicely for someone like Thiel, who'd been portrayed not as a conservative firebrand, but as quirky and interesting. In truth he was a key business partner of George W. Bush's CIA and a major investor in a company with a billion-dollar aerospace contract, all while advocating for a drastically different relationship between the United States and the Muslim world. But in the hands of the prominent tech scribe Kara Swisher, who visited the Clarium offices in 2007, he was simply "Silicon Valley's most interesting venture capitalist and all-around great character."

"I gotta say, Peter, you've got class," she enthused, praising his office. Later in the interview: "I love your positive outlook."

Denton respected Thiel, but did not love him. The two men shared a libertarian worldview and an extreme skepticism for elite institutions—along with a willingness to attack those institutions in public. He seemed, for instance, to hold the Ivy League and *The New York Times* in as low esteem as Thiel did. Like Thiel, Denton was also extremely ambitious, which may be part of why he seemed to understand, in a way the rest of the press did not, that Thiel was more than a quirky rich guy; he was building a power base.

Like Thiel, Denton also happened to be gay. But unlike Thiel, he made no effort to hide his sexuality. "Maybe because I was gay, I grew up hating open secrets," he'd later say. "Usually if someone's gay it's a pretty open secret. Their friends know, their family knows, but out of some misplaced sense of decency nobody talks about it. Generally, my view is that, let's just have it out. The truth will set you free."

All of this made Denton almost uniquely dangerous to Peter Thiel, who had not shared the information about his sexuality widely, who had conservative parents and friends, and who had investors in Middle Eastern countries where homosexuality was exceedingly taboo. Thiel had spent years carefully crafting different versions of himself and presenting them to different constituencies. To Wall Street, he was the brainy contrarian hedge fund manager; to Silicon Valley, he was the risk taker who cared only about empowering young founders; to Washington, D.C., he was the tech genius who could save us from terrorism. These were all inventions—and Nick Denton would make it his mission to expose them as such.

VALLEYWAG'S EARLY COVERAGE of Thiel in 2006 had been typical of the tech press. The site had marveled at his quirky philanthropic donations and at his success as an investor. But after Denton arrived at the end of the year, the blog became much more skeptical, referring to Thiel in one of his early posts as a "founder now recast as investing genius."

Denton had a knack for keying in to any bit of information that might undermine that narrative. He published Musk's "alternate history" of PayPal, and informed readers that their favorite quirky VC had been connected to the homophobic slurs that Keith Rabois had hurled at Stanford. *Valleywag* called him "Keith 'Hope You Die of AIDS' Rabois." Denton also brought up Thiel's "weakness for libertines" in connection to Sean Parker's alleged cocaine use, and he mocked "the Grotto," a party house owned by two Founders Fund partners.

Gawker eventually hired a full-time *Valleywag* editor and Denton went back to running the media company, but his tech blog continued to criticize and mock anyone and everyone in Thielverse. It also began to drop hints about Thiel's sexuality. In July 2007, the new editor, Owen Thomas, who was also gay, made a winking reference to a "fabulous" Fourth of July party at Thiel's house. Then, a few months later, in October, the site noted that a speech that he'd given at the University of Tennessee at Chattanooga had failed to attract a very big audience—a standard *Valleywag* dig. But then Thomas mentioned that there had been a lone autograph seeker, a woman. "If that girl was hoping to score more than just an autograph from Thiel," Thomas wrote, "she's due for a double-dip of disappointment." After that, Thomas returned to the trope, writing about a male real estate blogger who'd termed Thiel "dreamy": "Well, handsome enough we'd say," Thomas wrote. "At any rate, we hate to break it to you . . . but Thiel's taken. If he weren't, though, you'd have a better shot than that Tennessee girl who lined up to get his autograph."

Thomas told me these were intended as in-jokes, since Thiel's sexuality was an open secret by this point. As Thomas, and many within San Francisco's tech and finance worlds knew, Thiel had a serious boyfriend, a BlackRock vice president named Matt Danzeisen, who was based in New York, where Thiel had a second home. Danzeisen had flown to California for the Clarium Christmas party at Thiel's house, and Thomas had seen Thiel's Friendster profile, which made clear that he was interested in men. "It wasn't even an open secret," said a former longtime Thiel employee. "It was just open."

Thiel had never been one to ignore a potential adversary, and he began asking staffers to find a way to get Gawker Media off his back. A Clarium source who was involved in the effort told me that the firm interviewed security professionals and at one point hired a private investigative firm to dig into Denton's personal life and finances, the beginning of a dirty-tricks campaign worthy of far-right politics and one that would continue for another decade. Unfortunately for Thiel, the private eyes were unable to find anything useful. Denton was, as he'd said, an open book.

In December Thomas made explicit what he'd been gently implying all year long. PETER THIEL IS TOTALLY GAY, PEOPLE, his headline read. The story idea had been Denton's. He'd mentioned it to Thomas as a possible thread for *Valleywag* to report. The assignment seemed reasonable to Thomas, who was all for throwing open the closet. "I see the whole assumption that there is a closet that people are in or out of it as problematically reifying heteronormativity," he said. In this view, hiding that one is gay perpetuates inequity and discrimination. The kind of outing Denton proposed was also not unusual at the time. Six months earlier, *Out* magazine had included Anderson Cooper and Jodie Foster— celebrities who were widely known to be gay but who'd never made it explicit—on its cover under the headline THE GLASS CLOSET.

Thomas structured his post as a commentary about intolerance in Silicon Valley. Techies, he said, embraced all sorts of contrarian thinking, but for reasons that seemed odd and hypocritical, were prudish about sex. This was a soft bigotry, he argued. VCs weren't outright homophobes, but they'd often decline to invest in a gay founder out of a fear that some other, more conservative counterparty—a later-stage investor, a customer, a banker—would be intolerant. Thiel, as a gay billionaire and a contrarian, didn't have to worry about those second-order prejudices, which was why he was able to be somewhat open about his identity:

> How many out gay VCs do you know? I think it explains a lot about Thiel: His disdain for convention, his quest to overturn established rules. Like the immigrant Jews who created Hollywood a century ago, a gay investor has no way to fit into the old establishment. That frees him or her to build a different, hopefully better system for identifying and rewarding talented individuals, and unleashing their work on the world. That's why I think it's important to say this: Peter Thiel, the smartest VC in the world, is gay. More power to him.

Thomas didn't see this as an outing in the conventional sense. Everybody he knew—like everybody at Clarium—knew about Thiel's sexuality. Instead Thomas insisted he was piercing a prudish taboo that others in the Valley were respecting unnecessarily. Thiel was not in the closet, but his peers had effectively chosen to closet him anyway. "It's a strangely conservative industry," Thomas told me, summing up his thinking at the time. "Let's talk about that."

The post wasn't widely read—it got only a thousand or so page views when it was first published, which made it a dud even by the standards of a small blog like *Valleywag*. Nor did it cause much of a stir in the press; Gawker publications routinely speculated about the sexuality of all-but-out public figures, including Anderson Cooper, and would out Tim Cook years before he outed himself. A Thiel representative complained to Thomas, privately, but Thomas said he was never accused of outing Thiel, and he assumed that there were no hurt feelings. A few days later, he published a parody by another Gawker writer about Thiel's fondness for Ayn Rand: PETER THIEL IS TOTALLY OBJECTIVIST, PEOPLE. In a follow-up post, the site referred to Thiel as "openly Objectivist."

At first, Thiel didn't let his anger show at Clarium. Nobody thought of Thiel as closeted and the company was on such a roll anyway that most employees, who didn't realize the boss was closeted in the first place, weren't even aware that he had been outed. Thiel was a regular fixture in *The Wall Street Journal* and *Barron*'s; *Valleywag* was minuscule by comparison. Nobody talked about it in the office the next day, and most employees remained blissfully unaware that anything remotely destabilizing had happened.

PRIVATELY THOUGH, Thiel was stunned, especially after he noticed a note Denton had left in the comments section at the bottom of the piece. "The only thing that's strange about Thiel's sexuality," Denton wrote. "Why on earth was he so paranoid about its discovery for so long?" Thiel read into this—deeply. It was, as he saw it, a veiled suggestion that he was psychologically unstable. Denton, in Thiel's view, hadn't just outed him; Denton had outed him in a way that embodied the worst impulses of liberal elites. The blog had implied there was something wrong with wanting to live, at least partly, in private. It felt cruel and unfair.

He was rattled, which may have been why, the following January, Thiel did something that seemed to employees as almost inexplicable.

He gathered Clarium's traders and told them that he was moving the fund to New York. Employees could either relocate or take generous severance packages. Thiel said the reason was simple. "If you want to be a movie star, you move to Hollywood," he told them. "If you want to be a politician you move to Washington. If you want to be a hedge fund manager, you move to New York."

Especially coming from a contrarian, it sounded thin. The firm, after all, had just moved from Downtown San Francisco, supposedly to get away from the hedge fund herds. Now Thiel claimed he wanted to join them. The real reason, some employees later came to believe, was personal. "He never said it, but the real reason was Gawker," said one. "He wanted to get away."

Around the same time, Thiel sent an overheated letter to Clarium investors explaining the firm's economic outlook. Clarium did this regularly, but always under the byline of an analyst; this was Thiel's first time writing a letter personally, and the result was extreme. In the ten-thousand-word essay, "The Optimistic Thought Experiment," Thiel argued that the world was heading to end times. Investment analysts often employ religious metaphors, speaking of the "second coming" of bond yields or an equities "apocalypse," but Thiel was not speaking metaphorically. "The entire human order," he wrote, "could unravel in a relentless escalation of violence—famine, disease, war, and death . . . Against this future, it is far better to save one's immortal soul and accumulate treasures in heaven, in the eternal City of God, than it is to amass a fleeting fortune in the transient and passing City of Man." He made this case with arguments from history and through the liberal use of quotations from the Book of Revelation.

Thiel pointed out that because investors couldn't hope to profit during a future in which everything collapsed, they would continue to systematically overvalue everything—leading to bubbles in housing, tech, and finance. The essay's title referenced what Thiel regarded as the best-case scenario—an "optimistic" future in which there would be a political backlash against globalization and a catastrophic financial crisis. There were ways to make money on this—Clarium could short stocks, for instance—but Thiel undercut this analysis by focusing on the worst-case scenario, recommending prayer and repentance in lieu of investment analysis. "The agon between globalization and its alternative will be close—at least in the sense that individual choices will prove to be of decisive significance," he concluded. "In this, we are opposed to the reigning faith in efficient markets. Unlike the faith in efficient markets, however, ours is a faith that seemingly still cannot be named."

Friends saw this as a proof of Thiel's fearlessness and originality of thought, which it surely was. It was also, fair to say, far out for an investor letter—almost the finance industry equivalent of a suicide note. Thiel was broadcasting to the institutions that had trusted him with $8 billion by mid-2008 that he had no confidence he would be able to preserve it.

Around this time, in an all-hands meeting, Thiel predicted that markets would "explode" and warned employees that the brokers that Clarium used to trade equities might collapse. The firm would have to go to cash, immediately, and should consider other measures. One analyst suggested they buy gold bricks and bury them. "It was like some sort of Randian fever dream," said another former employee, recalling the mood.

The fever dream spread throughout the Thielverse. Around the same time, Joe Lonsdale appeared at Palantir's headquarters in Palo Alto and ordered an administrator to pull $100,000 out of the company's bank account. The thinking was to have cash on hand in case of a full-blown collapse of the U.S. economy so that employees wouldn't starve. "We had $1,000 for each person," said a Palantir staffer. "They thought the apocalypse was coming."

THIEL'S CRAZY PREDICTION turned out to be right to a meaningful degree. On September 15, Lehman Brothers, a Wall Street institution that had survived the Civil War, the Great Depression, and 9/11, but that had been aggressively underwriting securities tied to subprime mortgages, collapsed and filed for bankruptcy protection. Later that month, Washington Mutual, which had been founded in 1889 and which had earlier in the decade boasted about becoming the "Wal-Mart of Banking," failed, causing a bank run.

A deep recession followed in which regular people lost their jobs and, having been locked into mortgages they couldn't afford, lost their homes. The fund managers who'd anticipated this pain and found trades to exploit it got ridiculously rich. Most famously, John Paulson made $4 billion buying credit default swaps as the market collapsed, which inspired Gregory Zuckerman's book *The Greatest Trade Ever*. An obscure hedge fund manager, Steve Eisman, made a similar bet that would be made famous by Michael Lewis's *The Big Short*.

But Thiel did not get rich—precisely because he could not convert his big idea into a trading strategy. It wasn't a failure of imagination, according to former colleagues, it was a failure of management. "It was the court of the sun king," said an early employee. "We weren't structured to find the micro-opportunities," said another. "We could have been the Big Short. We looked at some of those same opportunities. But we couldn't take advantage."

At PayPal, Thiel had allowed employees to operate with near-total freedom, and the results had been spectacular. The company had developed a groundbreaking anti-fraud algorithm, groundbreaking (if ethically dubious) viral growth mechanisms, and a crafty corporate development strategy that forced eBay to buy it—all amid a technology collapse. That was a triumph of Thiel's hands-off management style. But at Clarium, his traders and analysts went too far. They'd watch Thiel come up with a brilliant contrarian thesis and, instead of trying to make investments based on Thiel's worldview, they wound up devising contrarian takes to his original contrarian take.

Sources spoke of "overthinking" and "trying to catch the knife." Clarium considered shorting banks but decided that was a bad idea because the banks were going to be nationalized, which could actually send their stock prices higher, squeezing the shorts. Thiel believed that the government would reinflate the bubble before it crashed further. Before the bankruptcy of Lehman Brothers in mid-September 2008 that started the financial crisis, he had invested only a small sliver of his portfolio in publicly traded stocks. Suddenly though he decided that equities, which had been losing value since the previous October, had fallen as far as they were going to fall and started buying like crazy. He put $800 million into Google and Yahoo each, and another $1 billion in a basket of bank stocks—betting that they would all bounce back when the government inevitably bailed them out.

These moves proved to be the end of his career as a professional hedge fund manager. The stock market continued to drop and by the end of the year, Thiel had lost all the money he'd made during the first half. He'd missed out on a huge profit that could have come from his belief that the financial industry was collapsing. He ended the year down roughly 5 percent. By the time the bounce-back came, Thiel had tacked again and dumped his stocks, missing out on the recovery. The losses were magnified by a wave of redemptions. Pensions and sovereign wealth investors began pulling their money out of Clarium, so that by the end of the year what had been a $6 billion fund was down to just $2 billion—and investors were still asking for their money back.

It might have been Thiel's bad investments—but it was hard to ascribe the redemptions *only* to poor performance, since Clarium had actually done better than the stock market and most hedge funds. (The S&P 500 had lost nearly 40 percent of its value in 2008; hedge funds, on average lost, 18 percent.) Moreover, Thiel had been right about the rebound in stock prices, which started in December 2008, thanks to action by the Federal Reserve and the Bush and Obama administrations. He'd only missed the market's bottom by a couple of months.

Rightly or wrongly, Thiel came to believe that the real reason for the mass redemptions was Gawker Media. Some of Clarium's big investors, according to former employees, were Arab sovereign wealth funds, controlled by governments that considered homosexuality to be a crime. Thiel has never explicitly acknowledged this, but he has hinted at why he might have wanted to keep his sexual orientation out of view. "If we talk about outing it's never a simply factual thing," Thiel said in a 2018 interview. "It's never Peter [is] gay, FYI. It's more like: Peter Thiel is gay and we have no idea why he didn't want us to talk about it. Maybe it's because his parents don't know and they'd be embarrassed. Or maybe it's because he's trying to get money out of Saudi Arabia."

Moreover, it wasn't just Thomas's post about Thiel's sexuality that would cause him to feel "targeted," as he later put it. Gawker affiliates continued to needle him and his close associates throughout 2008 and 2009—never missing an opportunity to point out Clarium's failings, or Thiel's latest hypocrisy, or Sean Parker's latest infamy. On Martin Luther King Day, 2008, *Valleywag* noted, apropos of nothing in particular, a recent Thiel donation to the campaign of Ron Paul, who'd been associated with racist newsletters. In September, the blog pointed out that Clarium had lost $900 million—more than Thiel had made on Facebook to date—noting Thiel hadn't even been asked about these losses at a recent tech conference. When Thiel flew to Davos, Switzerland, in early 2009—a key chance to project strength to the investor class—*Valleywag* referred to him as a "so-called visionary," noting that his fund had shrunk by $5 billion over the previous six months. Later in 2009, it claimed that Thiel had been inflating his net worth.

Throughout this period, it was unclear to those in the Thielverse whether Gawker was covering Thiel's failures as an investor or causing them, by undermining investors' confidence in his firm and Thiel's confidence in himself. "The way I think about it is he had a terrible crackup," said a former Clarium analyst, referring to Thiel's losses in 2008. "He got wrong-footed, and it was hard to get right."

Silicon Valley was losing some of its confidence too. In October 2008, Sequoia began distributing a PowerPoint presentation encouraging its companies to cut costs and conserve cash. The presentation, titled "R.I.P. Good Times," signaled a rejection of the blitzscaling playbook. No longer would there be enough money for startups to ruthlessly buy market share; they'd have to generate revenue instead. Facebook had seemed destined for an IPO; now that was off the table. Instead the company raised $200 million from Yuri Milner, a Russian investor with ties to the Kremlin. An IPO—and way for Thiel to realize some of his paper gains on the company's stock—was still years away.

Then, in November 2008, Barack Obama easily beat John McCain in an election that was viewed as a repudiation of the Bush-era national security policies. Obama had won the Democratic nomination, in part, because he'd opposed the Iraq war and, also, thanks to support from Silicon Valley. His campaign's social media efforts represented the first time any candidate had taken the medium seriously. They were led by one of Zuckerberg's Harvard classmates and a Facebook cofounder, Chris Hughes—"The Kid Who Made Obama President," *Fast Company* claimed. Some were calling 2008 the "Facebook Election," and Silicon Valley's startup elite contributed so heavily to Obama's campaign that the *Atlantic* termed the campaign "the year's hottest start-up." Never had Thiel seemed more out of step with his peers.

STRANGELY, HE DIDN'T seem miserable during this period; he seemed, for the first time in years, free. The hedge fund—and the pressures of being covered by the Wall Street press and having to please investors—had pushed him inward. He'd thrown around money after his exit from PayPal, but he'd done so bloodlessly, acquiring the accoutrements of extreme wealth while taking no apparent joy in them. Now, having lost most of his investors' money, having given up on trying to hide his secrets, he could follow his intellectual passions and, once again, play the role of provocateur.

At Stanford, Thiel had gravitated toward younger right-wing intellectuals and he did so again, beginning with a Google engineer named Patri Friedman. Small, sinewy, and handsome, Friedman had a master's degree in computer science from Stanford, which he was putting to work writing quality control software for Google while experimenting with exhibitionist alternative lifestyles. He'd explored pickup artistry, acrobatics, professional poker, paleo diets, communal living, and polyamory—blogging about all of it. "I had no concept of how I would see myself in ten years," Friedman told me. "I was just like, 'I'm an intellectual rebel. I'm going to write whatever the fuck I want.'"

Friedman's most sustained passion was seasteading, or the idea of libertarian utopias on floating platforms in international waters. These seasteads, as adherents described the open-water settlements, would be outside the control of any government, giving residents the freedom to experiment with illicit substances and enjoy any other pleasure currently denied by the world's two-hundred-odd countries. He teamed up with a couple of other techno-utopians to write a paper, which he posted online, explaining the ideology and practicality of "water-based lifestyles." It covered the pros and cons of incinerating human feces, the possibility of using inexpensive Chinese-made cruise missiles to defend against attacks from hostile naval fleets, and the promise of creating a society free of taxation.

Friedman's blog was popular among Thiel's libertarian employees, and he began corresponding with Jeff Lonsdale, younger brother of Palantir founder Joe and a Clarium vice president, who invited him to a meeting at the hedge fund's offices. Friedman initially hoped this might lead to a job, but instead it got him a dinner with Thiel. During the meal, Thiel grilled Friedman about his plan, which involved building a series of scale models, starting with a bathtub-scale platform and working his way up to Atlantis-size from there.

Thiel liked Friedman—who was, like so many of his protégés, young, male, attractive, facile with language, and willing to say the exact things that were not said in polite society. Moreover the idea of seasteading was viscerally appealing, a physical manifestation of PayPal's approach to skirting financial laws. Rather than launch a political campaign for lower taxes on billionaires or for reduced regulation of cryonics providers, a seastead could, in theory anyway, just make those policies real and challenge the government to shut it down. By the time the rest of the world noticed what was happening, he reasoned, it'd be too late. There was a final enticement: Friedman's project presented an opportunity for Thiel to ally himself more deeply with the conservative movement, since Friedman was the grandson of the great libertarian economist Milton Friedman.

"You should quit Google," he told Friedman at the end of the dinner, offering him $500,000 to start a nonprofit. He promised to match future donations and indicated that he would lend his name to the fundraising effort. "Decades from now, those looking back at the start of the century will understand that seasteading was an obvious step towards encouraging the development of more efficient, practical public sector models around the world," Thiel said in a press release announcing the donation. "We're at a fascinating juncture: the nature of government is about to change at a very fundamental level."

Critics saw seasteading as dangerous and reactionary—and also just kind of goofy. The founding of the institute "should live on in internet lore for confirming the dream that two guys with a blog and a love of Ayn Rand can land half a million dollars to pursue their dream, no matter how off-kilter or off-grid it might seem," *Wired* wrote. NPR ran a tongue-in-cheek report that began with joking promotional copy: "Tired of the rat race and following all the rules imposed by the man? Tired of being denied the opportunity to live on a floating ocean capsule?" host Mike Pesca asked. Gawker mocked Friedman relentlessly, mining his confessional blog and social media stream for the most ridiculous bits of inanity. LIBERTARIAN UTOPIANIST PATRI FRIEDMAN WANTS TO BE YOUR BABY'S DADDY was one headline in reference to his polyamory.

Clarium employees expected Thiel to be horrified by the attention.

"For years we'd been trying to suppress stuff, but at a certain point he just didn't care," said a former employee, referring to efforts to quash negative press. "He just embraced it. Not just the gay thing, but seasteading, his politics—everything." Thiel seemed ready to "let his freak flag fly," this person said.

He threw himself more deeply into another interest, funding technologies and research that might allow him to live forever. He continued to put money into the Methuselah Foundation and a spinoff, the SENS Research Foundation, which was dedicated to anti-aging research. The two organizations had been created by Aubrey de Grey, a Cambridge-trained academic with a wild beard, who'd given a TED Talk in 2005 that suggested old age could be reversed. Thiel donated more than $1 million in 2007 and 2008, and another $2 million in 2010.

In 2008, Founders Fund had invested around $500,000 into Halcyon Molecular, a startup founded by William Andregg, who'd started the company with his brother Michael when he was just nineteen, with a modest plan of developing inexpensive genomic sequencing technology in order to cure aging. In 2009, during his freak-flag stage, Thiel met with the Andreggs and was almost instantly enamored with their enthusiasm and approach. Thiel is not normally emotive, but he was on this occasion. "He actually jumped up and down," William Andregg recalled. "He was like, 'We have to solve this or we're all gonna die.' That was the first conversation."

Thiel would personally invest $5 million in the live-forever company and was a constant presence at the company's offices, with Founders Fund kicking in another $5 million on top of that. "He was spending so much time, it was like, 'Okay there's only so much advice you can give,'" Andregg said. "We had to start doing actual work."

He also gave more than $1 million to the Singularity Institute, a non-profit dedicated to research into super-intelligent computers that could one day host our brains and allow us to be immortal in software. To the extent that these donations attracted mockery, he now seemed to welcome it. He boasted to a crowd at a Singularity Institute event that he'd funded de Grey over the objection of his parents. "My parents, who live in the Bay Area, freaked out," he said. "They called me up and said, 'This is so embarrassing. What are the neighbors going to think?'"

DURING HIS EARLY hedge fund days, Thiel had kept his politics relatively bottled up, but after the outing, he reverted to form. Clarium's May 2008 letter to investors heralded "a bull market in politics," which, the letter said, would be characterized by a breakdown of the consensus of the "globalist elite." These globalists had argued for decades that opening borders and increasing trade would lead to prosperity. The policies had been embraced by Bill Clinton and George W. Bush, but Thiel saw a turning point. A year earlier, Bush had attempted to enact comprehensive immigration reform, which would have included a path to citizenship for undocumented immigrants, stepped-up border enforcement, and the addition of a guest worker program. But Bush's effort failed, which Thiel ascribed to "an unprecedented Internet campaign that had been going on for months."

Thiel was much more familiar with this anti-immigration reform campaign than his letter let on. Over the past few years, he'd been quietly cultivating a new crop of nativist politicians, including Kris Kobach, the chairman of the Kansas Republican Party, who'd served as a lawyer for an anti-immigration group, the Federation for American Immigration Reform, or FAIR, which had been suing state governments for allowing undocumented immigrants to pay in-state college tuition rates. FAIR was affiliated with NumbersUSA, a far-right nonprofit dedicated to the idea that the United States should reduce the total number of immigrants allowed into the country each year. The group, which the Southern Poverty Law Center has said is linked to white nationalists through its founder, had been relatively obscure until Bush's push for comprehensive immigration reform. NumbersUSA automatically sent faxes on behalf of supporters complaining about the dangers of runaway immigration to U.S. senators. More than a million faxes were delivered this way—so many, in fact, that the Senate's phone network crashed in the run-up to the vote.

In 2008, *Valleywag* reported that Thiel had made a $1 million donation to the group through an intermediary. (Thiel didn't comment on the report at the time, but several sources familiar with his political activities have told me the reported donation was real.) When *Valleywag* pointed out that this was inconsistent with Thiel's supposed libertarian values and suggested that he was "turning away from an embrace of freedom," Thiel responded by upping the ante. In early 2009, he and Friedman contributed essays to a journal published by the Cato Institute, the libertarian think tank cofounded by Charles Koch. The theme of the issue of *Cato Unbound* was "From Scratch"—that is, the idea of simply creating libertarian enclaves outside of the framework of normal democracy, which Friedman regarded as flawed "folk activism." Instead of voting or starting political parties, Friedman advocated for a concept that would come to be known as "competitive governance"—in which committed libertarians would leave their countries and start new ones in the same way that an entrepreneur who'd decided he didn't like his local coffee shop might see a market opportunity and create a competitor.

Thiel's essay, titled "The Education of a Libertarian," drew on similar themes but was more pointed and seemed calibrated to cause a reaction. "I no longer believe that freedom and democracy are compatible," Thiel wrote, arguing that the United States had been on a downward trajectory for most of the previous century. "The 1920s," he wrote, "were the last decade in American history in which one could be genuinely optimistic about politics. Since 1920, the vast increase in welfare beneficiaries and the extension of the franchise to women—two constituencies that are notoriously tough for libertarians—have rendered the notion of a capitalist democracy an oxymoron."

He argued that there were three signs of hope—not inconsequently all signs in which he was an investor—that might allow humanity a return to freedom and wealth, and a break from the tyranny of women voters and welfare beneficiaries. These were the internet, Facebook in particular; outer space, where, he said, new rocket technologies were making space colonies more likely; and, of course, seasteading. It was in the tradition of the *Stanford Review*'s outrageousness, but unlike the most inflammatory posts Thiel had published at the college paper, he was the author of this one.

Needless to say, the idea that humanity should celebrate Peter Thiel's attempts to build an offshore tax haven but mourn the passage of the Nineteenth Amendment did not lead to universal acclaim. "Facebook backer wishes women couldn't vote," wrote Thomas in *Valleywag*, calling Thiel "loopy."

Thiel posted a clarification to Cato's website, in which he offered a non-apology for his comments about women. "While I don't think any class of people should be disenfranchised, I have little hope that voting will make things better," he wrote. Amazingly, this explanation, however thin, sort of worked. George Packer, in his otherwise rigorous account of Thiel's thinking in *The New Yorker*, reported that "Thiel didn't want to take away women's right to vote—instead, he wanted to find a way around democracy, which was incompatible with freedom," as if that was somehow exculpatory. It wasn't that Thiel wanted to take away women's votes; he wanted, it seemed, to take away everyone's.

In any case, Thiel's opinions on the matter were irrelevant since according to the essay, he was off politics for good:

> I believe that politics is way too intense. That's why I'm a libertarian. Politics gets people angry, destroys relationships, and polarizes peoples' vision: the world is us versus them; good people versus the other. Politics is about interfering with other people's lives without their consent. That's probably why, in the past, libertarians have made little progress in the political sphere. Thus,

I advocate focusing energy elsewhere, onto peaceful projects that
some consider utopian.

A few months later, he told a private equity industry trade journal
that *Valleywag* was "the Silicon Valley equivalent of Al Qaeda," suggesting that the company's employees "should be described as terrorists, not
writers and reporters." He continued: "Terrorism is obviously a charged
analogy, but it's like terrorism in that you're trying to be gratuitously
meaner and more sensational than the next person, like a terrorist who
is trying to stand out and shock people. It's an interesting theoretical
question, whether, if *Valleywag* went away, something else would fill in
to replace it."

Thiel would be working on answering that question for much of the
next decade, while dramatically expanding his political project even as
he claimed he was winding it down. He didn't just want to protect his
image, but also to destroy those who had sought to damage it. He didn't
just want to break into government contracting; he wanted to take it
over. He didn't just want to persuade college administrators to root out
campus political correctness; he wanted to turn fears about political correctness into an issue that could swing an American election.

10

THE NEW MILITARY-INDUSTRIAL COMPLEX

Most histories of the American tech industry begin in September 1957, at a laboratory in Mountain View, California, when a group of the country's best young engineers at Shockley Semiconductor announced that they had decided to quit. The Traitorous Eight, as they would become known, would go on to start Fairchild Semiconductor. Led by the brilliant physicist Robert Noyce, the group developed a process to etch transistors—the building blocks of computers—onto a piece of glass. This was the first commercially viable computer chip—the *silicon* that made Silicon Valley.

The Apollo program would buy hundreds of thousands of Fairchild-designed chips, setting off an economic boom up and down the San Francisco Peninsula that ultimately led to personal computers, websites, cryptocurrencies, smart watches, and really all of twenty-first-century capitalism. Fairchild employees, a PayPal Mafia before the PayPal Mafia, fanned out across the Valley, starting many of the most important tech companies and venture capital firms.

In the popular imagination—colored by the successes that have come since, especially those of Steve Jobs—the story of the Traitorous Eight has come to represent the spirit of rebellion that is said to pervade the tech industry. When I was starting in journalism, in the mid-2000s, Silicon Valley was seen, at its core, as an antiestablishment movement. "We owe it all to the hippies," as the futurist (and countercultural activist) Stewart Brand famously put it, positing that the "real legacy of the sixties generation is the computer revolution."

But Silicon Valley—the real Silicon Valley—had never been about subverting the military-industrial complex. Silicon Valley, in its purest form, *was* the military-industrial complex. Its founders weren't dropping LSD. They were proud squares, with politics that were closer to those of David Starr Jordan than to the radicals of Stewart Brand's imagination. The man who'd coined the phrase "traitorous eight" (and the boss whom those eight men rebelled against) was William Shockley, a physicist who worked on radar for B-29 bombers during World War II, then invented a new kind of transistor, and then, after closing his company and taking a job as a professor of electrical engineering at Stanford, picked up Jordan's mantle to become the campus eugenicist. Starting in the late 1960s he'd argued that instead of addressing racial inequality with social welfare programs, U.S. policy makers should pay Black Americans to get themselves sterilized.

This was extreme, though much of the tech industry was extremely conservative, with a special hostility to the counterculture. Workers at Fairchild, HP, Intel, and others were being fed and clothed thanks to the endless Cold War–era defense budgets and were grateful for it. Their transistors were guiding the missiles that the Left wanted to decommission. Noyce left Fairchild in 1968 to start Intel, which also started largely as a defense contractor. He saw the Left as a countervailing force against technological progress. "They wanted to destroy the new machines," as Tom Wolfe put it in a 1983 *Esquire* profile of Noyce. "They wanted to call off the future." This was mostly forgotten in Silicon Valley by the early 2000s, when Apple and Google were preaching individual empowerment and books like John Markoff's *What the Dormouse Said* were arguing that LSD had, in some spiritual way, created the internet, when in fact it had been created with funding from the Pentagon's Defense Advanced Research Projects Agency (better known as DARPA).

Thiel saw tech the way Noyce had seen it—as fundamental to the rise of Western civilization and American power. The counterculture, on the other hand, had stopped tech in its tracks. Thiel dated American decline, as he'd write in a *National Review* essay, to Woodstock, three weeks after the moon landing. "This was when hippies took over the country," he wrote. "And when the true culture war over Progress was lost." The enemy of progress was "endless fake culture wars around identity politics." The values of multiculturalism in his mind were no longer just a threat to Stanford, as he'd argued in *The Diversity Myth*. Now they were a threat to American hegemony itself.

The fix, he'd come to believe, included redirecting government spending away from social programs and toward mega-scale technology projects of the kind that employed Noyce and his contemporaries. "The state can successfully push science; there is no sense denying it," he wrote. But, he continued, "I am not aware of a single political leader in the U.S., either Democrat or Republican, who would cut health-care spending in order to free up money for biotechnology research—or, more generally, who would make serious cuts to the welfare state in order to free up serious money for major engineering projects."

This would become one of Thiel's most important projects: to bring the military-industrial complex back to Silicon Valley, with his own companies at its very center.

THIEL HADN'T JUST PREDICTED the housing crash, he'd also predicted a rise in defense spending, which a 2008 Clarium letter had praised as "the one major sector in which the U.S. enjoys advantages in skilled labor, technology, and trade pathways." This was a shrewd reading of the times. Although Barack Obama had run as an antiwar candidate, he'd been mostly talking about the Iraq War, rather than Bush's war on Al Qaeda. In fact, Obama argued, Bush hadn't done enough. The country had "taken our eye off the ball," by using military resources in Iraq when they should have been used to capture Osama bin Laden. That meant investments in intelligence work and a troop "surge," in which he sent thirty thousand troops to Afghanistan in 2009.

Palantir was almost perfectly positioned to take advantage of the shifting political winds. In March of that year, a Canadian research team announced that it had identified a Chinese malware operation, which it called Ghostnet. The researchers said that hackers, likely working on behalf of the government in Beijing, had used emails and fake websites to install software that allowed them to control computers that were operated by the aides to the Dalai Lama, along with a host of other targets including embassies, foreign ministries, news outlets, universities, and even a computer inside NATO headquarters. The researchers issued a report that included screenshots of Palantir's software, showing a web of connections like the ones that PayPal had used a decade earlier on Russian credit card fraudsters.

The company's role in the investigation seems to have been limited, but the spiderweb diagrams and the fact that they came from a company founded by the PayPal guys enlivened what otherwise would have been an abstract story, and those diagrams and a prominent mention of Palantir appeared in an article published by *The New York Times*. The *Times* noted the PayPal connections as well, but failed to mention that buried on page 51 of the report on Ghostnet was a disclosure: Palantir had paid to help underwrite it. Though anyone who read the report would understand that Palantir's role seemingly had been confined to generating the diagrams, readers of the *Times* would leave with the impression that Palantir had been essential to the operation. This was part of a years-long effort to convince the world, and especially the U.S. Army, that it should throw out its existing data analysis software and instead give the money it was spending on software to Peter Thiel.

This was no easy task, in part because the Army had already agreed to spend $10 billion or so to build its own system, known as DCGS-A (pronounced "d-sigs"), using a group of traditional defense contractors that included Lockheed Martin, Raytheon, and Northrop Grumman. That meant that landing an enormous Army contract was next to impossible—that is, if Palantir approached the problem the old-fashioned way, which would have entailed lobbying Pentagon officials and modifying its software to work with the existing system. Instead, Thiel used a variation of the approach that had worked for PayPal—spending vast sums of money to market the service to directly to potential users, in the hopes of creating a network effect that would then influence the top brass in the same way that eBay sellers' adoption of PayPal had persuaded Meg Whitman to give up on her PayPal competitor.

Palantir adapted this strategy by targeting mid-level Army commanders who might be open to trying out something new, giving them free versions of the software to try. It provided them with training and made its engineers available to tweak the software to suit their needs. One of these commanders was Colonel Harry Tunnell, who led the Army's 5th Stryker Brigade of the 2nd Infantry Division.

Tunnell's career had been unconventional. He'd served in Iraq and had been seriously wounded in 2003. His patrol had been ambushed, and he'd been shot in the leg during the fight. Tunnell had been saved by two soldiers who'd pulled him into a ditch; he was later airlifted to a German hospital. The experience, which he wrote about in a 2006 book while recuperating and attending the Naval War College, had led him to conclude that the United States' counterinsurgency tactics, which relied on cultivating local allies and winning "hearts and minds," weren't sufficiently aggressive. He advocated a "counter-guerilla" approach that aimed to seek out insurgents and kill them. His motto for the brigade was starker: "Strike and destroy."

Tunnell's hawkishness and his willingness to buck convention made him a perfect target for Palantir's forward-deployed software engineers—as the company described its engineer-salespeople—who met with him while his 5th Stryker Brigade began training to deploy to Iraq in 2007. Tunnell had asked if Palantir could modify its software so that he could use it in the field to find insurgents. This was a tall order. Intelligence analysts typically worked on speedy computers with high-speed internet connections to giant government servers; field commanders worked on laptops, often without an internet connection of any kind. "At first the answer was no, that's ridiculous—we can't deploy to the Army," said someone who worked on the project.

Over the course of a few months, however, Palantir engineers modified their software to allow soldiers to access the database offline, add information as they checked houses for insurgents, and upload the modified data once they got back to their base and could use the internet. The result was that individual squad leaders could build on each other's work in the same way a team might collaborate on Google Docs or Slack. Palantir did this work for free and provided Tunnell the software to use in training. Tunnell deployed in 2009 and convinced the Army to pay for a version of Palantir for use in Afghanistan in early 2010. Soldiers in the brigade would later claim that this months-long delay contributed to the unit's more than thirty casualties, a claim that Palantir would use in years to come when selling its services.

Word spread in Afghanistan, and several other brigades also got their hands on the software, which allowed them to share intelligence with one another and created the beginnings of the PayPal-style network effects. This caught the attention of the military's head of intelligence in Afghanistan, a major general named Michael Flynn. Like Tunnell, Flynn was a critic of the United States' counterinsurgency approach who had been arguing for a more muscular campaign that would take advantage of intelligence gathered by soldiers on the ground. In early 2010, Palantir's forward-deployed engineers gave Flynn a demo and he responded by making an urgent request to the Department of Defense to buy enough Palantir licenses for the entire force in Afghanistan, while criticizing the Pentagon's existing database software as inadequate. "Intelligence analysts in theater do not have the tools required to fully analyze the tremendous amount of information currently available," Flynn wrote. "This shortfall translates into operational opportunities missed and lives lost."

The military's leadership would try to ignore Flynn, but his comments, with Tunnell's, would be worth a fortune to Palantir and Thiel. They found a receptive audience in Duncan Hunter, the San Diego representative who Palantir cultivated by way of a lobbyist, Terry Paul, whom it hired in 2011 and who was close to Hunter's father, Duncan Sr. After leaving the military, Tunnell complained that his Army superiors had slow-played his requests for better software, prompting Hunter to demand hearings. Flynn would continue to push the Army on Palantir as he rose to become the head of the Defense Intelligence Agency (DIA) under President Obama.

Tunnell and Flynn deviated from the military on more than just their love of Palantir. Flynn would be forced out of the DIA, ostensibly for mismanagement. The FBI would eventually investigate Flynn's contacts with Russians while at the DIA and afterward when he was a lobbyist. During the same period, he was unofficially lobbying for Palantir. Tunnell meanwhile would leave the military after members of his brigade were charged with war crimes. Tunnell was never implicated, but after he retired, an Army report said his more aggressive posture made it easier for soldiers to cross the line. Hunter, Palantir's champion in Congress, was eventually charged with campaign finance violations, conspiracy, and wire fraud. He pled guilty to a lesser charge and resigned his seat in early 2020.

None of these misdeeds were connected to Palantir, but those close to the company acknowledge that they were indicative of the type of person Palantir cultivated. "We were finding mercurial people—a little bit eccentric, a little bit bombastic—who we could ally with," said a former Palantir executive who worked on the effort. Thiel, who'd turned Sean Parker's drug arrest into a selling point, had never had a problem with doing business with a little ethical baggage and did nothing to discourage any of this. In meetings with Palantir staff he tended to present the company's work in terms that were ideological and revolutionary. "He was our spiritual guide to the idea that this system is corrupt," this person said.

Inevitably the grassroots approach and the desire to find fellow pot-stirrers led Palantir into arrangements that employees would later find troubling. In 2010, Palantir employees began working with two other security firms, HBGary and Berico, to win a $2 million a month contract to help build an intelligence operation to dig up damaging posts on social media by critics of the Chamber of Commerce. While working on the proposal, the trio also pitched Bank of America on a similar operation, aimed at Wikileaks. Palantir had proposed pressuring pro-Wikileaks journalists, including Pulitzer Prize winner Glenn Greenwald. "These are established professionals that have a liberal bent," a slide from a Palantir presentation read, "but ultimately most of them if pushed will choose professional preservation over cause."

To the outside, the project, which became public when members of Anonymous, the hacker group, published emails from the HBGary CEO in February 2011, was scandalous. Greenwald wrote a blistering column attacking what he saw as the "lawless and unrestrained . . . axis of government and corporate power."

But within the company's Palo Alto headquarters the incident was seen less as a scandal and more as an unfortunate product of the company's approach to sales, which—like everything in the Thielverse—was decentralized. "We'd given the business development people a lot of rope and put a lot of pressure on them to make things happen," said a former engineer. "It was hard to fault these people for trying really hard."

Alex Karp publicly apologized, cut ties with HBGary, and told employees that he hadn't known about the proposal to intimidate journalists. "The right to free speech and the right to privacy are critical to a flourishing democracy," he said in a statement. He also announced that Palantir would set up an ethics line so that in the future employees could report such troubling work. Even so, it wasn't clear whether Karp or Thiel truly regretted the proposal to strong-arm journalists. The former engineer said that some employees whispered that the Palantir staffers who'd been party to the plan—including a twenty-six-year-old engineer, Matthew Steckman, and a manager, Eli Bingham—were simply doing their jobs. Palantir put Steckman on leave, but he returned to the company and was later promoted, ultimately becoming the head of business operations and a senior adviser to Karp, before leaving in 2017. Bingham was also promoted and put in charge of the company's machine learning operation.

They remained in Thiel's good graces. Steckman would later become chief revenue officer at Anduril, a Palantir-like defense contractor that Thiel funded. Bingham became a vice president of engineering at Affirm, a PayPal-like finance company founded by Levchin and backed by Thiel. They would not be the last Thiel associates to be publicly chastised and privately rewarded.

If Palantir employees were discouraged by the HBGary episode, their discontent didn't last long. At the end of April, employees began to whisper that one of the company's most secretive clients had done something big. "You're going to want to watch the news for the next day or two," an employee recalled hearing.

ON THE FIRST SUNDAY EVENING in May, President Obama appeared in the East Room of the White House and announced that the United States had killed the world's most wanted terrorist. Osama bin Laden had been hiding out in a walled compound in Abbottabad, Pakistan, when a team of U.S. Navy SEALs found him. Speaking somberly, the president described a "painstaking" intelligence-gathering operation, led by the CIA, that had ended in a clandestine raid earlier in the day.

"On nights like this one," Obama said, "we can say to those families who have lost loved ones to al Qaeda's terror: Justice has been done." In the frantic hours that followed, the atmosphere at Palantir was electric; in emails, on internal forums, and in the company's offices in Palo Alto and Washington, employees began asking the obvious question: *Was this us?* The response from those in a position to know was "Maybe," though they said it in a way that almost certainly meant yes.

In *The Finish*, a bestselling account of the hunt for bin Laden published the following October, the journalist Mark Bowden credited two technological breakthroughs that he said had allowed analysts to find the Al Qaeda leader. The first was the development of the Predator drone, which could circle continuously over a town area and give commanders a detailed view of anyone, or anything, coming in or out. The second, which worked in concert with the drones by creating a record to make sense of a potential target's movements and contacts, was the Total Information Awareness program.

Officially, Poindexter's concept had been killed, but Bowden argued that the basic approach survived, helped along by Silicon Valley. "A startup called Palantir, for instance, came up with a program that elegantly accomplished what TIA had set out to do," he wrote. "The software produced from this very unlikely source would help turn America's special forces into deadly effective hunters."

Speaking at an all-hands meeting after Obama's press conference, Karp was careful not to take credit—and careful not to *not* take credit. He noted that it was public knowledge that Palantir worked with intelligence agencies and that those agencies had done something spectacular. "It was a coy smile," said another witness—another instance of Karp's *Inception*-like salesmanship.

The company would adopt this line when talking to the press, refusing to answer questions about the hunt for bin Laden but letting reporters know, off the record, that there was something there. An early employee told me that staff weren't supposed to direct anyone to Bowden's book, because it contained information that had been classified, but they could tell people to type "Palantir Bin Laden" into Google, which would lead them straight to the passage where Bowden referred to the company as one "that actually deserves the popular designation Killer App." That Google search would ultimately be worth billions of dollars to Palantir's valuation—as reporters repeated the claim as if it were true. A rare exception was Gawker, which noted that Palantir had used the claim to goose sales and that there was "no proven link." Years later *New York* journalist Sharon Weinberger would write that "no one I spoke with in either national security or intelligence believes Palantir played any significant role in finding Bin Laden."

Indeed, Bowden had been vague about Palantir's exact role and didn't discuss the software in any real detail. What did it actually do? Not as much as it seemed to promise, it turns out. A former intelligence analyst who used Palantir in these years said that the company's software was exceedingly limited. Though it was widely believed to be a tool that digested raw intelligence data, this person says it was actually more of a visualization aide—a way to create diagrams showing connections based on databases the military had already built. Palantir insiders would argue that this description was unfair and that the company provided valuable analysis tools, though they acknowledged that its software was not as automated as many believed at the time.

Analysts would figure out whom they wanted to target, and then create a spiderweb on Palantir and send it to their superiors. This was worth something—bosses like charts—but you had to make the chart more or less manually. "It was just the tool you'd use to put the final report together," the analyst told me, referring to claims about Palantir's intelligence prowess as "this totally fake thing." In reality, Palantir's role in the bin Laden killing would have been limited to "making a pretty picture and then taking a screenshot and putting it at the end of a PowerPoint that was sent to leadership." In other words: exactly how it had been used in the case of Ghostnet.

But what role, if any, Palantir had was more than enough for Karp. Palantir's wink-wink caused media interest in the company to explode. The combination of Karp's weirdness—in keeping with the *Lord of the Rings* theme, the company referred to its government work as "protecting the Shire" and called employees "hobbits"—and the company's perceived involvement with cloak-and-dagger operations was irresistible. A *Businessweek* article declared it "The War on Terror's Secret Weapon" and included a description, from a company sales pitch, of a Palantir-powered operation in which the CIA used the software to stop a terrorist attack on Walt Disney World. It was a hypothetical example, necessary to protect "the sensitive work of its clients."

The American Civil Liberties Union chimed in, warning that Palantir was supporting "the misguided strategy of sifting through millions of innocent people's communications and activities," and the press produced ominous takes about the dangerous implications of Palantir's technology, unaware that at that point, Palantir's technology was very much a work in progress. *The Guardian* warned of a "sinister cyber-surveillance scheme." *Forbes* titled its profile, which included Karp's smiling face on its cover, "Meet Big Brother." It opened with the "rumors"—which, of course, had been started by Palantir employees—that the company had "helped to kill Osama bin Laden."

Karp and Thiel did little to combat suggestions that its technology enabled government overreach, and, in fact, sometimes encouraged them, reasoning that a privacy panic might actually help support Palantir's claim that it was a game-changing surveillance technology. If people thought it was dangerous, all the better. That's why they had named it after Sauron's orb in the first place. As Thiel explained the strategy to a friend, "I'd rather be seen as evil than incompetent."

He was right. Prospective clients—financial services companies, corporate security departments—didn't care if Palantir was too good. In fact if it was too invasive, so much the better. They wanted military-grade technology, to hire the company that got bin Laden, and Thiel and Karp were ready to sell that to them. "It felt like we were on top of the world at that point," said a longtime employee. "A lot of people started knocking on our doors." Palantir's success would enrich Thiel dramatically, as the company's valuation would grow from $2.5 billion in 2011 to $9 billion two years later.

It would also give him something more. For years, Thiel had been projecting more power than he actually had—self-publishing books, paying to put on conferences, essentially paying for influence however and wherever he could—but now, with Palantir's rise and success, he suddenly had actual clout. Palantir had been straining for years to get attention from generals and politicians; now those generals were calling him. He was no longer just a techie; he was the guy behind the company that had proved game-changing to national security, and he had grand plans for what to do with that renown.

11

THE ABSOLUTE TABOO

In the summer of 2010, l met Thiel at a West Village coffee shop. I arrived with a vague notion that I might profile him for *Inc.*'s recurring "How I Did It" feature, in which successful businesspeople explained the winding road they'd followed to fame and fortune. These pieces were inevitably a bit schlocky, but it was a kind of schlock that seemed refreshing amid the economic devastation of the moment.

The Great Recession was technically over, but things felt somehow desperate, at least from my vantage point in New York. I was twenty-eight—still young, but also not quite young anymore. My friends, who mostly had degrees from prestigious universities, all seemed to be struggling, going through breakups and career setbacks. They were contemplating moving back home or applying to graduate school. Over the previous eighteen months a media company had seemed to fold or lay off half its staff every few weeks, and I found myself dreading—or maybe fantasizing about, it was hard to tell—the day when I too would get laid off.

Thiel showed up wearing a crisp blue dress shirt and joined me at a table without ordering anything or making any effort at pleasantries. Then he launched into an impromptu dissertation on the three recent economic bubbles. The first, of course, was the technology bubble; then came the bubble in subprime mortgages. Then, there was the bubble we were currently in: "Higher education," he said.

He explained his thinking, pausing on several occasions to draw on my notebook. Tuition prices had been soaring, and we'd been paying those ever-increasing premiums with federally guaranteed student loans, taking on ever-increasing debt loads—debt that, by the way, could not be discharged in bankruptcy. What, exactly, was it all for? Why was the government subsidizing useless art history degrees, which, after all, were really degrees in drinking and sex? Why in the world were we willingly paying $150,000 for the privilege of a four-year party?

The higher education bubble wasn't just like the bubble in subprime mortgages, he said. It was worse. At least with a subprime mortgage you had a house. With college—even an Ivy League college—you had nothing. The smartest people, he said, were dropping out and starting companies. I left the interview feeling convinced by Thiel's argument, but also confused by what I'd just experienced. I'd expected the normal give and take of an interview, and instead got a long-winded macro-economic discussion that seemed destined to end with me crying into my liberal arts degree.

This feeling is familiar to anyone who spends long stretches of time with Thiel—whose primary conversational mode is a one-sided series of riffs that he repeats and refines over time. That's what I thought at the time, anyway. But Thiel's anti-college thesis was more than just a riff—it was part of a larger strategy designed to expand his influence well beyond investing and tech. It would play out in three new domains: politics, the law, and, as I was about to learn, education—or rather the movement against it. I didn't realize it at the time but I was getting a sneak preview of Thiel's most ambitious startup effort yet: an attempt to win over every disaffected young person in America.

———

THAT OCTOBER, *The Social Network* premiered. David Fincher's film was based on *The Accidental Billionaires*, which used documents made public during Mark Zuckerberg's dispute with Eduardo Saverin over the ownership of Facebook. It was, all in all, an acid portrait of Silicon Valley's most craven impulses. Justin Timberlake played Sean Parker as a greedy, hard-partying conman. Jesse Eisenberg was devastating as Zuckerberg—affectless, sociopathic, and, above all else, lonely. Wallace Langham, known for his recurring role as a lab technician on *CSI: Crime Scene Investigation*, portrayed Thiel as a square investor in a blue button-down shirt.

As Aaron Sorkin's script told it, the inspiration that led to Facebook had come to Zuckerberg in a sexist reverie after a breakup. Then he'd swirled in some intellectual property of questionable origin and produced something that swallowed the social fabric of an entire generation, replacing it with a sad, blinking Like button. That was how most film critics saw *The Social Network*, anyway, which made sense because it was, more or less, what had happened in real life. But it would be emphatically *not* how America's budding technologists experienced the film. They would see it as a model to follow—and they would be led in that belief by Zuckerberg, and even more so by Thiel.

Thiel's strategy was simple: He didn't bother attacking the liberties the filmmakers had taken with the facts; instead he focused on what he saw as an incorrect interpretation of Zuckerberg's *mindset*. According to Thiel, Zuckerberg hadn't founded Facebook to get revenge, or get girls, as the movie implied; he'd started the company out of a pure desire to build something that would advance humanity. To believe otherwise was to fall prey to the "Hollywood, or governmental, win-lose mentality" that Thiel said had guided the production. "The one very positive thing about the movie is that it is going to encourage—in spite of the worst intentions of the producers—it will encourage a lot of people to go into the tech industry," he said at the time. "So, on that, I think it's a very positive thing."

He started a press push at TechCrunch Disrupt, a widely attended tech conference in San Francisco put on by the news site *TechCrunch*, a few days before the film's release. While onstage, he criticized the film, and then announced that, like the unwitting producers of *The Social Network*, he was going to do his part to entice aspiring Zuckerbergs into tech. "One of the initiatives that we're going to be starting over the next few weeks is a program, offering grants of up to $100,000 to up to 20 people under age 20, for starting something new," he said. "A lot of the great companies have been started by people who've been quite young, and we think [we should] actually encourage that."

Thiel had already been doing something like this. In 2009, Founders Fund partnered with *TechCrunch* to give out what it called "Genius Grants for Geeks," awarding $50,000 to promising tech figures to invest in a startup. The idea had been Sean Parker's—he saw it as a sneaky way for the firm to find new investments, and the program was structured so that the venture capital firm got half the equity—but a year later, Thiel was adding a twist. The new "20 Under 20" program would be limited to teenagers, and it would be entirely philanthropic. They would call the young entrepreneurs Thiel Fellows, and the grants would come with no strings attached. The only condition was that they would have to drop out of school, just as Zuckerberg had.

The project was written up in the tech press and by the libertarian blogs that Thiel had been cultivating. But even better, as far as Thiel was concerned, it was skewered by mainstream journalists. Writing in *Slate*, Jacob Weisberg, the online magazine's editor-in-chief and now the CEO of the podcasting company Pushkin Industries, who also happened to be a Yale graduate and Rhodes Scholar, accused Thiel of trying to clone himself, "perhaps literally." Thiel Fellows would "have the opportunity to emulate their sponsor by halting their intellectual development around the onset of adulthood, maintaining a narrow-minded focus on getting rich as young as possible, and thereby avoid the siren lure of helping others or contributing to the advances in basic science that have made the great tech fortunes possible." The essay was eloquent, and it attracted even more applications; Thiel would include excerpts from it in a promotional video. The provocation was working.

IN MARCH 2011, Thiel flew forty-four teenagers and their parents to San Francisco. They were there to present ideas, listen to talks, mingle with fifty or so members of the PayPal Mafia, and compete with one another to be one of what would be twenty-four final winners. They'd been selected from a pool of about four hundred who'd submitted applications online, answering questions including "How would you change the world?" and "What do you believe that no one else does?"

The room that greeted Thiel when he stepped up to a lectern to welcome them was less a reflection of intellectual diversity than it was a reflection of his own idiosyncratic interests and vanities. They shared Thiel's politics, interests, and predilections. In their essays, the students had written about radical libertarianism, or how stupid college was, or how awesome it would be to live forever. They were—nearly all of them— boys, and, almost to a person, they shared Thiel's social awkwardness.

"We have nothing against education," Thiel told the group. But, he added, "great education tends to have an autodidactic component." The fellowship would be a "small step for each of you, a great step for humanity."

Not long after, Thiel sent out acceptance letters. "The future will not take care of itself," he wrote. "Now let's change the world." His foundation released the list of names of twenty-two men and two women who would be dropping out of some of the nation's most prestigious universities. They came, the press release noted, from MIT, Harvard, and Yale, and there was even a teenage fourth-year Stanford PhD candidate in neuroscience who was also taking a break from his studies to try his hand at entrepreneurship. One eighteen-year-old wanted to mine asteroids; another one wanted to build a DIY mass spectrometer. There was a seventeen-year-old hoping to extend human lifespans by at least three hundred years and a sixteen-year-old developing a workaround to China's Great Firewall.

The press release also included a lengthy biography of the fellowship's founder, complete with a guide to pronouncing Thiel's last name (the *h* is silent). He gave interviews that emphasized the transgressive quality of the project. "Education may be the only thing people still believe in in the United States," he said. "To question education is really dangerous. It is the absolute taboo. It's like telling the world there's no Santa Claus."

Thiel hired a local film crew to follow the first group, producing short documentaries that glorified the project. He was interviewed in a dark room with dramatic lighting, and a few of the fellows were taped in their hometowns, reality-TV style, as they packed their bags and said goodbye to their parents. Thiel also partnered with a friendly journalist, Alexandra Wolfe Schiff, who happened to be the daughter of Tom Wolfe, to write a book about the project. The idea was to remake the elder Wolfe's *The Electric Kool-Aid Acid Test*, but with Thiel traveling the country by bus like some modern-day Ken Kesey, picking up fellows and bringing them to Silicon Valley.

The fellowship, and the accompanying media push, constituted a major element of Thiel's attempt to change his public perception. He'd spent the early 2000s playing a role that wasn't his—the heterosexual, high-living hedge fund manager—now he was fashioning a new character: a bold, risk-taking investor with a burning desire to blow up the system.

In truth, Thiel's image needed a rebrand. Founders Fund had been struggling to bring in new investors in part because Thiel was known as the guy who'd presided over the destruction of the hottest hedge fund in America. Yes, Thiel had invested in Facebook, but he'd declined to invest much in Facebook's 2006 round because he'd judged the company's

$500 million valuation to be way too expensive. By 2010, it was already clear this was a boneheaded call. "It was one of Peter's great regrets," said a former Founders Fund investor.

Thiel's recent investments hadn't looked so hot either. He had bought into SpaceX before Musk's third rocket blew up, but Musk waited to announce the deal until *after* the accident, as a way to signal to NASA and other potential customers that he had enough capital to keep the company going. That was great marketing for SpaceX and less great marketing for Thiel, who now looked as if he'd paid for a giant fireball. Shortly after the failure of the launch, an investor who'd been considering backing the fund wrote an email complaining that Thiel had taken the firm off the rails. "This is exactly why I didn't fund you guys—for ridiculous bets like this," the investor said.

The rebrand allowed Thiel to reframe this concern as a selling point. In July 2011, Thiel and his colleagues posted a five-thousand-word manifesto about slowing technological innovation under the title "What Happened to the Future?" Though written by a Founders Fund partner, Bruce Gibney, the ideas were the ones that Thiel had been working out for years. Its tagline compared the science fiction dreams of Thiel's youth with ostensibly diminished aims of the world's most successful tech companies: "We wanted flying cars, instead we got 140 characters." (This was a reference to Twitter, which had been heralded in the press as a potential Facebook-killer.)

VCs, Thiel argued, had once funded ambitious semiconductor companies, drug developers, and hardware enterprises—iconic names like Intel, Genentech, Microsoft, and Apple. Now they were backing lame consumer software, "fake technologies" that solved "fake problems." As a result, returns had been flat since 1999. "The future that people in the 1960s hoped to see is still the future we're waiting for today, half a century later," Gibney wrote. "Instead of Captain Kirk and the USS Enterprise, we got the Priceline Negotiator and a cheap flight to Cabo."

The essay was great rhetoric—even if it didn't exactly describe the Founders Fund investment portfolio, which consisted in large part of the kinds of companies that Thiel was criticizing and had only a handful of the firms that spoke to his high-minded ambitions. Founders Fund had backed Facebook—a social network, just like Twitter—as well as Path, Gowalla, and Slide, which were all also social media companies. The last one, which had been started by Thiel's PayPal cofounder Max Levchin, was known for something called SuperPoke, which allowed users to virtually "slap," "punch," and "grope" their Facebook friends and was about as far from the Randian ideal as one could imagine.

There was a similar disconnect between rhetoric and reality with the Thiel Fellowship, as the lucky teenagers who'd been selected would soon discover. Thiel's announcement at TechCrunch Disrupt of a major fellowship, for which two dozen people would upend their lives to accept, had not been the product of some sort of deep consideration but had been first conceived on a flight back to San Francisco the day before the conference. And though Thiel had certainly been brooding on problems with higher education, the problem he was actually trying to solve—as one of his close advisers would acknowledge years later in an interview with *City Journal*, the conservative magazine—was much more pedestrian. He'd gotten his hands on Aaron Sorkin's script for *The Social Network*, which the movie's producers had shared with Facebook, and was worried about his portrayal as the cold-blooded investor who'd set into motion a power play that the movie suggested amounted to the theft of the company. This, of course, was accurate, but it did not fit with Thiel's new image as an intellectual radical. "He wanted to get a jump on that with some good news," as former fellowship codirector Michael Gibson said. "We went to his house, we got into a car, and we went to this conference. And on the fly, we're coming up with—okay, well, what do we call this thing? How much money? How many years?"

Gibson and those in Thiel's orbit would celebrate the spur-of-the-moment nature of the fellowship as proof that Thiel was living on the edge, outthinking liberal Hollywood on the fly. But for the children and very young adults who would upend their lives to participate, the lack of preparation was obvious—and disastrous for some. They showed up in California only to find out that the actual execution of the fellowship was basically an afterthought once Thiel had achieved his marketing goal.

There was no structure to speak of beyond that suggestion, and the requirement that they not enroll in school or take a full-time job. There were no required readings or behavioral guidelines; no classes; no office hours and no faculty, except for the Thiel Foundation staff members who were responsible for the program. These were Jim O'Neill and Jonathan Cain, who were part of a pseudo-political operation that Thiel operated inside of Clarium, plus Gibson, a PhD dropout who'd been a seasteading blogger when Thiel hired him at Clarium, and a fourth staffer, Danielle Strachman, who'd started a K-to-8 charter school in San Diego, making her the only one of the four with anything close to relevant experience.

Fellows were granted a quarterly meeting with Gibson and Strachman and were invited to some networking events at Thiel's house. These sounded promising, but they were often desperate affairs with dozens of young people jockeying for a few minutes with the boss. "They are the most depressing parties you've ever been to," a former fellow told me. "Anytime anyone talks to him there's always an angle." If they were lucky, fellows might get to have a breakfast with Thiel, which involved sharing the table with five or ten other entrepreneurs. Thiel would hold forth continuously, riffing about some pet policy issue, pausing only, perhaps, to order a second breakfast when he took a bite forty-five minutes later and realized it was cold.

The $100,000 check was paid out in two annual installments, meaning fellows had $50,000 to live on. That was nice, but it wasn't a lot after taxes and San Francisco rent, and especially not if you'd never had to manage your own expenses. To help make things easier, the foundation rented a house on the outskirts of San Francisco one summer and the fellows slept four to a bedroom. But they were on their own starting in the fall. "It was, 'Here's a house, do your thing,'" said Thomas Sohmers, who applied to the fellowship for the first time as a fourteen-year-old in 2010 and was accepted into the third class two years later.

There were positives. All the buzz around the program meant that Thiel Fellows could land at least a meeting with pretty much any investor or tech company. On the other hand, it was hard not to see this as a little disappointing in itself. The Thiel program, one fellow told, promised libertarian capitalism and a supportive community that would reward creativity rather than Machiavellian maneuvering. "What I found was comically *not* that," he said. It was college without the classes, a residential community, or studying—in short, most of what was enriching about college. It wasn't an attack on a credentialing system; it was another credential.

Many others, especially the younger fellows, just felt lost. To show up in San Francisco at age sixteen, as Thomas Sohmers did, without friends, a home, or a boss, and on top of that, to be told to try to start a company more ambitious than Google, was an impossibly daunting directive. Sohmers had been assigned a mentor. The mentor was twenty-three. Another would-be mentor, Aron D'Souza, a handsome young Australian, gave a talk to the fellows in 2011 as an expert on intellectual property law despite the fact that he was fresh out of graduate school. He had a PhD from the University of Melbourne and a law degree from Oxford, but to the Thiel Fellows he seemed to have no obvious experience that would qualify him as a mentor to startup founders—except, of course, that he was a good-looking man Thiel seemed to like.

The fellowship was often compared to Y Combinator, a startup incubator that invested $100,000 in very early-stage companies and was famously hands off. But Y Combinator forced companies to show up every two weeks for "office hours," which created a sense of discipline for the founders and helped them make friends and contacts. The Thiel Fellowship offered neither of these things. "I was like, 'Here I am in Silicon

Valley,'" one said. "I don't know anyone at Stanford. I can't just go to a bar since I'm under twenty-one. I can meet with any CEO, but I don't need that. I just need someone to hang out with."

When fellows complained or asked for help, the response from Thiel's employees was exactly what one might expect from a bunch of ultra-libertarians. "This is a great problem for you to solve through business," they'd say, an ideologically reasonable response that was entirely unhelpful to a lonely teenager.

Some of these young people suffered. I heard of an early Thiel Fellow who seemed to be wrestling with mental health issues and drug addiction, but, according to two early fellows, administrators were slow to intervene. Another Thiel Fellow was quietly removed from the program, but only after police showed up at a house he shared with a few other fellows. The two fellows said that San Francisco police told them they were investigating his involvement with a cryptocurrency Ponzi scheme.

Many fellows described feeling like second-class citizens within Thiel's orbit. They were told that Founders Fund would not, as a rule, invest in any Thiel Fellows out of fear that that would create the perception of picking favorites. But the policy was always shifting—a handful of companies raised small sums—and Thiel himself put $2 million into Hello, a manufacturer of a $149 alarm clock and sleep tracker founded by James Proud, who entered the fellowship at age nineteen and whom Thiel said "stood out from the start." That was well and good for Proud's startup, which would fold in 2017, but it meant that anyone who didn't raise money from Thiel looked like an underperformer. Many of these companies would struggle, in turn, to raise their own funds.

When launching the Thiel Fellowship, Thiel had made much of the example of Halcyon Molecular, the company that pledged to solve the problem of aging, cofounded by a teenaged William Andregg. For George Packer's *New Yorker* profile in 2011, Thiel even had Packer sit in on a meeting at the end of which he'd urged Andregg and his brother and their staff to start aggressively recruiting more engineers. Write down the names of the three smartest people you know, Thiel had said, and then hire them.

But months after Packer's profile published in 2011, a British company beat Halcyon to market and began promoting small, disposable DNA sequencing machines that it expected to sell for $900 each—more than the $100 that Halcyon had aimed for, but much less than the $10,000 the machines had previously cost. Andregg attempted to shift his focus, but Thiel eventually had to shut the company down. There was no point in having the second-best sequencing method. By August 2012, Andregg was trying to find his employees new jobs within Thiel's empire. Thiel hired Aaron VanDevender, a physics PhD who'd worked at Halcyon, making him Founders Fund's chief scientist and a principal investor. On the day the company announced it was shutting down, he invited Andregg over to his house, where he mercilessly crushed him in a game of chess, and then used it to teach a business lesson. He pointed out that several turns before he'd gotten Andregg into checkmate, the younger man had more than a dozen possible moves. "When you're deciding what to do next, you should be very careful about making moves, because you'll end up in a situation where you're constrained," Thiel said, sending Andregg and his brother off into the world to figure out their next act.

Andregg would start another company, Fathom Radiant, which would build advanced artificial intelligence chips for supercomputers and would ask Thiel to invest. Thiel agreed to meet with him, but then canceled their meeting at the last minute. It was never rescheduled. Founders Fund, Andregg concluded, had become "more business focused."

Andregg bore no ill will toward Thiel, but came to regret spending his early twenties—maybe the best years of one's life, if you didn't, in the end, discover the fountain of youth—on a business model that in retrospect seemed ill conceived. "Don't run on a strategy that was formulated by your nineteen-year-old self," he said. "It's kind of obvious in hindsight."

Just as Thiel had distanced himself from the Andreggs, as well as his college friend Barney Pell's company, when both had apparently served their purpose, he eventually backed away from the Seasteading Institute, the freedom-loving nonprofit founded by Patri Friedman that Thiel had used to burnish his image as an intellectual radical. In 2011, he left the board of the foundation. He told Friedman that the nonprofit would have to "stand on its own" and eventually scaled back his donations as well. Friedman tried to start a for-profit company that would build a private city in Honduras, and Thiel invested. But the company ran into legal problems when the country's Supreme Court ruled the idea unconstitutional and shut the company down. He was broke—he had two kids, was getting divorced, and had been paying himself a salary that worked out to an average of $35,000 per year over the previous five years. "It was just a full burnout in every sense," Friedman said. And so, he went back to Google in 2013 for the money and the benefits. He barely spoke to Thiel for years.

WHAT SUCCESS THIEL Fellows enjoyed was so painfully rare that in 2015, Thiel grew frustrated with Gibson and Strachman and replaced them with Jack Abraham, an up-and-coming venture capitalist who shared his politics. Abraham changed the rules to allow for fellows who were as old as twenty-two—twenty had sounded good at Disrupt, but it was too young in practice—and began recruiting entrepreneurs who had already raised capital. Thiel set Gibson and Strachman up with their own fund, 1517, which invests in companies started by young people.

Fellows who failed to start world-beating startups would eventually be eased out of the network—left off of emails and no longer invited to the annual alumni retreat. They'd come to regard their time with Thiel not as some profound intellectual exercise, but rather, as one told me, "a super-smart PR move." This former fellow continued, "He spent $2 million a year and he bought enormous respectability. Without the fellowship he doesn't teach the class."

The class—this was the second part of Thiel's attempt to win over America's youth. In March 2012, Stanford's catalog included a course called "CS 183: Startup" in the computer science department, listing Thiel as the instructor and promising "accounts from the early days of startups including PayPal, Google and Facebook" featuring "entrepreneurs who have started companies worth over $1B and VCs (venture capitalists) who have invested in startups including Facebook and Spotify." Somehow, after spending the past year and a half railing against elite colleges in general, and after writing a book, op-eds, and speeches decrying Stanford specifically, he'd convinced his alma mater to let him teach a class on entrepreneurship.

The class was a hit on campus—it reached its 250-student limit within a matter of days—and caused a ruckus among the faculty, some of whom still remembered Thiel's antics as a student. But Stanford was not Thiel's intended audience. PETER THIEL, UNIVERSITY-HATER, HEADS TO CAMPUS was the Reuters headline. "If I do my job right," a spokesman boasted on Thiel's behalf to the newswire, "this is the last class you'll ever have to take." There was lots more media attention, including a *60 Minutes* segment and an essay by the *New York Times* columnist David Brooks.

He had even more success on social media. Once the classes started, detailed transcripts appeared on the internet, written by a young protégé, Blake Masters. He was a Stanford Law student who'd worked at Founders Fund the previous semester and was a typical Thiel acolyte—handsome, extremely conservative, verbose, ambitious. Masters had gone to Stanford for his undergraduate degree, majoring in political science, and worked as a clerk in a U.S. Attorney's office. Masters, like Thiel, was a member of the campus Federalist Society and a gym rat. Starting that spring, though, he became Thiel's Boswell, posting detailed prose versions of each class, complete with charts and graphs supplied by Thiel. The notes went viral almost immediately, showing up on the front page of Hacker News, a widely read tech and entrepreneurship forum, nearly every week, as well as on Facebook, Twitter, Reddit, and everywhere else ambitious young people came to connect with each other.

Thiel's delivery could be uncertain—his prepared speeches tend to be crisp on the page but full of circuitous digressions when delivered—and the structure of the lectures was a bit scattered, especially early on. Thiel gave mostly standard-issue startup advice at first. In one lecture on corporate cultures, he made the recommendation that companies should have them. But he enlivened even these bland lessons with guest appearances from his friends and former employees, including Max Levchin, Reid Hoffman, and Marc Andreessen.

And as the class went on, though, Thiel diverged from pat advice and became more philosophical, infusing his business advice with his unique brand of apocalyptic politics. The eleventh lecture was about secrets; the thirteenth, delivered in late May, was about the primacy of personal agency. In that one, which he titled "You Are Not a Lottery Ticket," Thiel argued that the world had basically gone downhill since around the time of his birth, when people had definite ideas about progress. Progress back then meant beating the Soviets and driving flying cars. Since then, the world had come to embrace what he diagnosed as "indeterminate optimism." This, he claimed, was a deceptively pernicious worldview that took many forms, including the rise of index investing, the general sense that it's okay to get old and die, and Los Angeles's traffic. The world was screwed up, Thiel said, and then argued that the driven students in the audience—who were by this point crowding the aisles and sitting on the floor—and the tens of thousands of young people following the lectures on the web, had the power to change it. They could fix the traffic in Los Angeles or even live forever—and get wildly rich along the way. Anything seemed possible as long as they freed themselves from the liberal, politically correct world of higher education.

The promise of a pathway toward economic certainty, even wealth, post-recession, coupled with a chance to stick it to the elites was too much for the young and tech savvy to resist. "There are lots of young ambitious people who want to feel like it's okay to be ambitious," said Louis Anslow, who was a twenty-year-old college student in southern England. Anslow loved Thiel's idealistic futurism and his confidence that even death could be overcome by science. Also, Anslow didn't like college either. So he dropped out, resolving to adopt Thiel as his guru.

He began writing to Thiel's employees and associates, offering to organize local events. "I was just determined to get as close to him as I could," he said. Eventually he was invited to a Thiel Foundation Summit, an event for aspiring fellows, as well as a handful of subsequent get-togethers.

To Anslow, and to others like him, it wasn't just that Thiel's ideas were perfectly pitched to the moment; it was also the way they were pitched. Thiel was transgressive and esoteric, and those in his network seemed to have access to secrets unavailable to the outside world. When in 2014 a Thiel employee gave him an advance copy of *Zero to One*, the book based on Thiel's Stanford lectures, Anslow told me he was filled with something like reverence. "You worship this guy and you're given this exclusive copy of this sacred text," he said. "It was all very religious."

Thiel had always been an unlikely sort of leader, but he'd been creating these networks based on loyalty for decades. Before the Thiel Fellowship there had been the PayPal Mafia, and before that there was the tiny crew of angry young college men he'd gathered at the *Stanford Review*. But now Thiel was working on an industrial scale, grooming young, ambitious, like-minded people—people who, as Stanford's Martin Hellman observed, "recognized him as the leader and would not fight with him." The students who joined the Thiel Fellowship, and those who, like Anslow, merely aspired to it, were—by giving up on college, by forgoing normal teenage socialization, and by molding their beliefs to his—effectively committing themselves to work for Thiel and his companies for years, if not for the rest of their careers. It felt, Anslow said, like being part of a mass movement. This movement would form the core of a new, much larger mafia that Thiel would deploy in business and politics.

12

BUILDING THE BASE

In late 2011, *Details* magazine, the now-defunct "metrosexual bible"—as *The New York Times* had described it—attempted a profile of Thiel, during which he submitted to an interview while walking in the Presidio, not far from the Founders Fund office. Thiel successfully followed a tried-and-true formula, presenting himself as a wildly ambitious investor—headline: THE BILLIONAIRE KING OF TECHTOPIA. But he froze up when asked about his life outside of work. "You know, it ends up being, um . . . it ends up being a lot of, uh . . . a lot of, uh . . . it's mostly, uh, pretty basic simple social things," he sputtered. This went on for five more lines until he finally brought the sentence to its conclusion: "It's nothing that, uh . . . nothing that insane or exciting."

It was, perhaps, hard to understand how a man who couldn't put a sentence about his interests together could be a charismatic object of fascination for a generation of young people. But of course, Thiel's most fervent followers weren't typical readers of urbane monthly magazines; they were engineers who didn't necessarily fit into the traditional social scene. These aspiring entrepreneurs had watched and rewatched *The Social Network* and taken in the message, reinforced by the Thiel Fellowship, that intelligent misanthropes could make good. It didn't matter if you couldn't hack it at Harvard; in fact, being rejected by (or, better, rejecting) that establishment could make you superior to your boring, rule-following contemporaries.

Thiel had recognized that this attitude was marketable, pushing the fellowship to the public in blog posts by his staff and a series of organized events that chiefly served to promote Thiel and his interests. There were happy hours, organized by Thiel Foundation employees and staffed by volunteers, as well as the Thiel Foundation Summit, a sort of minor league conference for aspiring fellows or people who'd already applied for the fellowship and gotten rejected. And of course, there was social media: For someone who hated the medium, Thiel associated with lots of people, like Michael Gibson and Patri Friedman, who used it constantly to promote his ideas, in blog posts and on Twitter.

The message, always, was simple: College and traditional careerism was pointless at best, and, at worst, it was an intellectually bankrupt exercise in debt accumulation. Your ambition—to change the world, and, as a consequence, to be rich—was good. It was Objectivism, in other words, and no less appealing to young strivers than it had been when Thiel had read Ayn Rand as a young man.

Across the United States and beyond, teenagers schemed to get close to Thiel. They responded to and amplified the blog posts that his surrogates published. They stalked his inner circle on Twitter and adopted his own language as their own. A young army of Thiel acolytes—most of whom simply wanted to start companies and get rich, ideally with Thiel's money—started talking like techno-utopians or contrarians.

They had their own language—many identified as "rationalists"— and their own literary canon. It included Tolkien and Rand, of course, along with arcane texts that venerated technology, among them *Harry Potter and the Methods of Rationality*, a 600,000-word fan fiction epic that

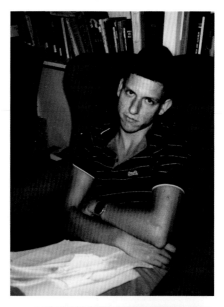

Thiel as a freshman at Stanford University in 1986. His intelligence and his standoffishness were legendary among his dormmates. "He was a strange, strange boy," said one.

Thiel was not much of a drinker at Stanford, though he couldn't resist a challenge to a game of "beer chess," in which players had to chug each time they lost a piece. He won easily.

Thiel and then PayPal CEO Elon Musk, posing to promote the banking ambitions of PayPal in 2000. That year, Thiel would lead a coup to replace Musk.

Thiel's PayPal cofounder, Max Levchin, was a twenty-three-year-old coder when he pitched Thiel in the late 1990s. Thiel's cultivation of Levchin, the technical genius behind the company, marked the beginning of his transformation into a tech power broker.

Thiel's friendship with Reid Hoffman dates to their sophomore year at Stanford. Hoffman served as PayPal's executive vice president and became a key player in the PayPal Mafia.

Thiel saw potential in law school classmate Alex Karp, a left-wing bohemian who briefly pursued an academic career in Germany. When Karp returned to the U.S., Thiel deployed his friend's quirky-genius affect in fundraising efforts for Founders Fund before making him CEO of his surveillance company, Palantir.

Steve Bannon, former executive chairman of *Breitbart News*, chief strategist to Trump in the White House, and Thiel's foremost ally inside Trumpworld.

Senator Josh Hawley, a beneficiary of Thiel's largesse, attacked tech companies and embraced some of the most extreme elements of Trumpism.

Charles Johnson, journalist, entrepreneur, and Thiel's entrée into the world of the alt-right.

In December 2016, the CEOs of some of the largest tech companies in the U.S., including Apple's Tim Cook and Amazon's Jeff Bezos, plus Elon Musk and Alex Karp, met with Trump at Thiel's invitation. "You're a very special guy," Trump said, thanking Thiel for setting the meeting.

Sean Parker (played by Justin Timberlake) and Mark Zuckerberg (Jesse Eisenberg) wait to pitch Thiel in the Hollywood version of the Facebook story, *The Social Network*.

The "blood boy" episode from HBO's *Silicon Valley* made light of Thiel's interest in parabiosis, a life-extension therapy involving the use of blood from younger donors.

In 2018, Facebook cofounder Mark Zuckerberg was called to testify in Congress about Facebook's commitment to user privacy and its involvement with 2016 election manipulation.

Palantir's work with the Immigration and Customs Enforcement agency, and its perceived complicity with President Trump's immigration policies, led to protests across the country, including in New York in 2019.

Terry Bollea, a.k.a. Hulk Hogan, a.k.a. Thiel's proxy in his campaign to destroy Gawker Media. Bollea sued Gawker after it published a sex tape that he said had been recorded without his consent. Thiel, who'd nursed a grudge against the New York publisher for years, secretly covered Bollea's legal fees.

Thiel soaking it in during his speech in support of Donald Trump at the 2016 Republican National Convention.

adapted J. K. Rowling's wizard story by imagining that Harry incorporates the scientific method into his magic. Another favorite: *The Last Ringbearer*, which was part of the ever-growing corpus of *Lord of the Rings* fan fiction, and which seemed apt for the founder of Palantir. In the book, which was first published in Russia in 1999 and then translated into English on the web in 2010, Tolkien's good guys—Gandalf and the elves—are warmongers who try to destroy Mordor because its peaceful progress threatens their feudal rule. "Gandalf's the crazy person who wants to start a war," Thiel told *Details*. "Mordor is this technological civilization based on reason and science. Outside of Mordor, it's all sort of mystical and environmental and nothing works."

One of Thiel's favorite books was *The Sovereign Individual*, a little-known political screed—that is, until Thiel started talking it up. The book, published in 1997 by a venture capitalist, James Dale Davidson, and a journalist, William Rees-Mogg, is a cyber-libertarian manifesto that predicts the end of the nation state. The book, which was reissued in 2020 with a preface by Thiel himself, likely influenced his wilder comments about PayPal's mission to do the same in the late 1990s and early 2000s. Davidson and Rees-Mogg argue that wealthy people should free themselves from their nationalities—and, of course, "the nationalist burden of taxation" and "the exploitation of the capitalists by workers"—by hiring private militias, securing citizenship in low- or no-tax countries, and enjoying a new libertarian paradise. The ideas would influence seasteading, of course, and a recent Thiel-funded project, Pronomos Capital, which is led by Friedman and is seeking to build "charter cities" in developing countries.

Thiel's budding movement also had a house political philosopher: Curtis Yarvin, who was then only known by his pen name, Mencius Moldbug. Yarvin, like so many in Thiel's orbit, was a verbose and dyspeptic geek with an abiding distaste for the mainstream Left. He'd graduated from Brown and then dropped out of a computer science PhD program at Berkeley. After taking a job at a tech startup that went public during the dot-com bubble, he'd become a full-time blogger, writing about political theory, culture, and race and drawing on obscure nineteenth- and twentieth-century philosophers, as well as the usual Thielverse standbys of *Star Wars*, *Lord of the Rings*, and *The Fountainhead*. "Moldbug reads like an overconfident autodidact's imitation of a Lewis Lapham essay," an essay in the left-wing journal *The Baffler* put it, referring to the famously dense prose of the former *Harper's* editor. "If Lewis Lapham were a fascist teenage Dungeon Master."

Yarvin's blog, *Unqualified Reservations*, focused on a theory that he called "formalism," which he defined as a project to reduce violence. Yarvin argued that the government of the United States should be replaced by a corporate structure and a dictator, democracy being "an ineffective and destructive system of government." Thiel's comments about the incompatibility of democracy and freedom in *Cato Unbound* would closely hew to Yarvin's view, and Patri Friedman would recommend *Unqualified Reservations* in a companion piece in the same issue. During his Stanford lectures, Thiel would rail against democratic decision making inside of companies. "Startups and founders lean toward the dictatorial side," he'd said, which of course was a virtue. "It is more tyrant than mob because it should be."

Yarvin's views would eventually harden into a full-blown ideology, "neo-reaction," which included positions like the belief that climate science was largely a fraud perpetrated by elites; that inflationary currencies, like the U.S. dollar, are "diabolical"; and that genetic differences cause some groups to be "more suited to mastery," while others (including Africans, he said) were "more suited to slavery." Thiel, of course, subscribed to the first two views, if not the third. Yarvin also had views on apartheid similar to those ascribed to (though denied by) the undergraduate Thiel, and had compared Nelson Mandela to the Norwegian mass shooter Anders Breivik. Neo-reactionary thought came with its own vocabulary: To "red pill" someone meant to open their eyes to this new worldview. "The Cathedral" was the elite orbit occupied by government officials, the media, and, most of all, university professors.

Thiel was also making connections with other far-right provocateurs. In 2010, he'd given $100,000, making him by far the largest donor to a newly formed group for gay conservatives, GOProud, launching the initiative with a party at his house that featured Ann Coulter, the firebrand pundit and the founder of a *Dartmouth Review*–style paper at Cornell University, *The Cornell Review*. GOProud was unique among gay political groups—and distinct from the more mainstream Log Cabin Republicans—in that it didn't focus on advocating for gay rights.

"An awful lot of Republicans want to get out of the gay issue in general," he told a *Politico* reporter who attended the event. Thiel's invitation of Coulter, a close friend, made the point well. In 2007, she'd referred to John Edwards, a Democratic candidate for the 2008 presidential nomination, as a "faggot" during a speech at the Conservative Political Action Conference—a joke, she told the crowd at Thiel's house. During her remarks she expressed opposition to gay marriage and attempted a racial joke while disputing the notion that gay Americans were an oppressed group. She cracked: "Blacks must be looking at the gays saying, 'Why can't we be oppressed like that?'"

THIEL'S IDEAS WERE SO EXTREME that they didn't easily fit into any political ideology. There was no political party for neo-reactionaries or right-wing contrarians—but there was a candidate: Ron Paul. The bushy-eyebrowed Texas representative was, like Thiel (and Yarvin), fond of the extreme free-market capitalism of the Austrian economics school as well as general doomsaying. Paul, like Thiel, was a climate change skeptic and, like Thiel, had a long history as a far-right provocateur.

In the late 1970s until the mid-1990s, he'd published newsletters, with names like *Ron Paul's Freedom Report* and *The Ron Paul Survival*

Report, that had, among other things, referred to Martin Luther King Jr. Day as "our annual Hate Whitey day" and had claimed that the 1992 Los Angeles riots had ended "when it came time for blacks to pick up their welfare checks." On the issue of South African racial equality, Paul, too, had been a skeptic, referring to the end of apartheid as a "destruction of civilization" and the greatest tragedy ever to befall sub-Saharan Africa. He later claimed he never wrote the newsletters, even though they were frequently published under his name and in the first person.

Paul's long-shot presidential campaign in 2008 had elided this history and focused on his economic hawkishness—he favored a return to the gold standard and an end to the U.S. Federal Reserve—and his opposition to the Iraq War. These ideas put him well outside the Republican Party mainstream, but they were gold on the internet, where Paul managed to recruit tens of thousands of followers, mostly younger voters drawn to his antiwar and antiestablishment messaging, to his social media accounts. Throughout the campaign, Paul polled in the low single digits, but he consistently won online polls conducted after debates and he raised millions of dollars from donors in online fundraising efforts his campaign called "moneybombs." On December 16, 2007—the 234th anniversary of the Boston Tea Party—57,000 Paul supporters kicked in an average of $50 each to help him raise $6 million, a record for a single day's fundraising. Paul had received no support to speak of from the mainstream party or the donor class, but a week later Peter Thiel donated $2,300—the first time he had backed a candidate for president.

Paul's 2008 campaign failed, but the Great Recession allowed him to raise his profile substantially. He was packing Tea Party rallies and drawing huge crowds on college campuses. His book *Liberty Defined: 50 Essential Ideas That Affect Our Freedom* became a bestseller in 2011. In media appearances, Paul showed a genius for picking up on and amplifying youthful obsessions. He called for ending federal student loans, which he argued had made tuition unaffordable, and undertook a gonzo quest to legalize all drugs.

Back then, some liberal Democrats were getting away with coming out in favor of medicinal marijuana and civil unions. Ron Paul went onto a debate stage in Greenville, South Carolina, in May 2011 and told Chris Wallace of Fox News that he was in favor of getting rid of federal laws prohibiting not only weed and gay marriage, but also cocaine, heroin, and prostitution. He compared attempts to stop people from using illicit substances to government encroachment on religious freedom. "It's amazing that we want freedom to pick our future in a spiritual way, but not when it comes to our personal habits," Paul said, to cheers and laughter.

"I never thought heroin would get applause here in South Carolina," Wallace said, dumbfounded.

By December, with the Iowa caucuses less than a month away, Paul was polling competitively in Iowa and was out-fundraising everyone but the front-runner, Mitt Romney. Amid the excitement, Thiel saw an opportunity for influence and, more importantly, to use Paul's growing celebrity to enhance his own.

On December 12, he gave $50,000 to Revolution PAC, a group supporting Paul's candidacy. Four days later, on another Tea Party anniversary, Paul's campaign once held a moneybomb drive—but this time, small donors weren't the only ones who participated. Along with the $4 million raised from the usual supporters, Thiel gave $85,000 more to the group. He also quietly began funding a Super PAC, Endorse Liberty, seeding it with $2.6 million—more, by a huge margin, than Paul had raised from anyone else. "Men and women who want freedom and growth should take action," Thiel said in a statement in late January 2012 when the filings became public. "A good place to start is voting for Ron Paul."

PAUL AND those close to him found the idea of a tech billionaire throwing his weight behind their campaign thrilling—and a little perplexing. Paul had no major supporters in the business world—though that was part of the point of his antiestablishment candidacy. Moreover,

Thiel's Super PAC was just odd. It was run not by political types or stalwart libertarian activists, but by a group of political neophytes that included Stephen Oskoui, a Stanford-educated online marketer who was friends with Luke Nosek of Founders Fund, and Jeffrey Harmon, who was known as the guy who'd popularized the Orabrush, a $5 "tongue cleaner" that supposedly combated bad breath. In an earlier era, the Orabrush would have been sold primarily through TV infomercials, but Harmon, who'd learned about the product while studying at Brigham Young University, made a series of YouTube videos featuring a giant talking tongue. ("The biggest tongue we could find.") After the Orabrush, he would start a digital ad agency with several of his brothers that promoted other novelty products, including Poo-Pourri (an anti-odor toilet spray) and the Squatty Potty. ("Scientists say this popular bathroom accessory really does help you poop better.")

Harmon's specialty is in making the weird and unpalatable, palatable—*From Poop to Gold* is the title of a book about his ad agency's work, and also the title of its podcast—and he used Thiel's money to sell Paul the same way he sold bathroom products. The Thiel-funded PAC produced a series of low-budget parody videos under the banner "Fake Politicians Network," featuring impersonators of other candidates, as well as documentary-style short films promoting Paul as a true conservative who wouldn't cave to Democrats, bankers, or the media.

The videos, some of which were ten minutes long or more, were unusual at the time for their length and their interactivity. Harmon had pioneered the use of a new Google advertising category that allowed marketers to pay to put links inside their videos. "Tribute to Our Troops," a documentary-style commercial, blamed 9/11 on U.S. military action and included testimonials from veterans who were voting for Paul. Viewers could click and immediately share the video on Facebook, a first for political advertisements.

In the end, it didn't make much of a difference, partly because Thiel and Paul's campaign worked at cross-purposes. Paul was focusing on

smaller caucus states where it was cheap to campaign and where enthusiastic volunteers could win delegates. It had decided to ignore Florida,
in part because the state's three major media markets—Tampa, Miami,
and Orlando—make it expensive to advertise there. But Florida was one
of the states where Endorse Liberty focused. Paul flopped, winning just
7 percent of the vote and coming in fourth in the state. "It was weird,"
said Brian Doherty, who followed the campaign as an editor at *Reason*
magazine and who is the author of *Ron Paul's Revolution: The Man and
the Movement He Inspired*. "I would love to know how those yutzes got
Thiel to give them millions of dollars."

The Paul campaign was similarly confused. Officially, of course,
Super PACs and campaigns operate independently, but normally committee leaders are close allies of the candidate, which ensures that even if
they don't talk, they're operating from the same playbook. "We had
none of that with Peter," said Jesse Benton, Paul's campaign chairman.
Neither Benton nor Paul had so much as shaken Thiel's hand before the
2012 campaign. "We read about it in the press," Benton told me. Back
then, Benton told *Reason* that Endorse Liberty had been counterproduc-
tive. "We haven't seen how any money they spent has done anything
effective," he said not long after it had become clear that Paul had lost.

The PAC stopped operating shortly thereafter. "There's not much
story to tell," Harmon said. "Peter and I had a very brief relationship."
The thing was, Thiel didn't really care about helping Ron Paul get the
Republican nomination. He'd found a relatively inexpensive way to try
to syphon off Paul's movement, with the ultimate goal of incorporating
it into his own. Speaking to young activists at the Students for Liberty
conference in late February, Thiel didn't even mention Paul, focusing
instead on his tech stagnation thesis. He complained that passenger planes
weren't getting any faster and suggested that better pharmaceuticals
would be developed if the FDA stopped regulating drugs based on their
efficacy and safety. To make the point, he suggested students try to imagine how terrible the world would be if the FDA had forced the popular

Facebook video game, Farmville, to prove that it didn't cause harm. "If you were to apply the standards you have in biotech to video games, you would not have a video game industry," he said.

When a journalist asked about Paul, Thiel could barely muster any enthusiasm—not for Paul, nor for democracy itself. "I'm sort of skeptical of how much voting actually works," he said, before giving a techno-utopian answer that seemed straight out of Yarvin's Moldbug. "One of the things I like about technology is that when technology's un-regulated you can change the world without getting approval from other people. At its best, it's not subject to democratic control, and not subject to the majority, which I think is often hostile to change."

So what in the world was he doing with Paul? "We're just trying to build a libertarian base for the next cycle," he explained. "The campaign really is for 2016."

THE THEME OF the 2012 Republican convention, held in late August in Tampa and delayed a day and a half by Hurricane Isaac, was "A Better Future." For three days, a series of speakers—including South Carolina governor Nikki Haley, New Jersey governor Chris Christie, and the actor-director Clint Eastwood accompanied by an empty chair—tried to establish that Obama's presidency had failed to live up to its promises and that the perception of Romney as a plutocratic businessman was flawed. The wrestler Hulk Hogan, one of Tampa's most famous celebrities, and a recent Romney convert, pitched in on Fox News, talking up his business ventures and his excitement about the election. "America's getting a chance to reinvent itself, kind of like I have," he said. "It's just a fresh start."

Notably absent from the official proceedings was Paul, who'd refused to endorse Romney and was given no speaking slot. Paul lost half his delegates in Maine, a state where he'd won almost all the delegates despite coming in second in the state's caucus, after a committee ruled that there had been irregularities with how they had been selected during the state's caucus. A group of the Maine delegates walked out of the convention in protest as supporters chanted, "Seat Maine now! Seat Maine now!" The Romney campaign made peace, agreeing to add to the party platform Paul's plan to audit the Federal Reserve—red meat for the base Thiel was helping to build—and producing a four-minute tribute video that played on the third night, just before Paul's son, Senator Rand Paul, addressed the convention.

All this was meant to placate the thousands of Paul supporters who'd converged on Tampa—a group that included more than a hundred delegates, campaign staff and volunteers, and one extremely socially awkward billionaire who had his own ideas about building "a better future." After Paul had suspended his campaign, Rob Morrow, a Clarium Capital partner and one of Thiel's political fixers at the time, called Benton, Paul's political director, telling him that Thiel wanted to come to Tampa. He asked for Benton's help securing tickets.

Whatever reservations Paul's advisers might have had about Thiel's approach during the campaign, they saw an opportunity to deepen the relationship. In July, Paul signaled that he would deemphasize this goal of getting rid of the Federal Reserve and would instead focus on the cause of "internet freedom," or ensuring that the big technology companies would be subjected to as little regulation as possible. Paul pledged to oppose net neutrality, the collection of rules that prevented big tech companies from paying to have their websites and apps load faster than competitors, and that he would oppose efforts to regulate the collection of private information by tech companies.

It was a brazen attempt to court Thiel and others in his circle, which continued at the RNC when the Paul camp finagled all-access passes for Thiel and Morrow and sent them a list of young activists. A Ron Paul staffer arranged a meeting between Thiel and Rand Paul, who was expected to take over his father's organization and run for president in 2016.

Though the topic was officially the future of the libertarian movement, Paul's allies understood it as an interview of sorts.

The idea, said someone familiar with the details of the meeting, "was that Rand would take the helm and expand" the movement. Thiel seemed to be on board. "The relationship seemed good," this person continued. While in Tampa, he threw his party for Paul campaign volunteers, posing for pictures with the young delegates.

After Paul had lost, Thiel had turned his efforts to the future of the Republican Party. He'd focused on ultra-conservative House and Senate candidates, giving $1 million to the Tea Party–affiliated Club for Growth Action fund to help finance the long-shot primary campaign of Ted Cruz. The former state solicitor general—whom Thiel backed in an race for Texas attorney general in 2009 with contributions that tallied to more than $240,000—had risen to national prominence by helping to strike down Washington D.C.'s handgun ban and by defending the appeal of a case built initially on a Mexican death row inmate who claimed the state of Texas had violated his rights under international law.

Cruz, who'd been endorsed by Sarah Palin and other Tea Party figures, came in second during the primary against the state's lieutenant governor, a heavy favorite with the backing of the state party. But he got enough votes in late May to force a runoff, setting up a frantic campaign that Thiel continued to fund, donating another $1 million through Club for Growth Action, just before the primary in July. Cruz won by fourteen points and *The Washington Post* called it "arguably the Senate upset of the cycle." He easily won in the general election—and just like that, Peter Thiel had helped elect his first senator. Gawker, naturally, showed up with ridicule, mocking Thiel's support of a candidate adamantly opposed to the expansion of gay rights and noting that it was "no crazier than paying kids to drop out of school, cure death, or create a floating libertarian utopia."

Thiel's support of Cruz, who was also seen as a 2016 contender, should have been a clue to Rand Paul's advisers that Thiel might be something other than the hardcore libertarian they'd taken him for. Ron Paul, for instance, was against capital punishment and saw Cruz as overly friendly to the financial services industry. "They think he's for the free market," Paul would spit in 2016. "He's owned by Goldman Sachs." Instead, the Paul team believed that Thiel would support Rand's inevitable 2016 run.

But in March 2013, with his star rising, Rand Paul made an attempt to broaden his appeal. The plan was to give a speech at an event convened by the U.S. Hispanic Chamber of Commerce—which, his advisers hoped, would signal his seriousness as a national candidate. It would also convey to mainstream Republicans that he didn't have the racial baggage of his father. In doing so, he would lose the support of his potential patron.

Paul began the speech by apologizing in Spanish for not having better command of the language. He recalled having played alongside Latino children as a boy and working with immigrants while mowing lawns as a teenager. He said that he'd asked one of the Hispanic laborers how much he made, and when the man told him $3, Paul assumed he meant $3 per hour. In fact, that was the day rate. These experiences had opened his eyes to the way that America, and in particular the Republican Party, had let down immigrants, he said. "Somewhere along the line Republicans have failed to understand and articulate that immigrants are an asset to America, not a liability," Paul said. He also proposed improving the visa system and border security, which he said would "enable us to let more people in and allow us to admit we are not going to deport the millions of people who are already here." He quoted Gabriel García Márquez and Pablo Neruda and called for a "new attitude toward immigrants, an attitude that sees immigrants as assets and not liabilities."

The speech was more conciliatory in its tone than in its policy prescriptions. Paul hadn't, as some had expected, argued for allowing current undocumented immigrants amnesty. The hope was that it would win a few moderate votes while keeping the extreme conservatives happy. Around this time, Thiel stopped joining the finance committee calls, indicating through an intermediary that he would be supporting another candidate. A person familiar with Paul's campaign said that he believed that the speech and Thiel's resistance to expanded immigration had driven a wedge between the two men. Paul would joke years later that Thiel's immigration strategy amounted to a "plan to make the Statue of Liberty into a digital stop sign." He later deleted the tweet.

Paul declined to mend the fences with Thiel, assuming, it seemed, that he would inherit the youth movement that his father had created and unaware that he'd never really had it in the first place. "All this time, I thought they were voting for libertarian Republicans," Kentucky representative and Paul ally Thomas Massie would say of the campaign's supporters. "But after some soul-searching I realized when they voted for Rand and Ron and me in these primaries, they weren't voting for libertarian ideas—they were voting for the craziest son of a bitch in the race."

This was Thiel's political genius, what he'd meant when he'd said he was focused on 2016. He'd seen Ron Paul's movement not in the idealistic terms that the media saw it, but as something useful. This emergent political base wasn't libertarian; it was, like Thiel, neo-reactionary. Paul had disavowed his racist newsletters and generally cleaned up the unsavory parts of his past. But Paul's supporters preferred the old Ron Paul—the Ron Paul who'd talked like one of Thiel's old *Stanford Review* columnists, who'd published a newsletter that said 95 percent of Black men in Washington, D.C., were criminals and said "I miss the closet" about gay rights. Like Thiel, they wanted to stick it to the Cathedral. He was ready to help them.

13

PUBLIC INTELLECTUAL, PRIVATE REACTIONARY

L et us in, let us in," they chanted. "No NSA, no police state!"

The protestors were outside the auditorium, but their chants—which referred to allegations that Palantir had been violating the civil rights of ordinary Americans—were audible from the stage where Thiel sat. Besides the two dozen or so demonstrators who showed up that evening in December 2014 on the campus of the University of California, Berkeley, a few hundred students had filled an auditorium to watch a member of the Berkeley Forum, an undergraduate public affairs group, interview Thiel about his new book, *Zero to One: Notes on Startups, or How to Build the Future.*

The protests came at the heels of demonstrations in cities across the country after grand juries in New York and St. Louis had declined to indict the officers involved in the deaths of Eric Garner and Michael Brown, and Thiel seemed amused to find himself in the middle of all of this. "Wow," he said, smirking. "This is really Berkeley, huh?"

A university official appeared onstage, suggesting that it might be prudent to end the event. Thiel shrugged, throwing his hands up. "I think we should keep going," he declared.

The crowd cheered, and Thiel nodded his head, settling into his chair for the next question. But seconds later, a sympathetic student inside the auditorium opened the door for the protestors, who took their chant onto the stage. Amid the chaos, Thiel's mic was cut off, and he was quickly escorted out. The event was over.

The moment was clearly thrilling to Thiel—proving his point about the power of the activist left—but it encapsulated the precariousness of his position. For years, he had been walking a line, attempting to use provocations to win mainstream recognition. Thiel's contrarianism was essential to his appeal, as he recognized when he'd insisted on carrying on above the protests. But his flirtations with extremist politics and ethically dubious business practices also carried risks. There was always a chance that he would push things too far, either by supporting something, or someone, truly odious and would be unable—or, more likely, given his impulses, unwilling—to pull back.

For the most part, his reputation within the broader world had never been better. On HBO's tech industry send-up, *Silicon Valley*, which premiered earlier that year, he'd been lovingly portrayed by Christopher Evan Welch as an out-of-touch but brilliant investor. In an early scene, the Thiel character—who is known in the show as Peter Gregory and who shares Thiel's affectless demeanor, his love for seasteading, and his disdain for elite universities—is successfully manipulated by a promising engineer who threatens to go to back to college. The show's writers had been unsparing with other tech figures, incorporating aspects of the Google founders and Oracle's Larry Ellison into the villainous Gavin Belson—a greedy big tech executive with a persecution complex and full-time spiritual adviser—and savagely mocking the investor and NBA team owner Mark Cuban, whose fictional double is obsessed with his own net worth and a failed but financially remunerative tech product he created in the 1990s. The Thiel character, on the other hand, comes off as sweetly innocent, more out of touch than conniving.

Though Gawker was still as critical as ever—"Thiel is spinning so much bullshit," *Valleywag* complained in late 2014, referring to Thiel's argument about a slowdown in innovation—the rest of the press had mostly acceded to the Hollywood view of the man. *The Washington Post* featured him in a series of Q&As with people who were "shaking up philanthropy," focusing on his support of research into life extension. "I've always had this really strong sense that death was a terrible, terrible thing," he said. "I think that's somewhat unusual." He added that he hoped his work to extend the human lifespan would be his legacy.

At the moment, Thiel's investment firm, Founders Fund, was throwing money behind the hottest Silicon Valley trend: the "sharing economy." The term described a class of startups in which unemployed people, or those looking for extra income, offered professional services on smartphone apps—Thiel's firm invested in most of the biggest players. There was Lyft, a ride-hailing app that replaced taxi drivers with regular people driving their own cars. (Lyft developed this idea; Uber would copy it and make it famous.) The Founders Fund portfolio also included Airbnb, a lodging service to let people rent out spare bedrooms or vacation homes; TaskRabbit, where "gig workers" offered to do odd jobs, like laundry and dogwalking; and Postmates, a similar service, except the gig workers delivered you gourmet food instead of putting together your IKEA furniture.

Though the apps had a few detractors, the press focused almost exclusively on their promise. "This is powerful," wrote *The New York Times*'s eternally optimistic tribune of globalization, Thomas Friedman, predicting that the sharing economy would allow unskilled workers to adapt to the modern economy. *Wired* focused less on economics and more on cultural potential. "How Airbnb and Lyft Finally Got Americans to Trust Each Other," a feature proclaimed. It argued that these Silicon Valley companies had the potential to return us to a form of "the neighborly interactions that defined pre-industrial society."

But, of course, Airbnb and Lyft also had implications beyond neighborliness. They were projects designed to reshape labor markets, removing the protections that workers had enjoyed since the New Deal, which was among the worst developments in American political history, as far as Thiel was concerned. Uber and Lyft drivers, TaskRabbit and Postmates workers, and the part-time hoteliers of Airbnb were not employees and couldn't be by definition. That meant the app companies they worked for—Thiel's portfolio companies—were under no obligation to provide for their health insurance or retirement or to negotiate with unions that represented them. There was no minimum wage for gig workers since they got paid by the gig. Moreover, this newly popular labor model wasn't limited to the sharing economy; businesses everywhere were stripping workers of rights by switching from full-time to gig-based contract workers. Now Airbnb, Lyft, and the rest of Thiel's portfolio provided an ideology to back up the shift. Stripping workers of their rights wasn't about corporate greed; it was *the future*.

THIEL'S NEW BOOK, *Zero to One*, attempted to walk the line between provocation and mainstream acceptance. He and Blake Masters, now functioning as his de facto chief of staff, shaped his Stanford lectures into a sort of startup manifesto that was a bit milder than the lectures had been. They cut the lengthy history on human sacrifice, the discussion of the ancient Scots and their blood rituals, and the phrase "Founder as God." Instead, Thiel emphasized competition, and his belief that successful people should do everything in their power to avoid it by seeking to achieve monopoly dominance of a market. He used Google as the archetype of a tech company that, he said, had created a monopoly for itself by eliminating or avoiding confrontations with would-be competitors.

The press deemed *Zero to One* a very good airport business book. "Yes, this is a self-help book for entrepreneurs, bursting with bromides and sunny confidence about the future that only start-ups can build," the *Atlantic*'s Derek Thompson noted before praising its "provocative thesis" as "an ingenious framing device—just controversial enough to arouse debate, but commonsense enough to make an incrementalist acknowledge its virtue." He continued: "Entrepreneurs should at first seek to dominate a small market. In other words: They should try to build a mini-monopoly."

Thiel was both pleased by this reaction—he was being suddenly welcomed into polite society after throwing bombs at it since his Stanford days—and, also, let down by it. He'd expected *Zero to One* to be a little bit inflammatory. But readers had largely ignored the argument about tech stagnation, which blamed the phenomenon on entitlement spending and which Thompson called "skippable." They also seemed to have failed to appreciate that he'd accused Google of being a monopoly. A well-known venture capitalist taking on one of the biggest, most beloved tech giants might have prompted regulatory action, or spurred a debate in Congress, or at least generated some controversial op-eds.

Nope. Nobody, to Thiel's disappointment, called for Google's breakup. Nobody really bothered pointing out that Thiel, a proud Straussian with a fondness for hidden meanings, might have intended a subtext. Instead they read him like a self-help author: Google is a monopoly, and you can too!

Thiel didn't publicly correct anyone, and some associates had the sense, watching him in 2014 and 2015, that he was holding back, just as he'd held back during the early days of his hedge fund. William Andregg, the entrepreneur whom Thiel had promoted as a possible candidate to cure death, said he found the book and its rollout puzzling—"as if someone watered it down," he said. Here was the swashbuckling critic of higher education—who liked to say that Harvard was basically Studio 54 for the elite, who had been so profoundly dismissive of MBAs at

PayPal that the MBAs who worked for him would hide their degrees from him—launching his book with an event at that great monument to management science, Harvard Business School. Here was the disrupter, appearing in a magazine profile in *Fortune* that described him as "perhaps America's leading public intellectual." In the profile Thiel seemed a embarrassed about seasteading, his gloriously controversial project to create floating libertarian utopias. Now he spoke of it "almost in the past tense," as *Fortune* put it.

In September, Thiel showed up at New York's General Society of Mechanics and Tradesmen to debate David Graeber, the left-wing academic who'd helped inspire the Occupy Wall Street movement, and found common ground. When a *New York Times* reporter asked what Thiel thought of an essay, published by the event's sponsor, *The Baffler*, that noted Thiel's fondness for neo-reactionaries, especially Curtis Yarvin, Thiel laughed this off, calling the article, which ran under the title "Mouth-Breathing Machiavellis Dream of a Silicon Reich," "vaguely flattering," but a "full-on conspiracy theory." In truth, Thiel said, "there's nobody sitting around plotting the future, though sometimes I think it would be better if people were."

Thiel was fond of this particular trick—proclaiming himself fully rehabilitated, while often winking that maybe in his heart of hearts, he wasn't quite falling in line to the degree he seemed to be. During an April 2015 Q&A with Tyler Cowen, the George Mason University economist who runs a fellowship, Emergent Ventures, which was started with $1 million in seed funding from Thiel, he was asked about the Cato essay in which he'd seemed to come out against women's suffrage and democracy. "Writing is always such a dangerous thing," Thiel said, coyly, and then pivoted to a riff about how the U.S. government wasn't really a democracy anyway because it was run by "these very unelected, technocratic agencies."

He didn't use the phrase "Deep State," which hadn't been brought into the lexicon by the Trump administration yet, nor did he nod to

Yarvin, who'd also advocated dramatically reducing federal bureaucracy in order to concentrate power in the hands of the chief executive. But the criticism would have sounded familiar to anyone following the Far Right and the neo-reactionary movement. Cowen, who'd praised Thiel lavishly at the beginning of the event as "one of the greatest and most important public intellectuals of our time," left the idea unchallenged, and then pivoted to a question about New Zealand. "Overrated or underrated?" Cowen asked. Underrated, Thiel responded.

Thiel, who has often described himself as "both a total insider and a total outsider," was playing a delicate game. From the outside—to Cowen's audience, for instance, or to the hosts of *CBS This Morning*—he was an up-and-coming thought leader whose controversial past was behind him. But, in fact, at the same time he was playing public intellectual and yucking it up with members of the press, Thiel was making moves in secret. He didn't just *like* New Zealand, he had secretly acquired citizenship in the country. And while he was jousting with reporters at book parties, he had secretly launched a media coup—one that aimed to settle the score with Gawker after years of criticism while sending a message to any other journalist who attempted to write about him critically.

THE CAMPAIGN AGAINST GAWKER was led, at least initially, by the handsome intellectual-property law expert who'd appeared mysteriously at a Thiel Fellows event. In April 2011, Aron D'Souza and Thiel had met for dinner in Berlin, where Thiel was attending a conference. D'Souza, who was enrolled at Oxford at the time, traveled there to see him. They'd met, D'Souza would say, through an unnamed mutual friend. "Peter attracts these types," author Ryan Holiday wrote of D'Souza in his book about Thiel and Gawker, referring to "a fit young man of indiscernible origin" who apparently had read Machiavelli's *Prince* at age thirteen and was "fascinated by power." Holiday, who'd been a guest at Thiel's parties, enjoyed extensive access to Thiel—and came away seeing

Thiel in epic terms. At various points in the book he compared the venture capitalist to General Sherman, the Count of Monte Cristo, and Andrew Carnegie, John D. Rockefeller, and Cornelius Vanderbilt combined.

D'Souza had come to that dinner meeting—eight courses, followed by several hours at a hotel bar—with a plan for Thiel to get revenge on Gawker. He proposed that Thiel use him as a cutout. D'Souza would set up a secret shell company that would anonymously fund lawsuits against Gawker, overwhelming it with litigation until it shut down. He asked for $10 million. By 3 a.m. that night, Thiel was in.

D'Souza visited Thiel in New Zealand and San Francisco, the two men refining their approach. They considered bribing employees to sabotage Gawker's operations, spying and then attempting to embarrass Denton, or even bugging the newsroom. "There were all these things that you could be tempted to do and it's not clear they would work any better," Thiel would later say. "So we decided very early on we would only do things that are totally legal, which is a big limitation."

That's how Thiel would portray the story, anyway, though others say that he also pursued tactics that would seem, at the very least, to be ethically questionable. One such example occurred when a Gawker systems administrator received an email from a Palantir recruiter. The job on offer was much more senior than the one he had at the media company, and the engineer worried that he might not be qualified for it.

The interviews—all five rounds of them—got weirder from there. The engineer told me that the Palantir executives repeatedly steered the conversation to Gawker. What were their servers like? Which security vendors did they use? How many people worked at the office overnight? What version of Linux were they running? He made it all the way to a final interview and never heard from Palantir again. It was only later that it occurred to him he'd divulged enough to mount a successful hack. "You could really attack a place with all that," he said. After Thiel was exposed, the engineer told Gawker's executives that he believed that he'd inadvertently become a source in an information operation. There was a similar probing from a Silicon Valley law firm, which purported to represent private equity investors and that attempted to interview Gawker executives. The company later concluded that that, too, was likely an attempt to gather intelligence.

An important ethical limitation for Thiel, at least as he would tell the story in retrospect, was that he and D'Souza would not fund libel or defamation claims against Gawker, even though these are the most common lawsuits brought by those unhappy with journalists. Thiel would tell friends that this choice had come from a high-minded desire to limit the scope of the ruling so that it didn't create a precedent that would undermine freedom of the press, but at other times he would suggest that he'd picked the case not because he had any special fealty to the U.S. Constitution, but because it was winnable.

Working through D'Souza he charged Charles Harder, an entertainment lawyer, with undertaking an opposition research operation more extensive than the one he'd attempted years earlier at Clarium. Harder and his team scoured Gawker's ugliest posts, looking for potential plaintiffs, and dug up memos and public statements by founder Nick Denton that could be used against him in court. In a memo to staff, Denton had written that "the staples of the old yellow journalism are the staples of the new yellow journalism: sex; crime; and even better, sex crime." Eventually, investigators working for the Thiel-funded effort would interview former employees, find out that Gawker had been using unpaid interns, and arrange for those former unpaid interns to sue the company.

Harder would bring several cases against Gawker, including one from a man who claimed to have invented email and who had been mocked by the website, another from an independent journalist whom Gawker had suggested might be suffering from "a paranoid freakout." His most promising case, however, involved Terry Bollea, better known as the professional wrestler Hulk Hogan.

On October 4, 2012, just a few months after Hogan's star turn at the

Republican convention in Tampa, Gawker published a one-and-a-half-minute clip of Hogan having sex with a friend's wife, Heather Clem, under a sardonic headline. EVEN FOR A MINUTE, WATCHING HULK HOGAN HAVE SEX IN A CANOPY BED IS NOT SAFE FOR WORK BUT WATCH IT ANYWAY, editor in chief A. J. Daulerio wrote. Gawker initially ignored Bollea's demand that it take down the video, which Bollea said had been filmed without his knowledge or consent, arguing that the couple were public figures. (Clem's husband was a Tampa radio host whose legal name is Bubba the Love Sponge.) Bollea complained to the press about the tape, which attracted Harder's attention.

Later that month, Harder sued Clem, whom Bollea alleged had recorded the encounter without his consent. In December, he filed an amended complaint naming Denton and Daulerio as well as Clem. The suit noted Hogan's status as "a twelve-time world wrestling champion" and asked for $100 million in damages.

Gawker's staff, along with the outside world, assumed that Hogan's lawsuit was another performance, or, at worst, an attempt to wring a few million dollars from a well-capitalized media company. As it would turn out, Bollea had been trying to suppress another, more damaging audio recording, in which he used racial slurs. ("I'm a racist, to a point," Hogan said on the tape. "Fucking n———." Hogan later acknowledged the comments. "I said something horrible," he said. "But that's not me, that's not who I am.") Denton figured that Hogan's lawsuit was aimed at Clem and any other leakers and instructed his lawyers to begin negotiating with Bollea's team about a settlement.

At first, the wrestler seemed willing, even eager, to settle—and at least, at one point, had agreed to a payout, according to people on both sides of the dispute. But then, just as the deal was reached, his lawyers disappeared and then returned to the negotiating table to announce that the deal was dead. To Gawker employees it felt like someone was playing a game.

Gawker's media insurance policy didn't cover invasion of privacy suits—

but the site did have a general liability policy protecting it from personal injury claims, and while battling to get Bollea's suit dismissed, the company had also been fighting with the liability insurer, arguing that because Hogan had claimed "emotional distress" its insurance should kick in. But then Bollea did something unexpected: In December 2014, he dropped the claim that Gawker had caused him emotional distress.

This was damaging to Gawker, effectively killing any chance of getting insurance. It was also deeply strange. Normally plaintiffs don't want to bankrupt a defendant if they hope to collect a judgment or settlement, but Hogan was suddenly acting as if Gawker's bankruptcy, rather than a large cash payment, were his goal. Why would he try to limit Gawker's ability to pay him?

Another mystery: Harder's firm had few cases, but seemed to have an unlimited budget. At court appearances Bollea's lawyers would stay at the city's nicest hotel. Where was the money coming from? Was someone compensating Hogan for pursuing the lawsuit?

In early 2015, Gawker reporters began looking into the case. Was Hogan paying his own legal bills, they wanted to know? And if not, who was? Gawker's reporters began assembling a list of their employer's enemies.

RYAN HOLIDAY'S BOOK mentions in passing that Gawker had other foes. These included Charles Johnson, an increasingly influential figure associated with members of the young alt-right. The movement was at once trollish, silly, and dangerously extreme. Members of the movement flirted with racism and even Nazism—anything to provoke liberal outrage—and its leaders used social media to attack anyone they saw as part of the center-left mainstream—which included Democratic Party figures, Black Lives Matter activists, and a number of Gawker writers. Thiel proclaimed himself disgusted by this crew. "These people," he told Holiday. "It's not that they are willing to do anything in the name of the ideology . . . The similarity is the nihilism: a mask for no ideology at all." Holiday noted that Johnson had sued Gawker, too, but described him as one of several "people who have nothing to do with Peter Thiel."

This was, if not a lie, a very careful evasion. In reality, Johnson and Thiel had been close for nearly a decade, and Johnson was, by this point, an important political adviser and confidant—and would come to take on a role in the Gawker campaign that was arguably as significant as that of D'Souza's. They first met around 2008 when Johnson was a nineteen-year-old college freshman, and bonded two years later at a conference put on by the conservative Claremont Institute. Like so many of Thiel's protégés, he was brilliant, but combative, verbose, and aggrieved by the liberal world around him.

Johnson had grown up in and around middle-class Milton, Massachusetts, a suburb just outside of Boston, and won a partial scholarship to attend the local prep school. He excelled at Milton Academy, the town's $25,000-a-year Ivy League feeder. (The price has since doubled.) It had not been an easy transition. He considered himself a townie among the sons and daughters of bankers, and, perhaps as a consequence of this, adopted an intense and confrontational sort of conservatism that would have been familiar to any reader of the *Stanford Review*.

After five members of the school's hockey team were expelled after a sexual encounter with a fifteen-year-old sophomore, Johnson defended the hockey players at a school assembly. He caused another mini scandal when he weighed in on an online forum discussion over comments made by Bill Bennett, Thiel's old boss at the Department of Education who in 2005 had suggested that doctors "abort every black baby in this country." (Bennett defended this as a thought experiment rather than a serious policy prescription.) Improbably, Johnson also befriended Alan Dershowitz, the Harvard Law School professor famous for the O. J. Simpson acquittal, after Dershowitz came to campus for a talk.

After graduating from Milton, he landed at Claremont McKenna

College, the liberal arts school outside Los Angeles known for nurturing right-wing intellectuals. There he attracted even more attention by starting a blog, the *Claremont Conservative*, and adopting an identity as the campus's right-wing provocateur. In one incident after a comment he'd left on an online forum about gay marriage had been deleted by the student moderator, he argued that the moderator, a student named Ross Boomer, was biased because he was gay. Boomer considered this an attempted outing since his family hadn't known of his sexuality. When *Mother Jones* reported the incident, Johnson said he hadn't known Boomer, who was out to his peers, had been closeted to his family. His classmate, he said, had been "like running around being gay on campus." Years later, he told me he regretted the incident and felt it had been blown out of proportion. During these years, Johnson was also immersing himself in conservative intellectual life, attending conferences dedicated to the works of Strauss and Machiavelli. It was at one of these conferences, held at the end of his junior year, that he first talked at length with Peter Thiel. Over a boozy dinner, they discussed their shared enmity for elite institutions, especially liberal colleges.

Thiel and Johnson stayed in touch after Johnson graduated. He landed a regular gig writing for the *Daily Caller*, Tucker Carlson's conservative news outlet, and published a book about Calvin Coolidge. By this point, Johnson's star was rising in right-wing circles to such an extent that Carlson, U.S. Senator Ted Cruz, and John Yoo, the lawyer who'd advocated on behalf of the Bush administration for torture during the Iraq War, all provided quotes endorsing it. He eventually started his own site, *GotNews*, a sort of Gawker for the right, where he stoked a backlash against Michael Brown, the eighteen-year-old Black man who was shot while unarmed by a police officer in Ferguson, Missouri, setting off a wave of Black Lives Matter protests. Johnson sued St. Louis County for any juvenile court records it might have on Brown—the request was denied because, the judge said, no records of serious felonies existed—and collected screenshots that purported to show the slain man's "violent streak." He claimed he had sources that said Brown was a member of a gang.

Then, in late 2014, Johnson reported that a *Rolling Stone* article describing an alleged gang rape at the University of Virginia was flawed and unsubstantiated. In December he published the full name of the alleged victim—breaking a longstanding taboo in both journalism and law enforcement—along with a photo that he said was her picture at an anti-sexual violence rally. Johnson seemed to have the right name, but he was wrong about the picture, which was of another woman. He apologized for the photo.

This caught the attention of Gawker. WHAT IS CHUCK JOHNSON, AND WHY? asked a Gawker headline shortly after he outed the alleged victim, referring to him as "The Web's Worst Journalist." Six days later, the site ran another post including a series of "rumors," all of which Johnson had denied and which were attributed to anonymous sources. The post attempted to give Johnson a satirical taste of his own medicine and included one claim that he'd defecated on the floor of his college dorm and another involving bestiality. "There is no evidence that Chuck Johnson was arrested in 2002 for pinning a sheep to a fence and fucking it," wrote Gawker's J. K. Trotter. "Johnson is, however, the kind of guy about whom random people make up and circulate rumors about him being arrested in 2002 for pinning a sheep to a fence and fucking it."

Johnson went to war on Twitter, railing against Trotter and Denton. "How much would you pay to end the career of a very liberal journalist?" he asked at one point. He became obsessed with the cause—blaming Gawker for the dissolution of his marriage and promising friends that he would destroy the outlet for what it had done to him. "I hated them," he said. After Gawker raised funds from a Putin-connected billionaire, Viktor Vekselberg, in early 2016, Johnson developed a theory that the site was connected to Russian intelligence. Around this time, Jeff Giesea, a longtime friend of Thiel's who'd worked at his hedge fund in the late 1990s, got in touch on Twitter and told Johnson he should talk to Peter Thiel.

The next time they had dinner at Thiel's home in San Francisco, sitting at a table with Blake Masters and other Thiel employees, Johnson had already figured it out. "You're funding the Gawker lawsuits," he said, fixing his eyes on Thiel.

"I—uh," Thiel stuttered, then turned beet red and confessed, asking Johnson to keep it a secret. Johnson told him he wanted in. "I know how to do this," he said.

As the two men bonded over their shared enmity, they talked and met more frequently, and Johnson became a second helper in the anti-Gawker campaign. There were dinners and breakfasts at Thiel's homes in Los Angeles and San Francisco, and phone calls, sometimes for hours at a time. Thiel found Johnson terrifying and amusing. "Charles, you're too extreme," Thiel would say when Johnson would rant, fantasizing about the demise of Nick Denton, or about why Peter should make the 20 Under 20 the "twenty million under 20," or about how little he thought of other members of the Thielverse.

Johnson, could, like Thiel's other courtiers, flatter him—he called him "Sensei Thiel"—but unlike most of the other insiders in Thiel's circle, he was more than willing to insult Thiel to his face. Johnson would tell Peter that the tech companies were parasitic—that is, the companies that Thiel had built and that everyone else in his circle venerated. He would tell Peter he was "full of shit" when making a point, and the crazy thing was that Thiel didn't seem to mind.

Many in Thiel's inner circle worried that Johnson's online persona would hurt Thiel publicly, but they may have also resented Johnson's growing influence. Although D'Souza was still nominally in charge of the Gawker case, Johnson began to advocate for a more muscular strategy.

Instead of D'Souza's plan to meticulously identify bulletproof cases, while preserving Thiel's secrecy at all costs, Johnson favored total war. He taunted Gawker executives on social media. Heather Dietrick, then Gawker's general counsel, had gotten emotional during a settlement negotiation, noting that if Bollea bankrupted Gawker, people would lose their jobs. The plea failed, and somehow word got back to Johnson, who tweeted that he'd heard that Gawker's lawyer had been crying.

With Thiel's blessing, Johnson began crisscrossing the country looking for anyone, anywhere who'd been aggrieved by Gawker. These included Pax Dickinson, a former executive at *Business Insider* who'd been fired after Gawker reporters dug up tweets that had railed against feminism, and woke culture generally, often in crass fashion. Dickinson used the n-word in one instance, and, in a sentiment reminiscent of Thiel's essay, tweeted that "women's suffrage and individual freedom are incompatible." Also potentially useful to Johnson was Hoan Ton-That, a young web developer who'd pushed the envelope as an entrepreneur. When Gawker pilloried a spammy app Ton-That had created, it also paused to mock Ton-That's Twitter profile page, where he referred to himself as an "anarcho-transexual." He was, as Owen Thomas put it, "a very San Francisco software developer." Johnson became friendly with him, along with Mike Cernovich, another conservative whom Gawker had called out for supporting the so-called Men's Rights movement. "Stop being fags," Cernovich had once tweeted. "Who cares about breast cancer and rape? Not me." Cernovich, who'd adopted positions on date rape roughly in line with those expressed by Thiel and David Sacks in *The Diversity Myth*, later deleted the tweet and moved on to politics.

Thiel was pleased enough with Johnson's brand of activism to provide him with financial support. After Johnson was banned from Twitter for suggesting that he was going to raise money for a project aimed at "taking out" DeRay Mckesson, the Black Lives Matter organizer, he started WeSearchr, a crowdfunding company that, unlike Kickstarter, promoted itself as unregulated and, as a result, was open to alt-right content. (Johnson told me he was speaking metaphorically about Mckesson; he said he was planning on publishing a story about the activist.) Around this time, Thiel gave him a check between $100,000 and $200,000. It was a gift, according to Johnson, not an investment, but it would prove awkward for Thiel. Johnson would later attract attention for suggesting on Reddit that nowhere near six million Jews had died in the Holocaust, and his crowdfunding company would help the neo-Nazi website *Daily Stormer* to raise $150,000. Like Rabois in 1992, Johnson said that both incidents were provocations designed to test the bounds of freedom of speech. His Reddit comments were a performance designed to determine if the site would censor its users; his crowdfunding site was open to all ideologies. He said neither reflected his true beliefs.

This gonzo persona made Thiel uncomfortable, but it brought an upside. The following year, it would be Johnson who would bring Thiel into the orbit of Donald J. Trump.

THIEL NEVER FULLY EMBRACED the alt-right. "He thought they were losers," said Johnson, but he also found them interesting—maybe even potentially valuable. In 2015, Thiel became friendly with Marcus Epstein, the founder of an activist group dedicated to opposing racial diversity called Youth for Western Civilization and a writer for VDARE, the far-right website that had been popular among Clarium Capital employees in the mid-2000s. Epstein had also started another group, the Robert A. Taft Club, with two prominent white nationalists, Kevin DeAnna and Richard Spencer. Epstein has adamantly denied that his writing was racist but, in 2007, while walking in Washington, D.C., one evening, he spotted a Black woman and started shouting insults. He then approached the woman, whose name was withheld by police, and, according to a court document, "uttered 'N——-,' as he delivered a karate chop to Ms.—'s head." Epstein entered a so-called Alford plea—essentially conceding the case without admitting to the crime.

In mid-2016 Thiel had dinner with DeAnna, the Taft Club cofounder and a frequent contributor to VDARE. The Southern Poverty Law Center identifies DeAnna as a key "ideological architect" of the white nationalist movement. Around this time, Johnson arranged for Thiel to meet with Milo Yiannopoulos, the *Breitbart* tech editor who had become famous for helping fuel the Gamergate movement, which directed harassment at several women in journalism and video games.

Thiel refused to meet with Richard Spencer, perhaps the most notorious member of this clique, who would attract attention in 2016 when he led a crowd in a Sieg heil–style salute, chanting, "Hail Trump! Hail our people!" "Peter's not a Nazi," said Johnson. "Nazi-curious, maybe." He told me later he was being glib, and meant only that Thiel's intellectual interests ranged widely. Another friend of Thiel's offered a similar assessment, noting that although Thiel met with members of the alt-right, the meetings rarely progressed to anything deeper. "The alt-right was ascending," this person said. "It's not surprising at all to me that he meets with these people. It's far more telling what happens next."

But Jeff Giesea, a close associate of Thiel's and an early employee of Thiel Capital, knew Spencer. According to a *HuffPost* report, he donated $5,000 to Spencer's nonprofit, the National Policy Institute. Katie McHugh, a former white nationalist who has since turned whistleblower, has also claimed that Giesea was the author of a widely circulated guide, "How to Fund the Alt-Right," which listed groups, including Spencer's and the *Daily Stormer*, and explained ways to keep donations secret. Giesea denied writing the guide.

During this time Thiel also drew closer to Curtis Yarvin, who'd become a sort of house philosopher for the alt-right. In late 2014, John Burnham, the idealistic teenager who'd been one of the faces of the Thiel Fellowship three years earlier, got into a business dispute with Yarvin over the management of their company, Tlon. A 2014 lawsuit filed by Yarvin alleges that Yarvin attempted to fire Burnham despite the fact that they were 50-50 partners and that Burnham was the CEO of the company. In justifying his rationale in the legal filing, Yarvin said that Burnham promised he would resign anytime if asked. He also noted that Burnham had been inexperienced when they founded the company, and "had almost no college education."

It was, from the point of view of the Thiel Fellowship, an odd complaint. After all, having no college education—especially for a Thiel-connected entrepreneur like Burnham—was supposed to be desirable. But when Burnham refused to leave, Yarvin's investors, a group that included Thiel and another libertarian venture capitalist, Balaji Srinivasan, sided with Yarvin. Burnham was removed from the Tlon office in October. A month later, Yarvin shared plans with Thiel and other investors to rectify what he called "the John disaster" by stripping Burnham of his 50 percent share in the company. Burnham eventually left the company, and the lawsuit was dropped.

But the incident, an echo of Zuckerberg's firing of Eduardo Saverin, would cut against Thiel's reputation for helping to protect the rights of founders above all else. Not only had he been complicit in the removal of a founder, but Burnham was one of his young mentees—somebody who'd given up college, and really everything, to chase a dream with the great man himself. Instead, it appeared that Thiel had taken the side of Yarvin, a guy who'd defended slavery. Maybe this was what Thiel really believed too? Did he believe in anything?

14

BACKUP PLANS

Locals called it the Plasma Screen House. It was carved into Queenstown Hill and overlooked one of the most beautiful places in the world: Lake Wakatipu, a deep glacial body of water cut into the mountain spine of New Zealand's rugged South Island. The name came from the home's defining feature: a nearly fifty-foot-long picture window that, from the outside, looked a bit like a giant flatscreen television. After Peter Thiel bought it, he added something else: a panic room.

He would have homes around the world—Japan, Brazil, New York, San Francisco, Los Angeles—and was living well. In addition to the constant networking, Thiel was partying. These weren't the desperate soirées filled with anxious aspiring entrepreneurs; they were ragers, with bartenders wearing "assless chaps," and drugs and sex out in the open, according to two sources familiar with the affairs. It wasn't clear how much Thiel, who was still dating Danzeisen, really partook in the bacchanals.

He tended to show up with an entourage of attractive young men, before disappearing into some back room.

The New Zealand house, as well as a roughly five-hundred-acre parcel of farmland some forty miles north that he later acquired, wasn't about partying; as the panic room suggested, it was an escape plan. Like many within his network, Thiel was a bit of a prepper—a term used to describe people who believed that the end of the world, or civilization at least, would take place within their lifetime, so they stockpiled gold and firearms, sometimes in underground safe rooms. This was, in other words, another kind of hedge, and New Zealand—remote, English-speaking, and with a right-leaning government then led by a wealthy former foreign exchange trader, John Key—was an attractive destination for a conservative billionaire with a paranoid streak. Thiel was looking for more than a bunker; he wanted a backup country.

He said nothing about this publicly—and at the time of the Q&A with Tyler Cowen in which New Zealand came up, made no mention of his Kiwi citizenship. He was becoming an important supplier of software to the U.S. military and a patron of far-right politicians who railed against globetrotting elites—which to non-contrarians might have seemed inconsistent. On the other hand, the notion of abandoning the United States had been floating around the Thielverse for years. It formed the basis for much of Thiel's work at PayPal, which had promised untraceable Swiss bank accounts for all and a broader "erosion of the nation state." It was also, of course, part of the basis for seasteading, whose proponents hoped that their floating settlements would serve as tax shelters for their residents (as well as home bases for pharmaceutical companies hoping to experiment on human subjects without regulatory oversight, among many other ideas).

Thiel had picked up this concept from the 1997 book *The Sovereign Individual*. It was one of his favorites and had recommended that elites seek out foreign citizenship and free themselves from the undue burdens of nationhood. The work's influence had also shown up in a talk by

Thiel's friend Balaji Srinivasan, a libertarian venture capitalist who'd invested alongside him in Curtis Yarvin's company. At a Y Combinator event for young entrepreneurs in 2013, Srinivasan had drawn a distinction between democratic engagement—"voice," he called it—and secession or emigration, or "exit." He'd advocated for his audience to consider the latter, freeing themselves from the bonds of traditional citizenship by starting companies that could successfully thwart regulations or even by absenting themselves from their country entirely.

Thiel's exit plans began to take shape in 2010, when he began taking an interest in New Zealand's tiny and relatively obscure tech scene. That year, the don of the PayPal Mafia made a $3 million investment in a little-known Wellington-based maker of accounting software. A friendly journalist for *Business Insider* showed up to explain that Thiel loved New Zealand and was "clearly in it for the long run." The article declared that Thiel was launching a New Zealand venture capital fund, Valar Ventures, to find more deals—all part of a plan to turn the country "into the libertarian utopia of his dreams." The following April, he wrote an $800,000 check to relief efforts for those impacted by the Christchurch earthquake. Both the investment and the donation were out of character— Thiel rarely put money into business software, and almost all his philanthropy to date had been explicitly ideological. (If he'd given to the relief efforts in New Orleans to recover from Hurricane Katrina, which had killed ten times as many people as the Christchurch disaster, he'd done so in private.) And in the summer of 2011, he flew to Auckland to speak at a conference organized by a government-backed nonprofit dedicated to supporting Kiwi entrepreneurship. His fourteen-minute speech—ironically focused on the dangers of globalization—was the centerpiece of the event.

Thiel's interest in the country and its tech sector seems less than sincere in retrospect. Despite the *Business Insider* story, Valar had no staff in New Zealand and was run by a team of loyalists that included Matt Danzeisen, his longtime boyfriend, and Andrew McCormack, the Thiel assistant who'd opened Frisson and who now worked at his hedge fund. At that moment, Thiel was secretly pushing the government to make him a citizen. New Zealand has some of the world's most liberal immigration laws, allowing skilled workers or anyone with more than $2 million or so in investment capital to stay indefinitely. But getting full citizenship typically required an intent to relocate to the country and a lengthy stay before applying—rules Thiel had no intention of following. So, over the course of six months, his lawyer furiously lobbied the government to consider his recent track record of investment and philanthropy to supersede the statutory requirements. Instead of spending the usual 1,350 days in the country, Thiel had spent 12.

Immigration officials were taken aback by the audaciousness of this request, but ultimately went along with it after Thiel sat down with Prime Minister Key. There were also meetings with the senior government figures, who secured Thiel's agreement to invest in a government-backed venture capital fund. In a secret ceremony, the future America First nationalist would take the New Zealand oath of allegiance at a consulate in Santa Monica.

That was effectively the end of Thiel's courtship of the country. Valar only made one more investment in New Zealand and never set up operations there. Thiel eventually exercised a buyout clause for his stake in the government fund. Thiel, as *The New Zealand Herald* would put it, "ghosted" his new homeland.

In New Zealand, the decision to fast-track Thiel's citizenship would be seen as a scandal—proof that the country had effectively sold a passport to a foreign billionaire. Back in the United States, it was interpreted merely as a sign of Thiel's prepper impulses. Reporters wrote stories that imagined the underground bunker he might be building on his newly acquired plot. However, those who knew him well suspected the real reason had little to do with the prospect of a nuclear war, pandemic, or revolution. It was about the thing Thiel really feared more than anything: the U.S. government.

ON THE OUTSIDE, Thiel had never been more successful. But from the inside, his empire felt vulnerable. In 2014, venture capital—and the technology industry it funded—was changing, in a way that threatened Thiel. He'd built his wealth to a great extent by cultivating a network—the PayPal Mafia—and using his rhetorical talents and contrarian instincts to further his influence, which earned him access to the most promising startups. But thanks to social media, and especially Twitter, networks and influence were suddenly easier to come by, and Thiel was no longer the only venture capitalist with a following of young protégés. Meanwhile, public-market investors such as Fidelity and Tiger Global Management, wooed by the growth potential of the new crop of private-market "unicorns," were suddenly competing for stakes in companies that normally would have been the exclusive domain of Silicon Valley VCs. In an effort to keep up and not see their lucrative ownership stakes in their funds' winning bets whittled down, venture capitalists started raising larger and larger funds. Thiel could play this game, to a degree—in March 2014, Founders Fund raised $1 billion for its fifth fund—but even this was still a fraction of the $2 trillion or so Fidelity had to play with.

And then there was politics. Thiel despised and feared Obama, who'd won election based on a campaign that appealed, in part, to the sort of multiculturalism that Thiel regarded as corrosive. Since taking office, Obama had pursued policies—including health-care reform and the economic rescue, which had used government money to bail out banks and prop up car companies, while providing stimulus checks to consumers—that Thiel regarded as tantamount to communism. He'd also engineered the economic rescue that had staved off a crash, which in turn contributed to Clarium's collapse. Making matters worse, Obama's success looked especially durable—with a clear successor, Hillary Clinton, in place to run in the next presidential election. Even though her husband had been president during the boom that enabled Thiel to create PayPal, Clinton seemed even more hostile to Thiel's interests than Obama—and was expected to bring antitrust scrutiny to tech companies and to raise capital gains tax rates. He felt, as he put it at a 2013 National Review Institute event, a "pincer movement of the upper class and the very poor against the center," a group in which, however unrealistically, he seemed to consider himself to belong.

Thiel had reason to take this personally. During the 2012 presidential campaign, Mitt Romney had disclosed that his individual retirement account, or IRA, had more than $100 million in it—a stunning admission to most Americans (and even to some in the private equity world) who struggled to see how anyone could accumulate that much money given that the government limits contributions to around $30,000 per year. Steve Rattner, the money manager who oversaw the Obama administration's auto bailout, noted at the time that Romney, who like Rattner had made his fortune in private equity investing, seemed to have "pushed the envelope all the way to the edge" in ways that were ethically dubious. "I've asked fellow private equity guys," Rattner told CNN. "None of us had even known this was a possible trick." The answer to how Romney had done it lay in understanding what *The Atlantic*'s William Cohan called the "alchemy" of private equity, whereby investors generate enormous returns based on tiny capital contributions—assuming they pick the right companies.

Thiel knew about Romney's "trick," of course, but he'd socked away many times what Romney had. And unlike Romney, who'd used a traditional IRA, meaning his withdrawals would be taxed as ordinary income, Thiel had used a Roth IRA, which meant he'd done so under even more stringent contribution limits of $5,000 per year at the time. It also meant he would pay no further taxes at all. According to four sources familiar with the structure of his finances, his Roth IRA is worth at least $3.5 billion, and likely a lot more. All of that money will, when he starts withdrawing it after his sixty-fifth birthday, be tax-free. That is as long as the government doesn't change the rules.

Many in Thiel's network saw this as a scandal in the making. Roths had been created in the late 1990s as part of a set of tax cuts passed by the Republican Congress and signed by Bill Clinton. As part of the Contract with America, House Speaker Newt Gingrich had sought to balance the budget while cutting capital gains taxes. But that required raising revenue elsewhere—hence the Roth IRA, which allowed investors to convert a traditional IRA into a Roth IRA, as long as they paid the tax beforehand. That's how Thiel, one of the wealthiest Americans, had wound up with an enormous, tax-free nest egg.

Roths were celebrated at the time they'd been created but had come under increased scrutiny during Obama's second term, with the president repeatedly proposing to limit Roth IRA contributions. Meanwhile, in 2014, the Government Accountability Office released a report announcing that it had identified an estimated 314 taxpayers with IRA balances of more than $25 million, specifically mentioning "founders of companies who use IRAs to invest in non-publicly traded shares of their newly formed companies"—that is, people who'd done exactly what Thiel did at PayPal. The report noted that the IRS planned to investigate these holdings and recommended that Congress pass laws to crack down on the practice. Not long after, Thiel told a friend he was being audited by U.S. tax authorities.

He was never sanctioned—the audit apparently never turned up anything illegal, but it seemed to make him paranoid. Investing in startups where you were the founder or one of the key investors—as Thiel had in both Facebook and Palantir—was theoretically fine, since Thiel was careful to keep his ownership stakes below 50 percent. But this practice was a gray area within a gray area, and everyone knew that Thiel exercised enormous influence over these companies.

All it would take would be a change in the way the IRS interpreted the rules around control of a company for it to force him to pay taxes on the entire $3 billion or more. Or a disgruntled former partner at an investment firm might draw attention to the extent to which Thiel exercised influence over his companies in a way that made it sound like control. "If he violates a single rule, puts the toe in the wrong direction, the government can tax the whole thing," said someone familiar with the arrangement.

This was scary, and according to several longtime colleagues, Thiel's vulnerability to a change in tax policy or a shift in how the IRS approached enforcement seemed to loom over all his relationships with those around him. It was the single dominant thing, one said. He seemed to worry constantly, these people say, that some former colleague or friend would turn on him and, as a result, tended to give former partners enticements not to do so—often by writing generous checks for funds started by former employees.

He was, when you got down to it, isolated—"deeply lonely," as one confidant put it. For someone who'd made his career on the strength of his network, Thiel had few real friendships or relationships of any kind that were entirely separate from his professional life. His longtime boyfriend, Matt Danzeisen, wasn't just his partner but was—like almost everyone close to Thiel—his employee. A member of the Thielverse noted that Danzeisen and Thiel seemed distant from one another in public, rarely standing next to each other or holding hands.

On a day-to-day level, Thiel's anxieties had little direct impact on his portfolio companies. Lower-level employees of Palantir, and even Founders Fund, thought little about Thiel's political obsessions, if they thought about them at all. But the nature of Thiel's empire—an empire that was full of people who'd molded their own beliefs and behaviors to resemble his, who saw his approval as central to their own self-worth and future prospects—is that his feelings had a way of filtering down, even when he wasn't directly in control. This was what was happening at Palantir, which was scrambling to find a way to justify its lofty valuation—as if reacting to Thiel's sense of vulnerability. In doing so, it would compound that sense of vulnerability further.

Ostensibly, Palantir was Thiel's thoroughbred unicorn—the key to his long-term financial success as well as his reputation as a brilliant futurist. Its story was well known and made it much admired—its ultra-secretive technology had supposedly tracked down bin Laden, the story went, and its founder was America's leading public intellectual. At the end of 2013, Palantir had raised more than $100 million at a $9 billion valuation, making it three times as valuable as hot-startup-of-the-moment, Uber. Alex Karp, the CEO Thiel had picked to run Palantir, was becoming a business celebrity in his own right. Earlier that year, *Forbes* had run a puffy profile presenting him as a sort of Silicon Valley bad boy, a "deviant philosopher" who boasted about going to "skanky" Berlin nightclubs, who strongly hinted that he'd smoked pot on occasion, and who just so happened to run a massive data company. There were canned quotes from famous generals. David Petraeus told the magazine it was "a better mousetrap when a better mousetrap was needed." And the article spoke of a huge, growing corporate line of business. Palantir was "emerging from the shadow world of spies and special ops to take corporate America by storm," *Forbes* said.

This all came as a surprise to many of Palantir's employees, who knew that JPMorgan Chase had mostly stopped using the technology. In fact, most of the big corporate deals that Karp and the Inception team had struck were falling apart. "It was very shaky ground," said Alfredas Chmieliauskas, who was hired by Palantir in 2013 to help set up a new line of business in Europe. "We had nothing," Chmieliauskas continued. "It was desperate." He hadn't talked publicly about the effects of that desperation until I reached him at his home in rural Spain—and the story he would tell me would shed light on one of the most curious chapters in Thiel's rise to power: the Cambridge Analytica scandal.

The context that caused Palantir to get sucked into the British consulting company's scheme to manipulate the 2016 U.S. election was this desperation. Palantir's main corporate product, Metropolis—the one that had been originally incubated inside of Clarium Capital—was a "disaster," in the words of one senior executive. It had been designed to help hedge fund managers create models based on data, such as prices or historical weather reports. For the software to analyze mortgages for JPMorgan, the company had to extensively modify it and send an army of forward-deployed engineers to the bank simply to maintain the code, acting more like consultants than Silicon Valley product developers. Customizing Metropolis to, say, keep track of raw materials for a big company's supply chain, required even more twisting—and never seemed to live up to the magic of Karp's salesmanship. "It kind of worked, but it took a lot of effort," said one former engineer. "It was a bit like a dancing bear."

Palantir's government product worked a little better, but the company was struggling in that sector too, especially with the most important decision makers inside the U.S. Army and the Obama administration. Yes, the intelligence agencies and a handful of special forces units liked the software, but the Army, the military's biggest branch and Palantir's largest potential source of revenue, showed little inclination to dump the contractors who were working on its main database software, DCGS. In fact, at a 2013 congressional hearing, the Army's chief of staff, Raymond Odierno, had exploded at Palantir's top political ally, California representative Duncan Hunter, after Hunter implied that the Army was failing soldiers in the field by not allowing them to buy Palantir.

"I'm tired of somebody telling me I don't care about our soldiers," the general said, his voice rising. He defended DCGS as a huge improvement over the technology that he'd used as a division commander during his deployment in Iraq in 2003 and suggested that Hunter didn't understand it. The encounter, which left Hunter looking stunned, went viral in defense circles—ODIERNO LETS THE FUR FLY AT A HOUSE HEARING was an *Army Times* headline—and Army secretary John McHugh defended Odierno, calling Hunter's analysis "not correct."

"The general officer corps circled the wagons after the Odierno thing," said someone involved with Palantir's Pentagon work. "That changed the dynamic forever." In the years that followed, as the Army was preparing to open bidding on a new version of DCGS potentially worth $8 billion, it began to signal that it was planning on hiring a traditional defense contractor to build a custom system rather than buying software from a commercial vendor like Palantir.

This was a disastrous turn for Palantir, which would be prevented from even submitting a bid on the contract. The company tried to apply pressure through its allies in Congress, including Hunter, and through Thiel's friend Glenn Beck, whose media company aired a documentary, "Armed and Unaccountable," that claimed the government's failure to buy Palantir was evidence of corruption. Those efforts didn't work either—and Palantir executives had begun considering the possibility that they'd have to give up on the idea of being a major government contractor and instead remake themselves as a consultancy. But because venture capitalists value software companies more highly than consultancies, that move, which might be necessary to save Palantir as a going concern, would have instantly wiped out a big chunk of the company's valuation—and Thiel's net worth.

In 2014, Karp had pulled the plug on the U.S. commercial business, relocating to Europe, where the Palantir's brand and its shortcomings were less well known, and quietly ordering senior engineers to throw out the Metropolis code and build a replacement from scratch. The plan was to focus on marketing Gotham—the software it had been selling to intelligence agencies—to large European industrial companies on the strength of the company's reputation for intelligence work, and, as ever, on the charisma of Karp and anyone he could hire.

This was where Alfredas Chmieliauskas came in. He was, like Karp and so many who find their way into Thiel's circle, idiosyncratic. Born in communist Lithuania, he'd moved to the West for college in 1999, and had, like Thiel, started a macro hedge fund in the mid-2000s, before entering academia and enrolling in an economics PhD program. He was politically agnostic, with wild hair and a desire for adventure. He quickly concluded that Palantir's software was lacking, but he embraced the com-

pany's culture, especially the cloak-and-dagger identity that it had cultivated in promoting its intelligence work. He liked the idea of playing spy.

Karp's shtick—the casual free-spirit—hadn't played as well in Europe, where executives expected formality from business partners instead
of athletic wear, as it had in the United States. Working closely with
Karp, Chmieliauskas said he had been part of a new approach, which
became known inside the company as "Team Rogue." It roughly meant
doing whatever had to be done, even pushing ethical limits. It's unlikely
that Thiel knew about Team Rogue, but Chmieliauskas said that Palantir's senior leaders certainly did, and in any case Chmieliauskas was following one of the most important rules of the Thielverse: Ignore the
rules when necessary. Palantir's actions to justify its valuation were in the
same spirit that had animated PayPal in its efforts to recover from crisis
under Thiel's leadership.

When bidding on a project for a large European bank, hoping to use
Palantir to find traders who weren't following protocol, Chmieliauskas's
team developed a tool so that the bank's IT department could read employee emails. This had not been part of the original assignment, which
involved analyzing trading patterns, not collecting intelligence—and it
also struck him as a potential violation of privacy, since Palantir's software made it easy to snoop on personal matters, like who at the bank
was sleeping with whom—but the client liked it. "We were trying to do
anything and everything," he recalled. Palantir won the business, its first
big deal in Europe.

Chmieliauskas was, in other words, moving fast and breaking things—
bigger things than he could've imagined. Because of Palantir's associa-
tion with the CIA, clients often assumed that the company specialized
in counterintelligence, and Palantir was happy to at least try to oblige
them if there was business to be won. "I'd worked on much shadier deals
before Cambridge Analytica," he said.

Cambridge Analytica had been founded by an aristocratic Brit, Alexander Nix, whom Chmieliauskas met in 2013. Despite the haughty-sounding

name, the company had little to do with Cambridge University—in fact, its office was in London—but Nix's plan had been to market ideas that had been developed at Cambridge about using people's Facebook data to guess their personality type. He would raise money from Steve Bannon and the ultra-conservative Mercer family, led by the patriarch Bob, who'd gotten rich at a quantitative hedge fund, and his daughter Rebekah. The Mercers were backers of Bannon's news outlet, *Breitbart*, and had invested in Nix's pitch to adapt the Facebook concept for use in electoral politics, enabling political campaigns to scan someone's social network profile, predict who they were going to vote for, and serve them ads to get them to show up to the polls.

Nix said he was modeling his effort on Palantir, which made Chmieliauskas, who knew that Palantir's software hadn't always lived up to Karp's salesmanship, instantly suspicious that Cambridge Analytica might be basically a con job. Then again, Nix's admiration for Palantir made him an attractive mark, and Chmieliauskas began cultivating him. He said he did this partly out of curiosity, and partly because he figured Cambridge Analytica might become a client someday. Indeed, in 2013 and 2014, the two companies discussed partnering, but Palantir executives refused, a spokeswoman would later say, because the company didn't want to get involved with political work.

Even so, in 2014, Chmieliauskas began sending Nix suggestions on how best to get his hands on the data the company thought it needed. Facebook did not sell data to outside marketers, which Zuckerberg had said was a matter of emphatic principle—though it was probably partly because by keeping the data for itself, it was able to offer advertisers the exclusive ability to target messages to Facebook users. Nix's plan had been to buy or license data that two Cambridge professors, Michal Kosinski and David Stillwell, had collected legally from Facebook, which permitted data gathering for research purposes. But when the professors demanded $500,000 plus half of anything that Cambridge Analytica made, Nix decided he didn't want to pay.

Chmieliauskas offered an alternative: Why not just create another Facebook app that could scrape data from the social network by collecting the personal information of anyone who used it as well as the personal information of all of their Facebook friends? Over the next few months, Nix took Chmieliauskas's idea and ran with it. Instead of buying Kosinski's data, he paid another researcher, Alexander Kogan, to create an app that would harvest the Facebook data of 87 million Americans, ultimately in support of Donald Trump, who would rely on using targeted Facebook ads to raise money and turn out voters, spending around $100 million on the social media platform.

The Cambridge Analytica scandal would lie dormant for years and would come out only after whistleblowers at the company revealed what they'd done to *The New York Times* and London's *Observer* newspaper. The revelation that data taken from Facebook might have helped Trump win caused an outcry, especially among Democrats, who blamed Zuckerberg.

The Facebook founder had insisted that his company had been the victim of Cambridge Analytica's bad behavior as the Americans who'd had their data stolen, but this argument began to seem weaker when it became clear that a Facebook board member was connected to the scandal. Christopher Wylie, a former Cambridge Analytica employee who'd turned whistleblower, said that he'd seen Palantir engineers in the Cambridge Analytica offices, where they were given Cambridge Analytica logins and helped build additional apps, like Kogan's quiz, to harvest more private data from Facebook users. If Facebook had been a victim, rather than a willing accomplice of Cambridge Analytica, why had the consultancy been working with a company controlled by Zuckerberg's mentor?

Chmieliauskas was eventually fired, and Palantir said that he was a rogue employee who'd been working "in an entirely personal capacity." This, he told me, was sort of true, in that his Cambridge Analytica work had been off the books and didn't get very far, but also misleading. He'd been paid to do just this kind of business development—and in fact, Palantir had worked with social media data for other clients in the past and had no policy against it. He was a rogue employee, yes, but he'd been doing that job in a semiofficial capacity. "They threw me under the bus," he said.

None of this would solve Palantir's underlying issues—and by early 2016, the company's difficulties, and Thiel's by extension, had been discovered by the press. On May 6, *BuzzFeed* reported that a number of the company's prominent corporate clients had been firing it—recent departures included American Express, Coca-Cola, and NASDAQ. Around this time, Thiel was secretly attempting to arrange a sale to Oracle, the big database provider, with Michael Ovitz, the Hollywood mogul, who was friendly with both Thiel and Oracle cofounder Larry Ellison, playing the role of matchmaker.

There was a lunch with the three men and another investor, Marc Abramowitz, but the potential deal fell through, and, as the presidential election heated up, Thiel needed a candidate who would ensure that his wealth would be protected, as well as one who would be open to buying the kind of software that Palantir was selling. None of the choices—Carly Fiorina, Ted Cruz, Rand Paul, and the wildcard, Donald Trump—were a perfect fit with the reactionary ideas that Thiel had been cultivating. But he'd spent the past decade building social and political capital, along with a network of far-right political allies who were ready and willing to help him. He would suddenly have a chance to spend it.

15

OUT FOR TRUMP

n his initial assessment of the jockeying for the Republican nomination for the 2016 presidential race, Thiel had thrown his weight behind Carly Fiorina, a well-known tech executive who'd been on the cover of *Fortune* magazine's "Most Powerful Women" issue in 1998 when she was a senior executive at Lucent Technologies, the telecommunications equipment business spun off from AT&T, and who had later served as CEO of Hewlett-Packard. "She was the only one who understood what a fucking algorithm was," said Steve Bannon. "That's his kindred soul."

But Thiel hadn't been entirely enamored of Fiorina. Her business career had ended disastrously in 2005, after she pushed HP to acquire Compaq, just as the personal computer industry was beginning to contract. The merger is now considered by many to be one of the worst business deals in modern history and coincided with several waves of layoffs. In all, nearly thirty thousand people lost their jobs, including Fiorina, who had then reinvented herself as a mainstream conservative Republican. This put her far to the left of Thiel on issues like trade and immigration. "He didn't think Carly would win," said a friend. Backing her "was a way to say, 'I'm not on anybody's team.'"

In August 2015, Thiel gave $2 million to Fiorina's Super PAC, leading to a big ad buy that, along with a strong debate performance, helped contribute to a brief surge in the polls. By September, Fiorina was in third place, behind the two vanity candidates, Trump and the neurosurgeon Ben Carson. She was seen, for a fleeting moment, as the likely pick of the Republican party establishment. She hit a high point in mid-September shortly after Trump had been sufficiently rattled by her to make a sexist quip to *Rolling Stone* about her appearance. "Look at that face!" he said. "Would anyone vote for that?"

But Fiorina dipped in the polls in late September after Trump toned down the misogyny and began attacking her business record, which he called "a disaster." When the press followed up by scrutinizing the Compaq merger, Thiel would have been a natural surrogate to help her respond to the attacks. Fiorina's poor job performance had come during a brutal tech downturn that almost killed PayPal too. Thiel could have testified to that, but instead he did nothing—declining to donate any additional funds or to speak on Fiorina's behalf. She only received 2 percent of the votes at the Iowa caucus and 4 percent in the New Hampshire.

After Fiorina withdrew, the race quickly winnowed to just three candidates: the centrist Ohio governor John Kasich, Trump, and Ted Cruz. Thiel and Cruz, of course, also had a history that included the donation to support Cruz's Senate campaign in 2012. Thiel admired Cruz, who embodied some of the same contradictions that existed in Thiel's own relationship with elite institutions. Cruz was, like Thiel, a sort of Ivy League populist, who'd nurtured his sense of a class struggle between liberal elites and regular Americans at Princeton University, and who, like Thiel, had attended a top law school. In a 2014 interview with the *Daily Caller* Thiel had praised Cruz, comparing him favorably to the typical Republicans in Congress, who he said "are somewhat lower IQ than the people on the other side." This all made Cruz a natural next choice.

After Fiorina dropped out on February 11, Thiel and Charles Johnson had dinner in Dallas with Hal Lambert, an investor and Cruz's finance chair. Thiel had told people he planned to donate $1 million and to throw his support behind the Texas senator, whom he hoped would consolidate the Never Trump vote, win backing from mainstream Republicans, and then take the nomination. But at the end of the dinner, Thiel made no move to offer his support.

"What are you thinking?" Johnson asked over drinks, after Lambert left the table without having secured a commitment.

Thiel said he'd been thinking about President Obama's notorious comments about working-class white voters. "You go into some of these small towns in Pennsylvania, and like a lot of small towns in the Midwest, the jobs have been gone now for 25 years and nothing's replaced them," Obama had said at a 2008 fundraiser in San Francisco. "And it's not surprising then that they get bitter, they cling to guns or religion or antipathy to people who aren't like them or anti-immigrant sentiment or anti-trade sentiment, as a way to explain their frustrations."

Surprisingly, given that he considered Obama a communist, Thiel agreed with the analysis. Not the part about clinging to guns and religion, but the sense that the bipartisan consensus on globalization had failed. Americans, he said, were angry about trade and immigration—which they blamed, correctly in his view, for making them poorer. And they were angry about the globalization of information, as their culture was defined increasingly by the big internet companies. It was a powerful admission, almost a self-hating comment, for an immigrant tech entrepreneur who'd made a career based on moving money across international borders. Thiel didn't care.

"Politics is going to be all about globalization," he told Johnson. "And Trump is going to win."

Thiel wasn't ready to publicly support Trump, but he asked Johnson for a favor. Could he secure Thiel a place as a delegate for Trump at the Republican National Convention?

Thiel had never particularly *liked* Trump. They are, in almost every respect, polar opposites: Trump, the libidinous New Yorker incapable of preserving an inner monologue; Thiel, the introverted citizen of three countries whose every utterance is measured and qualified. In the same *Daily Caller* column in which he'd praised Cruz's intelligence, he'd dumped on Trump as "sort of symptomatic of everything that is wrong with New York City." And yet, Trump was, in many ways, a perfect avatar for the political project Thiel had been pursuing. He was, like Ron Paul, in favor of an extreme crackdown on illegal immigration. His campaign platform, like Paul's in 2012, included ending birthright citizenship and fortifying the border. Nor was Trump, like Paul, averse to white identity politics—his views on race in New York in the 1980s and '90s were roughly in line with the positions expressed in Paul's newsletters from the same period. Most of all—and most importantly—Trump, like Paul, could play, to perfection, "the craziest son of a bitch in the race." He was the candidate always willing to say the unsayable—and for this Thiel would love him. "It was almost like a spiritual connection," said Johnson. "He thought Trump was something special."

The real estate mogul pitched his candidacy as a direct rebuke to the same issue that had first animated Thiel in his political evolution: the great scourge of liberal political correctness. "We have to straighten out our country," Trump said on *Meet the Press*, just as the campaign for the Republican presidential nomination was getting underway. "We have to make our country great again, and we need energy and enthusiasm. And this political correctness is just absolutely killing us as a country. You can't say anything. Anything you say today, they'll find a reason why it's not good."

WHILE THIEL QUIETLY drew toward Trump, he was also monitoring developments in the Gawker case, where a trial was just weeks away. Bollea's legal team had caught something of a break. His case had been shot down by a federal judge, so he sued Gawker in state court, which meant that the trial would be in the Tampa Bay area, where Bollea lived. The judge in the case, Pamela Campbell, seemed likely to be sympathetic to Bollea and was not at all averse to a media circus. She'd represented the parents of Terri Schiavo, who sued to prevent her husband from removing her feeding tube after Schiavo was declared brain-dead by doctors. Given the venue, and the fact that the jury would almost certainly include a few Hulkamaniacs, Bollea's legal team seemed sure to argue that a sadistic New York media company had railroaded a local hero.

Gawker's editors had made the case easy for them. During depositions, former Gawker editor A. J. Daulerio had quipped sarcastically that he would have published a sex tape involving a child, as long as the child was at least five years old. Nick Denton had come off as glib and unrepentant, claiming that by publishing the sex tape Gawker was paying a compliment to Bollea by "humanizing" him. This led to a dramatic moment at the trial, when one of Bollea's lawyers asked Denton to read the description from Gawker's write-up of the sex act, which Gawker had called a "dutiful blowjob." "Use your most humanizing tones," Hogan's lawyer instructed. Denton complied, reading the passage to the courtroom.

Gawker might have saved itself if it could have proven that Bollea's case was getting secret funding, and the company was getting close to doing so. In January, David Goldin, a crisis PR operative hired by Gawker, heard a rumor from a local lawyer with connections in Tampa. The source told him that Terry Bollea's lawsuit was being backed by a billionaire whose gay son the blog had outed.

Gawker executive editor John Cook and reporter J. K. Trotter frantically scoured the site's archives. They failed to find a billionaire who fit the bill exactly, but they did find several possible candidates. The most likely, they believed, was Peter Brant, a hedge fund manager whose son, Peter Brant II, is gay and had once written an angry letter after Gawker posted a series of paparazzi shots of the then-eighteen-year-old kissing his mother, the supermodel Stephanie Seymour. A slightly less likely possibility: Peter Thiel. He wasn't the gay son of a billionaire, but a gay billionaire who obviously hated Gawker, having compared it to a terrorist organization and mused about its demise as "an interesting theoretical question" in 2009. By the time the trial started in March, that was the extent of the evidence, and it was nowhere near enough to go public with their suspicions.

In court, Gawker never had a chance. Bollea's legal team, led by Harder, made an argument that was at once subtle and crude. Harder argued that when Bollea had talked about his sex life in the past—bragging about the length of his penis in a radio interview and yucking it up about the publication of the tape in an interview with *TMZ*—he'd done so in *character*, as the Hulkster—a muscled, sexed-up maniac. Yes, perhaps, Hulk Hogan was newsworthy, Harder conceded. But, he pointed out, Gawker had also invaded the privacy of the private man who'd played Hulk Hogan. "Terry Bollea's penis is not ten inches," the former wrestler told the jury, in one of a few surreal moments during the trial.

The less subtle part of the argument amounted to a populist attack on a New York media company. Gawker, Bollea's team argued, was evil. It was run by a "porn king," Denton, who "ruins lives." It took six hours for the jury to deliver the death blow to the out-of-towners: Gawker owed Hogan $115 million. Another $25 million was added in punitive damages for a grand total of $140 million. When he learned of the verdict, Thiel was overcome with relief and even joy. "It's the most philanthropic thing I've ever done," he began telling friends.

He said nothing about any of this publicly—not yet anyway. Privately, though, he was bragging, and the word was getting out. As the trial was starting, Dan Abrams, the lawyer and media entrepreneur, published a blog post in which he speculated that "a Gawker hater" was paying Hogan's legal bills. After the trial, a member of Gawker's sales team reported that he'd heard that Thiel was backing Gawker while chatting with a friend who'd recently attended a Facebook company party. The strange thing about this, this Gawker employee said, was how he'd mentioned it almost as an aside, as if everyone already knew.

Gawker would file for bankruptcy in June, but the site was still publishing, and Denton announced plans to appeal the ruling. Johnson urged Thiel to press his advantage, and Harder went on the attack. No longer especially concerned about discretion, he began filing defamation lawsuits on behalf of a number of clients who were much less sympathetic than Hogan had been.

One involved a freelance journalist, Ashley Terrill, who'd claimed a Gawker employee had defamed her in an article about her fight with the online dating site Tinder. Her suit was scattered and included a laundry list of general grievances that seemed to have little bearing on the case. Another was on behalf of Shiva Ayyadurai, an entrepreneur who'd said he'd invented email in 1978, even though most historians considered electronic messaging to have come into use years earlier. Both suits named editor John Cook as well as Sam Biddle, a young Gawker writer who'd frequently criticized Thiel's friends and members of the alt-right. The second portrayed Biddle as an unreliable narcotics abuser based on a personal essay he'd written about anxiety and depression. It was exactly the kind of innuendo Gawker had perfected—now trained on one of the site's junior employees.

On May 9, Trump's campaign submitted its delegate slate for California's Republican primary. Among the three names listed for California's third congressional district was Peter Thiel. This prompted a few head-scratching headlines that put Thiel's Trump support in the context of his other contrarian bets, like seasteading and the 20 Under 20. But this turned out to be a prelude to what happened two weeks later, when Andrew Ross Sorkin of *The New York Times* published an interview with Denton, who told him that he suspected that a Silicon Valley billionaire had been funding the Gawker lawsuits. Sorkin's article may have pushed one of Thiel's confidants to finally leak that he was behind it because the following day, in *Forbes*, Ryan Mac and Matt Drange broke the news that it was Thiel.

Thiel then made his own call to Sorkin, who published the interview the following day. In Sorkin's column, Thiel used the same formulation he'd used on the day of the judgment. Killing a small media company over a negative story wasn't a typical oligarch's grievance—it was, he insisted, a public service. He wasn't attacking the press, he was helping it by ridding it of a bad actor. "It's precisely because I respect journalists that I do not believe they are endangered by fighting back against Gawker," he said. "It's less about revenge and more about specific deterrence."

THE REACTION TO Thiel's emergence as both a Trump supporter and the architect of a decade-long conspiracy to destroy a media company was intense. "When the backlash starts in earnest & everyone in tech is hated, it'll be because of bond villain shit like this," tweeted Anil Dash, CEO of the software firm Glitch. A *Guardian* columnist, Marina Hyde, warned, presciently, that the case would presage a new era in which powerful people use the courts to bully media outlets. "People even remotely tempted to sympathize with Thiel's imperious 'philanthropy' claim should wonder if they'll apply the same designation when the next angry billionaire follows his lead and sets out to destroy a media outlet they respect," she wrote. "It is certainly possible to imagine, say, a defeated Donald Trump embarking on a round of score settling. Thiel has given him the road map."

The disdain was not the exclusive domain of reporters. At Recode's annual conference, Jeff Bezos said he thought secret lawsuits of the type Thiel pursued should be illegal. "The best defense against speech that you don't like about yourself as a public figure is to develop a thick skin," he said. "You can't stop it."

Now that people were looking for them, Thiel's connections to the alt-right were surfacing. Earlier that year, he'd agreed to speak at a conference in Turkey on the subject of "corporate monopoly" organized by the Property and Freedom Society. After he was revealed as the backer of the Gawker suit, the Southern Poverty Law Center published an article noting that the conference had frequently attracted white nationalists, including Richard Spencer. Thiel pulled out of the event the following month.

Still working behind the scenes, Johnson ensured that Thiel got as much mileage as possible from the controversy. With his network of right-wing activists, he circulated messages on Twitter thanking Thiel for bringing down Gawker. The hashtag #ThankYouPeter spread quickly and was listed on Twitter's site as a top trending topic. Spencer, Milo Yiannopoulos, and Mike Cernovich all promoted the hashtag, urging their followers to thank Thiel. Yiannopoulos compared him to Batman: "The hero Silicon Valley needed," he wrote in a *Breitbart* post.

Johnson also used his crowdfunding company, WeSearchr, to finance a campaign to uncover evidence that Denton had committed a crime so that he could be sent to prison. The WeSearchr page, which included an illustration of Denton wearing stripes and behind bars, raised $50,000, much of it contributed by Johnson himself. Because few people outside of the shadowy world of far-right politics knew of Thiel's patronage of the alt-right, the press mistook it as a grassroots uprising. The journal *Quillette*— an outlet that Thiel was secretly funding, according to Johnson—used the trending hashtag as proof that "ordinary readers" were on Thiel's side, effectively making Johnson's information operation look organic. *Breitbart* and *Fortune* carried versions of the same claim.

Johnson and Thiel's connections were still a secret at this point, but

Johnson felt safe enough to expose himself slightly. He gave an interview to Tucker Carlson's *Daily Caller* in which he announced that he was offering an "olive branch." He said he would drop his own lawsuit if Denton would publish an essay by every victim of the site's snark. "He says he wants a meeting with Peter Thiel?" he said. "Well I'm ready for my meeting with him anytime."

It was a curious comment. Denton had not publicly mentioned a meeting with Thiel. In fact, though, they were set to meet later that month. The conversation had been arranged by an intermediary, Thiel's old PayPal colleague Jeremy Stoppelman, who was still running Yelp and who was also friendly with Denton. He had encouraged the two men to try to reach a settlement that would spare them the agony of continued litigation. The rationale for a deal was obvious: Denton could save himself financially, get Thiel to drop the lawsuits against his writers, and preserve Gawker in some form. By being merciful Thiel would make his "philanthropic" point without having to actually destroy a media company—and without risking an embarrassing loss in appeals court. It would be a win-win.

That wasn't even close to what happened. During the meeting, and in the months that followed, Thiel pressed his advantage, making it clear that he had no interest in preserving Gawker as a business or allowing Denton any measure of dignity. He wanted the media company gone and he wanted Nick Denton financially crippled.

"Listen," he said, when the possibility of a settlement came up. He promised to "wipe out your publication."

By this point Gawker Media had filed for bankruptcy, but its flagship website was continuing to publish. Denton had put the company's other blogs up for sale and had been planning to appeal the Florida verdict. But Thiel's resolve broke Denton's, pushing him into personal bankruptcy in early August. Three weeks later, just before his fiftieth birthday, he published Gawker's final post. "Peter Thiel has gotten away with what otherwise would be viewed as an act of petty revenge by reframing the debate on his terms," Denton noted. He identified Thiel as a member of a new elite—a group of "techlords flush with monopoly profits" who were "as sensitive to criticism as any other ruling class, but with the confidence that they can transform and disrupt anything, from government to the press."

Denton would exit bankruptcy eventually, but only after Gawker dropped its appeals and agreed to pay Bollea $31 million, plus an additional sum from Denton. Ashley Terrill got $500,000, Shiva Ayyadurai got $750,000, and Johnson got around $800,000. In a blog post described the settlement in November, Denton explained that he had given up his appeals because Thiel had made clear that he would never back down. Given Thiel's intransigence and his endless resources, it would be impossible to raise money to continue funding the case. That was the end of it: Thiel had effectively ruined the owner of a major media company.

WHAT WAS HAPPENING TO PETER? some of his close friends wondered. He seemed to be suddenly picking fights with the entire world. There was his intransigence over Gawker, his support of Trump, and the increasingly indiscreet connections with the alt-right. "Every time I read" about Peter Thiel's support of Trump, Max Levchin said, "I typically check the calendar because I'm not completely sure it's not April 1." Others, especially those who knew Thiel from the hedge fund world, were considerably less shocked. Thiel didn't look so much like a crazy person as someone who was making a bet. Maybe he knew something that they didn't.

That summer, *Bloomberg*'s Lizette Chapman and I began calling friends and former colleagues of Thiel's to try to suss out his approach to the 2016 election. We reported that Thiel saw his bet on Trump as a high-upside, low-risk wager. Thiel had already offended everyone there was to offend in Silicon Valley with his views on seasteading, women's rights, immigration, and so on. What would adding one more quirky position really do to his status? He was, we wrote, "the Valley's preeminent kooky libertarian." But, if Trump won, he would be "the U.S. president's kooky libertarian."

That would mean, potentially, easier access to contracts for SpaceX and Palantir. It would also give Facebook a way to get as close to the White House as Google had been. "It was my least contrarian bet," Thiel would later joke.

Of course, Thiel rarely did anything without a hedge, and Palantir, especially, needed a backup plan, in case Thiel was wrong and Trump lost. The company was still struggling to sell software in Europe, and although it had managed to raise more money at an even higher valuation, $20 billion, it still had made no progress with the Army. Thiel was so pessimistic about the company's prospects that Founders Fund's valuation of Palantir was 40 percent lower than the official $20 billion figure. The company's Washington, D.C., employees were also getting desperate. They devised what was known internally as the "Trojan horse strategy." Palantir would attempt to mend fences with Army brass and try to establish the company as a subcontractor to whomever won the $8 billion DCGS contract. Then, somehow, the company would take over the whole contract at a later date.

But in late June, just a month after Thiel had revealed his support of the Gawker suit and switched candidates to Trump, Thiel's company did something that was as shocking in the defense world as his attack on Gawker had been in the media world. He sued the U.S. Army. In a legal complaint, Palantir's lawyers, led by Hamish Hume of the powerful corporate firm Boies, Schiller and Flexner, argued that the Army, in failing to allow Palantir to submit a bid for the contract for its big software database, had violated a 1994 law that had been passed to prevent overspending by the federal government. According to that law, which had been passed amid outcry over the Pentagon's supposed purchase of $600 toilet seats, the Army was required to consider cheaper, commercial products wherever possible rather than those that had been marked up by big defense contractors. By setting up DCGS as a consulting arrangement, the Army had cut out Palantir, a commercial product, the suit argued.

The Army and the broader defense community were flabbergasted. Contractors typically attempted to seduce bureaucrats—sometimes crossing the line into bribery. Palantir hadn't quite played this game, but under Karp it had tried to seduce in its own geeky way. Now it had launched an attack against a potential customer.

If the move surprised the Army, it didn't surprise anyone who'd followed the Thielverse closely. Two years earlier, SpaceX—the Thiel-backed rocket company founded by Elon Musk—had successfully tried the same trick, suing the Air Force after it awarded a contract to a competitor, United Launch Alliance, or ULA. "Everyone said, 'If you sue NASA, that's your future customer, and they'll never work with you again,'" Musk recalled. "I was like 'Okay, they're definitely not gonna work with us if we *don't* sue, so at least there's a chance they'll work with us if we do sue them and win.' So it was a small chance versus nothing." Musk paired the lawsuit with an appearance before Congress where he noted that ULA used Russian-made engines. The Air Force backed down, agreeing to ensure that SpaceX could bid on its contracts, and the company's valuation would soar.

Now Palantir was trying the same move. The complaint included a litany of testimonials from the midlevel commanders Palantir had been courting and quoted from Michael Flynn's supportive memo. It also claimed that the Army had suppressed reports praising Gotham, Palantir's main government product. Palantir wanted the federal judge to throw out the DCGS bidding and start again.

The lawsuit was a "calculated risk," according to someone who worked on it, that also functioned as a potential hedge, presenting a chance for Thiel to win no matter what happened in November. Trump could win and disrupt the Army; but even if he lost, Palantir's lawsuit might do the same.

THE REPUBLICAN NATIONAL CONVENTION, held in mid-July in Cleveland, was characterized by a reality-show insanity befitting th TV star turned candidate. Trump had won the nomination handily, bu he'd done so in part by insulting a large subset of the Republican elite The runners up, Kasich and Cruz, had indicated that they had no inten tion of endorsing the candidate. Trump had also repeatedly mocked for mer president George W. Bush, as well as the two previous nominees Mitt Romney ("One of the dumbest and worst candidates") and John McCain ("I like people who weren't captured"). None of the past nomi nees would even show up.

The mainstream business community had also stayed away from Trump Not a single CEO from one of America's one hundred largest companies had given to his campaign, and many longtime Republican donors had declined to offer support. Some, like Meg Whitman, whom Thiel had tangled with when she ran eBay, were openly critical.

Silicon Valley had been especially averse to Trump. Zuckerberg had criticized him earlier in the year, albeit with the sort of deliberate ambi guity he seemed to have picked up from Thiel. "Instead of building walls, we can help people build bridges," he'd said in April, referring to Trump's proposal to build a wall on the U.S.-Mexico border without naming the candidate himself. In June, Intel's then-CEO, Brian Krza nich, whose company, with its enormous U.S. manufacturing operation, seemed poised to benefit from Trump's economic nationalism, had planned to host the nominee and other tech executives at his home. But he can celed at the last minute when news of the event leaked.

Filling the vacuum in Cleveland were members of Trump's immedi ate family—six Trumps were listed as headline speakers—and what Bannon would describe to me as a "dog's breakfast" of supporters. These included Joe Arpaio, the famously anti-immigrant Arizona sheriff who'd recently been held in contempt of court for racial profiling; the 1990s underwear model Antonio Sabato Jr.; and Scott Baio, better known as Chachi from *Happy Days*.

To the extent that there were corporate leaders in Cleveland, they were rather scruffy ones—Willie Robertson, founder of the hunting supply business made famous by *Duck Dynasty*; Dana White, the cage fighting mogul; Phil Ruffin, the owner of Circus Circus in Las Vegas; and Thomas Barrack, the real estate mogul who introduced Trump to Paul Manafort. None of these men seemed likely to lead the manufacturing renaissance that Trump was promising. *Those* people would still mostly be voting for Hillary Clinton or sitting the election out. Just days before the convention, a group of 150 or so well-known tech executives and investors published an open letter condemning Trump for his "anger, bigotry, fear of new ideas and new people, and a fundamental belief that America is weak and in decline."

Of course, the idea that America was weak and in decline was one that Thiel had been pushing for years. He wasn't the only CEO in the Valley who believed Trump's basic message, but he was the only one willing to say so publicly. That made his support exceedingly valuable, according to Trump insiders, and was why the convention organizers asked him to speak. He was a business celebrity, but without the slightly slimy aspect that defined so many in Trump's circle. "Trumpworld was replete with people who were trying to accomplish things, but who didn't have great track records in the outside world," explained Bannon. "There were very few people who'd gone to Ivy League schools, very few people who had achieved anything in capital markets or the corporate world. He brought all those talents to the movement."

Thiel was placed in prime time on Thursday, the night Trump was set to formally accept the nomination. He would speak just after Jerry Falwell Jr.—the Liberty University president who'd given the twice-divorced Trump a key boost among evangelicals when he'd endorsed him over Ted Cruz earlier in the year—and just before Thomas Barrack. The technologist and the real estate entrepreneur would hammer home

Trump's key message: that his success in business, such as it was, qual
fied him to be president. They would be immediately followed by Ivank
Trump, and then by the candidate himself.

Thiel began his speech by identifying himself as a "builder," lik
Trump, before hitting an uncharacteristically personal note. He talke
about his parents, Klaus and Susanne, who'd emigrated to the very cit
where he was now addressing the crowd. "They brought me here as
one-year-old," he said of Cleveland. "This is where I became an Amer
can."

The convention hall was noisy, and Thiel looked a bit unsteady, espe
cially at first. He stood at the podium, hunching slightly, while wearin
a painted-on smile that was all teeth, as his gaze pivoted robotically be
tween the two teleprompters. He'd rehearsed, clearly—he managed t
drop his characteristic speech disfluency, his normally heavy use of fille
words—but he spoke too quickly, forgetting to pause between sentence:
and few of his lines seemed to land, aside from a crack about Hillar
Clinton's emails.

The camera panned to the crowd, where Donald Trump Jr. and hi
then-wife, Vanessa, joined Tiffany Trump at their seats. They shifte
around, chatting with one another, appearing only to half listen as Thi
delivered a searing indictment of the state of technology in the Unite
States. To those who were paying attention and who'd followed his wri
ing, this theme would sound familiar: The United States had lost its wa
sometime in the 1980s and no longer had the ambition to make the fu
ture happen, he said. Trump would be the man to bring it all back.

"Our government is broken," Thiel declared. American nuclear powe
plants still used floppy discs. Some fighter jets didn't work in the rair
Government software was useless. "This is a staggering decline for th
country that completed the Manhattan Project," he said. "We don't ac
cept such incompetence in Silicon Valley, and we must not accept it fror
our government."

At this point, about three minutes into the speech, he allowed th contrived smile to drop, looking more serious, but also looking like he might be actually starting to enjoy himself. The crowd quieted as Thiel noted that when he was a boy, "the great debate was about how to defeat the Soviet Union." He continued: "Now we are told the great debate is who gets to use which bathroom. This is a distraction from our real problems. Who cares?" He said the last two words loudly, almost angrily, and got his first real show of applause. Even the Trump kids were clapping.

Then Thiel delivered the line that everyone would remember. "Of course," he said, "every American has a unique identity. I am proud to be gay. I am proud to be a Republican. But most of all I am proud to be an American." A faint "USA! USA! USA!" chant rang out for a gay immigrant from members of a party that had been generally hostile to both. The Trumps were on their feet, along with everyone else.

Charles Johnson watched the speech from the VIP section, along with Hoan Ton-That, who'd been mocked by Gawker. They were becoming friends, and were scheming about starting a company with Thiel's help. That week, Johnson had introduced Thiel to Ton-That and the men had bonded over the destruction of Gawker.

"I would give you a kiss if I knew you well enough," Ton-That had said.

Thiel had squirmed slightly but nodded enthusiastically. "Yes, yes, yes!" he'd said, beaming.

He'd agonized over those final lines about his identity. "I want them to know that gays have always been a part of America, and that America is the best country for gays," he told Johnson. He'd never spoken publicly this way about his sexuality—hell, he never spoke about it directly with most of his friends. But he wanted "people to know the full me." "He never had a coming-out moment," Johnson said. "That was it."

The personal turn was useful, giving authority to Thiel's argument that political correctness was somehow getting in the way of American greatness, and insulating Trump from criticism that he'd been simply trading on intolerance. The Republican platform, under Trump, supported "traditional marriage and family," condemned the 2015 Supreme Court case declaring that gay marriage was legal in all fifty states, and claimed that equal legal rights for transgender Americans, which the Obama administration had tried to establish based on an interpretation of the 1972 education law, Title IX, were part of a project to reshape the United States "to fit the mold of an ideology alien to America's history and traditions." It suddenly became easier for Trump to argue that being anti-PC wasn't just about the freedom to insult protected classes.

What's more, the speech put Thiel and his companies in a strategically advantageous position—assuming Trump could somehow defy the odds and win. Beyond a wall, Trump had been vague on how, exactly, he planned to govern. Thiel's speech had suggested a possible framework: Trump could embrace the kinds of big technology projects for which Thiel had long been an advocate. Build a big beautiful wall, sure, but Trump's infrastructure projects could and should include improvements in the software the government used. Washington could look to Silicon Valley—especially the parts of Silicon Valley where Thiel had a stake.

16

THE THIEL THEORY
OF GOVERNMENT

You were terrific," Trump told Thiel at the conclusion of the convention. "We're friends for life."

Mostly though, the New York real estate mogul seemed indifferent to his Silicon Valley backer. "Peter is outside the area that Trump admires," said Bannon. What Trump seemed to care about was Thiel's money—and the legitimacy it conferred on Trump—as well as about the potential to use Thiel as a conduit to reach other tech billionaires.

For his part, Thiel hadn't instantly appreciated Trump's value either. After the convention, Thiel enjoyed his boundary-breaking role—he had been the first gay person to talk openly about his sexuality from the stage of the Republican convention—but resisted when Bannon and other members of the campaign attempted to involve him further. Trump had caught up to Clinton in the polls immediately after the convention, but subsequently fell way behind. Thiel told associates he was worried Trump was going to lose and resolved to keep his distance.

And then, on a Friday afternoon in early October, Thiel—along with most of America—watched a leaked video, published by *The Washington Post*. In it, Trump could be seen bragging to the host of *Access Holly-wood*, Billy Bush, about his sexual escapades, including an attempt to sleep with a TV host by taking her furniture shopping. "I did try and fuck her," Trump, who'd married Melania nine months earlier, explained. "But I couldn't get there." He also boasted about forcing himself on women. "I just start kissing them," he said. "When you're a star, they let you do it. You can do anything. Grab 'em by the pussy. You can do anything."

The consensus view was that Trump was cooked. Mitch McConnell, the Senate majority leader, called Trump's comments "repugnant" and urged him to "take full responsibility for the utter lack of respect for women shown in his comments on that tape." And Paul Ryan, the House speaker, declared himself "sickened," and said that Trump was no longer welcome at an event the following day in Ryan's home state. Many prominent Republicans urged Trump to step aside and allow his vice-presidential nominee, Mike Pence, to take the top spot on the ticket.

Thiel was encouraged by Johnson to take a different view. Johnson told him that the worst thing about the tape from a political point of view was not the apparent endorsement of sexual assault, nor the adultery. It was the failed seduction—a "beta" move, in alt-right parlance. The rest, he said, was just how heterosexual men talked in private. Heterosexual men would respect Trump more, not less. "You should double down," he advised.

Johnson suggested a plan: Thiel should make a big contribution to Rebekah Mercer's political action committee, Make America Number 1. (The PAC was originally known as the Defeat Crooked Hillary PAC, but adopted the slightly more staid name because, as an official told Bloomberg at the time, "If we call it 'Defeat Crooked Hillary,' it's an FEC violation.") Since Mercer was a longtime patron of Steve Bannon and *Breitbart*, a substantial donation would give Thiel access to Trump's inner circle and set him up as the campaign's savior if Trump somehow squeaked out a win.

The proposed donation would be the first part of Johnson's role in the rehabilitation of the beleaguered candidate. The second would involve the next presidential debate, in St. Louis. Johnson and the conservative author Candice Jackson arranged for three women who'd accused Bill Clinton of sexual assault over the years, along with a fourth woman, Kathy Shelton, to travel to St. Louis for a press conference just before the debate.

The three Bill Clinton accusers—Kathleen Willey, Paula Jones, and Juanita Broaddrick—were household names among Clinton critics; Shelton's story was less well known. When she was twelve years old, in 1975, Shelton had accused a forty-one-year-old man of raping her. Hillary Clinton, then a young lawyer running a legal aid clinic, had defended the man in part by claiming that Shelton had been "emotionally unstable with a tendency to seek out older men." Her client ultimately pled guilty to a lesser charge.

Johnson's company WeSearchr raised the funds for Shelton to travel to St. Louis and promoted her story on its website. Trump appeared with the women in a Facebook Live video that was broadcast just before he went onstage, and he told the Shelton story during the debate when pressed about his vulgar comments. "Kathy Shelton, that young woman, is here with us tonight," Trump said. "So don't tell me about words."

The following week, Thiel got a final push. *The Advocate,* the queer newsmagazine, published an essay criticizing his endorsement of Trump. "Peter Thiel, the Silicon Valley billionaire who made news this summer for endorsing Donald Trump at the Republican convention, is a man who has sex with other men," Jim Downs, an author and American studies professor at Gettysburg College, wrote. "But is he gay?" Downs made the case that Thiel's politics—in particular his dismissal of transgender rights as a distraction in his convention speech—constituted a betrayal of gay culture. He portrayed the speech, which Thiel has seen as his own personal coming-out moment as a setback for the LGBT community, rather than a boundary-breaking moment.

The following day, someone close to Thiel leaked word that he would give $1.25 million to Trump's election effort, with the vast majority of it earmarked for the Mercer PAC, just as Johnson had urged. A few weeks later he explained himself in a speech at the National Press Club. "I don't agree with everything Donald Trump has said and done—and I don't think the millions of other people voting for him do, either," Thiel said. "We're voting for Trump because we judge the leadership of our country to have failed."

In the speech, he argued that the liberal scolds saying that Trump's "grab 'em by the pussy" comments made him unelectable were the immoral ones because they were ignoring the country's more pressing issues. He brought up the *Advocate* column. "The lie behind the buzzword of 'diversity' could not be made more clear," he spat. "If you don't conform, then you don't count as diverse, no matter what your personal background." It wasn't so much a defense of Trump as it was a defense of Trump's defenders—a version of the arguments he'd been making since his Stanford days.

During a Q&A after the speech, he suggested that the media should ignore Trump's outrage and focus on the substance of his critique—to take Trump "seriously, but not literally." For instance, Thiel said, Trump's comments about banning Muslim immigration or building a Great Wall of China on the U.S.-Mexico border should be interpreted impressionistically. Trump didn't *literally* want to ban Muslims or build a thousand-mile barrier—he wanted, as Thiel put it, "a saner, more sensible immigration policy" that would "strike the right balance between costs and benefits." Thiel likely cribbed the seriously-not-literally line from an *Atlantic* article by journalist Salena Zito, who was explaining how heartland voters were able to ignore Trump's constant prevarications. But it went viral anyway. PETER THIEL PERFECTLY SUMMED UP DONALD TRUMP IN A FEW SENTENCES was the CNBC headline.

The money and the speech would be significant news—Trump hadn't lined up any major tech donors prior to Thiel's contribution, which helped reverse the sense that Trump's campaign was collapsing—but it was not the only way that Thiel's empire helped the president. Mark Zuckerberg, after initially seeming to oppose Trump, had been supporting the candidate in his own way.

ONE SECRET—understood by the conservatives who had attended the peace summit convened with Thiel's help in May 2016 between influential right-wing pundits and Facebook executives, but which somehow seemed to elude many of the company's actual executives—was that actions by a few liberal Facebook employees were beside the point. Facebook wasn't biased against conservative media; it *was* conservative media. That was because the company's news feed was essentially a popularity contest, and inside of Facebook, the Trump ideology, which combined white identity politics and economic populism, was more popular than anything else.

"I don't think Silicon Valley has come to grips with this," said an attendee of the Facebook meeting, David Bozell. Google's treatment of news had long focused on established media organizations, while Facebook, on the other hand, featured whatever Newsmax piece or right-wing meme happened to be trending, which was much more likely to be shared than a *New York Times* article or left-wing meme. The right-wing content was getting the most clicks. Trending Topics had been an effort to rectify this—to tilt Facebook, not against the right, but toward more ostensibly legitimate news sources. But Zuckerberg, seeming to follow Thiel's advice, had opted to kill the effort and go back to the popularity contest, giving Donald Trump, a candidate made for memes, a huge advantage.

Trump built on this edge by attracting help wherever he could find it. This included, most infamously, assistance from the Russian government, which distributed hacked materials on social media, and reached 126 million people through a Facebook network of fake accounts and groups aimed at discouraging liberals from supporting Clinton while firing up conservatives to vote Trump. It also included Cambridge Analytica, where Bannon had been a board member: After Trump's nomination, the company provided some voter data to the campaign, which it used to raise $80 million in July 2016. During this period, it's possible that some voter information that had been stolen by the company from Facebook, with the help of Palantir, found its way into Trump campaign donor lists.

But the most significant assist, by far, came from Facebook itself. The company's algorithm allowed for targeting that was vastly superior to anything that Cambridge Analytica could deliver. A team of Facebook engineers embedded inside Trump's campaign, training the candidate's digital guru, Brad Parscale, to use a technique that allowed advertisers to target extremely specific groups of potential voters. These included pro-Trump groups—for instance, people who'd visited the campaign's website but hadn't donated—as well as groups that Trump perceived to be favorable to Clinton, including women and Black people, who were served ads reminding them that Clinton had defended her husband against sexual harassment claims and had used the racist formulation "super-predators" in 1996 when describing gang violence.

Clinton's campaign had refused this kind of help, a decision Facebook executives later suggested might have cost her the election. Andrew Bosworth, a close ally of Zuckerberg, would praise Parscale's work in a memo as "the high-water mark of digital ad campaigns." "Was Facebook responsible for Donald Trump getting elected?" he asked rhetorically. "I think the answer is yes."

ON ELECTION NIGHT, Thiel threw a party at his Presidio mansion in San Francisco, inviting anyone he knew who might be a Trump supporter. It was not a huge crowd—maybe twenty people, including Thiel's assistants, a few good-looking college-aged men, and a handful of well-known CEOs. Naval Ravikant, then CEO of AngelList, was there, a was Luke Nosek, the PayPal cofounder who'd convinced Thiel to back Elon Musk's SpaceX. So was Curtis Yarvin, the neo-reactionary blogger and then CEO of Tlon, a company in which Thiel had invested.

The mood was subdued at first. Chairs had been arranged in several rows before a big TV that was tuned to CNN. Thiel sat in the front, keeping his eyes on the screen while holding court. In private, he was generally friendlier to the candidate's most extreme positions than he was in public. Yes, he might distance himself from Trump's wall comments in a speech at the National Press Club. But when he was among friends, as he was now, he would clarify: He might not agree with the exact policy prescription, but he was thrilled that Trump was speaking frankly about immigration. "I love that he's saying it," he would say.

A sense of excitement started to build around 8 p.m., when news networks announced that Trump had won North Carolina and Ohio in quick succession, while opening up leads in Michigan and Wisconsin, two must-win states for Clinton. Pennsylvania, a state that Clinton was supposed to win with some ease, was nearly tied. Thiel's prediction about Trump and the Midwestern voters clinging to their guns was coming true.

"Is this really happening?" someone asked.

Champagne was passed out and the TV was switched to Fox News. How confident had Thiel been, someone else wanted to know. "You're never totally sure," Thiel said. "But he had all these elements. He was silly enough to get all this attention. He was just serious enough to actually do it." The tone turned celebratory, and not just because their man had won. "The big attitude was, 'I'm so happy everyone in Silicon Valley is unhappy about this,'" according to an attendee.

Thiel started getting calls at what seemed like a frantic pace. Word spread among the partygoers that one of the suiters was John Bolton, the hawkish former U.N. ambassador, who'd been the most prominent public supporter of the Iraq War. He was getting in touch to ask Thiel to support him for a State Department position. (A Bolton spokeswoman said he was on set at Fox News and didn't call Thiel on election night.) Not long after, Thiel disappeared.

The group moved to the nearby Founder's Fund offices, where they continued drinking and tried to unpack what had just transpired. How had it come to be that Peter Thiel—nerdy, socially awkward tech guy— was being courted by the likes of John Bolton? Thiel was, by this point anyway, an outspoken dove, who'd railed against "the era of stupid wars" during his RNC speech. Was it possible that Bolton, an architect of that era, was now paying tribute to a venture capitalist and political neophyte? It was surreal. Not only had Thiel's long-shot bet paid off, but he was already a key voice in the new administration—even on matters that would have seemed far from his area of expertise.

Thiel's aides were operating as if Trump's victory was the most natural thing on earth. Michael Kratsios, his young chief of staff, and Jim O'Neill, the Thiel Foundation president, were already buzzing about the transition. Thiel was going to be named as a member of the executive committee in a matter of days, they said, and the Trump campaign had promised to give him a substantial portfolio.

"The conversation," said someone who attended the party, "was basically, 'Where do you want to work?'" Attendees were made to understand that if they wanted, they would have a shot at an administration job.

There had never been a more exciting time to be in the Thielverse. The few liberals in Thiel's inner circle were grudgingly respectful—hey, he'd called it—and conservatives were over the moon. Few of them had liked Trump, but the win, and Thiel's involvement, allowed them to see possibility in the new presidency. Trump was a disrupter, after all, and he was a businessman, which by Thielverse logic made him potentially better than a normal politician, even if he wasn't exactly their preferred brand of businessman. Maybe he'd be amendable to embracing the kind of policies that Silicon Valley's intellectuals fantasized about.

They imagined four to eight years of business-friendly tax policy, an embrace of Silicon Valley by the military-industrial complex, and de regulation of the Food and Drug Administration, a potential boon to venture capital–backed biotech companies. Maybe—and this was really dreaming, but maybe—Trump would embrace cryptocurrencies like Bitcoin. Even Trump's anti-China position wasn't as bad as it might appear. A U.S. crackdown on trade might hurt some factories in the Midwest but could be a boon to tech companies that manufactured domestically, such as Musk's companies, SpaceX and Tesla Motors, as well as chip companies like Intel. Who knew how far the tech-friendly policies could extend? Even those Silicon Valley leaders who'd opposed Trump tended to see Thiel's position of influence in the White House as an encouraging sign.

"He's *the* supporter for the tech side of things," said a Thielverse member, summing up the general mood. "That's the whole thing about proximity to Thiel. If you have his support, Trump will almost do whatever he says." At Founders Fund, this sense of Thiel's power was so pronounced that employees took to referring to him by a new moniker: Shadow President.

ON NOVEMBER 11, Trump announced that Thiel would be on the executive committee of his transition team, alongside Bannon, who'd been named chief strategist, as well as Rebekah Mercer, the Trump children, Jared Kushner, Reince Priebus, and others. Bannon would take charge of staffing Trump's cabinet, and Thiel's role would be to appoint people who could disrupt "the administrative state"—the alphabet soup of agencies that sit below the cabinet level, including the FTC (Federal Trade Commission), the FCC (Federal Communications Commission), the SEC (Securities and Exchange Commission), the FDA (Food and Drug Administration), and much smaller groups like the OSTP (Office of Science and Technology Policy). These agencies employed tens of thousands of people, including hundreds of political appointees who represented a sort of government within a government. According to Bannon, Thiel's job was to appoint people who could "break it up."

As a libertarian, Thiel seemed to relish the role. He'd spent his career attacking the government's regulatory power—going all the way back to PayPal and the dream of Swiss bank accounts, to his 2009 essay in which he'd attacked democracy, to the 2015 interview with Tyler Cowen when he'd complained about "these agencies [which] have become deeply sclerotic, deeply nonfunctioning."

The Trump administration would adopt this rhetoric, complaining about an administrative apparatus so powerful that even the words "deep state" undersold it, according to Bannon. "It's not deep, it's in your fucking grill," he told me, crediting this as "Peter Thiel's theory of government."

"The progressives understood something," Bannon continued. "They said sometimes we win and sometimes we lose elections, but if we expand the functions of the federal government into these alphabet agencies, and then inside the agencies themselves, we'll have our own legislative branch, our own executive branch, our own courts. This was everything Peter went after."

While Thiel suggested administrators who'd be inclined to gut the architecture of the New Deal and Great Society, Trump would appoint libertarian judges who wanted to overturn the Chevron deference doctrine. The precedent had been established in 1984 when the Supreme Court ruled that the Reagan administration's Environmental Protection Agency could change its interpretation of the Clean Air Act, signed into law by Jimmy Carter, to allow it to go easier on the oil company Chevron. The ruling allowed federal agencies to adjust how laws were enforced as long as the interpretation of the law was reasonable—giving political appointees wide latitude. Libertarian-leaning legal groups, like the Federalist Society, had railed against this for years. Bannon suggested to Thiel, a longtime Federalist Society member, that his project could be to undo the administrative state from the inside.

Peter Thiel showed up in Trump Tower about a week after Election

Day ready to work. The Trump staffers hadn't known quite what to think of him. They assumed that while he might gamely offer suggestions for, say, EPA commissioner, he was really just aiming for a photo op, some face time with the president, and the chance to advance a handful of self-serving policy ideas. Many in Trump's orbit were opportunists and shameless self-promoters after all, and transition team staffers were constantly trying to hustle their way into a few minutes with the president-elect. Strangely, Thiel never asked to see Trump at all.

This was odd—though not nearly as odd as the entourage Thiel brought with him. Of course, it was common for executive committee members to show up with an aide or two; Thiel brought a half dozen. They were all young men, and all were disconcertingly attractive; "they looked like male models," said Bannon. Bannon cleared out a dingy office on the fourteenth floor of Trump Tower that Stephen Miller, Peter Navarro, and Curt Ellis—Trump's policy team—had been using and gave it to Thiel. A long table was installed, and the team of hunks set up laptops, Silicon Valley–style. From November through January, they worked shoulder to shoulder, cranking out a list of possible appointees and working late into the evening, after most of the rest of the staff had gone home.

Thiel produced a list of 150 names for Trump to consider for senior government positions. Many were ultra-libertarians or reactionaries; others were more difficult to categorize. "Peter's idea of disrupting government is *out there*," said Bannon. "People thought Trump was a disrupter. They had no earthly idea what was being pitched" by Thiel.

For Trump's science adviser, he suggested Princeton's William Happer, the country's most prominent climate change skeptic, who'd taken up the ultimate contrarian position on the subject. Happer had argued that carbon dioxide was not only *not* harming the planet but that it was actually good for the earth, since trees need the gas to grow. He had likened "the demonization of fossil fuels" to Hitler's treatment of the

Jews. Thiel seemed enamored with the physicist when he visited, failing to appreciate that there was no earthly way that Trump or his staff would put a denier of man-made climate change up for Senate confirmation, no matter how brilliant they thought he was. In 2018, Trump appointed Happer to a lesser position—as head of emerging technologies at the National Security Council. "I never thought of Peter as very strong in technology, unless you narrow down the definition of technology to ways to profit from the internet," Happer later told me. He left the Trump administration in 2019, complaining that he'd been undermined by White House officials who'd been "brainwashed" into believing in the dangers of climate change.

Thiel had another candidate for the job of presidential science adviser: Yale's David Gelernter, an anti-PC warrior whose book *America-Lite: How Imperial Academia Dismantled Our Culture (and Ushered in the Obamacrats)*, read like a version of *The Diversity Myth* updated for the 2000s. He blamed "post-religious, globalist intellectuals" for the liberal takeover of academia. More controversially, Gelernter made clear that by globalists, he meant Jews, whom he argued were naive and belligerent by nature. He was less extreme than Happer on questions around earth science, but he'd also argued that climate change skepticism was one of many "commonplace truths that every reader of objective, unbiased news has known for years."

When his name leaked, the press pointed out that Gelernter wasn't affiliated with any of the major scientific societies—which could have proven problematic if the White House needed to scramble to address a crisis such as a natural disaster, an oil spill, or, as *The Washington Post* presciently pointed out, a pandemic—and Bannon initially tried to talk Thiel out of putting Gelernter in front of Trump. But Thiel insisted. Gelernter was the smartest computer scientist he knew, he said—and, on top of that, Thiel added, Gelernter had been blown up by the Unabomber. In 1993, not long after publishing a book about the coming prevalence of virtual reality, *Mirror Worlds,* he received a package from Ted Kaczynski, the former Berkeley mathematician who'd been sending letter bombs to technologists and others whom he believed were contributing to a dystopian future. Gelernter was severely injured and lost part of his right hand in the explosion.

In a way, this made Gelernter a technology martyr, which impressed Thiel, though it completely derailed the conversation with Trump. Trump focused intently on Gelernter's injury, asking Gelernter a series of questions about the explosion, his health, and the Unabomber more generally, before dismissing him curtly. "You didn't get the job," Trump said.

THIS BECAME A PATTERN: Thiel would suggest some bold and entirely ridiculous name, who would be promptly rejected and replaced with someone more acceptable. For Food and Drug Administration commissioner, he attempted to nominate candidates who shared his belief that the FDA's main role—regulating trials for drugs—was unnecessary.

The consensus view among drug developers, even many in Silicon Valley, has been that "you don't want to put individuals at risk," said Zach Weinberg, the cofounder of Flatiron Health, a Silicon Valley–backed medical research firm that is now owned by the pharmaceutical giant Roche. "Peter Thiel's view is that will slow things down. His whole game is if a few people get hurt and that creates progress, he's willing to take that trade."

One of Thiel's allies in this crusade, and his top pick to lead the FDA, was Balaji Srinivasan, the Stanford computer science lecturer and cryptocurrency entrepreneur who'd invested alongside Thiel in Curtis Yarvin's company and shared Thiel's views on the wisdom of Silicon Valley elites leaving the country. He'd given a talk in 2013 urging techies to leave the "paper belt" and "build an opt-in society, outside the United States, run by technology." Srinivasan also had something of a bug about the FDA.

Namely his view seemed to be that it shouldn't exist. "For every thalido-mide," he'd tweeted, "many dead from slowed approvals." He deleted the tweets before his interview with Trump.

Thiel had argued much the same, but it was a far out position for a serious candidate to head the FDA, since the agency's refusal in the early 1960s to approve thalidomide, a sleeping pill, is regarded as one of the great administrative success stories. In Europe, where a less-regulated mar-ket allowed thalidomide to be prescribed to pregnant women, thousands of babies were born without fully formed limbs. The incident prompted Congress to require drugmakers to prove their drugs worked before seek-ing approval—essentially creating the modern pharmaceutical regulatory regime. But instead of requiring proof of efficacy through tightly con-trolled clinical trials, Srinivasan had argued that the FDA could be re-placed by a decentralized database where doctors and patients rated their experiences with experimental therapies—a "Yelp for drugs," he'd called it, referring to the Thiel-backed restaurant-rating service.

Thiel's other choice to run the FDA was Jim O'Neill, who'd run the Thiel Foundation and had since worked as an investor at Mithril, Ajay Royan's venture capital firm. O'Neill was more circumspect than Srini-vasan, and he had actual government experience—having worked as a speechwriter at the Department of Education and the Department of Health and Human Services—but he'd never worked in a position of scientific oversight and had spent much of his career in PR. He also be-lieved in rolling back the FDA mandates about drug efficacy.

Bannon brought O'Neill and Srinivasan to meet Trump, but did not endorse either pick. "Balaji is a genius," he said. "But it was too much." Bannon knew that it was unrealistic to nominate a computer scientist who'd implied he wanted to get rid of the FDA—"a man with two brains," as he called Srinivasan—to run said agency.

Doing so would have gotten Trump branded a radical—and not in a good way. Bannon continues, "That's not a confirmation hearing you're going to win in the first 100 days. Remember, we're a coalition, and the

Republican establishment was aghast at what we were doing. And Thiel got turned off by that."

IN JANUARY, Thiel's longtime collaborator, Jeff Giesea, threw a party for young alt-right activists that he dubbed the Deploraball. The tongue-in-cheek reference to Hillary Clinton's putdown of Trump supporters—"basket of deplorables," she'd said, referring to the GOP's "racist, sexist, homophobic, xenophobic, Islamophobic" members—made clear that this was the Trump inauguration party for types of conservative media personalities that Thiel had been cultivating. Thiel, of course, would be there.

Even so—and even as Thiel agitated for maximal disruption within the White House, allying with Bannon and trying to bring burn-it-down libertarians into the Trump administration—his network was beginning to close ranks. In December, one of the organizers of Giesea's political group, Tim Gionet, better known as the man behind the alt-right Twitter account Baked Alaska, had been tweeting conspiratorially about Jewish control of media using "JQ"—an alt-right shorthand for the "Jewish Question," which Hitler had attempted to answer with his Final Solution order of 1942. In response, Giesea and Mike Cernovich took Gionet off the list of speakers and informed him that he was not welcome. They also nixed Richard Spencer after his pro-Trump Hitler-style salute.

Thiel attended the party, hanging off to the side and leaving after just half an hour. He'd been—at least in the minds of his staff—Shadow President for two months and had little to show for his efforts. Out of the 150 names he'd put forth for administration positions, only a dozen or so had gotten jobs, though he did have a few successes to be happy about. His longtime hedge fund idea man, Kevin Harrington, would be named a deputy assistant to the president at the National Security Council, and his chief of staff, Michael Kratsios, would be deputy chief technology officer. Kratsios would eventually be elevated to chief technology officer in 2019, the only Senate-confirmed appointment Thiel managed. In mid-2020, he would see his purview expand, as acting Under Secretary of Defense for Research and Engineering, which put him in charge of the Pentagon's R&D budget for the waning months of the Trump presidency.

Aside from Harrington—who commands respect from many of Thiel's longtime associates—these were not the most accomplished people in his circle, nor were they the genius disrupters that Thiel had tried to install at high-level positions. They were mostly inoffensive bureaucrats. A never-Trump member of the Thielverse theorized—probably as part of a fanciful exercise in wishful thinking, or perhaps professional jealousy—that Thiel had staffed the White House with "his useless people" in order to undermine the president.

Bannon and the other more radical members of Thiel's circle saw Thiel's failure to install more allies in the Trump White House for the washout it was. "He took a full shot, he got a few wins, and he had more defeats," Bannon said. "He failed because Trump turned out not to be a revolutionary."

Of course, if Thiel really failed, it was partly because he'd cast his lot with Bannon, who only lasted seven months in the White House. "They basically allied themselves with the alt-right," said another person who worked on the transition, referring to Thiel and Blake Masters, who served as his deputy. "They chose disruption over normalcy and it backfired." In this view, the moderates in Trump's circle, led by his daughter and son-in-law, had squashed the revolution that Bannon and Thiel had plotted.

But Thiel had never counted on a revolution. He always had a backup plan, a hedge. And as the Trump administration began—even as Thiel himself suffered a political setback—the pieces for his next move were set up well.

17

DEPORTATION FORCE

On December 14, just a month after Thiel had joined the transition, and a month before the inauguration, he sat near the center of a long table in a boardroom on the twenty-fifth floor of Trump Tower. The president-elect was planted, as was customary, in the center, looking deeply satisfied. His closest advisers were there: Bannon, Pence, Priebus, Kushner, Stephen Miller, Ivanka Trump, plus Eric and Don Jr. But the real stars were the CEOs of the United States' largest and most important tech companies, and their shepherd in all things Trump, Peter Thiel.

He sat at Trump's left elbow, with Pence on the other side. To his left was Apple's Tim Cook. Arrayed around the table, interspersed between Trump's advisers and children, was a group that included Facebook's Sheryl Sandberg and Amazon's Jeff Bezos, as well as the CEOs of Microsoft, Cisco, Oracle, Intel, and IBM.

"These are monster companies," Trump said, beaming before lavishing praise on Thiel. He credited the Silicon Valley investor for having seen "something very early—maybe even before we saw it." Thiel had tucked his arms under the table to make room for Trump's broad shoulders and seemed to shrink away from the president-elect, who was having none of it. As Trump spoke, he reached below the table groping for Thiel's hand, found it, and raised it above the table. "He's been so terrific, so outstanding, and he got just about the biggest applause at the Republican National Convention," Trump said, rubbing Thiel's fist affectionately. "I want to thank you, man. You're a very special guy."

Though Thiel found this moment of bro tenderness embarrassing, he was thrilled. The meeting at Facebook earlier in the year had been awkward and strained, but now Silicon Valley's best and brightest had come to Trump Tower to pay their respects to the same movement they'd mocked. He was smiling. He'd bet on Trump when no one believed in him, and he'd won.

In addition to playing power broker, Thiel also had a chance to settle scores. The meeting included representatives from the biggest American tech companies in terms of market capitalization. Thiel had also invited representatives from two smaller companies—he had a financial stake in both. To the left of Tim Cook was Elon Musk, whose car company, Tesla, had a market capitalization at the time that put it at about one fifth the size of the next biggest invitee, Cisco. On the other side of the table was the CEO of an even smaller firm, Alex Karp.

Karp, of course, was one of Thiel's close friends, running a company that Thiel had founded and (though it wasn't yet public knowledge) still effectively controlled. Karp also, suddenly, had a lot to gain from Donald Trump. Just before the election, a federal judge had ruled in Palantir's favor in its lawsuit against the Army. That meant that the Army would have to rebid its contract, considering Palantir and other commercial software makers as potential candidates for work that could be worth hundreds of millions of dollars.

The court order didn't mean the Army would buy Palantir's software, only that it would give it a "hard look," as Hamish Hume, the company's lawyer put it. Now Karp had a chance to make a personal appeal to the commander in chief. He promised Trump that his company could "help bolster national security and reduce waste." When asked, Karp would say he had no idea why he'd been invited to the meeting, saying all he knew was that Thiel had organized it. "There's probably a longer version I don't know about, but they had a selection process and I was asked and I said yes," he said. Of course, Thiel had declined to invite any other defense contractors, including Karp's main competitor in the bidding on the Army deal, Raytheon, to the meeting.

MUCH HAD BEEN made during the 2016 campaign about the gulf between Silicon Valley and Trump. The president-elect, somewhat famously, despised Amazon and its founder, Jeff Bezos—because of both Bezos's ownership of the liberal *Washington Post* and Amazon's "monopolistic tendencies that have led to the destruction of department stores and the retail industry," as Trump had put it. On the campaign trail Trump had repeatedly suggested that he would retaliate against Bezos by bringing antitrust action in response to negative articles in *The Post*. At other times, he'd attacked Apple for making phones in China, and had suggested he'd roll back one of the big tech companies' favorite programs, the H-1B visa. Facebook and Google had argued that the visa, which grants temporary residency to skilled workers and is especially popular in Silicon Valley, should actually be *expanded*.

Given Trump's general hostility to the positions favored by tech founders and to the tech founders themselves, it wasn't surprising that almost everybody in the room had supported Clinton during the campaign. Days after the election, Larry Page and his Google cofounder, Sergey Brin, hosted an all-hands meeting during which Brin said he found the election of Trump "deeply offensive" and that it "conflicts with many of our values." Bezos had once joked he'd like to send Trump to outer space.

Pundits had predicted that the post-election tumult would pit Trump against these mostly liberal leaders, who favored globalization, immigration, drug legalization, and gay rights—and indeed early accounts of the meeting, based on the four or so minutes during which media were allowed in the room, suggested that this was what had happened. *Business Insider* published a photo of Sandberg, Page, and Bezos grimacing under the headline THIS PERFECTLY CAPTURES THE FIRST MEETING BETWEEN TRUMP AND ALL THE TECH CEOS WHO OPPOSED HIM.

But after the press was shooed out, the tone changed. With the cameras gone, the tech CEOs were solicitous, thanking Trump profusely and repeatedly for the opportunity to meet, even as Trump continued to insult them. Trump negged Bezos over his ownership of the *Post* and Cook over Apple's balance sheet. "Tim has a problem," Trump cracked. "He has too much cash." At one point he referred to the group as "the greatest liberals in the history of the world."

The tech CEOs smiled through all of it, flattering Trump, pleasing his aides, and avoiding opportunities to privately air disagreements. Most had voted against Trump; now they wanted to show him they could work with him. "Those guys were so impressed," said Bannon. "It was like they finally got invited to lunch with the quarterback of the football team."

Trump had gone in ready to be grilled over his comments about H1-B visas. Instead the executives said they were willing to be convinced. "We have people who are very concerned about this issue," said Chuck Robbins, the Cisco CEO, referring to H1-B. "If you can talk about this it would help calm people down." That was the toughest challenge Trump got during the course of the entire hour, and he sidestepped it without conceding anything.

"We're going to do a whole thing on immigration," Trump said. "We are going to get the bad people"—the reference was to numerous campaign promises to deport millions of undocumented Americans.

No one objected to this, nor did any of the CEOs attempt to inveigh against another policy that Trump had signaled he was considering: creating a registry to track the entry of Muslims into the United States. Instead, they attempted to sidestep the discussion, implying that it would be fine to crack down on illegal immigrants as long as Trump could supply their companies with enough skilled workers. "We should separate the border security from the talented people," Cook said. He suggested the United States try to cultivate "a "monopoly on talent." Thiel, who'd often privately made the distinction between immigrants who embraced American values and those who did not, offered that the United States could adopt a system along the lines of New Zealand's, which uses points to make it easier for well-educated immigrants with good language skills to enter the country and harder for low-skilled immigrants.

Stephen Miller seconded Thiel's proposal for a points-based system, adding that Trump would crack down on outsourcing firms that were abusing H1-B visas. Miller had attracted attention during the campaign for his extremism on immigration. He'd riled up crowds with promises of building the wall high and tall, and profiles had noted that in college he'd written a series of columns that seemed to walk a fine line on race, including defending Bill Bennett's comments about aborting black babies, which he said had been taken out of context. Not only did none of the tech CEOs speak up for the Mexican immigrants who'd be denied entry or even deported under this scheme, they all seemed impressed. Google chairman Eric Schmidt suggested a name for Trump's carrot-and-stick approach to immigration reform. "Call it the U.S. jobs act," he said.

There were other issues of concern that the tech CEOs could have raised with the soon-to-be most powerful man in the world. They might have questioned him about his threats to use antitrust law to break them up, or they could have asked if he realized how damaging his anti-immigrant rhetoric was to their existing workforces. They might have brought up Trump's promise to withdraw from the Paris climate accord, or about his plans, which he'd first tweeted about in 2014, to end net neutrality—repealing a law that many in the room regarded as fundamental to the modern internet—or about the numerous ways that Trump had seemed, during the campaign, hostile to technology, science, and the future.

But the room ignored all of that, steering the conversation to Trump's signature issue, China. Bezos complained that Amazon had spent years trying to get a business license in China and blamed the government's protection of the Chinese ecommerce giant Alibaba. "As soon as you get close to getting a license, they change the rules," he said, adding that Chinese companies were stealing his company's intellectual property and engaging in "economic espionage." He also complained about the low postage rates the U.S. Postal Service charged Chinese manufacturers shipping goods to the United States. Other CEOs raised similar gripes.

"These guys understood," said Bannon. "The H-1B visa was a sideshow. China was the issue. They were supposed to be the biggest enemies we got and they're basically making a nationalistic case."

This was what Bannon and others saw as Thiel's most important contribution to the Trump presidency: not the dozen or so appointees, but the ability to get the most powerful and respected businesspeople in America to put themselves in Trump's orbit—even if they despised him privately. Obama's 2011 dinner in Silicon Valley had included heavy hitters, but not every single one of them—and unlike that dinner, which had led to a disagreement between Obama and Steve Jobs, there was very little visible dissent.

This was not the official line from Silicon Valley, which positioned itself as part of a burgeoning resistance movement, nor from Trump, who'd spend much of the next four years threatening to tax, regulate, or even break up the big tech companies. There was a word for this that Thiel loved: *kayfabe*, the professional wrestling term that refers to the way that bouts are scripted by television producers—and both sides played it beautifully.

In January, Trump signed an executive order suspending entry to people from seven predominantly Muslim countries: Iran, Iraq, Libya, Somalia, Sudan, Syria, and Yemen. The order applied to refugees and, until the White House backtracked, green-card holders. It also noted that when immigration from those countries resumed, refugees who'd been persecuted based on "a minority religion" would have priority. Trump clarified that by this he meant that Christians would have an easier time getting U.S. visas than Muslims.

This was the promised Muslim ban that Trump had touted on the campaign trail. It was immediately decried by liberals and civil libertarians, who noted that it not only seemed to cross the line into religious discrimination but also that it put those who'd lived in the United States for years but who happened to be traveling abroad in January in a terrible position. More than seven hundred people who'd legally traveled to the States, many with families in the country, were detained at airports as authorities prepared to deport them.

The following day, protestors gathered at the international arrivals area of New York's Kennedy Airport. Taxi drivers went on strike, and thousands rallied that night as a federal judge ordered the deportations halted. The New York demonstration was widely covered and protestors began showing up at their local airports, including in San Francisco, where Sergey Brin, the Google cofounder, told reporters, "I'm here because I'm a refugee." Brin said that he'd come in a "personal capacity," but Google's CEO, Sundar Pichai, made clear that it also reflected Google's corporate values. In an email to staff, Pichai said he was "upset about the impact of this order and any proposals that could impose restrictions on Google employees and their families." Similar statements were released by Netflix, Apple, and Microsoft.

The corporate response was praised endlessly by San Francisco's tech press, which leaned left and still tended to see Silicon Valley executives in heroic terms. "The Tech Resistance Awakens," *Wired* proclaimed. The truth was more complicated. Yes, some companies, most notably Google, were setting themselves up in opposition to Trump in response to activism by their employees, but most were attempting to find some middle ground, hoping to avoid antagonizing the president.

This was especially pronounced among the companies where Thiel had influence. Mark Zuckerberg, who had cofounded a pro-immigration lobbying group, FWD.us, would have seemed a likely opponent of the Muslim ban, and he was—but his statement in opposition was notably weaker than those of most of his peers. He wrote in a Facebook post that he was "concerned about the impact of the recent executive orders signed by President Trump," but he also praised Trump for having promised to "work something out" for undocumented immigrants who'd come to the United States as children—and who'd been granted legal status under an executive order by President Obama. Trump would not follow through with this vague pledge and canceled the program that September. In his statement, Zuckerberg also praised Trump for being supportive of attracting highly skilled immigrants—a business priority for Facebook. Casey Newton, a tech columnist then at *The Verge*, noted the Facebook's CEO's post "doesn't quite rise to the level of criticism."

Elon Musk was more direct in his opposition to the Muslim Ban, calling it "not the best way to address the country's challenges." But Musk found common ground with Trump in other areas, joining Trump's standing economic advisory council alongside a group of heavy hitters that included IBM's Ginni Rometty and Disney's Bob Iger, as well as a second council, on manufacturing, along with Intel's Brian Krzanich and General Electric CEO Jeff Immelt. Both councils would be disbanded by year's end, and Musk left in mid-2017 in protest over Trump's withdrawal from the Paris Climate Agreement, but at the time they were lauded by the White House.

Karp had seemed to despise Trump, slamming him in the run-up to the election in a meeting with Palantir employees. He boasted that he'd declined to meet with Trump previously, referred to Trump's wealth as "fictitious," and described him as a "bully." "I respect nothing about the dude," he'd said. "It'd be hard to make up someone I'd find less appealing." But after Karp's performance at Trump Tower, the company moved aggressively to sell to the Trump administration, taking advantage of Thiel's connections where possible.

During the early days of the transition, Thiel had urged Trump to fire Francis Collins, the longtime director of the National Institutes of Health, an accomplished geneticist who'd headed up the Human Genome Project under Bill Clinton and George W. Bush, before taking over the NIH under Obama. Thiel was convinced that the NIH had become stultified and needed shaking up—and, according to Bannon, suggested Andy Harris, a Republican congressman and former anesthesiologist from an extremely conservative district on Maryland's rural Eastern Shore. Harris was a staunch Trump supporter and a member of the House Freedom Caucus who'd attracted attention in early 2016 when, in what normally would have been a routine vote, he was one of eight Republicans to oppose naming a post office after the poet and civil rights activist Maya Angelou. One of the most celebrated Black artists in American history had been, he claimed, a communist sympathizer. Harris would acquire further renown during Trump's presidency by voting "present" on a resolution condemning QAnon, by opposing COVID stay-at-home orders and what he called the "cult of masks," and by supporting Trump's efforts to overturn the results of the 2020 election. He was also a longtime advocate for NIH reform, proposing that Congress force the agency to make more grants to younger researchers—a pet cause of Thiel's.

Bannon had resisted this plan. The optics of firing a decorated geneticist with more than twenty years of government service and replacing him with a far-right firebrand who was known for picking a culture-war fight with the U.S. Postal Service was too much, even for Bannon. But he agreed to ask Collins to come to New York in early January to interview for the job.

According to documents later disclosed by the Trump administration, the vetting of Collins included an interview at Trump Tower, plus a lunch with Thiel and Blake Masters. In a follow-up email after the lunch, Collins agreed that Thiel was right that some aspects of the NIH were outdated and mentioned an eagerness to learn more about Palantir. He said he was meeting with Shyam Sankar, Palantir's top business development executive.

It appears, in retrospect, to have been the beginning of a very successful sales pitch. Collins would be renominated, and, the following year, the

NIH would give Palantir a $7 million contract to help it keep track of the research data it was collecting. There would be many more contracts.

THIEL DID TRY to create some distance between himself and Trump on immigration policy. In an interview where he otherwise praised even some of the president's most questionable qualities—his closeness with Vladimir Putin, the rampant conflicts of interest within his businesses, and even his haircut—Thiel noted that Trump's plans to build a Muslim registry were a nonstarter, at least at Palantir. "We would not do that," he told Maureen Dowd of *The New York Times*.

But the man who was now criticizing the Muslim registry was one of the key backers of the plan's most prominent supporter, Kris Kobach. The secretary of state of Kansas had known Thiel for more than a decade, first meeting him when he was a lawyer for the Federation for American Immigration Reform, an anti-immigration group affiliated with Numbers-USA, the far-right nonprofit that Thiel had donated to in the mid-2000s.

Thiel and Kobach had become friends during that period—a time when Kobach attracted attention by, among other things, suing the state of California to prevent undocumented immigrants from attending the state colleges at in-state tuition rates and defending cities that sought to prevent undocumented immigrants from obtaining housing. A person familiar with Thiel's political operation estimates that Thiel funneled at least $5 million to Kobach's political campaigns and causes for which he advocated between 2005 to 2020. Not long after the 2016 election, Kobach was photographed walking into Trump's New Jersey golf club carrying a "strategic plan for [the] first 365 days" that included a plan to reinstate a 9/11-era database to track "aliens from high risk areas" and asking prospective immigrants about their thoughts on Sharia law. Trump supporters had defended the proposal, pointing out that such registries had been used on Japanese Americans during World War II.

Moreover, Palantir was already doing businesses with the agencies that Trump would seek to press into service as part of his immigration crackdown. On the campaign trail, Trump had boasted of a massive "deportation force," a policing effort that would rely on the Immigration and Customs Enforcement agency, or ICE, with whom Palantir had already a $41 million contract thanks to a deal the company had signed with the agency since 2014.

In February, the White House announced policy changes that would result in dramatically more deportations and raids. Previously, the Obama administration had directed ICE to focus on deporting undocumented immigrants who were also perceived as a threat—for instance, because they were in a gang or had been convicted of a violent crime. Immigrants convicted of misdemeanors were generally left alone. Trump changed that, ordering ICE to deport anyone charged with a crime, however minor, and ending the "catch and release" policy in which immigration agents would allow people caught crossing the border to go free while they applied for asylum in the United States. The new instruction was to either place these individuals in detention centers or send them to Mexico while they waited. The policy memos noted that parents who crossed the border with children might be deported, even while their kids were held in the United States.

Palantir, despite Thiel's assurances, would play an important role in this enforcement plan. Public records would show that the company had created a database, called FALCON, not unlike the ones it had created for the military and intelligence services, designed to help agents catch smugglers and other border criminals. The company had also secretly helped create a second database, the Analytical Framework for Intelligence, which creates individual risk scores that the Customs and Border Protection agency uses to evaluate travelers and immigrants.

These disclosures—combined with Thiel's support of Trump—generated intense outcry, first within Silicon Valley and then beyond it. In January, the Tech Workers Coalition, an activist group, had staged a march in front of Palantir headquarters to protest the company's work with Trump. Two months later, after the FALCON story broke, a group of protestors showed up at Thiel's home in San Francisco carrying signs that read: PALANTIR: WAKE UP! YOU ARE COMPLICIT, DON'T BUILD SOFTWARE FOR MORDOR and PETER THIEL IS A VAMPIRE. These would be the first of many such protests over the course of the next four years, and they would serve to solidify the link between Palantir and some of the most controversial policies of the Trump era.

Palantir's support of the Trump administration was still indirect, but Thiel was not above directly linking his business interests with Trump's most controversial policies. In 2017, Charles Johnson persuaded Thiel to invest in a new venture that he was developing with Hoan Ton-That, the anti-Gawker enthusiast who'd met Thiel at the RNC. It was called Clearview—and the idea, as Johnson explained to Thiel, was simple: He and Ton-That had written software to browse Facebook profiles, as well as profiles uploaded to other social networks, and then to download every picture that users had ever posted, storing a copy along with that person's name. They would offer this database to police departments and other law enforcement groups along with a facial recognition algorithm. These tools working in concert would allow police to take a picture of an unidentified culprit, upload it into the software, and get a name back. The two men would recruit Richard Schwartz, a former Republican political operative in New York City, to be cofounder and president, with Ton-That serving as CEO. Johnson, who would receive a third of the company's equity, had no formal operational role. His job would be to raise money for the company and to help sign up customers.

Johnson boasted that this software would be ideal for Trump's immigration crackdown. "Building algorithms to ID all the illegal immigrants for the deportation squads" was how he put it in a Facebook post. "It was a joke," Johnson later said. "But it became real." Indeed, Clearview would eventually sign a contract to give ICE access to its technology—and would have Thiel's help. After hearing Johnson's pitch, he provided $200,000 in seed capital to the effort.

THIEL'S COMFORT WITH TRUMP and his proximity to figures like Johnson and Bannon was enough to drive some of his closest friends away. A few longtime confidants simply stopped speaking to him altogether. Others just avoided politics around Peter, attempting to keep his views about Trump separate from his work as a technologist.

Thiel had never taken criticism well, which had made criticizing him publicly impossible if you hoped to ever take his money. But a handful of his confidants took that step. Shortly after election day, Geoff Lewis, a Founders Fund partner who'd led the firm's investment in Lyft, wrote a blog post attacking Trump with several veiled swipes at his boss. "If we take Trump seriously," Lewis wrote—alluding to Thiel's suggestion that Trump be taken "seriously, but not literally"—"it may not be safe for me to write a post like this a year from now. . . . If some of the most frightening rumors circulating already are true, then I will face retaliation just for writing these words today." Lewis noted that he hoped to be proven wrong but added that, "from all I've seen thus far, a world in which President Trump makes any sense at all is not the world I want my grandchildren to inherit." He later edited the post to remove the references critical of Thiel, as well as the line about his grandchildren.

In 2015, Thiel had accepted a part-time position at Y Combinator, the early-stage incubator that was sometimes compared to the Thiel Fellowship. YC—as it was known—had since expanded to include venture capital investing and had displaced Founders Fund as the hot firm of the moment in Silicon Valley. The firm was, like Founders Fund, committed to entrepreneurs and entrepreneurial control—and fanatical about ambitious companies. The Founders Fund manifesto had mentioned fast airplanes; YC had actually funded one, Boom Supersonic, along with a fusion power company, a driverless car company, and more seed-stage biotech firms than any investor.

Thiel had been close to Sam Altman, YC's young president. Altman, who'd supported Hillary Clinton in 2016, considered Thiel a mentor and had defended him ahead of the election, promising that he would not "fire someone for supporting a major party nominee." But the following fall, the firm quietly removed Thiel's name from its list of partners, amending the blog post that had welcomed him to the firm. "Edit: Peter Thiel is no longer affiliated with Y Combinator," an update read. Although Altman never offered a public explanation, the move was widely seen as a repudiation of Thiel's politics.

The reaction was stronger at further levels of remove in the Thielverse. Louis Anslow, who'd once idolized Thiel, had dreamed of receiving an investment term sheet from Thiel. Now he flipped. Anslow proposed a sort of anti-PayPal Mafia, urging fellow startup-minded futurists to refuse to accept any capital from Thiel's firms as part of a #NeverThiel movement. "My dream is to a get a term sheet from him and tell him to FUCK OFF," he wrote in a blog post. He compared Thiel's support of Trump with Henry Ford's of Adolf Hitler, and Thiel and Trump's shared hatred of political correctness with Ford and Hitler's shared anti-Semitism. It wasn't subtle, but it captured a new strain of serious tech industry pushback on Thiel's brand of influence.

Thiel Fellows had once been guaranteed a call back if they tried to get a meeting with a venture capitalist or a potential business partner. But in 2017, the calls were slower to come. "I have a standard line when I introduce this," said a pre-2016 Thiel Fellow who went on to start a successful tech company when I asked about the potential negative reaction to Thiel's link to Trump and the alt-right. "I'm always like, 'I was part of the Thiel Fellowship when Thiel was a tech figure, not a political figure.' And people sort of get it."

This person said he'd always found the stories about Thiel's callousness unpersuasive—that is, until before the election. "It definitely changed how I look at him," he said. "That was the first time I thought the supervillain thread had any credibility." Others chose to look at Thiel's bet on Trump as a matter of pure power. He'd realized, one prominent Silicon

Valley software entrepreneur said, "I can pay $1 million and have a cabinet position."

This in the end was how most of Silicon Valley processed Thiel's support of a reactionary reality television star: cynically. They chose to ignore his proximity to the alt-right and the ways the white supremacist threads of Trumpism fit with Thiel's own feelings toward immigrants. These were perhaps the necessary moral compromises made by any real disrupter—and no different from the growth hacking at PayPal, or the privacy violations at Facebook, or the lies that Thiel and his peers had told throughout their careers to hasten the advent of the future. "It almost doesn't matter if you agree with it or not, he was right," said former Thiel Fellow Austin Russell, now the CEO of Luminar, which makes sensors for self-driving cars. "If you really want to change the world, you have to have a seat at the table."

Indeed, perhaps if only to placate his friends, Thiel sought to put some distance between himself and Trump, explaining the endorsement as a practical matter of allying with the likely winner—as Austin Russell had. "Supporting Trump was one of the least contrarian things I've ever done," he would often say, noting that, after all, half the country had agreed with him. He was more blunt in private. At a dinner for the Thiel Foundation, a longtime investor at Thiel's firms told a group of founders that his boss had backed Trump as a visceral attack on the elite institutions he'd always despised. "He wanted to watch Rome burn," this person said.

ROME STARTED BURNING in the late summer, when Bannon tried to secure Thiel's nomination to the White House's Intelligence Advisory Board. The position was part time, but prestigious: His predecessors would include former senator Chuck Hagel, former National Security Advisor Brent Scowcroft, and former chairman of the Joint Chiefs of Staff William Crowe. The job, which he would have shared with Safra Catz of Oracle, one of the only other prominent tech industry Trump supporters, would also carry lots of potential influence, giving Thiel a platform to advocate for greater investments in Silicon Valley–style software, which would likely help Palantir and could give him a chance to cut out the company's rivals.

But then came the Unite the Right rally in Charlottesville, the murder of a protestor, Heather Heyer, by a white supremacist, and Trump's comments in the aftermath that there were "very fine people on both sides." Bannon left days later, in what was interpreted as a rebuke of the alt-right's place within the administration. This severed Thiel's most important connection with the White House.

Thiel began to waffle, worrying about how the proposed position would impact his companies—surely there would be charges of corruption when Palantir won its next contract. He told a confidant he was worried about what it would mean for his personal life and his privacy. Sometime that fall he informed the White House that he was backing out of contention for the Intelligence Advisory Board. That October, Thiel turned fifty. For someone who'd lived in fear of death his whole life, the milestone wasn't entirely welcome, but he and his longtime partner, Matt Danzeisen, invited friends to Vienna, Austria, to celebrate anyway. When guests showed up, they were informed that they'd been summoned not for a birthday party, but for a wedding. Thiel was getting married.

From the outside, it was easy to mistake Thiel's pivot away from the Trump administration for a retreat. He no longer wanted to be in the position of having to defend the president's controversial immigration policy or to face scrutiny as Robert Mueller's Russia probe intensified. He was settling down, socially at least, and he and Danzeisen were thinking about having children. But although he was absenting himself from public life, he was not leaving politics or tech. Instead, he was embarking on a campaign to solidify his influence in Washington and ensure that his companies stood to benefit from that influence. The Trump administration was getting ugly, but it would be the most profitable four years of Peter Thiel's career.

18

EVIL LIST

n early 2019, I made my way down Sunset Boulevard to a glass office tower, not far from the sceney clubs of West Hollywood. The Thiel Capital suite, on the building's eleventh floor, was brand new—full of expensive-looking midcentury furniture and devoid of any obvious signs of life, just as Thiel's homes had been described. It was pin-drop quiet, and most of the offices seemed to be empty. An assistant appeared, led me to a glass conference room with a breathtaking canyon view, and served me an espresso on a nice-looking saucer. A few minutes later, Thiel walked in, wearing an open-collar polo shirt, jeans, and a smile. The conversation was off the record and lasted a little more than an hour, ending suddenly when Thiel simply stood up and left, and I awkwardly tried to figure out if someone was going to return to show me out, or if I was just expected to leave on my own. It was a strange exit—not rude exactly, but as if he'd simply run out of things to say and hadn't thought to say goodbye.

During the interview, I attempted to draw him out on his vision of the future—what came after Trump? I also tried to figure out why he seemed to have it in for Google. The open hostilities had started in 2012, when Thiel was teaching his class at Stanford. During one of the lectures, he'd noted Google's monopoly in internet search and then maintained that it had presented itself as a general-purpose tech company in order to avoid scrutiny from the U.S. Department of Justice and other antitrust regulators. This self-presentation, Thiel said, was a lie; Google's businesses in driverless cars, social networks, and everything else were there because "politics demand that the cash be spread around."

At the time, most people who heard it or read about Thiel's statement assumed that he meant it as an interesting observation, maybe even a compliment. But it wasn't exactly that. In 2001, Thiel had used the threat of antitrust scrutiny during PayPal's fight with eBay, and then in 2011, the same executive who'd worked on that effort, Vince Sollitto, showed up in Hawaii to make a presentation at the Conference of Western Attorneys General on behalf of another Thiel-affiliated company, Yelp. The company's CEO, Jeremy Stoppelman, had been a junior engineer at X.com. Despite having been hired by Elon Musk, he'd survived the coup. Then, after the company was sold, and after he'd spent a year at business school, he'd shown up at the Clarium offices for an internship. Instead of putting Stoppelman to work, Thiel passed him off to Levchin, who'd started a business incubator, and it was there that Stoppelman came up with the idea of creating a website where regular people reviewed restaurants and other businesses.

Yelp had thrived—until Google copied it, releasing a clone called Places, which appeared next to the company's search results for restaurants and other businesses. In his 2011 presentation, Sollitto noted that Places was lifting reviews from Yelp, essentially stealing its content, and then using that content to draw traffic (and revenue) away from its competitor: the classic behavior of an illegal monopoly.

Google stopped the practice, but later that fall, Stoppelman appeared before the Senate Judiciary Committee. Google, he said, was engaging in unfair competitive practices and should be prevented from using its market power to take over other parts of the internet. "Today represents a rare opportunity for the government to protect innovation," Stoppelman said. "Allowing a search engine with monopoly market share to exploit and extend its dominance hampers entrepreneurial activity."

In July 2012, a few months after he'd attacked Google at Stanford, Thiel was set to appear onstage with Google chairman Eric Schmidt at a conference in Aspen, Colorado, in what was billed as a debate about the future of technology. Schmidt had spoken first, praising the presence of the tech industry, and Google especially, in the developing world. "In our lifetimes, we'll go from a very small number of people having access to the world's information to virtually everyone in the world having access to all the world's information in their own language," he said.

Thiel, who wore a sport coat over a shirt with two open buttons, clenched his teeth and then broke into a smile. "Eric, you do a fantastic job as Google's minister of propaganda," he said, launching into a version of his view that the tech industry had stopped innovating. "There are obviously individual companies that do quite well, especially if they have world-class monopolies like Google has in search."

"Legal monopolies," the moderator, Adam Lashinsky, corrected him.

"They're legal as long as they don't try to tie in and oppress other companies by extending their monopoly power unfairly," Thiel said, without smiling. "It's quite legal to have a monopoly as long as you don't abuse it."

Schmidt laughed it off, saying he'd take that as a compliment, but Thiel's broadsides continued for the next half hour. He said that Schmidt and his colleagues "like computers more than people, in many cases" and then suggested that Schmidt had inappropriately taken credit for the Arab Spring, the wave of revolutionary fervor that was sweeping the Middle East. "The actual facts on the ground are that food prices rose by 30 to 50 percent in the previous year and you basically had people who had become—you had desperate people who had become more hungry than scared, who revolted," Thiel said. "Then Eric goes around and says, 'Let them eat iPhones.'"

Finally, Thiel focused his complaints on Google's balance sheet, which showed that the company had $30 billion in cash but was out of good ideas for what to do with the money. "The intellectually honest thing to do would be to say that Google is no longer a technology company," he said. "It's like a bank that generates enormous cash flows every year, but you can't issue a dividend because the day you take that $30 billion and send it back you've admitted that you're no longer a technology company."

Half a decade later, Google wasn't just a threat to Yelp. It was a sprawling conglomerate that competed for advertising dollars with Facebook and seemed poised to vie for high-tech defense contracts that might otherwise go to Palantir. Indeed, it presented, in one way or another, a threat to nearly every company in Thiel's portfolio.

Google was also uniquely vulnerable. Schmidt's closeness with Barack Obama and, later, Hillary Clinton—he'd infamously been photographed at Clinton's election night party wearing a staff badge—put him on the outs with Trump, who'd complained during the campaign that Google was filtering out negative results about Clinton. And it also served as a handy stand-in for the sins of big tech that were more uncomfortable for Thiel to acknowledge. Like Facebook, it had collected enormous quantities of data, often from customers who may not have realized they were being surveilled; like Facebook it had, effectively, given advertisers access to that data; and like Facebook, it had been manipulated by Russian trolls (by way of YouTube).

After Trump's election, Thiel began telling anyone who would listen that while the public—especially liberals smarting from the 2016 election—were focusing their anger on Facebook, the truly evil big tech company wasn't Facebook. Zuckerberg's company "has been given more of a bum rap than it deserves." If anyone deserved regulation, he implied, it wasn't Zuckerberg; it was his main rival. Behind the scenes, he was doing more than just talking.

THE CAMPAIGN INTENSIFIED after he'd left the Trump White House in 2017 and it began the way many of Thiel's companies and political projects had begun since his college days: with a culture war. Google was, not unlike Stanford, full of lefty idealists devoted to the company's lofty mission—"To organize the world's information and make it universally accessible and useful"—and its vaguely progressive-sounding politics that promised "don't be evil."

But Google also had a conservative contingent—young college graduates who'd been attracted to the growing company because it paid well, offered great job security, and had the reputation for hiring elite engineers. Many of them were well versed in the blend of prosperity gospel and libertarian politics of Peter Thiel. They'd watched *The Social Network,* they'd read *Zero to One,* and they'd cheered on Ron Paul and Donald Trump and the destruction of Gawker.

In July 2017, a twenty-eight-year-old Google engineer from the Chicago suburbs, James Damore, circulated a memo arguing that the company had been systematically discriminating against certain employees. This kind of complaint was common at the idealistic company where workers spent 20 percent of their hours on personal projects in a pseudo-academic atmosphere, publishing their thoughts about all manner of topics on company mailing lists. But whereas most Google staff believed the company discriminated against minorities and women—facts that were borne out in its diversity statistics, which showed that white and Asian men accounted for an outsized portion of the company's staff—Damore, who like Thiel had played chess as a boy and who'd recently gotten into the Men's Rights movement, had come to believe Google was in fact discriminating against conservatives. He'd watched a documentary,

The Red Pill, in which a self-described feminist comes to question her beliefs—the film's title used Curtis Yarvin's preferred term for enlightenment. He'd also been watching lectures by Jordan Peterson, the controversial Canadian psychologist and self-help author who inveighs regularly against affirmative action.

Peterson's ideas had persuaded Damore, who wrote that Google managers had been "shaming" conservatives "into silence" about the possibility that maybe women were underrepresented at Google, not because of discrimination, but because they were less interested in coding than men were. That made sense to Damore since women seemed more extroverted and neurotic, traits that Damore claimed were inconsistent with being a good coder. The tortured logic was debunked by Google employees who leaked the memo publicly in early August.

Google fired Damore, who went to the press. "They betrayed me," he told Bloomberg TV, claiming that he'd circulated the memo in good faith and was being punished unjustly, a charge that Thiel's network was happy to amplify. Eric Weinstein, a managing director of Thiel Capital, posted a tweet that suggested that Google, by firing Damore, was "teaching my girl that her path to financial freedom lies not in coding but in complaining to HR." He signed it, "thx in advance, A dad." Despite Weinstein's title, his most prominent role today is as the host of a podcast, *The Portal*, in which he interviews contrarians, including Thiel himself. He also leads a group of YouTube personalities, including Peterson, dedicated to complaining about political correctness, that he dubbed the Intellectual Dark Web.

Jeff Giesea, Thiel's friend from Stanford who'd become an alt-right activist, wrote a series of tweets defending Damore with a hashtag borrowed from Thiel's mid-1990s jeremiad against multiculturalism. "Let's get more people talking about the Google memo," Giesea wrote. "Hashtag: #DiversityMyth." He later delete the tweets.

The task of cultivating Damore was taken on by Charles Johnson, who set up a legal defense fund on his behalf on WeSearchr—his crowdfunding site that had been created with Thiel's support—complaining that "the radical Left has been whipping up hate mobs to get independents, libertarians, conservatives, and simple contrarians publicly shamed, bullied, and fired from their jobs." It raised $60,000. He also arranged for Damore to meet with Thiel and Harmeet Dhillon, a prominent labor attorney and the chair of the California Republican Party. Around the same time, Thiel also invited a group of disaffected conservative Google employees to his home. Johnson served as host to the group.

The following January, Damore and another former engineer filed a class action lawsuit against Google, claiming it had discriminated against white men and conservatives. The lawsuit suggested that the company's diversity initiatives, which included discussing white male privilege and praising departments in which 50 percent of the staff were women, constituted a violation of antidiscrimination laws.

Johnson, who'd been urging Thiel to find another vehicle for a Gawker-style legal attack, encouraged him to pay Damore's legal bills, but Thiel declined. "I don't know why he didn't back us," Damore told me. It may have been partly because Thiel had grander plans, which were playing out, at that moment, in a government building in Jefferson City, Missouri.

In November, while Damore was plotting his lawsuit, a *Stanford Review* alumnus named Josh Hawley announced that, as attorney general for the state of Missouri, he was opening an antitrust investigation into the dominant search engine, citing the company's collection of private data. "No entity in the history of the world has collected as much information on individual consumers as Google," Hawley said. The comments could have easily applied to Facebook or Palantir, but Hawley wasn't taking them on at the moment. "We should not just accept the word of these corporate giants that they have our best interests at heart." He vowed to investigate the way that search engines used content from competitors' websites and then biased its results against them—echoing the complaints that Yelp had made years earlier and that had since become a popular line of attack among those who favored antitrust action.

Hawley's lawsuit was laughed off in Silicon Valley. He'd just announced that he was considering a run for Senate and at thirty-seven was seen as an inexperienced opportunist. But he knew Peter Thiel— and Thiel had big plans for him. Hawley had gone to Stanford a decade after Thiel and had written for the *Review*. When Hawley announced a run for attorney general in 2015, Thiel donated $300,000—a huge sum for a race during which Hawley raised $4 million over two years. On November 9, 2017, Thiel made two donations to Hawley that together amounted to the federal maximum, $2,700 each, for his primary and general election bids. Four days later, Hawley announced his lawsuit.

Hawley would deny that Thiel's donations had influenced his action. But staff inside of Google saw a coordinated attack, backed by Thiel, who, after all, had sat on the board of Google's main competitor, Facebook.

THE FOLLOWING JANUARY, Thiel showed up at Stanford for an onstage chat with his old friend Reid Hoffman. The two men had been at odds over Trump—Hoffman and his wife, Michelle Yee, were bitterly opposed to Trump and had avoided socializing with Thiel after the election—but they were back on good terms. During the event, which was moderated by Thiel's friend the conservative historian Niall Ferguson, Thiel sparred with Hoffman on the question of whether social networks should attempt to regulate falsehoods—Hoffman thought it was sensible; Thiel disagreed—and reprised his attack on Google's "propaganda." He also suggested that artificial intelligence, which Google considered a core competency, was "communist." "It's about big data, about big governments controlling all the data, knowing more about you than you know yourself," he said. "The Chinese communist party loves AI and hates crypto."

Later, when Ferguson asked Thiel about the prospect of antitrust in the hypothetical event that the Democrats won back control of the White House, Thiel answered by flipping the question on its head. What if Trump went after the tech companies instead?

> THIEL: The thing I'm struck by, and that I worry about, is how poorly the big tech companies are playing the political game . . . The thing that maybe is idealistic or maybe stupid, or maybe just wrong, is that Silicon Valley is a one party state. It's all in on one party—and that's when you get in trouble, politically, in our society, when you're all on one side . . . You said that regulation may come from the left. It may well come from the Republicans at this point. And you're really in trouble when the Republicans want to regulate you.

> FERGUSON: How might they do that? I can't imagine Republicans doing a big antitrust action.

> THIEL: You know, there are a lot of—I'm not gonna give them ideas.

The coy hypothetical failed to acknowledge the role that Thiel was playing in the Republican crackdown on tech companies, and especially Google. Just as he'd been at the center of the populist uprising he'd warned about ten years earlier as a hedge fund manager—while secretly bankrolling that very uprising—Thiel was at the center of the campaign to regulate the tech companies. The reference to the one-party state was a nod to the grievances expressed by Damore and amplified by Johnson and others in Thiel's orbit—but it was also, to anyone watching carefully, a warning: Get on the Trump train, or get a visit from the FTC.

A few weeks later, Thiel resumed the culture war. He began telling friends, who in turn leaked to the press, that he was going to back away from the tech industry. He felt ambivalent about what the internet had done to polarize American society and how it had systematically reduced privacy. And so he was going to exit, leaving Silicon Valley for a home in the hills above the Sunset Strip, where he would also relocate Thiel Capital and his foundation. He sold the house on the Presidio, the house that had served as a statement of his ambitions as a hedge fund manager and technologist.

The move was pure kayfabe. Thiel had always traveled a lot—he owned more than a dozen homes on five continents, had owned the Hollywood home since 2012, and would still have a place in San Francisco. He wasn't moving Founders Fund, his most important investment vehicle, and employees there would say after the move that it was as if he'd never left. He was spending as much time in the office as before. But the move gave him a ready-made talking point: The man who'd built Silicon Valley had become its most vocal critic—even if that criticism stopped short of leaving the board of Facebook or distancing himself from Palantir. Few noted the inconsistency.

He would sometimes connect his move with the rising real estate prices in the Bay Area—complaining that as a venture capitalist, most of his investment capital was going to "urban slumlords," in the form of commercial rents and the high salaries demanded by employees to cover their housing costs—but mostly his complaints were political, a near faithful reprise of the barbs he'd first crafted as a Stanford undergraduate, and were pitched perfectly to conservative media. Silicon Valley, he would often say, was so ideologically oppressive that it resembled North Korea. It was, he said, full of very smart but "brainwashed" workers who'd been driven into political correctness, which Thiel diagnosed as the single most important problem in American society. His critics on the left would point out the obvious hypocrisy: A man who'd vindictively destroyed a liberal media outlet for writing things he didn't like was complaining about the oppressiveness of liberals—but on Fox and *Breitbart*, and among the commentators of the alt-right and the Intellectual Dark Web, he was a truth-teller, even a hero. "When people are unanimously on one side, that tells you not that they've all figured out the truth, but that they're in a sort of totalitarian place," Thiel told Fox Business anchor Maria Bartiromo. "Silicon Valley has shifted from being quite liberal to being a one party state."

THIEL MIGHT NOT HAVE succeeded exactly in his push to install friends, fellow travelers, and loyalists in positions of power inside the Trump administration—but he didn't entirely fail either. Besides Kevin Harrington and Michael Kratsios, Trae Stephens, a Founders Fund partner and former Palantir employee whom a Thiel insider described as "Peter's mini-me," was detailed to the Pentagon during the transition. Thiel helped install Michael Anton, a friend and conservative firebrand— he'd written an essay, "Flight 93 Election," that was credited with helping to bring some moderate Republicans around to the pro-Trump cause by comparing Hillary Clinton to the 9/11 terrorists—at the National Security Council. Justin Mikolay, a former Palantir marketer who'd previously served in the Navy, joined the Defense Department as a speechwriter and communications strategist to Secretary of Defense Jim Mattis.

Mattis himself subscribed to the disruptive ethos that Thiel, Alex Karp, and others close to the company had been preaching for a decade, and he wasn't the only one. His senior staff also included a chief of staff and a senior adviser, Anthony DeMartino and Sally Donnelly, who'd both done work for Palantir as consultants. In early 2017, Thiel and Stephens had visited the Pentagon and urged officials there to consider restructuring the government around computers and to make it easier for Silicon Valley companies to do business with them. "There is making mistakes, and then there's the mistake of making no mistakes," Thiel said in his talk. "And that is a very big mistake." It was "move fast and break things" for a new era.

Palantir arguably had an even more important ally at the National Security Council—if only briefly. That was Michael Flynn, the bellicose lieutenant general who, after being forced out of the military under President Obama, had refashioned himself into a globetrotting, Russophilic Make America Great Again keynoter. Of course, before that transformation he'd been the first high-level officer to publicly call for the Army to adopt Palantir. Flynn resigned as National Security Advisor after just three weeks on the job when it emerged that he'd lied about conversations he'd had with the Russian ambassador before taking office. He was replaced with H. R. McMaster, who was unlike Flynn in most respects—an institutionalist and career military man who'd never voted in an election. But McMaster, who'd distinguished himself during the first Gulf War and the Iraq counterinsurgency, had one thing in common with his predecessor: He'd also been an enthusiastic Palantir user and champion.

It's possible, of course, that appointment of military officials sympathetic to Palantir's brand of disruption had nothing to do with Thiel—these ideas were gaining currency in government circles even during the Obama administration, and in interviews Palantir executives insisted they had not benefited from preferential treatment. "It's completely and utterly ludicrous," Karp told me. "It takes ten years to build this kind of business." But Trump's appointments had the effect of seeding his administration with advisers who saw Palantir extremely favorably. The Army held a bakeoff between Palantir and Raytheon, the original DCGS contractor: Both companies would build a prototype system and present it to a panel of soldiers. It was exactly the kind of contest that Palantir had called for in a lawsuit a few years prior.

The Army had seemed skeptical of the company; now the officials in charge of DCGS were suddenly solicitous. Some Palantir insiders wondered if they'd been convinced on the merits—Palantir's software had indeed improved a lot over the previous decade—or if political pressure had been brought to bear. Either way, in early 2019, the Army announced that Palantir had won outright: The company would get its largest contract ever—worth as much as $800 million or more. The win created momentum, with the company suddenly in the hunt for more Pentagon work, worth hundreds of millions of dollars more.

Palantir wasn't the only way that Thiel would profit from the Trump presidency. Anduril, a startup defense contractor with a similar pitch to Palantir (and even a *Lord of the Rings* name to boot—Andúril is Aragorn's sword and means "flame of the West" in Elvish), had been founded by Trae Stephens and Palmer Luckey, a close friend of Johnson's whose previous company, Oculus, had received money from Founders Fund and been sold to Facebook. The company, which a Thielverse member described as "the next the iteration of Peter's project with Palantir," added three more cofounders—two more of whom had previously worked at Palantir—and quickly raised $17.5 million from Thiel's venture capital firm. Just as Palantir had tailored itself to a new political opportunity—Americans, reeling from the 9/11 attacks, were suddenly open to digital surveillance and data mining—Anduril was developing hardware and software for the U.S. border pitched to Trump's "build the wall" furor, which Thiel had said was not meant to be taken literally but which he was happy to financially support and profit from. The gear, starting with technology to help police the U.S. border, would be priced commercially, rather than on a contract basis—just like SpaceX's rockets and Palantir's software.

Palantir, of course, had relied on the CIA's patronage during its early years; for Anduril, the government agency keeping the lights on was the Customs and Border Protection agency. The CBP was flush with funds, newly empowered under President Trump to improve border security, deport undocumented migrants, and, most controversially, separate immigrant children from their parents. As a practical matter, the government had generally either released families with children before their court dates or detained them as a group. But a new "zero tolerance" policy, announced in April 2018, called for police to separate parents who were charged criminally—and who would be deported—from their children.

It was designed as a deterrent, but it was a remarkably cruel one. "If you don't want your child separated, then don't bring them across the border illegally," Attorney General Jeff Sessions said. "It's not our fault that somebody does that."

Until Trump reversed himself in June, the policy led to the separation and forced detention of thousands of children, including toddlers and infants in 2017 and 2018, prompting outcry from public health advocates, who warned of the inevitable trauma that the government was inflicting on children. In June, an eight-minute recording was published in which young children could be heard calling desperately for their parents—"Mami, Papa"—while border agents cracked jokes. "Well, we have an orchestra here," an agent said. "What's missing is a conductor."

Thiel never condemned the policy, and many of his closest political advisers praised it. Ann Coulter, Thiel's longtime friend, suggested on Fox News that the crying babies were "child actors." Kobach said the cages in which very young detainees were photographed had been established purely for the "children's safety." And Thiel's companies were happy to take money from the CBP. In 2018, according to documents released by the advocacy group Mijente, Anduril landed contracts worth $5 million to provide equipment as part of a "virtual wall" involving inexpensive cameras and other sensors, paired with advanced artificial intelligence. The group also released a document showing that Palantir's software was used by officers to find parents of unaccompanied children in the United States for arrest and deportation.

Protests against the company intensified in 2019. Palantir, like many Silicon Valley companies, used the online software repository GitHub— a sort of social network for coders, where engineers share software programs they've written and work out technical problems. In May, dozens of members of the Tech Workers Coalition posted the same message to Palantir's GitHub page: "ICE uses Palantir's software to deport families of migrant children." Two months later protestors showed up at an Amazon Books store in New York, demanding that the company, which offers cloud computing services to Thiel's data mining company, cut ties with it. Palantir would be near the top of *Slate*'s "Evil List." On the left, Palantir—and Thiel, by extension—became a stand-in for far-right authoritarianism and Silicon Valley creepiness. His name was a regular punch line on *Chapo Trap House*, the gonzo left-wing political podcast. Sam Seder's *Majority Report* had a running gag in which the late comedian Michael Brooks did an impression of Thiel as malevolent and stereotypically gay—an attempt to needle him about the Gawker case.

Over the summer, complaints about Palantir spilled over to its corps of employees, who distributed a petition demanding that the company donate profits from its ICE work to charity. When Karp refused, some resigned in frustration. "It feels really bad," a former engineer told me. He and several other employees privately pledged to donate any money they made by selling stock to RAICES, a Texas-based organization that provides legal services to help immigrants fight their deportations. "It feels like dirty money." This was exactly what Thiel had wanted: a full-blown Silicon Valley culture war—one that he'd spend the rest of Trump's presidency profiting from.

IN JULY 2019, Thiel flew to Washington to appear on the first night of the inaugural National Conservatism Conference. It was a new gathering for a new kind of conservatism, embracing, as the conference organizers explained, the populist and nationalist movements that had sprung up in the United States and Europe. This "national conservatism" was an attempt to expand upon Trumpism—to find a "Trumpism beyond Trump," as Thiel had been putting it to friends and colleagues. It was a turn away from the libertarian politics that had prevailed since the rise of Barry Goldwater and toward a vision Thiel had been promoting at least since his reactionary investor letters and his cultivation of figures like Curtis Yarvin—a politics of closed borders, mercantile trade policy, and populist industrial policy.

The Thielverse was well represented at the nationalist conference. Yarvin was in the audience, as was Jeff Giesea. The speakers list included Josh Hawley, now the junior senator from Missouri, who would have a keynote, plus Michael Anton and J. D. Vance, a former managing director at Mithril who'd since refashioned himself as a populist author with the book *Hillbilly Elegy*. Even John Bolton was on the program.

Thiel, of course, was the headliner, and the unsurprising focus of his speech was his favorite monopoly. Google, in Thiel's telling, was building "the *Star Trek* computer." This gave him an opportunity to give his standard riff on technological stagnation: There might be a computer that knew everything, but we didn't have a warp drive—we didn't even have the Concorde anymore! Of course, *Star Trek*, in Thiel's view, was a communist show—a universe without national borders or capitalism—and Google was, he argued, a communist company, which saw itself as above and beyond the reach of the United States. (There was an irony to this line of criticism: Thiel had often sought to put his own interests above and beyond the reach of the United States and had, in fact, nurtured an entire ideology around doing so.) Thiel then suggested, without offering evidence, that Google's artificial intelligence project had been "thoroughly infiltrated" by Chinese intelligence operatives. From there he twisted the knife.

A year earlier, under pressure from employees, Google had canceled a contract with the Department of Defense that had called for it to help the military process images from drones. Protestors had suggested that Google tech might be used for targeted killings, and, under pressure, CEO Sundar Pichai had been persuaded by their argument. Around the same time, Google had been pursuing a plan to build a Chinese-language search engine. The effort, Project Dragonfly, had required Google to censor content about topics that might embarrass the Communist Party and would have allowed Beijing to track Google users in China. The company continued attempting to build a Chinese search engine even after backing out of the U.S. military program, and Thiel wanted to know why. Why was Google being friendlier to the Chinese military than to the American one? he asked. He offered a pat answer: Google was "treasonous." An auditorium full of nationalist populists broke out in applause. "These questions need to be asked on a federal level by the United States," he said. "They need to be asked by the FBI, by the CIA. And, I'm not quite sure how to put this, I would like them to be asked in a not excessively gentle manner."

Thiel delivered his talk in his typically discursive style, which is to say, rather poorly. He stepped on his own jokes, he stuttered, and he missed punch lines. Yet the audience, even in the back with my fellow members of the "fake news," as one of the organizers had described us from the podium, was rapt. Not only was the world's most famous venture capitalist attacking an industry that he himself had built, he was suggesting that his primary business rival required investigation—perhaps forceful investigation—by the federal government.

Even as it circled some of Thiel's favorite themes and targeted his usual object of scorn, the speech was a radical departure from the rhetoric he'd adopted as a "public intellectual." Naturally, Johnson had a role, having helped arrange for Thiel to reprise the speech the following day on Tucker Carlson's Fox News show, knowing that Trump was a loyal viewer. Thiel was sweaty and uncomfortable, but the message came through. He not only accused Google of treason but suggested that there was "a broad base of Google employees that are ideologically super left wing, sort of woke," and, he added, "anti-American."

The following morning. Trump did exactly what Johnson had hoped. "A great and brilliant guy who knows this subject better than anyone!" Trump tweeted, referring to Thiel.

It didn't go anywhere—Treasury Secretary Steven Mnuchin quickly said that he'd looked into Google and found nothing worrying. But the comments certainly didn't hurt the chances for Palantir, which was competing for dozens of other government contracts and whose surrogates were happy to repeat Thiel's allegation. Joe Lonsdale, Thiel's old Clarium Capital employee and a Palantir cofounder, went on CNBC. "Peter and I built a patriotic company," he said. "Google is clearly not a patriotic company."

Just months later, Palantir took over Google's work on Project Maven—a deal that would be worth $40 million per year. That happened despite the fact that Palantir had limited experience in the kind of high-end image recognition software that Maven used to identify targets—and despite concerns from a government official, in an anonymous memo sent to military brass and first reported by *The New York Times*, that the company had received preferential treatment in landing the contract.

No matter: Maven became a new Palantir product and a way to further deepen the military's dependence on Thiel's company. Anduril, the latest member of Thiel's defense portfolio, also received a piece of the Maven contract. For Palantir, there would be yet another huge deal announced in December, this one worth as much as $440 million over several years. There was $10 million from Trump's brand-new military branch, the Space Force, and $80 million from the Navy. And Palantir ignored the objections of its own employees and immigration activists, renewing its contract with ICE, for another $50 million. After all, one rule of the Thielverse was that it was better to be seen as evil than incompetent.

19

TO THE MAT

The relationship was never perfect. Zuckerberg had regarded Thiel warily almost from the beginning, and Thiel had never embraced the function or philosophy of Facebook, even if it was the most successful bet he'd made in his career. For a man who'd at times obsessed over the destructive power of imitation and competition, of wanting what others want; for a man who'd railed about the dangers of the increasingly borderless world; for a man who'd complained that the best and brightest of his generation were wasting their time on piddling software companies— what, exactly, was Facebook? It was a social network of two billion people, built on the premise of transcending national boundaries, in which users competed with one another to see whose duckface selfie, or bare feet pointed to the surf, or just-so breakfast would get the most Likes. It was everything that Peter Thiel had warned about. And it had made him rich.

Nor had Thiel seemed to entirely buy into Zuckerberg's conception of the company as a force that would eventually come to subsume much of the internet. He'd urged Zuckerberg to consider selling the company after Yahoo! had offered $1 billion, and began selling stock shortly after

Zuckerberg flatly refused—"Eight-thirty seems about as good a time as any to turn down $1 billion," he said at an early-morning board meeting, cutting off any debate.

When the company finally went public in 2012, Thiel had been one of the biggest sellers of its stock, immediately offloading about 17 million shares at around $38 each, which was worth $640 million—in an echo of his sudden exit from PayPal to make hedge fund investments. Most IPOs are sold to investors at a price slightly below their true market value, which allows those who agree to buy in advance of the IPO to make a modest profit in exchange for their early bet and makes the company look good in the financial press. But Facebook's IPO never "popped," in suit-speak. As insiders, including Thiel, sold their shares, the stock's value plummeted, falling below $20 per share over the next few months.

The problem, even more so than the perception that insiders didn't believe in the company, was Facebook's fealty to its original website. Facebook.com was where the company made almost all of its money, but the rise of smartphones meant that desktop web browsing was becoming less common, especially among young people, which threatened the company's revenue. It was much harder to show people a lot of ads on small screens. "Without an earth-changing idea," *MIT Technology Review* predicted not long after the IPO, "it will collapse." Two pension funds, including a group of Arkansas teachers, filed a class action lawsuit, claiming that Zuckerberg, Thiel, Sheryl Sandberg, and Facebook's bankers had underplayed Facebook's difficulties on smartphones when they'd sold the stock during the IPO. Facebook eventually paid $35 million to settle the suit. "That was a terrible summer," said one former Facebook staffer. "People were talking about us like we were going to be a penny stock."

To cheer up the depressed staff, the company organized a series of motivational all-hands meetings. The head of partnerships, a former Amazon executive named Dan Rose, gamely recalled to employees that the stock price of the online retailer had cratered during the dot-com bust before it came back. He told them to block out the noise and trust that the company was on the right track. "The world doesn't know it, but we know what we're doing," Rose said.

There was also a less inspiring talk. Someone in the communications department had the bright idea that the company's longest-serving investor—a man who'd survived the dot-com bust, after all—might have something encouraging to say.

But Peter Thiel, unfortunately, did not play ball. "My generation was promised colonies on the moon," he said, after being introduced by Zuckerberg. "Instead we got Facebook."

Employees looked at one another with astonishment. Thiel—America's great public intellectual, the Godfather of Silicon Valley—had just told one of the most successful companies of the past decade that they kind of, sort of . . . sucked. They'd heard the old Founders Fund line, "We were promised flying cars, instead we got 140 characters," which had been funny since it had taken a dig at Facebook's competitor, Twitter, which nobody at Facebook took seriously anyway. "A clown car that fell into a gold mine," Zuckerberg had once called it. But Thiel had adapted his line to insult Facebook instead. Was there such a thing as a non-motivational speech?

Thiel's point seemed to be that in the scheme of things Facebook was basically inconsequential—not a world-changing or world-breaking technology—just another social network. Therefore, he said, it wasn't worth stressing out. This too would pass, and the staff should let criticism from the press and investors slide off their backs; the stakes were low.

But that was not the message that Facebook employees heard. Already, some had been asking in the internal forums the company maintained for employee questions and comments if a man who'd suggested that women's suffrage had set back the cause of freedom should be on the board at all. Now he'd told them what they were doing was pointless.

Thiel's comments could also be interpreted as a sort of mea culpa. He'd tended to describe the technology stagnation as the inevitable result of liberals' obsession with their racial, ethnic, and gender identities to the exclusion of good ideas. But, of course, he'd fanned the flames of the culture wars throughout his career. He'd bet money on the stagnation by shorting the U.S. economy and investing in Canadian tar sands, rather than investing all his capital in American startups. And, of course, he'd given capital to Mark Zuckerberg. The stagnation, like Facebook, might have been bad for America, but it had been damn good for Peter Thiel.

As part of the IPO, Facebook insiders had to agree to wait ninety days after the stock started trading to sell their equity. The ninety days were up on August 16, and Thiel sold most of the rest of his shares for around $20 per share for another $400 million. This was exceedingly poor timing as it would turn out. Facebook's stock would trade around $300 per share at the end of March 2021. Tellingly, Thiel barely used the service that had made him rich and could never quite seem to be able to bring himself to praise it publicly. You didn't have to know him well to understand that he felt ambivalent about an investment that his peers viewed as one of the all-time best in the history of venture capital.

THE FUNNY THING WAS, at least to Facebook employees who were close enough to the board to understand this dynamic, Zuckerberg never punished him for it. Sure, Thiel was effectively banned as a speaker at future all-hands meetings, and any time his name would come up in the press, his views about women would once again surface in the company's internal message boards. But Zuckerberg kept him close, and, in fact, seemed to take his advice more seriously.

This decision was partly strategic—having someone with Thiel's politics around shielded Zuckerberg from conservative ire—but it was also temperamental. In Facebook's structure, which Thiel had played a role in setting up, Zuckerberg possessed near-absolute power. The Facebook founder controlled a majority of the equity, he could fire the board at will, and he was a business celebrity—which meant that whenever he said something at Facebook, he was surrounded by executives who would compete with one another to agree the most fervently. "It really is like dealing with the court of a king," said someone close to him. "You had different factions and different interests, but they don't really challenge the king. And so it's very hard for the person at the center to get unvarnished advice."

This, of course, was a problem throughout the Thielverse as well; Thiel's own underlings sometimes used the courtier metaphor to describe their relations with their patron. But when Zuckerberg and Thiel talked, it was king to king. Thiel had been attracted to Zuckerberg's obvious lack of concern for what anyone else thought; Zuckerberg now found the same quality appealing in Thiel. Thiel's counsel could be rude, but it was always real.

Still, somehow it wasn't always clear where Thiel's loyalties lay, especially now that he'd dumped most of his Facebook stock. When he'd played host to the conservative pundits after the Trending Topics brouhaha, he hadn't bothered mentioning to anyone at Facebook that he was making a play for a role as a major kingmaker in conservative politics and courting the alt-right. That omission made the Trending Topics meeting look less like an effort to use his contacts to help Facebook, and more like an attempt to use Facebook to shore up Thiel's own standing among conservative media figures.

Several weeks after Thiel's endorsement of Trump at the Republican National Convention, and the day before a Facebook board meeting, a fellow board member, Netflix CEO Reed Hastings, sent him an email suggesting that the endorsement might disqualify him from serving further. "I'm so mystified by your endorsement of Trump for our President, that for me it moves from 'different judgement' to 'bad judgement,'" Hastings wrote. "Some diversity of views is healthy, but catastrophically bad judgement (in my view) is not what anyone wants in a fellow board member."

Zuckerberg ignored the tensions until the following August when someone leaked Hastings's email to *The New York Times*. The article by Nick Wingfield, which came out just as Thiel was encouraging the unrest at Google, noted, as the headline put it, THE CULTURE WARS HAVE COME TO SILICON VALLEY and attempted to put Damore's firing from Google into a broader context by pointing out two other prominent political disputes at Facebook. One was the firing of Palmer Luckey, the founder of Oculus, a virtual reality company that Zuckerberg had paid more than $2 billion to acquire two years earlier. Zuckerberg had dismissed Luckey in early 2017 after Luckey had been exposed as a donor to a pro-Trump political action committee that had been created by members of Reddit's forum for alt-right activists, The Donald. The other was the email that Hastings had sent to Thiel, which *The Times* published in full. A common thread was Thiel's friend Charles Johnson, who'd supported Damore, who was close to Luckey, and who had a copy of the Hastings email.

Zuckerberg suspected that Thiel might have had something to do with the article. He asked Thiel for a list of people with whom he'd shared Hastings's email, and then asked him to consider stepping down from the board. Thiel refused. "I will not quit," he told Zuckerberg. "You'll have to fire me." The Facebook founder backed down and allowed Thiel to stay on. Hastings would leave the board in 2019.

Not long after his confrontation with Zuckerberg, Thiel had Johnson over for a drink at his San Francisco home and recounted the conversation. "Charles, you and I have a weird relationship," Thiel said, smiling from behind a pair of dark sunglasses. "Mark asked me who I sent that email to. The only name I didn't give him was yours."

Johnson's plans for his facial recognition app, Clearview, which Thiel had invested in, were also hostile to Facebook. Hoan Ton-That had developed software to scrape millions of photos from the social network (as well as photos from Twitter, Instagram, and a few others). Facebook, which discouraged people from joining the site under a pseudonym, was particularly useful to the startup since each photo would be easy to match up with the person's full name, making it perfect for Johnson's vision of a comprehensive record of every American's face.

Using those photos and then offering them to police as a massive criminal investigation database might seem icky to some—and according to Facebook, it amounted to a violation of the company's terms of service, which prohibited scraping—but Johnson knew it was likely legal given that Facebook profile photos were publicly available on the internet. Scraping them was arguably no different from what Google called "indexing" websites, which involves creating a copy of every site and storing that information on its servers. Not only that, but as he explained to Thiel, it would have the happy side effect of exposing Mark Zuckerberg as the fraud that Johnson believed him to be. Zuckerberg had encouraged users to share as much personal information as possible while assuring them that they would always be able to control what they shared on the network and how that information was used. Clearview showed that that wasn't exactly the case. A photo that someone posted publicly on Facebook—perhaps when he or she was in high school or college—was now part of a massive law enforcement database. That photo could be used, years later, by a government or police department attempting to solve a crime—or, perhaps, to deport an undocumented worker. Johnson told Thiel that reality might make people less willing to share photos, which in the long run could "destroy" Facebook.

Despite the obvious conflict with Thiel's obligations to Facebook, he made a modest seed investment in the company, promising to make a follow-on investment through Founders Fund. But after a reporter with *The New York Times* began digging into Clearview in November 2019, Thiel moved to distance himself from Johnson and the company. Johnson had planned to attend the Founders Fund Christmas party as a guest of Cyan Banister, a partner at the firm, but at the last minute Thiel called and asked him not to come. Founders Fund would pass on the investment too, and Banister would leave the firm to join an early-stage venture capital fund. When the *Times* published its story, Thiel's spokesman described giving "a talented young founder $200,000, which two years later converted to equity in Clearview AI." The check had been Thiel's "only contribution." Johnson's role in the company, and his relationship with Thiel, was not mentioned.

Zuckerberg may not have realized the depth of Thiel's connection to Clearview, but in any case he never punished Thiel—not for Clearview, nor for Palantir's alleged involvement in the Cambridge Analytica scandal, nor, ultimately, for the media leaks.

When Project Veritas, which creates sting videos aimed at exposing supposed left-wing bias in media and tech, produced a report purporting to show that Facebook was suppressing conservative content in early 2019, the company fired a contractor who'd appeared on camera claiming she'd violated its employment policies. But it took no action against Thiel, who'd given a $10,000 grant to the Project Veritas founder, James O'Keefe, years earlier.

In April 2019, Reed Hastings and Erskine Bowles, the former Clinton administration official who'd at times supported efforts to rein in Zuckerberg's power, resigned from the Facebook board. The following March, Ken Chenault, the former CEO of American Express and another board member who'd raised concerns about Facebook's unwillingness to stop disinformation, followed suit. Zuckerberg replaced those critics with his friends and business partners, including Drew Houston, the thirty-seven-year-old founder of Dropbox, and Peggy Alford, a PayPal executive who'd worked at his for-profit philanthropic organization, the Chan Zuckerberg Initiative. By early 2020, the only board members whose tenure dated to before 2019, other than Zuckerberg and Sheryl Sandberg, were Thiel ally Marc Andreessen and Thiel himself.

ZUCKERBERG LIKELY ALSO tolerated Thiel's disloyalty because he was politically vulnerable. If Trump had won in 2016 because American voters had turned against globalization, then few companies were more exposed to those shifting winds than Facebook. It wasn't just the company's user base, or Zuckerberg's previous advocacy for immigration, or the vaguely anti-Trump comments the Facebook CEO had made during the campaign about building bridges "instead of building walls." It was that Zuckerberg was arguably just as guilty of the kind of "treasonous" behavior of which Thiel had accused Google.

Facebook, like Google, was banned in China—whose government Thiel bitterly opposed—but for years Zuckerberg had been courting China's leaders, especially Xi Jinping, the Communist Party general secretary who'd assumed near-dictatorial powers. Zuckerberg had taught himself Mandarin, and while hosting a top party official, he'd displayed copies of Xi's book, saying that he'd been presenting them to employees as gifts. The following year, just as Trump's anti-China rhetoric was propelling him to the front of the Republican field, Zuckerberg was laying it on thick with Xi in person. Over dinner at the White House with the Chinese leader—as well as President Obama, Apple's Tim Cook, and Microsoft's Satya Nadella—Zuckerberg, whose wife, Priscilla, was pregnant at the time, asked Xi to give his unborn child an honorary Chinese name. Xi declined.

Zuckerberg had bent over backward in 2016 to avoid being seen as anti-conservative, but it was becoming increasingly clear that the conservatives had maneuvered him into helping Trump win the election. During the campaign, Facebook had allowed numerous fake stories, most of them skewed against Democrats, to proliferate on its platform. It had also turned a blind eye to Russian propagandists who'd disseminated pro-Trump hoaxes. After the election, Zuckerberg treated the outcry over his company's failures like a sideshow, calling the idea that fake news on Facebook had swayed the election "a pretty crazy idea." Then he went on a nationwide bus tour in early 2017 to rehabilitate his image, doing laps at a NASCAR track in North Carolina with Dale Earnhardt Jr.—"This is fun," he said. "I understand why so many people love this."

During the tour, he was asked by a student at a historically Black college what he did personally to encourage diversity. He answered by praising Thiel. "We have a board member who is an adviser to the Trump administration," he said, referring to a man who'd written a whole book about the dangers of venerating diversity. "I think the folks who are saying we shouldn't have someone on our board because they're a Republican, I think that's crazy. I think you need to have all kinds of diversity if you want to make progress together as a society."

All the while, Trump, who had leaned hard on Zuckerberg to make

sure that Facebook stayed balanced in conservatives' favor, kept up th
pressure. The company "was always anti-Trump," the president tweeted
in September, comparing the social network with the "fake news" *New
York Times* and *Washington Post*. Bannon suggested that the White Hous
might go further, by regulating Facebook and Google like utilities—
essentially controlling prices on advertisements and ensuring that th
companies didn't skew content ideologically (that is, against conserva
tives); Trump would return to this threat throughout his presidency.

As the 2020 campaign began in earnest, Trump invited a group o
social media influencers—including those who promoted QAnon, a
pseudo-religious right-wing conspiracy theory that saw the president in
messianic terms—to a Social Media Summit where the president claimed
that tech companies, Facebook included, were censoring his supporters
He pledged to use his power as president to protect them.

Even in the face of this blowback from the White House, Zuckerberg
had reason to believe that the Democrats posted a greater threat to Face
book than Trump. By the end of April 2019 there were twenty declared
candidates for the Democratic Party's nomination, including several front
runners who seemed especially eager to rein in Facebook. In May, Kamala
Harris, the California senator who'd previously been seen as friendly to the
tech industry, told CNN that Facebook was "essentially a utility that ha
gone unregulated, and as far as I'm concerned that's gotta stop." Bernie
Sanders had promised "vigorous antitrust legislation in this country," sin
gling out Facebook. "We deal with it every day," he said. "They determine
who we can communicate with. They have incredible power—over the
economy, over political life in this country—in a very dangerous sense."

Radical as these ideas might have sounded during the Obama presi
dency, neither candidate was the most hawkish about Facebook in the
presidential field. That title went to Massachusetts senator Elizabeth
Warren, who'd released a detailed plan earlier in the year calling for the
breakup of Facebook. She promised to designate it a utility, and then to
force it to divest from Instagram and WhatsApp, the image-sharing and

social-messaging services it had acquired in 2012 and 2014 and that together accounted for much of the company's growth.

Zuckerberg took these warnings seriously. In a meeting with employees several months later, he warned that a Warren presidency would "suck for us." "If she gets elected president, I would bet that we will have a legal challenge," he said. "But look, at the end of the day, if someone's going to try to threaten something that existential, you go to the mat and fight." Zuckerberg was already girding for that fight, and Thiel was available to help.

HE'D REVELED IN the attention from his speech at the nationalist conference, publishing an op-ed in *The New York Times* that reprised the argument: GOOD FOR GOOGLE, BAD FOR AMERICA was the headline. He'd had big plans for 2020—there had been talk of starting a conservative media company or, perhaps, writing another book. But it was increasingly hard to ignore the unfolding disaster that was the end of the Trump presidency. And so Thiel did what he always did when a bet of his seemed to be failing; he bailed.

Thiel had felt confident enough just before the 2018 midterms to proclaim the Trump presidency "relatively successful," to call the suggestion of Russian collusion "a conspiracy theory," and, while struggling to keep a straight face, to respond to a question about Trump's propensity to lie by describing the lies as mere "exaggerations of the truth." But although the midterms went well enough for Thiel—one of his favored candidates, Hawley, had been elected to the Senate—it was a disaster for the Trump administration, with Democrats retaking the House. The new Congress at first resisted calls to impeach Trump, even after Special Counsel Robert Mueller suggested that he had received help in 2016 from Russian agents and then attempted to control and minimize the investigation. But then, September 2019 brought news of Trump's "perfect" call with the Ukrainian president, in which Trump asked him to investigate a political opponent—and Democrats finally acted.

Thiel spent 2019 and early 2020 mostly lying low, appearing in pub lic only a couple of times and always before friendly audiences. He me regularly with prominent conservatives, but always at home, where h could avoid being seen and didn't have to perform. In fact, he didn't ever have to get dressed. On one occasion, Thiel hosted a group that include Matt Gaetz, the Florida representative, wearing only a T-shirt and hi underwear. "Weird," Gaetz later wrote. "But OK!" Another visitor who experienced this treatment: Wilbur Ross, who was then U.S. labor secre tary. "That is a highly unorthodox attire," the eighty-seven-year-old Ros remarked to a colleague after the meeting.

Strange as his guests, especially the newcomers from D.C., may hav found his wardrobe choices, they were also struck by Thiel's idiosyn cratic mode of conversation. He didn't seem to want anything—just t talk. The D.C. crowd interpreted this as listlessness, though it may hav actually just been contentment. Thiel was, according to friends, enjoy ing a new phase of life: domestic bliss. He and Danzeisen had recently become parents to a baby girl born through a surrogate.

Despite the reclusiveness, Thiel still had juice, and in October 201 he flew to Washington to meet with Zuckerberg and Trump. The Face book CEO was in town to testify about his plan to create a new digita currency, Libra, which critics warned could one day displace the dolla as the world's reserve currency. Since the end of World War II, foreig governments have bought and held large quantities of dollars, which means that the United States can effectively borrow nearly unlimite amounts of money and can cut rogue nations out of the global financia system. If people began holding their money in digital currency like Libra borrowing could become more expensive for the United States and th global financial system would be outside of American control. That, o course, was exactly what Thiel had proposed doing at PayPal when h talked about giving anyone their own virtual Swiss bank account.

Zuckerberg's other task was to address growing criticism from Demo crats about Facebook's apparent willingness to amplify the president' lies. Earlier in the month, the Trump campaign had run ads that claimed that former vice president Biden had pressured Ukraine's government to drop an investigation into the business dealings of his son Hunter Biden. This was a lie. CNN refused to air the ads, but Facebook allowed them, citing a policy of not fact-checking things that politicians say. Senator Warren called Zuckerberg out, describing Facebook as a "disinformation-for-profit machine." She said it had "already helped elect Donald Trump once through negligence" and, by failing to fact-check the ads, was again putting its profits above any sense of civic duty.

Zuckerberg responded with a speech at Georgetown University. "I know many people disagree, but, in general, I don't think it's right for a private company to censor politicians or the news in a democracy," he said, citing Dr. Martin Luther King Jr.'s "Letter from Birmingham Jail," the Vietnam-era campus protests, and his own opposition to the Iraq War, which he implied had been the reason he'd started Facebook. Thiel's influence had been clear both in the style—Zuckerberg repeatedly used the word *voice*, to mean "democratic participation," a formulation that Thiel and his friends often used in seasteading discussions—and in the substance. The policy Zuckerberg was articulating was exactly what Thiel, and Trump, wanted.

During Zuckerberg's visit to Washington, Thiel and Danzeisen met Zuckerberg and Priscilla Chan, as well as Jared Kushner and Ivanka Trump, for dinner at the White House with the president and first lady. The exact specifics of the discussion were secret—but Thiel later told a confidant that Zuckerberg had come to an understanding with Kushner during the meal. Facebook, he promised, would avoid fact-checking political speech—thus allowing the Trump campaign to claim whatever it wanted. If it followed through on that promise, the Trump administration would lay off on any heavy-handed regulations.

After the dinner, Zuckerberg took a hands-off approach to conservative sites. In late October, Facebook launched a news app that showcased what the company called "deeply-reported and well-sourced" outlets.

Among the list of recommended publications was *Breitbart*, Bannon's site, even though it had promoted itself as allied with the alt-right and had once included a section dedicated to "Black crime." Facebook also seemed to go out of its way to help the *Daily Wire*, a younger, hipper version of *Breitbart*, which would become one of the biggest publishers on the platform. Facebook had long seen itself as a government unto itself; now, with Trump's blessing, the site would push what a person in Thiel's circle who spoke to him about the meeting called "state sanctioned conservatism."

Zuckerberg denied that there had been any deal, calling the notion "pretty ridiculous," though reporting from *BuzzFeed*, *Bloomberg*, and others would suggest that members of Facebook's policy team indeed intervened to protect conservative sites from getting punished for violating the company's rules against misinformation. (The company declined repeated requests for comment on this issue.) Through the rest of the campaign Facebook would go softer on Trump than its peers. Twitter hid a post by Trump, aimed at Black Lives Matter protestors, that seemed to admiringly quote a threat used by, among others, Alabama segregationist George Wallace: "When the looting starts, the shooting starts." Facebook allowed it, with Zuckerberg explaining that although he disagreed with the president, "I believe people should be able to see this for themselves, because ultimately accountability for those in positions of power can only happen when their speech in scrutinized out in the open." He continued to speak regularly with Jared Kushner, and Thiel continued to emphasize, publicly and privately, that Facebook was less bad than its competitors.

By early March 2020, the plan seemed to be working. Elizabeth Warren and Kamala Harris's campaigns had crashed, Bernie Sanders had sputtered, and Joe Biden, whom Thiel regarded as weak, seemed poised to win the nomination. Trump was seen, especially among conservatives, as likely to win reelection, and Thiel's influence on the right was more pronounced than it had ever been. It would take something totally unexpected—apocalyptic even—to throw off the plan he'd set in motion at Facebook four years earlier. It was all working.

20

BACK TO THE FUTURE

Just as the American public was coming to the realization that the coronavirus was spreading rapidly and that life was going to be profoundly different for some indeterminate amount of time, Peter Thiel left Los Angeles. Conventional wisdom had it that he'd gone to New Zealand—to the Plasma House and its panic room or perhaps to a bunker on the South Island farm he'd bought. New Zealand was living up to its reputation as an ideal apocalypse destination. The country had locked down early and closed its borders to noncitizens. It would suffer only twenty-five deaths from coronavirus through the end of 2020.

But Thiel never made it to New Zealand—and, in fact, he'd essentially ignored his newly adopted homeland since the end of 2017, when he'd attended Simon Denny's art exhibit *The Founder's Paradox*, which explored the mythology of tech founders as the godlike figures that Silicon Valley, and especially Thiel, had promoted. Denny's idiosyncratic medium for the show was board games—and he'd adapted a handful of well-known favorites including Operation and The Game of Life, as well as some of the games popular within the Thielverse, including Settlers of Catan and Descent: Journeys in the Dark, a D&D-like board game. Life was reimagined as a series of choices for a young Stanford graduate involving either socially conscious activities, like paying your taxes, or libertarian ones, like escaping to a tax haven. In Denny's *Descent* spinoff, Ascent: Above the Nation State, Thiel's likeness appeared on a plastic figurine, the "contrarian hero," fighting a dragon labeled "democracy," a lion labeled "fair elections," and an ogre labeled "monetary policy." "It's, uh, actually a work of phenomenal detail," Thiel had remarked to an attendee.

The giant plot of farmland remained untouched and undeveloped. There was no bunker—and Matt Nippert, the *Herald* reporter who'd broken the news of Thiel's citizenship, had begun to suspect that Thiel had given up on the idea shortly after Trump's election. "It was a hedge," he told me. Thiel, he concluded, was worried about Democrats changing U.S. tax policy. But after Trump won—and New Zealand's right-wing National Party government was replaced by the country's left-wing Labor Party under Jacinda Ardern in 2017—he lost interest.

Instead, Thiel hunkered down at his estate in Maui. He'd paid $27 million in 2011—a record price at the time—for a home with ocean views and 4,500 square feet of living space. It was located on an undeveloped stretch of the island, with a high stone wall separating Thiel from the only road in the region. The other side had a pool and 1.7 acres, almost all of it beachfront.

It was, in short, a perfectly lovely place from which to survey the chaos of the next few months. Starting in mid-March, New York and most other major American cities shut down almost entirely. News programs grimly displayed hospitals that looked like war zones, with bodies stacked in refrigerated trucks and nurses using garbage bags in lieu of surgical gowns because of a shortage of personal protective equipment. At the height of the initial outbreak, in mid-April, more than 2,200 people were dying each day in the United States alone.

Eventually government lockdowns paid off. Case numbers and deaths fell, and by early May it seemed reasonable to begin to think about reopening. Yes, seventy thousand Americans had died by that point, but the serious outbreaks had been arrested, and a sense of normalcy seemed within reach as long as social distancing and mask guidelines were followed and officials kept certain sectors of the economy, like bars and restaurants, closed and restricted indoor events. This would obviously look like wishful thinking in retrospect, but it seemed possible that workers could start returning to offices that summer. September seemed a sure bet for school reopening.

During this period of guarded optimism, I learned through intermediaries that Thiel was considering talking to me on the record about the coronavirus. He saw the virus as a vindication, which made a certain sense: There had been a sudden collapse of the economies around the world driven by an unlikely calamity related to globalization. He'd predicted some version of this twelve years earlier in the wild essays he'd published as a hedge fund manager. When he'd written "The Optimistic Thought Experiment," Thiel's anxiety about an apocalypse seemed laughable to his peers, and uncomfortably strange to some of his employees. He was a successful hedge fund manager, sitting on billions of dollars in capital gains, talking like a revivalist preacher about the dangers of the very forces that had propelled him to wealth—the rise of the technology industry, the explosion of trade, the free movement of information across borders. But who was laughing now? Not the "cosmopolitan" types, as Thiel had described them, who considered "this sort of hysterical talk about the end of the world . . . to be the exclusive province of people who were either stupid or wicked or insane (although mostly just stupid)." Thiel had been criticized for his hard-line immigration stance and mocked as a prepper when he'd acquired New Zealand citizenship. Now Trump was being criticized for *not* closing the U.S. border to Europe when he closed it to China, and regular Americans were hoarding toilet paper and trading tips on where to get the best dried beans.

Ten years earlier, the Thiel Fellowship had been seen as reckless. But Thiel had only convinced twenty students per year to skip going to Harvard. Now Harvard was forced to close its entire campus—effectively replacing a world-class $50,000 education, plus another $25,000 for room and board, with a bunch of Zoom classes that still cost $50,000. Thiel's view, that college was an overpriced mechanism for enforcing class distinctions, seemed a whole lot more reasonable than it had in 2010, and it seemed possible to believe that the education "bubble" he'd warned me about might be bursting. Not twenty students, but 20 *percent* of Harvard's incoming freshman class had chosen to skip the 2020–21 school year. Some of them would never be back, and smaller, less prestigious colleges, which were already struggling, faced serious financial hardship. The entire education sector seemed like it could conceivably collapse, just as Thiel had predicted it would.

Even Thiel's fruitless efforts to send the Trump administration in a far-right direction suddenly looked a little bit more reasonable. Balaji Srinivasan, his FDA candidate, whom even Trump's wildest adviser, Steve Bannon, had considered "crazy," raised the alarm about the dangers of a pandemic in January, when most government experts were advising calm. Thiel's instincts that government health agencies were sclerotic and in need of disruption also seemed at least more in the ballpark after the Centers for Disease Control insisted on developing a more complicated and ultimately flawed test, and the FDA refused to approve the simpler test that the rest of the world used. This put the United States roughly six weeks behind South Korea, which arrested its own outbreak quickly.

And then there was Silicon Valley. Factory workers had been laid off, restaurants had closed, shopping malls were abandoned—but the world that Peter Thiel inhabited was absolutely booming. All the predictions about the ways that technology would subsume aspects of our lives— "Software is eating the world," as the venture capitalist Marc Andreessen famously put it—were suddenly, forcefully, coming true. Every primary and secondary school in America suddenly needed a Zoom account, and every child needed a tablet. Amazon sales—on everything from cloth bandanas to 1,000-piece jigsaw puzzles—spiked so dramatically that the company had to triage its shipping times. Companies scrambled to sign up for Slack, and we joked about having "finished" Netflix. Online social networks might be a proxy for a real social life, but suddenly they were all we had. "The techlash is over," Srinivasan gloated on Twitter.

The tech surge was a financial phenomenon as well as a cultural one. After dropping precipitously following the lockdowns in March, the S&P 500 index recovered and was actually up for the year by July. Almost all of those gains were due to the handful of big tech companies that now dominated the index. Amazon was up 71 percent, Apple was up 51 percent, and Facebook was up 31 percent. Zuckerberg's net worth would cross $100 billion the following month. All this even as the unemployment rate was above 10 percent.

Thiel, too, was getting richer. The sudden embrace of ecommerce was good for Amazon, of course, but it was also good for Stripe, the payment processing company in which Thiel held a significant stake and which raised $600 million at a $36 billion valuation. A person close to Thiel estimated that his Stripe stake was worth around $1.5 billion, but that was before November, when Stripe reportedly began raising a new round, this time at a valuation of around $100 billion. Airbnb was weathering the sudden collapse of the travel industry better than the traditional hotel industry and was preparing to go public at a valuation that was said to be around $35 billion. By the time it happened, in December, the market cap was $87 billion. By March 2021, it was up to $110 billion. Founders Fund had 5 percent of that too.

Meanwhile, Thiel's decades-old bet on the military-industrial complex had never looked better. Anduril, the startup built on the back of Trump's promise to strengthen border security and founded by Johnson's friend Palmer Luckey, raised $200 million in July, doubling its valuation to $2 billion. SpaceX became the first private company to send humans into orbit, successfully launching two NASA astronauts, Bob Behnken and Doug Hurley, and docking them to the International Space Station. Trump, happy for any news not related to the pandemic, traveled with Mike Pence to watch the launch off of Cape Canaveral, Florida. "It's incredible—the technology, the power," Trump said a few hours after the launch, referring to Musk as "one of our great brains." Not long after, the Defense Department would announce that SpaceX had won another launch contract, worth more than $300 million, and the company's valuation would climb to $74 billion—with Founders Fund standing to benefit from its inevitable public offering too.

On top of these gains, much of Thiel's net worth was still tied up in Palantir, a company that was almost uniquely positioned to profit from the coronavirus and of which he held a little less than one-fifth of the equity, personally and through his investment firms. The virus was a problem for doctors, virologists, and epidemiologists to solve, but in the near term it was a data problem. While scientists raced to create a vaccine, governments and big hospital systems had to figure out where the hotspots were appearing and then allocate supplies accordingly. Palantir's software, rewritten after the company's attempt to win business in Europe, was already being used to manage some health care supply chains, but starting in early March, the company moved all its research and development employees to work on COVID-related problems, adding functions to its existing offerings that would, for instance, allow corporate clients to easily pull in government data about cases and hospitalization numbers and then incorporate that into their sales projections. For government health departments, which were all scrambling to find anything to help bolster their supply chains and modeling, the software was a natural fit and was used to distribute ventilators and personal protective equipment. The push led to more than a hundred new deals with customers in a matter of months, including dozens of public health agencies.

"Our company was forged and reforged through crises," Shyam Sankar, Karp's deputy, told me in an interview, rattling off a series of cata-clysms: 9/11, Palantir's raison d'être, followed by the financial crisis, the rise of cyber-attacks, and Palantir's work helping the military combat ISIS. "The pandemic, in some ways, is the most recent version of that."

Beyond its expertise in crisis management, Thiel's company had a second strength that was arguably even more important: extracting large sums of money from the U.S. government, and especially Donald Trump's government. In early May, the Department of Health and Human Services, which had already given Palantir a contract after Thiel and Sankar had met with NIH director Francis Collins, awarded it two more contracts, worth $25 million, to design a new software system that would be used by the White House Coronavirus Task Force to track cases, hospital data, supplies of personal protective equipment, and testing sites. The deals were classified as "emergency acquisitions," meaning they were awarded without competing bids.

The sense that the Trump administration had given a political ally a role in a matter so crucial and, given Trump's propensity to downplay the seriousness of the pandemic, politically sensitive was heightened in July when, as cases spiked in the southern United States, the administration ordered hospitals to stop reporting to the CDC—which had previously overseen data collection and which had been making its data available publicly—and send it to the new HHS system instead. Several lawmakers and a former CDC director accused Trump of making the change in order to conceal the severity of the outbreak from the public. "Rather than strengthening the public health data system to improve hospital reporting, the administration has chosen to hand data to an unproven, commercial entity, reporting to political appointees, not scientific experts," former director Tom Frieden tweeted. "People in Arizona, Texas, South Carolina, Florida and elsewhere are already paying the price for this."

The White House balked at accusations of mismanagement and, after briefly taking the CDC data offline, allowed the agency to begin disclosing it again. Palantir, meanwhile, denied that the no-bid contract it had received had come thanks to any preferential treatment. In interviews, company representatives emphasized that Thiel's involvement was minor anyway. "It's very interesting," said Sankar. "If you look at Palantir pre-Trump it was always described as Alex Karp's Palantir, which it is, by the way. And then post-Trump suddenly a switch flipped, and it became 'Peter Thiel's Palantir.' I think that relates more to external perception than to some sort of internal reality."

This was true in a sense—Palantir employees rarely saw Thiel—but it was also deeply misleading. In late June, Palantir announced that it had appointed a woman to its board, a necessary step if the company hoped to go public since California law requires public companies to have at least one female board member. There had been rumors that the company was courting Condoleezza Rice, but Palantir instead nominated Alexandra Wolfe Schiff, Thiel's longtime friend and the author of a flattering book about the Thiel Fellowship. She would be one of six board members, out of seven, with close ties to Thiel. (In November, Adam Ross, a former *Stanford Review* editor in chief, would leave the board; he was replaced in January by an Accenture managing director with no obvious ties to Thiel, Lauren Friedman.)

To those who knew Thiel well, the nomination of Wolfe Schiff seemed particularly brazen. Wolfe Schiff, who lives in New York, had often stayed at Thiel's house during visits to the West Coast, and during the mid-2000s, before Thiel was fully out, she'd posed as Thiel's girlfriend at Davos, according to the journalist Felix Salmon. Shortly after the announcement, an associate sent Thiel a text asking if he'd intended the Wolfe Schiff appointment as a troll. After all, offering Wolfe Schiff as the first woman on the Palantir board was quite the fuck-you to the PC police. Thiel's response: a winking emoji with its tongue sticking out.

LIKE EVERYBODY, Thiel spent the pandemic worrying—especially about the future of arguably his most important investment. Some days, he seemed sure that Trump was going to pull it off; the president's message of "law and order," a callback to Nixon, would win over the Democratic party's lurch to the left on racial politics. Other days, he was convinced that the coronavirus and the ensuing recession would make Trump unelectable.

It was hard to be dispassionate. Thiel had anticipated a global crisis that would bring the world economy to its knees, and he'd positioned himself to profit from that chaos, just as he'd called the financial crisis and set himself up to profit from the fallout. But, as in 2008, when he'd secretly encouraged the forces of disruption—sending out sober-minded letters to Clarium's investors warning of the dangers of anti-immigrant populism while secretly funding the very same movement—he'd also helped plant the seeds of the chaos that followed the spread of COVID-19. He'd helped Trump overcome Republicans who'd feared that his narcissism and authoritarian tendencies would be disastrous in a crisis, and he'd helped create and protect Facebook, which was now facilitating the spread of misinformation that encouraged Americans to shun masks, take unproven and potentially harmful treatments, like the antimalarial hydroxychloroquine and even industrial bleach. If the Trump presidency ended in failure, it would be Thiel's failure, too.

He began telling friends that he was considering buying property in Switzerland and might move there if Trump lost, presumably to protect his IRA from any changes in policy by the Biden administration, which he feared might attempt to finish what Obama had started. Palantir's IPO filing in September 2020 was of a piece with this thinking—as clear a sign as any, according to several associates, that Thiel was hoping to cash out as much as possible before capital gains taxes could be raised or the rules on IRAs revised. He'd spent two decades accumulating billions in assets tax-free. He had no intention of paying taxes now.

In conversations with friends, he'd taken to referring to Trump's White House as "the S.S. *Minnow*"—the hapless fishing charter that runs aground in the show *Gilligan's Island*. Of course, in this analogy,

Trump was the skipper. There were, as Thiel told a friend in a text, "lots of Gilligans." In an unrelated nautical metaphor, Thiel said that changes to Trump's campaign were the equivalent of "rearranging deck chairs on the *Titanic*."

Eventually, Thiel's employees leaked these gripes to the press, hoping to create some distance between their boss and the flailing Republican candidate. After *The Daily Beast* and *The Wall Street Journal* reported that he was souring on Trump, some assumed he judged Trump's coronavirus response to be an indictment of his presidency, and that perhaps Thiel would embrace more centrist politics. But this wasn't true. Thiel agreed with Trump that concerns about COVID were overblown, telling friends he thought the lockdowns were "crazy" and overly broad.

Nor was Thiel's inner circle moderating—if anything, they seemed disappointed that Trump had surrounded himself with centrist types and hadn't pushed for the hard-right populism that Bannon and others had initially promised. After Trump's Supreme Court pick Neil Gorsuch sided with liberals and moderates in ruling that gay and transgender workers were deserving of civil rights protection, Blake Masters, the Thiel adviser who'd cowritten *Zero to One*, complained that the party had betrayed conservatives. He wrote, sardonically, that the point of the Republican party seemed to be, among other things, "to protect private equity, low taxes, free pornography."

Masters, who'd moved to Arizona, had been flirting with the possibility of mounting a primary challenge to the reelection campaign of Republican senator Martha McSally, after complaining that she'd been insufficiently loyal to Trump. He decided against that, but Thiel was backing a similar candidacy in Kansas, where Kris Kobach, who'd helped create Trump's most extreme immigration proposals (and who also had a history of opposing gay rights) was now running for Senate as the Trumpist candidate against Roger Marshall, a moderate Republican.

Thiel donated $2.1 million to Kobach, becoming his main patron. This included two donations totaling $1.25 million in July, just before the Republican primary. Though Thiel had donated $5,600 directly to Kobach's campaign in 2019, he funneled these donations through a newly created political action committee, the Free Forever PAC, which promised "to secure our border, create America First immigration policy, take care of our veterans, end endless wars, and build an economy that works for American workers."

In addition to his usual nativist positions, Kobach had, in seeking the nomination, fanned the conspiratorial flames about the coronavirus. In an interview a week before the primary—and two weeks after getting his latest check from Thiel's PAC—Kobach told an interviewer that he believed hospitals and doctors were exaggerating the severity of the pandemic to hurt Trump, by recording accidental deaths, like car accidents, as COVID deaths. "I believe that the numbers are being cooked," he said. On primary day, he lost to Marshall by fourteen points.

EXPERTS HAD CALLED for a gradual reopening of the economy and the continued reliance on social distancing and masks. Trump dismissed all of this as political posturing, insisting, at various times, that the terrible virus was being vanquished by his administration, or that it actually was no worse than the flu, or both. He disparaged mask wearing as "politically correct," and touted unproven remedies and magical thinking. In Trump's mind, at least, the United States was continually "rounding the final turn." He discouraged state governors from testing patients (and recording cases) and, six months before vaccines would be available, insisted on holding indoor rallies with thousands of largely unmasked attendees.

And much of the United States reopened all at once, with Thiel's network often cheering on the lack of caution. Keith Rabois, Thiel's old friend from Stanford, tweeted endlessly about the prophylactic benefits of hydroxychloroquine, even as study after study showed it did not help prevent COVID cases or deaths. Rabois's response to this was the line that Thiel's FDA nominees had used: He blamed the bureaucracy of drug trials. "Randomized control trials are horrible ideas," he tweeted. When Weinberg, the Roche executive, argued with him, Rabois shot back, "Obviously someone is jealous of my success."

Musk used his platform to minimize the severity of the disease, to tout hydroxychloroquine, and to call for a complete reopening of the economy—which he was particularly interested in because Tesla was facing a substantial order backlog. "FREE AMERICA NOW," he tweeted. A week or so later, he ignored a county lockdown order and reopened Tesla's factory in Fremont, California. The result of this would be stark: according to public health data released as part of a freedom of information request, between May and December, there were about 440 cases among Tesla workers in Fremont.

As if on cue, cases began spiking again. There was a second wave that hit the Sunbelt starting in late May, with Texas and Florida each recording thousands of deaths in a span of several weeks, and then, just as Election Day approached, a third wave surged, starting in the Midwest and spreading to the rest of the country by December. At the high point of this spike, more than 4,000 Americans were dying each day. By now, Thiel's network had gone mostly silent about the pandemic and were back to tweeting about cryptocurrencies, the hideousness of the Black Lives Matter movement, and the social media companies' censorship of stories linking the Democratic presidential candidate Joe Biden's son Hunter to corruption.

The Trump administration, whose coronavirus response was now under the influence of a Hoover Institution–affiliated radiologist, Scott Atlas, had given up trying to stop the pandemic at all. Trump touted herd immunity as a strategy—that is, allowing the virus to infect a sizable enough portion of the population so that our broadly acquired immunity would protect society as a whole—mistakenly calling it "herd mentality." In October, the president himself contracted COVID, went to the hospital, and then shrugged it off, dismissing the potentially deadly virus as the "sniffles" when it was reported that his son, Barron, had also contracted the virus. Mark Meadows, Trump's chief of staff, appeared on CNN to question the helpfulness of mask wearing and other basic doctor-recommended mitigations. "We're not going to control the pandemic," Meadows said, comparing it to the flu.

WHILE THE COUNTRY continued to reel, Thiel was busy cashing out. On August 25, as the country surpassed 175,000 deaths, Palantir submitted its S-1 filing with the Securities and Exchange Commission—the formal document announcing its intention to go public. Karp had been saying for months that he was thinking about following Thiel out of Silicon Valley—and now he'd revealed his destination: Denver. The S-1 also included a stem-winder of a letter criticizing his former home base. "Our company was founded in Silicon Valley," Karp had written. "But we seem to share fewer and fewer of the technology sector's values and commitments." It continued:

> Software projects with our nation's defense and intelligence agencies, whose missions are to keep us safe, have become controversial, while companies built on advertising dollars are commonplace. For many consumer internet companies, our thoughts and inclinations, behaviors and browsing habits, are the product for sale. The slogans and marketing of many of the Valley's largest technology firms attempt to obscure this simple fact. The world's largest consumer internet companies have never had greater access to the most intimate aspects of our lives. And the advance of their technologies has outpaced the development of the forms of political control that are capable of governing their use.

It was a searing indictment of Silicon Valley, especially Facebook, delivered by the CEO of a company founded by Facebook's earliest and most significant backer. It also harked back to the vision of the Valley that had always interested Thiel: the starched-collar conservatism of the military-industrial complex.

It was also, to me anyway, familiar—months earlier Charles Johnson had sent me a similar memo about Clearview. "Silicon Valley companies say they want to make the world a better place, but they put fat ad profits over democracy and safety," he'd written. In Silicon Valley, he continued, "they take private data and sell it to advertisers." On the other hand, "Google hates the military." After the filing appeared, Johnson called me. "Sounds like everything I've written," he said, noting that he'd sent the same notes to Thiel.

The Palantir filing wasn't just an ideological statement—it presented a portrait of a company that was capitalizing on the pandemic, and more broadly on the Trump era. Sankar's boasts about thriving in a crisis were accurate. Palantir had taken in $466 million in revenue in 2016; it had generated more in just the first half of 2020. The U.S. Army accounted for $79 million of this—more than 15 percent of total revenue—and other government contracts, including the Maven deal and the company's work with ICE and HHS services, would add tens of million more.

Yes, Palantir was raking in enormous sums of money—$165 million during that period—and its losses were narrowing. Those losses wouldn't matter to Thiel, who was positioned to profit handsomely from the public listing regardless of Palantir's long-term fate. The S-1 showed a thicket of venture capital firms, investment vehicles, and entities connected to him in one way or another. He owned shares through multiple Rivendell funds, the name linked to his IRA, as well as through Mithril, Founders Fund, Clarium, PT Ventures, STS Holdings, and others.

This added up to roughly 20 percent of the company, but Thiel, who'd long been a fan of dictatorships, had arranged things to give himself far more control than even that would imply. Beyond a board of directors loyal to the founder, Palantir had created a new class of shares that would control just under 50 percent of the voting power. These shares would be held in a trust controlled by three men: Karp, Stephen Cohen, and Thiel—and at any time Thiel could choose to use some of his other shares to increase that percentage, giving him de facto control. Incredibly, they would maintain this level of control even if they sold large chunks of their stock, which Thiel was planning on doing immediately.

The stock opened at $10 a share, making Palantir worth about $20 billion. Thiel immediately began cashing out, selling shares worth more than $250 million personally, and then another $20 million or so through Founders Fund. The country might have been in crisis, and his political project was collapsing—but he was doing fine.

BETTER THAN FINE, ACTUALLY. The country was full of uncertainty as the votes were counted during the first week of November, as it became increasingly clear—to all but Trump and many in the Thielverse—that Trump had lost and the pandemic was getting worse, and that the president had no interest in doing anything to slow its spread or to provide further aid to workers during the Biden transition.

As Trump and his affiliates spread misinformation about voter fraud, claiming that the election had been stolen from them by a handful of crooked cities with majority Black populations, Thiel was silent. But the Thielverse was abuzz with anecdotes about secret uncounted votes in key swing states and about a general sense that the truth—that Joe Biden, the candidate supported by a decisive majority of Americans, had won the election—was somehow in doubt. Eric Weinstein, a Thiel employee and Intellectual Dark Web podcaster, tweeted videos of a purported postal service whistleblower (distributed by conservative journalist and provocateur James O'Keefe, another person who had once called Thiel a patron). He warned that Trump was being "played off" by the media without due process. Blake Masters, who was preparing for another possible Senate run, with Thiel backing his campaign, tweeted darkly about the Dominion voting machines used in Arizona, picking up on a conspiracy theory alleging that the electronic voting machine manufacturer somehow changed people's votes and claimed, offering no evidence, that dead people had voted in Milwaukee and Detroit. These all turned out to be false.

Curtis Yarvin, the neo-reactionary intellectual and Thiel's longtime friend, went much further. He published an essay that claimed that voters in "urban communities" had, through some mix of manipulation by organizers and actual voter fraud, stolen the election for Biden, or "China Joe," as he called the president-elect, referring to Biden's supposed deference to Beijing. Then Yarvin suggested that Republicans execute what he called a "very legal coup" to "steal the election back" by getting Republican-controlled state legislatures to invalidate the vote, and then having Trump claim emergency powers, ignoring any interference from Congress or the judiciary and using the National Guard to enforce his orders. After that, Yarvin argued, Trump could "liquidate the powerful, prestigious, and/or wealthy institutions of the old regime, inside and *outside* the formal government," which, he said, would be followed by the achievement of "a singular vision of utopia."

It was perhaps a joke or maybe a thought experiment—Yarvin conceded, with some regret, that Trump was too incompetent and weak to pull it off and he did, to his credit, say that he wasn't advocating a Stalin-like purge. But it was a near-perfect echo of Thiel's old thought experiment: a deliberate election loss, followed by military coup. Yarvin said the whole thing was going to work out just fine and had been rooting for Biden anyway. Trump's loss would cause Trumpism to thrive—as Thiel had always hoped. He predicted a restoration in 2024. "Red America's story gets much simpler and easier to sell," he wrote,

Amid the uncertainty and rising deaths, Palantir's stock price started to climb thanks to a collection of new COVID-related contracts, including a recently announced one to help the Department of Health and Human Services track vaccines. By early January, it was worth more than $40 billion. A headline that fall had summed it up succinctly: PETER THIEL'S PALANTIR IS SKYROCKETING AS TRUMP'S PROSPECTS GROW

DIM. For his entire career Thiel had been backing long shots, profiting from their unlikely success, and then ghosting them just before things went south. Now he'd done it with an American president.

AND YET, THE TRUMP ADMINISTRATION wasn't over—and although Thiel might have successfully absented himself from Trumpist politics to focus on business, the influence of the Thielverse was still very much felt in Washington.

Thiel remained, quietly, a Trump supporter as his allies and employees understood, even if he wasn't saying it out loud. The nature of the Thielverse—in which courtiers vied with one another to please him, acting independently in the hopes of securing further patronage—meant that even if he disappeared into a bunker indefinitely, they would ensure that the white identity politics he'd been nurturing since his college days would continue. Thiel's ideology is not especially coherent, but to the extent there was an ideology, it was that a less democratic America, purged of its multicultural delusions and pieties, would somehow lead to economic and technological progress. A critic might call this fascistic; Thiel called it going "back to the future."

His preferred 2024 candidate had long been Josh Hawley, the populist Missouri senator and diehard Trump ally. Hawley shared Ted Cruz's politics and had similar intellectual credentials, but he was a decade younger than Cruz, with a square jaw, a trim physique, and a deep voice. At the National Conservatism Conference where Thiel had attacked Google's complicity with China, Hawley had chosen for his target what he called "the cosmopolitan consensus." He used that anti-Semitic trope repeatedly to refer to a group of business leaders and university presidents who, he claimed, weren't loyal to America but to their own elite project. When Jewish groups suggested he apologize for the reference, Hawley saw an opportunity to score anti-PC points, tweeting that "the liberal language police have lost their minds."

So committed was Thiel's champion in the Senate to claiming the Make America Great Again mantle from Trump that he continued to imply that Trump might still win the election long after the vote counts were in. In late December—even after evidence failed to emerge that Dominion had changed any votes in Georgia, Arizona, and Michigan, and even as it was becoming increasingly clear that the stories about dead Democrats going to the polls in Milwaukee and Detroit were fanciful— Hawley announced that he would object to the congressional certification of the election on January 6, turning what is normally a formality into a moment of high drama. A few days later, Cruz made a similar announcement, along with ten other Republican senators.

Trump, who was attempting to pressure Vice President Mike Pence into trying to disrupt the certification, had encouraged supporters to amass in Washington that day. Thousands of them showed up—drawn in from QAnon and alt-right "Stop the Steal" groups that had formed and been nurtured on Facebook. They were angry, and some of them were armed for combat. Around midday, as Congress was preparing to vote, Trump hyped the protestors up further with a bellicose speech. He thanked the senators and others for holding the line and urged the crowd to march to the Capitol. "Fight like hell," Trump said. "If you don't fight like hell, you're not going to have a country anymore." As he walked into the Capitol, Hawley saluted the protestors with a raised fist.

In the hours that followed, Yarvin's thought experiment—and in some sense, two decades of Thielism—became suddenly, brutally literal. A violent mob chanting "Treason, treason" and "Hang Mike Pence" broke into the congressional chambers, attempting to end the certification of the election and ensure that Trump would remain president. They viciously attacked journalists and Capitol Police, including Officer Brian Sicknick. He died the following day, and two of his colleagues took their own lives not long after the insurrection. Four rioters died.

In a way, the failed attempt to overthrow American democracy had nothing to do with Thiel, who'd been quiet for nearly all of 2020. But just as, years earlier, he'd set in motion events that made inevitable the 2014 theft of user data by Cambridge Analytica's and Facebook's complicity in pro-Trump misinformation during the 2016 campaign, so had he planted many of the seeds that led to the failed insurrection. On January 11, with Hawley's career in apparent ruins, as moderate Republicans began speaking openly about a "big lie" perpetrated by him and others, *Axios* published a short item: WHAT PETER THIEL GOT WRONG ABOUT DONALD TRUMP. It blamed Thiel for having "helped establish and then cement a viewpoint through which even Trump's most egregious statements were taken at other than face value." That month, with Peter Thiel's political project in apparent ruins, Palantir's market capitalization would rise as high as $68 billion.

EPILOGUE

—

YOU WILL LIVE FOREVER

D espite Thiel's wide-ranging influence—despite the dozens of companies he has been associated with, the billions of dollars he's earned, and the role he's played in the rise of the far-right—many people still know him for one thing: his dalliances with a novel field of experimental biology known as parabiosis.

The term describes surgically joining two bodies so that their circulatory systems merge, creating, in effect, synthetic conjoined twins. Based on experiments that were conducted in the 1970s in which older rats were attached to younger ones, scientists and antiaging enthusiasts have speculated that the grisly procedure might hold the key to halting the aging process, and perhaps to ending death itself. It represents, for believers anyway, a possible fountain of youth.

A 2016 study on mice helped set off a flurry of interest about the prospect for adapting the idea to humans, by transfusing older patients with blood from young ones, which would supposedly rejuvenate them. It was, in other words, a sort of vampirism. "I'm looking into parabiosis stuff, which I think is really interesting," Thiel said in an interview published that year. He suggested that he'd considered injecting young blood as part of his own health regimen but noted that he had not pursued it yet.

Thiel's interest in parabiosis led to wild speculation—and lots of snark. Gawker heard a rumor that he had been paying $40,000 to get quarterly infusions from an eighteen-year-old. The following year, HBO's *Silicon Valley* dedicated an entire episode to the subject, having the show's evil corporate character, Gavin Belson, receive transfusions from a strapping "blood boy"—or as Belson described him, "my transfusion associate." (The actor who'd played the Thiel character had died during the series' first season, and some of Thiel's quirks found their way into Belson.)

In late 2018, during his last interview with a major U.S. media outlet before the pandemic hit—at *The New York Times*'s annual DealBook conference—Thiel addressed the issue. The conference's host, the financial columnist Andrew Ross Sorkin, had started to ask him a question about life extension research in general. Then he stopped, mid-sentence, and brought up the rumors. "By the way, true or not true?"

Thiel smirked, and started waving his hand. "I'm not even sure what I'm supposed to say," he began. "I want to publicly tell you I'm not a vampire."

The 2016 mouse study did have a Thiel connection. It had been funded by SENS, the nonprofit founded by Aubrey de Grey and backed by Thiel. The lab, which I visited in early 2020, just before the lockdown, was functional, if not fancy—a one-story office building next to a freeway interchange outside of Mountain View, California. De Grey had a Rip Van Winkle beard and had been working out of a cramped office just off the lab, with an overflowing bookshelf and a bicycle propped up against the wall. He credited Thiel for having seeded an entire generation of believers in his cause. The Thielverse, he told me, is made up of "people who grew up understanding that aging was a medical problem that we were in striking distance of fixing. They never had to be persuaded."

Thiel has declared that he sees SENS's work as part of his most important legacy and that it is at the very center of his religious faith. "The one part of the Christian view that I believe more strongly than anything," he said in a 2015 appearance with the theologian N. T. Wright, "is that idea that death is evil, that it is wrong, and that we should not accept it. We should fight it in every way that we possibly can." At the end of 2019, the organization recruited a new CEO, James O'Neill, a longtime employee at Thiel's companies (and one of Thiel's suggestions to run the FDA). At the time of my visit, SENS had been enjoying some modest success, having spun out several research projects into early-stage companies and attracted a number of new donors, including Vitalik Buterin, the creator of the technology behind the Ethereum cryptocurrency and, years earlier, a Thiel Fellow.

But the success was fleeting. In the summer of 2021, two female entrepreneurs accused De Grey of sexual harassment. De Grey denied wrongdoing, but was fired the following month. O'Neill resigned as CEO. Not that this affected Thiel. His last donation to SENS had been in 2016 and he'd kept his distance since. During my visit, De Grey had mentioned that, despite talking up SENS's work often in the press, Thiel had never actually visited the nonprofit's laboratory, which is located just eight miles from Palantir's Palo Alto office. At the time, this made me wonder if Thiel's live-forever messaging was sincere. Did he actually want to cure death? Or was this just a useful story that had helped him build his brand as a contrarian—a piece on the chessboard that he'd discard given the opportunity?

It became harder not to question Thiel's sincerity about the scourge of human mortality in the months that followed, as he stayed quiet while Trump shrugged through a humanitarian crisis without precedent in recent American history. How could anyone devoted to life extension not be moved by so many preventable deaths? By late March 2021 more than 550,000 Americans had died from COVID, making the pandemic deadlier than U.S. casualties in World War I and World War II combined. The United States had suffered one of the worst per-capita mortality rates in the world. How had those grim figures not moved him to break with Trump or to at least spend his money more ambitiously to try to help? How was it that his most ambitious donation of 2020 had been to the political action committee of one of America's most prominent nativists, Kris Kobach?

I tried to ask him about this, of course. But the promised interview never materialized, and as COVID-19 case levels soared anew, Thiel's representative stopped returning my emails. Instead, Thiel spoke to *Die Weltwoche,* a Swiss newspaper whose editor Roger Köppel is a member of the country's national-conservative People's Party. During an interview with Köppel, Thiel characterized the disease as a mental pathology rather than a physical one. "I see it as a psychological indicator that people know deep down: There is no way back to the old normal," he said.

He continued: "COVID-19 created a shift. There used to be this feeling that the future was being held back somehow. Changes that should have taken place long ago did not come because there was resistance. Now the future is set free." He was, it seemed, welcoming the pandemic as a chance to reset society according to his ideals and plans.

Nor did he break with Trump, as his employees had led the press to believe. "I still support him," he said of Trump, describing then-candidate Biden as "a slightly younger, more senile version of Pétain," the puppet head of state of Nazi-occupied France. Thiel believed Biden would sell the United States out to China, just as Marshal Pétain had sold out the French to Germany. For Trump, on the other hand, Thiel had nothing but praise for a "pragmatic" response. Trump "didn't stick with the extreme health experts who called for a total shutdown," he said.

Thiel remained loyal to Trump through the end, and, on the final day of Trump's presidency, helped secure a pardon for Anthony Levandowski, a driverless car engineer who'd been sentenced to eighteen months of prison after admitting to stealing intellectual property from Google. It was a final elbow to his longtime nemeses at Google, and a sign that even though Thiel might have gone quiet, he wasn't abandoning his extreme beliefs.

"He has not reverted back to Republicanism," Steve Bannon told me in late January, three weeks after the insurrection. "He's full MAGA."

THE CONTRAST BETWEEN Thiel's professed hatred of death and his apparent indifference to the many hundreds of thousands of deaths from COVID was one of the many examples that I encountered in the reporting of this book where Thiel's most deeply held beliefs seemed at odds with his Machiavellian actions. That these inconsistencies mostly have gone unnoticed, and that Thiel is regarded as a contrarian free-thinker rather than a calculating operator, is a testament to his singular facility for personal branding. He is self-created, a Silicon Valley Oz, who has, through networking and a capacity for storytelling, constructed an image so compelling that it has come to obscure the man behind it. This makes him a quintessentially American figure—even if exigencies of tax planning may at some point allow Germany or New Zealand (or some future seastead nation not yet built) to lay claim to him.

The Thiel mythology contains a good deal of truth: He has created companies that have defined our culture and economy over the past quarter century. The industry that Thiel helped build is responsible for trillions of dollars in wealth creation and hundreds of thousands of jobs. He has been the rare futurist who actually managed to accelerate the future—and for that, at least, he deserves history's respect.

And yet this is only half the story because Thiel has also contributed to a reactionary turn in our politics and society that has left the United States in a much more uncertain place than he found it in when he went into business for himself in the mid-1990s. He is a critic of big tech who has done more to increase the dominance of big tech than perhaps any living person. He is a self-proclaimed privacy advocate who founded one of the world's largest surveillance companies. He is a champion of meritocracy and intellectual diversity who has surrounded himself with a self-proclaimed mafia of loyalists. And he is a champion of free speech who secretly killed a major U.S. media outlet. "He's a nihilist, a really smart nihilist," said Matt Stoller, the anti-monopoly activist and author of *Goliath*:

The 100-Year War Between Monopoly Power and Democracy. "He's entirely about power—it's the law of the jungle. 'I'm a predator and the predators win.'" That, more than anything, may be the lesson that Thiel's followers have learned—the real meaning of "move fast and break things."

In the months after January 6, Thiel retreated from public life. He was a parent now, with a growing family—just as this book was going to press that spring 2021, there were whispers in the Thielverse that he and Danzeisen had added a second child—and parenthood has a way of subverting even one's most ambitious plans. Given Thiel's obsession with his own mortality, that shift might be even more pronounced. Parenthood, after all, offers a chance at a living legacy, literal life after death. Most of us would judge having a child and raising her well to be a far better investment in the eternal than even the most groundbreaking achievements in mouse surgery. Friends have said they've seen a softening; Thiel seems more at ease, maybe even happier. This could be a projection—one of Thiel's talents is to present a canvas onto which others can ascribe their own ideas—but it probably isn't.

Moreover, Thiel's legacy is assured, even if he were to withdraw entirely. His acolytes are some of the highest profile thought leaders emanating from Silicon Valley. Elon Musk can move markets with a single tweet—driving downloads of the secure messaging app Signal or helping to convince Reddit investors to buy shares in the money-losing mall retailer GameStop. Keith Rabois, an original satellite in the Thielverse, is a partner at Founders Fund and has been, on a daily basis, amplifying Thiel's message that the Bay Area should be abandoned by anyone with money or ambition. Rabois purchased a home in Miami Beach in December, complaining about California's high taxes and its COVID-19 restrictions. Thiel also relocated, acquiring two properties in Miami Beach at the end of 2020, a good spot for him given that Florida, unlike California, doesn't tax capital gains, and is not far from the de facto headquarters of the Republican Party, Donald Trump's Mar-a-Lago Club. Founders Fund opened an office in South Florida too.

Meanwhile, Max Levchin, Thiel's PayPal cofounder, wants to destroy credit cards and algorithmic credit ratings with his company Affirm, which went public in January 2021, at a value of around $25 billion. Another financial disrupter in Thiel's portfolio, Stripe, is seeking to displace current payment networks with its own high-tech payments system, just as Thiel envisioned decades ago. Stripe is one of the most valuable privately held companies in the world, and its cofounder, Patrick Collison, is a power center in his own right, promoting a Thielian vision of technology progress through his own book publisher, Stripe Press. Beyond his portfolio, Thiel has also seeded dozens of funds run by protégés—investors such as Sam Altman, William Eden, and Sarah Cone—often taking a substantial stake in their future performance bonuses, and thus ensuring that he will enjoy better returns than normal investors. And he's hired a new generation of bomb throwers, including Delian Asparouhov and Mike Solana, who have made it their mission to spread the Thielian gospel about the future and the dangers of the "woke mob."

Moreover, Thiel's impact is felt even among founders who've never met him. Just as Steve Jobs inspired a generation of monkish product visionaries, Thiel has inspired a generation of techno-contrarians who aspire to similar levels of success and power, and who, like the most practiced 1980s *Stanford Review* columnists, readily deploy (or hint at) sexism and racism to showcase their independence of thought. As one young tech founder put it in late November 2020 after advising thousands of Twitter followers not to "hire a hot young girl" early in a company's life, because naturally she would distract the male CEO from the real work, "IQ is real, bio sex is real, 0wn the libs, Hayek/Friedman ftw, 4 more years for DJT."

Beyond the tech industry, Thiel's political prospects are much less dire than they seemed immediately after January 6. Hawley defied his critics—including former senator John Danforth, his political mentor, who called supporting Hawley the "biggest mistake I've ever made in my life." He refused to apologize, and then used the controversy to his advantage. When Simon & Schuster canceled his forthcoming book, *The*

Tyranny of Big Tech, Hawley found a new publisher, Regnery, and went on a media tour in which he portrayed himself as the victim of a "cancel culture agenda" before millions of Americans. The book became a *New York Times* bestseller.

Hawley has said that he is not running for president in 2024, though he has plenty of time to change his mind. Ted Cruz will likely remain a force in Republican politics, and could also run for president, and there are other Thiel-friendly politicos waiting in the wings, including Fox News host Tucker Carlson and Florida governor Ron DeSantis.

And then there's the U.S. Senate, where Thiel had big plans for 2022. He was supporting two candidates: his longtime aide and coauthor, Blake Masters, and J. D. Vance, the author of *Hillbilly Elegy* and a former partner at Mithril, who spoke at the National Conservatism Conference with Thiel and is a contender to replace the moderate Ohio senator Rob Portman. In March 2021, a new Super PAC, Protect Ohio Values, announced that Thiel had pledged $10 million to support Vance's Senate run. Members of the Mercer family, longtime backers of *Breitbart* and Cambridge Analytica and allies of Thiel, were also said to be donors. At the time, two people in Thiel's circle told me they expected him to make a similar donation to Masters if he were to run, and the following month *Politico* reported that Thiel would do just that, contributing $10 million to a newly formed organization, the Saving Arizona PAC.

Masters is a committed Trumpist who visited the border wall shortly after the announcement of the Thiel donation. "Obviously this works," he said in a video posted to Twitter. Vance, on the other hand, opposed Trump in 2016 but has walked back this apostasy, appearing on Sebastian Gorka's podcast, warning of the dangers of Biden's universal child-care plan, and even tweeting what seemed to be a coded defense of QAnon. He met with the former president in Mar-a-Lago in the spring. Thiel was his chaperone.

As the primary campaign intensified, both candidates embraced platforms that parroted Thiel's views. Besides supporting hard-line immigration policies and *Stanford Review-style* views on race and gender, they both urged an end to Covid mitigation measures and said that the 2020 election had been fraudulent. They also were sharply critical of Facebook. In July 2021, Protect Ohio Values aired an ad in which Vance warned of "an elite who don't actually care about the American nation and the people who live in it." Among pictures of Hillary Clinton, Nancy Pelosi, and the Google headquarters was one of Mark Zuckerberg. There was no mention of the billionaire and Facebook board member who'd paid for the ad.

So it was not entirely surprising when in early February 2022, Thiel announced he was stepping down from board of Zuckerberg's company, which had been recently renamed Meta. In leaving a position he'd held since 2005—and one that had endowed him with otherworldly wealth and power—Thiel told associates that his intention was to focus on the restoration of Trump to political power. As if to make clear just how far he was willing to go, he hosted a fundraiser at his Miami home for a House candidate, Harriet Hageman. A crowd that included Donald Trump Jr. watched Thiel attack Hageman's primary opponent, Wyoming Representative Liz Cheney, who had been one of only a handful of Republicans to condemn Trump for inciting the assault on the Capitol.

The prospects of Thiel's 2022 candidates remained uncertain going into the primaries. But if they are successful, Masters and Vance will be among four U.S. senators who partly owe their seats to Peter Thiel's largesse. Moreover, Masters and Vance are different from Hawley and Cruz in that they don't just owe Thiel. They are, as two Thielworld insiders pointed out to me, extensions of him. Masters, as this book went to press, was COO of Thiel Capital and president of the Thiel Foundation; Vance, of course, is Thiel's former employee and counts Thiel as an investor in his venture capital firm.

Although it was hard to imagine that Thiel would be able to wield the same influence in the Biden administration that he did in Trump's White House, it was even harder to imagine that he'd have none at all. In the spring of 2021, Johnson told me he'd reconciled with Thiel, who had gotten over whatever qualms he'd had about Clearview and made a seed investment in Johnson's latest company, Traitwell. The genetic sequencing startup has designs of winning military contracts, following the model pioneered by Thiel at Palantir and later used by Anduril and Clearview. Johnson also mentioned that he'd recently come to a new and surprising realization about politics. The man who'd helped Thiel nurture the alt-right was now, he said, a Joe Biden supporter. He praised the Democratic president's defense and intelligence appointments, as well as his plan to create a DARPA-like agency focused on funding new healthcare technologies. Biden, he said, had the makings of a truly great president.

This conversion notwithstanding, Thiel had other contacts who were close to the Biden administration. Avril Haines, a 2020 campaign adviser and, in January, the new Director of National Intelligence, had served as a consultant for Palantir. A disclosure showed that just before joining Team Biden, she'd worked for Thiel's defense contractor, which paid her $180,000 in fees between July 2017 and June 2020. Meanwhile, one of the most prolific donors during the 2020 election was Reid Hoffman, who spent around $7 million personally and raised millions more to help Biden and the Democrats. Thiel and Hoffman may have their disagreements, but they remain close. The relationships forged by the PayPal Mafia will continue to pay off for years, if not decades.

———

BACK IN 2005, when Thiel was still trying on a new identity as a master of the universe, Steve Jobs gave a commencement speech at his alma mater. To this day, Jobs's Stanford University address is revered, both as a window into the Apple founder's psyche and a distillation of the rebelliousness of Silicon Valley in the 1990s and 2000s. Everyone in tech has watched it at least once; many know it nearly by heart.

"Truth be told, I never graduated from college," Jobs began. "This is the closest I've ever gotten to a college graduation." After explaining his decision to drop out from Reed College in the early 1970s before starting

Apple, Jobs revealed that he'd been diagnosed with pancreatic cancer and had been contemplating his death. He'd come to see mortality as a gift, he said—"the single best invention of life." "Remembering that I'll be dead soon is the most important tool I've ever encountered to make the big choices in life," Jobs continued. "Because almost everything—all external expectations, all pride, all fear of embarrassment or failure—these things just fall away in the face of death, leaving only what is truly important." He continued: "You are already naked. There is no reason not to follow your heart."

Thiel met Jobs a year later—a brief encounter at a wedding, during which Jobs didn't seem interested in having anything to do with Thiel. But Thiel seemed to have Jobs's commencement speech in his mind eleven years later, in May 2016, when he stepped up to a lectern at Hamilton College, in upstate New York, to deliver one of his own. It came at a turning point in his life and career—he'd just become a Trump delegate, and he was days away from being exposed as the architect of Gawker's destruction—and he used the speech to try to bury Jobs's New Age value system, while offering a new tech industry a new kind of founding myth.

The Apple cofounder had started his talk by declaring himself unqualified because he'd never graduated college; Thiel opened with a similar humblebrag. "You're about to begin working," he said. "I haven't worked for anybody for 21 years."

He then told the story of *his* decision to drop out—not from college, but from the world of corporate law. Jobs had presented his decision to leave college as financially motivated—he was wasting his parents' savings on an education that seemed of questionable value. Thiel, on the other hand, dropped out of a high-paying job as a form of rebellion against the establishment. "Familiar tracks and traditions are like clichés," he said, referring to his early life of careerist conformity.

Jobs had quoted the slogan of the lefty *Whole Earth Catalog*: "Stay hungry. Stay foolish." Thiel cited the great modernist poet (and fascist) Ezra Pound: "Make it new." Then, without naming Jobs, Thiel proceeded to attack the two maxims that the Apple founder's speech had turned on. Jobs had told graduates to follow their hearts. Thiel said the opposite. "Do *not* be true to yourself," he countered. "You need to discipline yourself, to cultivate it and care for it, not to follow it blindly."

Then Thiel moved on to the advice Jobs had given about death. "The best way to take this advice is to do exactly the opposite," he said. "Live each day as if you will live forever." Adopting this worldview "means you should treat the people around you as if they too will be around for a long time," he said. "You will get the best returns in life from investing your time to build durable friendships and long-lasting relationships."

The sentiment was perfectly on brand—a contrarian inversion that gestured at Thiel's interest in life extension. It also suggested an awareness of his own far-reaching influence. Thiel has surrounded himself with supporters and admirers who have protected him and enriched him. They—the PayPal Mafia, the Thielverse, and Silicon Valley itself, in all its hypocrisy and greed, and, yes, in its brilliance too—are part of his legacy.

And yet it is a legacy that feels a little bit shallow. Thiel has disseminated his reactionary ideas and made great sums of money, but he may be forever marooned in his own contrarianism—an ideology that is inherently isolating, after all. That makes the Hamilton speech surprising in that it addressed friendship at all. In his dealings, Thiel tends to treat interpersonal relationships in explicitly transactional terms, a fact that his own choice of words betrays: treating people well is not an end in itself but something one does in the expectation of "returns." The implication, of course, is that you don't have to treat people well if you don't think you'll have to deal with them again. As far as I could gather in my reporting for this book, Thiel's life has been full of important relationships, but few that seem to transcend money or power. Contrary to his own advice, he has built a world in which success, as he defines it, depends on a willingness—or really, a need—to shed ties and go it alone.

ACKNOWLEDGMENTS

This book grew out of fifteen years of reporting on the world of Silicon Valley's entrepreneurs, startups, and investors. Jane Berentson gave me my first opportunity in journalism, as a fact-checker at *Inc.*, and convinced me that business writing need not be dull. She became a mentor, a friend, and, at times, a surrogate parent. I also wouldn't be the journalist I am without Katherine Stirling (my editor at *Vanity Fair*) and David Lidsky (at *Fast Company*), who became two of my best friends in addition to teaching me how to be a better writer.

I am convinced there is no better place in the world to practice journalism right now than at Bloomberg, where my bosses generously allowed me the time and support to complete this project. I'm especially grateful to Brad Stone, Jim Aley, Joel Weber, Kristin Powers, and Reto Gregori—as well as to my amazingly talented colleagues, especially Josh Green, Ashlee Vance, Josh Brustein, Emily Chang, Sarah Frier, Austin Carr, Mark Bergen, Mark Milian, Caroline Winter, and Alex Shoukas, who contributed ideas, sources, and, sometimes, jokes to the final product.

The original framing and structure for this book grew out of a series of conversations with agent Ethan Bassoff at Ross Yoon. Without Ethan's edits and advice early on, this project would have never happened. I also owe thanks to Dara Kaye and Howard Yoon, whom I assume will represent my children as well someday.

I couldn't have found a better partner in Penguin Press. Thanks to Ann Godoff, Scott Moyers, Liz Calamari, Danielle Plafsky, Shina Patel, and, especially, to my editor, Emily Cunningham. Emily was tireless and incisive in her edits, approaching this project with good humor, intelligence, and humility. To the extent this book succeeds, it is mostly her doing.

Jana Kasperkevic provided research and fact-checking, and was my constant companion from the beginning. Kelsey Kudak was my brilliant guide through the fact-checking. Kaula Nhongo contributed reporting from Swakopmund. Diana Suryakusuma curated the images. David Lidsky was my coach throughout, provided a crucial early read, and gave me notes on some of the stickiest sections. Brad Stone provided hours of encouragement and commiseration, as well as an invaluable early read. Burt Helm and Jill Schwartzman provided friendship and emotional support.

The reporting of this book was informed by relationships with hundreds of sources. Most of the people who picked up the phone, or responded to my emails, or met with me in person did so at substantial risk and with little obvious benefit to them, personally or professionally. Their generosity of spirit and fearlessness will forever move me. Thank you for valuing journalism and for trusting me.

I also had help from researchers at a number of institutions and nonprofits. These include the Stanford Library's Special Collections department, the Case Western Reserve University Archives, and the *Western Mining in the Twentieth Century* oral history series maintained at the University of California, Berkeley. The Internet Archive, the Center for Responsive Politics' OpenSecrets.org, and ProPublica's Nonprofit Explorer were resources I relied on daily and are essential items in the modern journalist's toolkit.

Many reporters have covered Thiel's world extensively, and their work informs my own. While still a Stanford undergraduate, Andrew Granato wrote a thorough account of Thiel's role on the *Stanford Review*, which served as the starting point for my own research about the *Review*. Andrew obtained emails through a public records request concerning Thiel's relationship with the National Institutes of Health, which informed my reporting. Matt Nippert, of *The New Zealand Herald*, broke the story of Thiel's New Zealand citizenship and generously shared documents and insights with me. Corey Pein's book, *Live Work Work Work Die*, helped suggest some of the themes of this one. I also devoured everything by Lizette Chapman, Will Alden, Deepa Seetharaman, Ryan Mac, Jeff Bercovici, Brian Doherty, and George Packer. They are all on my perpetual jealousy list.

This book will be forever tied up with two events: the birth of my son, Leon, who showed up on the day that the world broke in March 2020, and the death of my brother Jackson Turner, who left us a few months later. Jackson was thirty-seven, a year younger than I was at the time. He was an inspiration to me and to so many others. I think about him every day.

As I look back on the last few years and especially on 2020, I don't know how I would have survived without the love and support of friends and family—especially my dad and mom, my stepmother, Laurie, and my brother Casey, who, with my sister-in-law Chelsea, provided me with a very comfortable futon in Oakland for weeks on end while I was on reporting trips.

My first reader, now and forever, is Christine, who has supported me in too many ways to count and who has shown me through her love, her strength, and her example the journalist and the person I aspire to be. Marrying her will always be the best thing that ever happened to me.

Our three little ones, Alice, Solly, and Leon, are not yet readers, but they will be soon, and I hope they will absorb these words in the near future: I love you. I owe you so many stories.

NOTES

INTRODUCTION

vii **"Age of Unicorns":** Erin Griffith and Dan Primack, "The Age of Unicorns," *Fortune*, January 22, 2015, https://fortune.com/2015/01/22/the-age-of-unicorns/.

vii **as his next act:** "The 'Anti-Business' President Who's Been Good for Business," *Bloomberg Businessweek*, June 13, 2016, https://www.bloomberg.com/features/2016-obama-anti-business-president/.

viii **NOT LEANING IN:** Drudge, archived homepage from May 9, 2016, http://www.drudgereportarchives.com/data/2016/05/09/20160509_144805.htm.

viii **FACEBOOK UNDER FIRE:** "Facebook Accused of Political Bias," Fox News, May 10, 2016, video, https://video.foxnews.com/v/4886941905001/#sp=show-clips.

ix **"advancing human potential":** Mark Zuckerberg, "A Letter to Our Daughter," Facebook, December 1, 2015, https://www.facebook.com/notes/mark-zuckerberg/a-letter-to-our-daughter/10153375081581634?fref=nf.

x **demanded his ouster:** Glynnis MacNicol, "Here's the Real Reason Glenn Beck and Fox News Are Parting Ways," *Business Insider*, April 6, 2011, https://www.businessinsider.com/glenn-beck-fox-news-fired-ratings-2011-4.

xi **whatever they wanted:** Nicholas Thompson and Fred Vogelstein, "Inside the Two Years That Shook Facebook—and the World," *Wired*, February 12, 2018, https://www.wired.com/story/inside-facebook-mark-zuckerberg-2-years-of-hell/.

xi **much of it in Trump's favor:** Craig Silverman, "This Analysis Shows How Viral Fake Election News Stories Outperformed Real News on Facebook," *BuzzFeed*, November 16, 2016, https://www.buzzfeednews.com/article/craigsilverman/viral-fake-election-news-outperformed-real-news-on-facebook.

xi **would eventually apologize:** Siobhan Hughes, "Mark Zuckerberg: Facebook Made Mistakes on 'Fake News,' Privacy," *The Wall Street Journal*, April 9, 2018, https://www.wsj.com/articles/mark-zuckerberg-facebook-made-mistakes-on-fake-news-privacy-1523289089.

xi **a voter suppression strategy:** Joshua Green and Sasha Issenberg, "Inside the Trump Bunker, with Days to Go," *Bloomberg Businessweek*, October 27, 2016, https://www.bloomberg.com/news/articles/2016-10-27/inside-the-trump-bunker-with-12-days-to-go.

xiii **from cable television:** Amy Mitchell et al., "Americans Who Mainly Get Their News on Social Media Are Less Engaged, Less Knowledgeable," Pew Research Center, July 30, 2020, https://www.journalism.org/2020/07/30/americans-who-mainly-get-their-news-on-social-media-are-less-engaged-less-knowledgeable/.

xiii **to rein them in:** Kaushik Viswanath, "How Uber and Airbnb Created a Parasite Economy," *Marker*, September 14, 2020, https://marker.medium.com/uber-and-airbnb-are-parasites-but-they-dont-have-to-be-36909355ac3b; Paris Martineau, "Inside Airbnb's 'Guerilla War' Against Local Governments," *Wired*, March, 20, 2019, https://www.wired.com/story/inside-airbnbs-guerrilla-war-against-local-governments/; Mike Isaac, "How Uber Deceives the Authorities Worldwide," *The New York Times*, March 3, 2017, https://www.nytimes.com/2017/03/03/technology/uber-greyball-program-evade-authorities.html.

xiv **tech founders are godlike:** Peter Thiel and Blake Masters, *Zero to One* (New York: Crown Business, 2014), 23, 168, 183.

xiv **1.25 million copies worldwide:** Blake Masters (@bgmasters), "Zero to One has now sold more than 1.25 million copies worldwide!" Twitter, January 31, 2016, https://twitter.com/bgmasters/status/693909418321141760.

xv **shortly after the 2016 election:** Maureen Dowd, "Peter Thiel, Trump's Tech Pal, Explains Himself," *The New York Times*, January 11, 2017, https://www.nytimes.com/2017/01/11/fashion/peter-thiel-donald-trump-silicon-valley-technology-gawker.html.

xvi **Thiel and his coconspirators:** Max Chafkin, "Entrepreneur of the Year, 2007: Elon Musk," *Inc.*, December 1, 2007, https://www.inc.com/magazine/20071201/entrepreneur-of-the-year-elon-musk.html.

CHAPTER ONE: FUCK YOU, WORLD

1 **built in the 1960s:** "Community Profile," Community, Foster City website, accessed January 20, 2021, https://www.fostercity.org/sites/default/files/fileattachments/community_development/page/3211/final-snapshot-030812-02-community-profile.pdf.

2 **killed himself in 1980:** William Robbins, "Brilliant Computer Student Dies from Gun Wound," *The New York Times*, August 18, 1980, https://timesmachine.nytimes.com/timesmachine/1980/08/18/111169520.html.

3 **a white-owned bar:** Mary Kilpatrick, "Cleveland Blamed 1966 Hough Riots on Outsiders—and It Wasn't True," *Cleveland.com*, June 3, 2020, https://www.cleveland.com/metro/2020/06/cleveland-blamed-1966-hough-riots-on-outsiders-and-it-wasnt-true.html.

4 **"to you one day":** George Packer, "No Death, No Taxes," *The New Yorker*, November 21, 2011, https://www.newyorker.com/magazine/2011/11/28/no-death-no-taxes; George Packer, *The Unwinding: An Inner History of the New America* (New York: Farrar, Straus and Giroux, 2013).

6 **facilities provided to whites:** Roger Moody, *The Gulliver File: Mines, People, and Land: A Global Battleground* (London: Minewatch, 1993), 665.

6 **Namibia Support Committee:** Greg Dropkin and David Clark, *Past Exposure: Revealing Health and Environmental Risks of Rössing Uranium* (London: Namibia Support Committee, 1992).

6 **behind the family's house:** Packer, *The Unwinding*, 120.

8 **on a Tandy TRS 80:** Packer, *The Unwinding* 121–22.

CHAPTER TWO: A STRANGE, STRANGE BOY

13 **speech that appeared:** David Starr Jordan, "Graduates Listen to Final Words of Advice from President Jordan," *Stanford Daily*, May 22, 1907, https://archives.stanforddaily.com/1907/05/22?page=7&section=MODSMD_ARTICLE15#article; Corey Pein, *Live Work*

Work Work Die: A Journey into the Savage Heart of Silicon Valley (New York: Metropolitan Books, 2018), 202.

15 **policy memo that led to Reaganomics:** John Makin, "The Godfather of Reaganomics," *The Washington Post*, June 5, 1988, https://www.washingtonpost.com/archive/entertainment/books/1988/06/05/the-godfather-of-reaganomics/9fae6dbf-a702-4897-8f9b-c5e2b6837b4f/.

15 **thirty of Anderson's Stanford colleagues:** Jeffrey Golden, "Hoover's Publicity Spurs Discussion of Academic Quality," *Stanford Daily*, November 18, 1981, 1, https://archives.stanforddaily.com/1981/11/18?page=1.

15 **White House reception:** Leon Lindsay, "Liberal-Conservative Debate at Stanford's Hoover Institute," *The Christian Science Monitor*, June 28, 1983, https://www.csmonitor.com/1983/0628/062846.html.

19 **according to Lythcott-Haims's account:** Julie Lythcott-Haims, "My Conversation with Peter Thiel about Apartheid . . . and Its Unfolding Aftermath," Medium, November 2, 2016, https://medium.com/indian-thoughts/my-conversation-with-peter-thiel-about-apartheid-and-its-aftermath-3fdf4249b08d.

19 **made by apologists:** Jacob Heilbrunn, "Apologists without Remorse," *The American Prospect*, December 19, 2001, prospect.org/world/apologists-without-remorse.

19 **confessed feeling "ambivalence":** Thomas Hays, "Chapel Dean Remembers South African Home," *Stanford Daily*, December 4, 1985, 14, https://archives.stanforddaily.com/1985/12/04?page=14&section=MODSMD_ARTICLE33.

20 **"somewhat rebellious undergrad":** "Peter Thiel on René Girard," ImitatioVideo, January 4, 2021, https://www.youtube.com/watch?v=esk7W9Jowtc.

23 **"the universe, and everything":** "Reid Hoffman and Peter Thiel Share the Secrets of Breaking into Tech's Most Exclusive Network", *Forbes*, May 2, 2012, https://www.forbes.com/forbes/2012/0521/midas-list-reid-hoffman-peter-thiel-inside-the-club.html#6ee83d3c6a46.

24 **thought of him:** Richard Feloni, "Before Billionaire LinkedIn Founder Reid Hoffman Met Peter Thiel in College, the 'Pinko Commie' Had Heard of the 'Libertarian Wacko'—Now, They've Been Friends for 30 Years," *Business Insider*, November 21, 2017, https://www.businessinsider.com/linkedin-founder-reid-hoffman-friendship-with-peter-thiel-2017-11.

24 **platform was anti-bureaucratic:** "ASSU Elections Handbook," *Stanford Daily*, April 9, 1987, 1, https://archives.stanforddaily.com/1987/04/09?page=1.

25 **a class trip to El Salvador:** Joseph Green, "El Salvador Trip Controversial," *Stanford Review*, June 9, 1987.

25 **Another front-page story:** Chris DeRosa, "Radical Politics Creates Western Culture Dispute," *Stanford Review*, June 9, 1987.

26 **new donations anyway:** The Black hair course, which debuted in 1992 when he was enrolled at Stanford Law School, would be of particular interest to Thiel. Three years later, Thiel and cowriter David Sacks quoted extensively from the syllabus of the class, complaining that it was "a parody of multiculturalism," and presented it as a symptom of the pernicious effects of racial tolerance. Peter Thiel and David Sacks, *The Diversity Myth: Multiculturalism and the Politics of Intolerance at Stanford* (Washington, D.C.: Independent Institute, 1995).

26 **"quite a bit of pressure":** Barbara Vobejda, "Bennett Assails New Stanford Program," *The Washington Post*, April 19, 1988, https://www.washingtonpost.com/archive/politics/1988/04/19/bennett-assails-new-stanford-program/68ca775f-f95c-499b-9e1d-cfc219d8b7ea/.

26 **"ace the LSATs":** Reid Hoffman, "Escape the Competition," *Masters of Scale*, podcast, November 8, 2017, https://mastersofscale.com/peter-thiel-escape-the-competition/.

27 **"Catholic Church 500 years ago":** Jennifer Kabbany, "Peter Thiel Predicts 'Reformation' of Higher Education in Speech to Student Journalists," *The College Fix*, December 1, 2018, https://www.thecollegefix.com/peter-thiel-predicts-reformation-of-higher-education -in-speech-to-student-journalists/.

CHAPTER THREE: HOPE YOU DIE

30 **Hitler Youth in the 1930s:** Alan Bloom, *The Closing of the American Mind* (New York: Simon & Schuster, 2012), 68–81, 208–14.

31 **tenure it had published:** Chuck Lane, "Crying Out in Ignorance," *Harvard Crimson*, June 7, 1982, https://www.thecrimson.com/article/1982/6/7/crying-out-in-ignorance-pbwhat -did/; Keeney Jones, "Dis Sho' Ain't No Jive, Bro," *Dartmouth Review*, March 15, 1982, https://journeys.dartmouth.edu/lesttheoldtraditionsfail/dis-sho-aint-no-jive-bro/; Dylan Matthews, "Dinesh D'Souza, America's Greatest Conservative Troll, Explained," *Vox*, May 31, 2018, https://www.vox.com/2014/10/8/6936717/dinesh-dsouza-explained; Matthew Zeitlin, "Tim Geithner Asked Dinesh D'Souza 'How It Felt to Be Such a Dick,'" *BuzzFeed*, May 11, 2014, https://www.buzzfeednews.com/article/matthewzeitlin/tim-geithner-asked -dinesh-dsouza-how-it-felt-to-be-such-a-di; Dudley Clendinen, "Conservative Paper Stirs Dartmouth," *The New York Times*, October 13, 1981, https://www.nytimes.com/1981/10 /13/us/conservative-paper-stirs-dartmouth.html; David Corn, "Remember How Dinesh D'Souza Outed Gay Classmates—and Thought It Was Awesome?" *Mother Jones*, January 24, 2014, https://www.motherjones.com/politics/2014/01/dinesh-dsouza-indictment- dartmouth-outed-gay-classmates/.

31 **parlayed his talent:** "Critical Monthly Rouses Princeton," *The New York Times*, April 19, 1984, 52, https://www.nytimes.com/1984/04/29/nyregion/critical-monthly-rouses -princeton.html.

32 **own book about the era:** Thiel and Sacks, *The Diversity Myth*.

32 **raging in the Bay Area:** Victor F. Zonana and Dan Morain, "Holocaust Image: AIDS Toll in S.F.: City Under Siege," *The Los Angeles Times*, August 22, 1988, https://www .latimes.com/archives/la-xpm-1988-08-22-mn-551-story.html.

32 **as a sort of addiction:** Tom Bethell, "Festive Foolery," *Stanford Review*, June 9, 1987, 5.

33 **anti-gay bias should be rebranded:** John Abbot, "Relentless Revolution: Homopho- biaphobia Paralyzes Stanford," *Stanford Review*, November 19, 1989; Nathan Linn, "'Homophobia'—the Big Lie," *Stanford Review*, March 9, 1992, 10.

34 **top of his lungs:** "New Light Shed on Otero Epithet Case; Officials, Students Clarify Circumstances," *Stanford Daily*, February 5, 1992, 1, https://archives.stanforddaily.com /1992/02/05?page=1&section=MODSMD_ARTICLE4; Thiel and Sacks, *The Diversity Myth*, 169.

35 **shouldn't be schoolteachers:** June Cohen, "Rabois' Comments on 'Faggots' Derided Across University," *Stanford Daily*, February 6, 1992, 1, https://archives.stanforddaily .com/1992/02/06?page=1&section=MODSMD_ARTICLE5.

36 **an impassioned defense of Stuart Thomas:** David Sacks, "From Statutory Rape to Stat- utory Red Tape," *Stanford Review*, January 21, 1982.

36 **graduation was in doubt:** Angie Chuang, "Thomas Sentenced to Service, $1,000 Fine," *Stanford Daily*, January 31, 1992, https://archives.stanforddaily.com/1992/01/31?page =1&section=MODSMD_ARTICLE4.

36 **Mike Newman complained:** Mike Newman, "Safe Sex: Simple Rules to Avoid Charges of Sexual Assault," *Stanford Review*, January 21, 1992, 8.

36 **a coauthor joked:** Mike Ehrman and Keith Rabois, "You Absolutely Know You Go to Stanford When . . . ," *Stanford Review*, January 21, 1982.

37 **complained that campus diversity:** David Lat, "In Defense of Ryan Bounds," *Above the Law*, July 20, 2018, https://abovethelaw.com/2018/07/in-defense-of-ryan-bounds/.

38 **would say years later:** Hoffman, "Escape the Competition."

40 **marking up contracts:** Thiel and Masters, *Zero to One*, 119.

41 **"victims demanding reparations":** Thiel and Sacks, *The Diversity Myth*, 145–46.

41 **"what they want to hear":** Julia Carrie Wong, "Peter Thiel, Who Gave $1.25 Million to Trump, Has Called Date Rape 'Belated Regret,'" *The Guardian*, October 21, 2016, https://www.theguardian.com/technology/2016/oct/21/peter-thiel-support-donald-trump-date-rape-book; Ryan Mac and Matt Drange, "Donald Trump Supporter Peter Thiel Apologizes for Past Book Comments on Rape," *Forbes*, October 25, 2016; Kara Swisher, "Zenefits CEO David Sacks Apologizes for Parts of a 1996 Book He Co-wrote with Peter Thiel That Called Date Rape "Belated Regret,'" *Recode*, October 24, 2016, https://www.vox.com/2016/10/24/13395798/zenefits-ceo-david-sacks-apologizes-1996-book-co-wrote-peter-thiel-date-rape-belated-regret; Andrew Granato, "How Peter Thiel and the Stanford Review Built a Silicon Valley Empire," *Stanford Politics*, November 27, 2017, https://stanfordpolitics.org/2017/11/27/peter-thiel-cover-story/.

42 **multiculturalism on college campuses:** David Sacks and Peter Thiel, "Happy Indigenous People's Day," *The Wall Street Journal*, October 5, 1995.

42 **conservative nonprofit dedicated:** Lizzy Ratner, "Olin Foundation, Right-Wing Tank, Snuffing Itself," *The New York Observer*, May 9, 2005, https://observer.com/2005/05/olin-foundation-rightwing-tank-snuffing-itself/.

42 **$40,000 grant to help publicize:** "Independent Institute," SourceWatch by Center for Media and Democracy, last accessed on January 20, 2020, https://www.sourcewatch.org/index.php/Independent_Institute.

CHAPTER FOUR: WORLD DOMINATION INDEX

45 **heralds of a new era:** James Collins, "High Stakes Winners," *Time*, February 19, 1996, http://content.time.com/time/subscriber/printout/0,8816,984131,00.html.

46 **$50 a copy:** John Quain, "Nothing but Netscape," *Fast Company*, October 31, 1996, https://www.fastcompany.com/27743/nothing-netscape.

47 **in 1993 he had urged Americans:** John Wilson, *The Myth of Political Correctness* (Durham, NC: Duke University Press, 1995), 7.

47 **complaints were a product:** T. J. Babbitt, "Ailing Review Sings 'Song of Myself,'" *Stanford Daily*, February 12, 1998, https://archives.stanforddaily.com/1998/02/12?page=5&section=MODSMD_ARTICLE16.

47 **an op-ed with Sacks:** David Sacks and Peter Thiel, "The IMF's Big Wealth Transfer," *The Wall Street Journal*, March 12, 1998, https://www.independent.org/news/article.asp?id=45.

47 **recent failures of Asian economies:** David Sacks and Peter Thiel, "Internet Shakes Up Complacent Press," *The San Francisco Chronicle*, March 10, 1998, https://www.independent.org/news/article.asp?id=60.

47 **lost investors' money:** Details on the fund's early structure and losses were revealed by a 2006 lawsuit filed by an early investor, Amisil Holdings, in a San Francisco state court.

48 **150-foot yacht:** Michael Lewis, *The New New Thing* (New York: W. W. Norton, 2000).

48 **$125 million divorce:** John Carney, "Netscape Founder Jim Clark's $125M Divorce," *Dealbreaker*, November 13, 2006, https://dealbreaker.com/2006/11/netscape-founder-jim-clarks-125m-divorce.

49 **Levchin later recalled:** Sarah Lacy, "I Almost Lost My Leg to a Crazy Guy with a Geiger Counter," *PandoDaily*, August 17, 2017, https://pando.com/2017/08/17/i-almost-lost-my-leg-crazy-guy-geiger-counter-max-levchin-and-other-valley-icons-share-their-stories-luck/.

49 **"How about tomorrow?":** Max Levchin, interviewed by Jason Calacanis, *This Week in Startups*, 4–6, https://www.youtube.com/watch?v=e48aSjtg1ds.

50 **"One day," he told Thiel:** Max Levchin, "A Fireside Chat with Max Levchin," *Pando-Daily*, July 17, 2004, 50:00–54:00, https://www.youtube.com/watch?v=wYSFom16CtY.

52 **boasted to a reporter:** Steve Bodow, "The Money Shot," *Wired*, September 1, 2001, https://www.wired.com/2001/09/paypal/. Thiel never specifically mentioned money laundering, but the use of anonymous bank accounts would almost certainly lead to money laundering and other crimes.

52 **a meeting later that year:** Eric Jackson, *The PayPal Wars: Battles with eBay, the Media, the Mafia, and the Rest of Planet Earth* (Los Angeles: World Ahead Publishing, 2004), 25.

53 **"no one even knew how to play":** Blake Masters, "Peter Thiel's CS183: Startup—Class 5 Notes Essay," Blakemasters.com, April 20, 2012, https://blakemasters.com/post/21437840885/peter-thiels-cs183-startup-class-5-notes-essay.

57 **one headline declared:** Mark Gimein, "High Tech's New 'It Guy': Elon Musk Is Poised to Become Silicon Valley's Next Big Thing," *Ottawa Citizen*, August 23, 1999, D1.

57 **strength of a demo website:** Max Chafkin, "Entrepreneur of the Year, 2007: Elon Musk," *Inc.*, December 1, 2007, https://www.inc.com/magazine/20071201/entrepreneur-of-the-year-elon-musk.html.

57 **"be done in two minutes":** Craig Tolliver, "X.com Opens Its Virtual Doors," *CBS MarketWatch*, December 10, 1999, https://web.archive.org/web/20000301165053/http://www.x.com/external_CBS_interview.htm.

59 **sign up for a PayPal account:** Jackson, *The PayPal Wars*, 57–61.

59 **"World Domination Index":** Jackson, *The PayPal Wars*, 19.

61 **caper at the *Dartmouth Review*:** Clendinen, "Conservative Paper Stirs Dartmouth."

61 **they were growing so slowly:** Bodow, "Money Shot."

CHAPTER FIVE: HEINOUS ACTIVITY

64 **Thiel bragged to:** Jason Sapsford, "PayPal Sees Torrid Growth with Money-Sending Service," *The Wall Street Journal*, February 16, 2000, https://www.wsj.com/articles/SB950653184492190214; William Trombley, "Reagan Library Strains Link between Stanford and Hoover Institution," *Los Angeles Times*, March 8, 1987, https://www.latimes.com/archives/la-xpm-1987-03-08-mn-13662-story.html.

66 **$1 million McLaren:** "Elon Musk: How I Wrecked an Uninsured McLaren F1," interview by Sarah Lacy, *PandoDaily*, July 15, 2012, https://www.youtube.com/watch?v=mOI8GWoMF4M.

66 **"didn't get any insurance":** Maureen Dowd, "Peter Thiel, Trump's Tech Pal, Explains Himself," *The New York Times*, January 11, 2020, https://www.nytimes.com/2017/01/11/fashion/peter-thiel-donald-trump-silicon-valley-technology-gawker.html.

68 **a Cantor Fitzgerald analyst:** Catherine Tymkiw, "Bleak Friday on Wall Streak," *CNNMoney*, April 14, 2000, https://money.cnn.com/2000/04/14/markets/markets_new york/.

68 **raised an additional $51 million:** Izabella Kaminska, "From the Annals of Disruptive Digital Currencies Past," *Financial Times*, November 4, 2014.

68 **bloodless subject line:** Jackson, *The PayPal Wars*, 108.

71 **deemphasize the PayPal brand:** Jackson, *The PayPal Wars*, 159–60.

CHAPTER SIX: GRAY AREAS

77 **shamelessly marketed to children:** Julia Belluz, "The Vape Company Juul Said It Doesn't Target Teens. Its Early Ads Tell a Different Story," *Vox*, January 25, 2019, https://www.vox.com/2019/1/25/18194953/vape-juul-e-cigarette-marketing.

77 **questionable financial products:** Max Chafkin and Julie Verhage, "Robinhood Thinks Bitcoin Belongs in Your Retirement Plan," *Bloomberg Businessweek*, February 8, 2018, https://www.bloomberg.com/news/features/2018-02-08/brokerage-app-robinhood -thinks-bitcoin-belongs-in-your-retirement-plan?sref=4ZgkJ7cZ.

78 **known as a captcha:** The original captchas asked users to read letters that had been slightly distorted; newer versions use pictures.

79 **its own conference room:** Paul Cox, "PayPal and FBI Team Up to Combat Wire Fraud," *The Wall Street Journal*, June 22, 2001, https://www.wsj.com/articles/B99263912388 8198275.

79 **a pair of Russians:** Brad Stone, "Busting the Web Bandits," *Newsweek*, July 15, 2001, https://www.newsweek.com/busting-web-bandits-154463.

80 **No charges were brought:** Greg Sandoval, "Investigations into PlayStation 2 Sales Mount," *CNET*, March 2, 2002, https://www.cnet.com/news/investigations-into-play station-2-sales-mount/.

80 **"who temporarily succeed":** Cox, "PayPal and FBI Team Up."

82 **in both those cases:** Matt Richtel, "PayPal and New York in Accord on Gambling," *The New York Times*, August 22, 2002, https://www.nytimes.com/2002/08/22/business/tech nology-paypal-and-new-york-in-accord-on-gambling.html; Dylan McCullagh, "PayPal Settles over Gambling Transfers," *CNET*, August 2, 2004, https://www.cnet.com/news /paypal-settles-over-gambling-transfers/.

85 **sign up for Billpoint:** Jackson, *The PayPal Wars*, 205.

86 **around 3 percent of the company:** The ownership stakes here have been estimated based on PayPal's original S-1 filing in September 2001, just after the stock grants were made. The grants would ultimately give Thiel an ownership stake of 4.6 percent at the time of the IPO the following February. Musk's share would be reduced to 12 percent.

87 **he used the proceeds:** The details of how Thiel structured the purchase were disclosed as an exhibit in an SEC filing before PayPal went public. PayPal Inc., "Registration Statement," filed September 28, 2001, exhibit 10.9, https://www.sec.gov/Archives/edgar /data/0001103415/000091205701533855/0000912057-01-533855-index.html.

87 **legal gray area:** Deborah Jacobs, "How Facebook Billionaires Dodge Mega Millions in Taxes," *Forbes*, March 20, 2012, https://www.forbes.com/sites/deborahljacobs/2012/03 /20/how-facebook-billionaires-dodge-mega-millions-in-taxes/#6a53c50c58f3.

88 **read one headline:** Jackson, *The Paypal Wars*, 225.

89 **told employees at the time:** Jackson, *The PayPal Wars*, 270.

CHAPTER SEVEN: HEDGING

93 **invited by the White House:** "Moneyline News Hour," CNN, March 28, 2001, 6:30 p.m. ET, https://web.archive.org/web/20021103202734/http://www.cnn.com/TRANSCRIPTS /0103/28/mlld.00.html.

93 **Kvamme was not:** Bush would later nominate John Marburger, a physicist, as the head of the Office of Science and Technology Policy.

95 **while employees cheered:** Jackson, *The PayPal Wars*, 293.

96 **got to profitability:** Budow, "Money Shot."

96 **"over the top"**: Gary Rivlin, "If You Can Make It in Silicon Valley, You Can Make It . . . in Silicon Valley Again," *The New York Times*, June 5, 2005, https://www.nytimes.com/2005/06/05/magazine/if-you-can-make-it-in-silicon-valley-you-can-make-it-in-silicon.html.

96 **"much better place than Earth"**: Jackson, *The PayPal Wars*, 295.

96 **a sense of the frontier:** Jonathan Miles, "The Billionaire King of Techtopia," *Details*, September 2011.

96 **"day-to-night lounge"**: Sarah Lynch, "Decorati + PayPal: From Start-Up to Finish," *California Home+Design*, March 17, 2011, https://web.archive.org/web/20140919063020/https://www.californiahomedesign.com/trending/2011/03/17/decorati-paypal-start-finish/.

97 **as one visitor remarked:** Deepak Gopiath, "Macro Man," *Bloomberg Markets*, January 2007, 39–50.

97 **"clear-sighted fusion"**: "Restaurant Review: Frisson, San Francisco," *Vinography*, September 2004, http://www.vinography.com/archives/2004/09/restaurant_review_frisson_san.html.

98 **"I was shocked"**: Gopiath, "Macro Man."

98 **a $10 million investment:** Karen Breslau, "The NASCAR Lifestyle," *Newsweek*, May 16, 2004, https://www.newsweek.com/nascar-lifestyle-128331.

98 **media reporter David Carr:** David Carr, "Where the Reader and the Rubber Meet the Road," *The New York Times*, May 5, 2005, https://www.nytimes.com/2004/05/05/sports/auto-racing-where-the-reader-and-the-rubber-meet-the-road.html.

100 **the market was peaking:** Gregory Zuckerman, "How the Soros Funds Lost Game of Chicken Against Tech Stocks," *The Wall Street Journal*, May 22, 2000, https://www.wsj.com/articles/SB95894419575853588.

101 **officer Ralph Ho put it:** Gopiath, "Macro Man."

101 **column that warned about:** Linn, "'Homophobia'—the Big Lie."

101 **white nationalist writing:** Sam Francis, "Abolishing America," *VDARE*, July 21, 2003, https://web.archive.org/web/20030801083024/http://vdare.com/francis/reparations_too.htm.

102 **glowing *Barron's* column:** Eric Savitz, "Game Theory," *Barron's*, March 1, 2004, https://www.wsj.com/articles/SB107792721619541724.

103 **Canada's barren far north:** Eric Savitz, "A Second Payday for PayPal Founder," *Barron's*, February 13, 2006, https://www.wsj.com/articles/SB113961793285971352.

103 **"most destructive oil operation"**: Stephen Leahy, "This Is the World's Most Destructive Oil Operation—and It's Growing," *National Geographic*, April, 2019, https://www.nationalgeographic.com/environment/2019/04/alberta-canadas-tar-sands-is-growing-but-indigenous-people-fight-back/.

103 **doubled in value:** Savitz, "Second Payday."

104 **explained it in 2006:** Gopiath, "Macro Man."

104 **$6.4 billion under management:** Dane Hamilton, "Clarium Hedge Fund Posts Gains of 57.9 Percent," Reuters, July 9, 2008, https://www.reuters.com/article/us-clarium-hedge/clarium-hedge-fund-posts-gains-of-57-9-percent-idUSN0948639720080709.

105 ***New York Post* observed:** Kaja Whitehouse, "Clarium Returns Climb," *The New York Post*, July 10, 2008, https://nypost.com/2008/07/10/clarium-returns-climb.

106 **enormous spam machine:** Mike Masnick, "Now That Plaxo Spam Has Annoyed Enough People, It's Time to Fade It Out," *TechDirt*, March 22, 2006, https://www.techdirt.com/articles/20060322/0317223.shtml.

106 **fired him anyway:** Steven Bertoni, "Sean Parker: Agent of Disruption," *Forbes*, October 10, 2010, https://www.forbes.com/global/2011/1010/feature-sean-parker-agent-disruption -napster-facebook-plaxo-steven-bertoni.html?sh=42f2099b7c28; David Kirkpatrick, "With a Little Help from His Friends," *Vanity Fair*, October 2010, https://www.vanityfair.com /culture/2010/10/sean-parker-201010.

108 **"seen in the wrong light":** Bari Schwartz, "Hot or Not? Website Briefly Judges Looks," *Harvard Crimson*, November 4, 2003, https://www.thecrimson.com/article/2003/11/4 /hot-or-not-website-briefly-judges/.

108 **Thiel told Zuckerberg:** David Kirkpatrick, *The Facebook Effect* (New York: Simon & Schuster, 2010), 89.

108 **startup of the decade:** Kirkpatrick, *Facebook Effect*, 103–4.

108 **behind the service:** Kirkpatrick, *Facebook Effect*, 89.

109 **instant message exchange:** Nicholas Carlson, "EXCLUSIVE: Mark Zuckerberg's Secret IMs from College," *Business Insider*, May 17, 2012, https://www.businessinsider.com /exclusive-mark-zuckerbergs-secret-ims-from-college-2012-5?op=1.

CHAPTER EIGHT: INCEPTION

115 **Silicon Valley firm:** Andy Greenberg and Ryan Mac, "How a 'Deviant' Philosopher Built Palantir," *Forbes*, September 2, 2013, forbes.com/sites/andygreenberg/2013/08/14 /agent-of-intelligence-how-a-deviant-philosopher-built-palantir-a-cia-funded-data -mining-juggernaut/.

116 **found Thiel and Karp arrogant:** Sharon Weinberger, "Techie Software Soldier Spy," *New York*, September 28, 2020, https://nymag.com/intelligencer/2020/09/inside -palantir-technologies-peter-thiel-alex-karp.html.

116 **which put in $2 million:** Shane Harris, "Killer App," *Washingtonian*, January 31, 2012, https://www.washingtonian.com/2012/01/31/killer-app/.

119 **this kind of abuse:** Peter Waldman, Lizette Chapman, and Jordan Robertson, "Palantir Knows Everything about You," *Bloomberg Businessweek*, April 19, 2018, https://www .bloomberg.com/features/2018-palantir-peter-thiel/?sref=4ZgkJ7cZ.

119 **was never charged:** David Kirkpatrick, "With a Little Help from His Friends," *Vanity Fair*, October 2010, https://www.vanityfair.com/culture/2010/10/sean-parker-201010.

119 **from investing in Facebook:** Matt Marshall, "Founders Fund Hires Sean Parker as Partner, to Launch Second Fund," *VentureBeat*, December 12, 2006, https://venturebeat.com /2006/12/12/founders-fund-hires-edgy-sean-parker-as-partner-to-launch-second-fund/.

120 **a "smear campaign":** Kirkpatrick, "With a Little Help."

120 **"venture capital 2.0":** Jessica Guynn, "The Founders Fund Emerges as Venture Capital 2.0," *San Francisco Chronicle*, December 13, 2006, sfgate.com/bayarea/article/The -Founders-Fund-emerges-as-venture-capital-2-0-2543274.php.

CHAPTER NINE: R.I.P. GOOD TIMES

123 **screaming about power, sex:** "Editorial: Google's Power Couple," *Valleywag*, February 2, 2006, https://web.archive.org/web/20060206211542/http://www.valleywag.com/tech /marissa-mayer/editorial-googles-power-couple-152210.php#more.

123 **framed as media criticism:** "Valleywag Exclusive: Oh Schmidt!" *Valleywag*, February 6, 2006, https://web.archive.org/web/20060208024001/http://www.valleywag.com/tech /top/valleywag-exclusive-oh-schmidt-153052.php.

124 **guilty of "intellectual douchebaggery":** Doree Shafrir, "From the Mailbag," *Gawker*, July 31, 2007, https://gawker.com/tag/adam-gopnik.

124 **"a primate on caffeine":** "'New York Times' Staff Explained for Math Majors," *Gawker*, July 18, 2006, https://gawker.com/188110%2Fnew-york-times-staff-explained -for-math-majors.

124 **produce a lengthy takedown:** Vanessa Grigoriadis, "Everybody Sucks," *New York*, October 12, 2007, https://nymag.com/news/features/39319/.

124 **page views per month:** Allen Salkin, "Has Gawker Jumped the Snark?" *The New York Times*, January 13, 2008, https://www.nytimes.com/2008/01/13/fashion/13gawker.html.

124 **"center of the new world":** Nick Denton, "Valleywag Update: Nick Denton Speaks," interviewed by Al Saracevic, *San Francisco Chronicle*, November 13, 2006, https://blog .sfgate.com/techchron/2006/11/13/valleywag-update-nick-denton-speaks/.

125 **the prominent tech scribe:** Kara Swisher, "Kara Visits Founders Fund's Peter Thiel," *AllThingsD*, November 1, 2007, http://allthingsd.com/20071101/kara-visits-founders -funds-peter-thiel/.

125 **"hating open secrets":** Belinda Luscombe, "Gawker Founder Nick Denton on Peter Thiel, 'Conflict and Trollery,' and the Future of Media," *Time*, June 22, 2016, https:// time.com/4375643/gawker-nick-denton-peter-thiel/.

126 **a winking reference:** Owen Thomas, "Peter Thiel's Fabulous Fourth of July," *Valleywag*, July 6, 2007, https://gawker.com/275650/peter-thiels-fabulous-fourth-of-july.

126 **failed to attract:** Owen Thomas, "Peter Thiel's College Tour," *Valleywag*, October 6, 2017, https://gawker.com/308252/peter-thiels-college-tour.gawker.com

127 **"but Thiel's taken":** Owen Thomas "Peter Thiel Crush Alert," *Valleywag*, November 27, 2007.

129 **out Tim Cook:** Owen Thomas, "Is Apple COO Tim Cook Gay?" *Valleywag*, November 10, 2008, https://web.archive.org/web/20090119085309/http://valleywag.gawker.com /5082473/is-apple-coo-tim-cook-gay.

129 **that he was psychologically unstable:** Ryan Holiday, *Conspiracy: Peter Thiel, Hulk Hogan, Gawker, and the Anatomy of Intrigue* (New York: Portfolio, 2018), 31.

132 **"Wal-Mart of Banking":** Peter Goodman and Gretchen Morgenson, "Saying Yes, WaMu Built Empire on Shaky Loans," *The New York Times*, December 28, 2008, https://www .nytimes.com/2008/12/28/business/28wamu.html.

134 **he has hinted at:** Dave Rubin, "Trump, Gawker, and Leaving Silicon Valley," *Rubin Report*, 1:34, https://www.youtube.com/watch?v=h10kXgTdhNU.

134 **to feel "targeted":** Thiel, *Rubin Report*, 1:33.

134 **donation to the campaign:** Nicholas Carlson, "Peter Thiel Supports Ron Paul, the Candidate Who Opposed the 'Black Agenda,'" *Valleywag*, January 21, 2008, https://gawker .com/347103%2Fpeter-thiel-supports-ron-paul-the-candidate-who-opposed-the-black -agenda; James Kirchick, "Angry White Man," *The New Republic*, January 8, 2008, https://newrepublic.com/article/61771/angry-white-man.

134 **about these losses:** Owen Thomas, "Facebook Backer Peter Thiel Loses Almost $1 Billion in a Month," *Valleywag*, September 9, 2008, https://gawker.com/5047074%2Ffacebook -backer-peter-thiel-loses-almost-1-billion-in-a-month.

134 **inflating his net worth:** Owen Thomas, "Give Me Liberty or Give Me Taxpayer Money," *Valleywag*, May 6, 2009, https://gawker.com/5243197%2Fgive-me-liberty-or-give-me -taxpayer-money.

135 **the "Facebook Election":** Soumitra Dutta and Matthew Fraser, "Barack Obama and the Facebook Election," *U.S. News & World Report*, November 19, 2008, https:// www.usnews.com/opinion/articles/2008/11/19/barack-obama-and-the-facebook -election.

135 **"the year's hottest start-up"**: Joshua Green, "The Amazing Money Machine," *The Atlantic*, June 2008, https://www.theatlantic.com/magazine/archive/2008/06/the-amazing-money-machine/306809/.

137 **it'd be too late**: Peter Thiel, "The Seasteading Institute Conference 2009," November 12, 2009, https://vimeo.com/7577391.

137 **in a press release**: "Introducing the Seasteading Institute," April 14, 2008, https://www.seasteading.org/introducing-the-seasteading-institute/.

137 **joking promotional copy**: "Libertarian Island: No Rules, Just Rich Dudes," NPR, May 21, 2008, https://www.npr.org/transcripts/90664406.

139 **nationalists through its founder:** Heidi Beirich, "The Nativist Lobby: Three Faces of Intolerance," Southern Poverty Law Center, February 1, 2009, https://www.splcenter.org/20090131/nativist-lobby-three-faces-intolerance.

140 **run-up to the vote:** Molly Ball, "The Little Group behind the Big Fight to Stop Immigration Reform," *The Atlantic*, August 1, 2013, https://www.theatlantic.com/politics/archive/2013/08/the-little-group-behind-the-big-fight-to-stop-immigration-reform/278252/.

140 **"an embrace of freedom"**: Owen Thomas, "Billionaire Facebook Investor's Anti-immigrant Heresy," *Valleywag*, November 14, 2008, https://gawker.com/5083655/billionaire-facebook-investors-anti-immigrant-heresy.

140 **start new ones:** Patri Friedman, "Beyond Folk Activism," *Cato Unbound*, April 6, 2009, https://www.cato-unbound.org/2009/04/06/patri-friedman/beyond-folk-activism.

140 **calibrated to cause a reaction:** Peter Thiel, "The Education of a Libertarian," *Cato Unbound*, April 13, 2009, https://www.cato-unbound.org/2009/04/13/peter-thiel/education-libertarian.

142 **"terrorists, not writers and reporters"**: Peter Kafka, "Why Did Nick Denton Think Peter Thiel Was behind the Hulk Hogan Suit?" *Recode*, May 24, 2016, https://www.vox.com/2016/5/24/11765246/peter-thiel-nick-denton-hulk-hogan-gawker-valleywag.

CHAPTER TEN: THE NEW MILITARY-INDUSTRIAL COMPLEX

144 **"We owe it all to the hippies"**: Stewart Brand, "We Owe It All to the Hippies," *Time*, March 1, 1995, http://content.time.com/time/subscriber/article/0,33009,982602-3,00.html.

144 **a 1983 *Esquire* profile:** Tom Wolfe, "The Tinkerings of Robert Noyce," *Esquire*, December 1, 1983, http://classic.esquire.com/the-tinkerings-of-robert-noyce/.

145 **as he'd write:** Peter Thiel, "The End of the Future," *National Review*, October 3, 2011, https://www.nationalreview.com/2011/10/end-future-peter-thiel/.

146 **essential to the operation:** "Tracking GhostNet," The Information Warfare Monitor, March 29, 2009, https://citizenlab.ca/wp-content/uploads/2017/05/ghostnet.pdf; John Markoff, "Tracking Cyberspies Through the Web Wilderness," *The New York Times*, May 11, 2009, https://www.nytimes.com/2009/05/12/science/12cyber.html.

147 **had already agreed:** Steve Brill, "Trump, Palantir, and the Battle to Clean Up a Huge Army Procurement Swamp," *Fortune*, March 27, 2017 https://fortune.com/longform/palantir-pentagon-trump/. The A in DCGS-A refers to the U.S. Army; other branches have their own DCGS systems. Throughout this book, for simplicity, I refer to the Army's system as DCGS.

147 **in a 2006 book:** Harry Tunnell, *Red Devils: Tactical Perspective from Iraq* (Fort Leavenworth, KS: Combat Studies Institute Press, 2003).

147 **"Strike and destroy"**: Anna Mulrine, "Pentagon Had Red Flags about Command Climate in 'Kill Team' Stryker Brigade," *Christian Science Monitor*, October 28, 2010, https://www.csmonitor.com/USA/Military/2010/1028/Pentagon-had-red-flags-about-command-climate-in-kill-team-Stryker-brigade.

149 **FBI would eventually investigate**: Adam Goldman et al., "F.B.I. Used Informant to Investigate Russia Ties to Campaign, Not to Spy as Trump Claims," *The New York Times*, May 18, 2018, https://www.nytimes.com/2018/05/18/us/politics/trump-fbi-informant-russia-investigation.html.

149 **resigned his seat**: "Report Blames Lapses on Stryker Commander," *Military Times*, March 27, 2013, https://www.militarytimes.com/2013/03/27/report-blames-lapses-on-stryker-commander-532-page-report-finds-colonel-ignored-doctrine-proper-procedure-in-leading-undisciplined-bct/; Julie Watson, "GOP Rep. Duncan Hunter Resigns after Corruption Conviction," AP, January 7, 2020, https://apnews.com/article/21f9320c1ab116538a9244941c11192b.

150 **dig up damaging posts**: Nate Anderson, "Spy Games: Inside the Convoluted Plot to Bring Down WikiLeaks," *Wired*, February 14, 2011, https://www.wired.com/2011/02/spy/.

150 **"The right to free speech"**: Andy Greenberg, "Palantir Apologizes for Wikileaks Attack Proposal, Cuts Ties with HBGary," *Forbes*, February 11, 2011, https://www.forbes.com/sites/andygreenberg/2011/02/11/palantir-apologizes-for-wikileaks-attack-proposal-cuts-ties-with-hbgary/?sh=6b6b7055585e.

153 **rare exception was Gawker**: Nitasha Tiku, "Leaked Emails Show How Palantir Founder Recruits for Global Domination," *Valleywag*, October 17, 2013, http://valleywag.gawker.com/leaked-emails-show-how-palantir-founder-recruits-for-gl-1443665496; Sharon Weinberger, "Techie Software Soldier Spy," *New York*, September 28, 2020, https://nymag.com/intelligencer/2020/09/inside-palantir-technologies-peter-thiel-alex-karp.html.

154 *Businessweek* **article declared it**: Ashlee Vance and Brad Stone, "Palantir, the War on Terror's Secret Weapon," *Bloomberg Businessweek*, November 22, 2011, https://www.bloomberg.com/news/articles/2011-11-22/palantir-the-war-on-terrors-secret-weapon?sref=4ZgkJ7cZ.

154 **a "sinister cyber-surveillance scheme"**: Barret Brown, "A Sinister Cyber-Surveillance Scheme Exposed," *The Guardian*, June 22, 2011, https://www.theguardian.com/commentisfree/cifamerica/2011/jun/22/hacking-anonymous.

154 **smiling face on its cover**: Greenberg and Mac, "'Deviant' Philosopher."

CHAPTER ELEVEN: THE ABSOLUTE TABOO

160 **"it's a very positive thing"**: "Peter Thiel on Facebook, Technology, and the Higher Education Bubble," interview by Tim Cavanaugh, *Reason.TV*, November 12, 2010, https://www.youtube.com/watch?v=P6qm7vVB5so.

160 **tech conference in San Francisco**: "Peter Thiel Talks about Investing," *Venturebeat*, September 27, 2010 https://techcrunch.com/2010/09/27/peter-thiel-drop-out-of-school/.

160 **"Genius Grants for Geeks"**: Michael Arrington, "Announcing the TechFellow Awards with Founders Fund," *Techcrunch*, April 16, 2009, https://techcrunch.com/2009/04/16/announcing-the-techfellow-awards-with-founders-fund/.

161 **about four hundred**: Sarah Lacy, "Peter Thiel: We're in a Bubble and It's Not the Internet. It's Higher Education," *Techcrunch*, April 11, 2011, https://techcrunch.com/2011/04/10/peter-thiel-were-in-a-bubble-and-its-not-the-internet-its-higher-education/.

162 **"there's no Santa Claus"**: Lacy, "We're in a Bubble."

164 **the day before the conference**: "20 Under 20 Introductory Episode," The Thiel Fellowship, December 15, 2011, https://www.youtube.com/watch?v=uVCbjehiwqo&t=173s.

164 **"get a jump on that"**: Tara Isabella Burton, "The Gospel According to Peter Thiel," *City Journal*, Spring 2020, https://www.city-journal.org/peter-thiel.

167 **"stood out from the start"**: Brian Solomon, "Peter Thiel's Chosen One," *Forbes*, January 3, 2017, https://www.forbes.com/sites/briansolomon/2017/01/03/james-proud-hello-sense -sleep-apple-amazon/.

167 **which would fold in 2017**: Michael Nunez, "Overhyped Sleep Tracker Backed by Peter Thiel Is on Its Death Bed," *Mashable*, June 6, 2013, https://mashable.com/2017/06/13 /hello-sense-sleep-tracker-shut-down/.

170 **"If I do my job right"**: Gerry Shih, "Peter Thiel, University-Hater, Heads to Campus," Reuters, March 12, 2012, https://www.reuters.com/article/us-stanford-thiel/peter-thiel -university-hater-heads-to-campus-idUSBRE82A0EO20120312.

CHAPTER TWELVE: BUILDING THE BASE

173 **now-defunct "metrosexual bible"**: Warren St. John, "Metrosexuals Come Out," *The New York Times*, June 22, 2003, https://www.nytimes.com/2003/06/22/style/metrosexuals-come -out.html.

173 **he submitted to an interview**: Miles, "Billionaire King of Techtopia."

175 **started talking it up**: Caroline Howard, "Peter Thiel: Don't Wait to Start Something," *Forbes*, September 10, 2014, https://www.forbes.com/sites/carolinehoward/2014/09/10 /peter-thiel-dont-wait-to-start-something-new/?sh=61f93f6e1e69.

176 **"destructive system of government"**: Mencius Moldbug, "A Formalist Manifesto," *Unqualified Reservations*, April 23, 2007, https://www.unqualified-reservations.org/2007 /04/formalist-manifesto-originally-posted/.

176 **"more tyrant than mob"**: "Peter Thiel's CS183: Startup—Class 18 Notes Essay," Blakemasters.com, June 6 2012, https://blakemasters.com/post/24578683805/peter-thiels -cs183-startup-class-18-notes.

176 **like the U.S. dollar, are "diabolical"**: Mencius Moldbug, "UR's Crash Course in Sound Economics," *Unqualified Reservations*, August 6, 2009, https://www.unqualified -reservations.org/2009/08/urs-crash-course-in-sound-economics/.

176 **"more suited to slavery"**: Mencius Moldbug, "Chapter 2: Why Carlyle Matters," *Unqualified Reservations*, July 16, 2009, https://www.unqualified-reservations.org/2009/07/why -carlyle-matters/.

176 **had views on apartheid**: Mencius Moldbug, "South Africa: The Solution," *Unqualified Reservations*, October 21, 2009, https://www.unqualified-reservations.org/2009/10/south -africa-solution/.

176 **mass shooter Anders Breivik**: Mencius Moldbug, "Right Wing Terrorism as Folk Activism," *Unqualified Reservations*, July 23, 2011, https://www.unqualified-reservations.org /2011/07/right-wing-terrorism-as-folk-activism/.

177 **he told a *Politico* reporter**: Ben Smith, "They're Gay, Conservative and Proud," *Politico*, September 25, 2010, https://www.politico.com/story/2010/09/theyre-gay-conservative-and -proud-042711.

177 **he'd published newsletters**: James Kirchick, "Angry White Man."

178 **a single day's fundraising**: O. Kay Henderson, "Ron Paul Touts His $6 Million 'Money Bomb,'" Radio Iowa, December 17, 2007, https://www.radioiowa.com/2007/12/17/ron -paul-touts-his-6-million-money-bomb/.

178 **drawing huge crowds**: Robert Smith, "Ron Paul: Why the Young Flock to an Old Idealist," *Morning Edition*, NPR, May 16, 2011, https://www.npr.org/2011/05/16/135990053 /ron-paul-why-the-young-flock-to-an-old-idealist.

179 **when the filings became public:** Alina Selyukh, "PayPal Co-founders Fund Pro-Paul Super PAC," *Reuters*, January 31, 2012, https://www.reuters.com/article/us-usa-campaign -spending-paul/paypal-co-founders-fund-pro-paul-super-pac-idUSTRE80U1OF20120131.

181 **"any money they spent":** Brian Doherty, "Ron Paul Revolution: What Now?" *Reason*, March 9, 2012, https://reason.com/2012/03/09/ron-paul-revolution-what-now-ron-paul-re/.

181 **that Paul had lost:** In 2016, Benton and another Paul campaign staffer, John Tate, would be convicted of violating campaign finance laws in connection with payments made to an Iowa state senator. In 2020, Donald Trump pardoned the two men.

181 **Speaking to young activists:** Students for Liberty, "Peter Thiel at the ISFLC 2012," February 26, 2012, https://www.youtube.com/watch?v=k3rp4jXTYJU.

182 **"how much voting actually works":** Dave Weigel, "Ron Paul's Billionaire," *Slate*, February 20, 2012, https://slate.com/news-and-politics/2012/02/investor-peter-thiel-is-the -billionaire-behind-ron-pauls-presidential-campaign.html.

182 **a recent Romney convert:** Kevin Robillard, "Hulk Hogan Ready to Rumble for Romney," *Politico*, August 30, 2012, https://www.politico.com/blogs/click/2012/08/hulk-hogan -ready-to-rumble-for-romney-133822.

184 **"Senate upset of the cycle":** Sean Sullivan, "The Biggest Upset of 2012," *The Washington Post*, November 28, 2012, https://www.washingtonpost.com/news/the-fix/wp/2012/11 /28/the-biggest-upset-of-2012/.

184 **showed up with ridicule:** Sam Biddle, "Reminder: Peter Thiel Is Ted Cruz's Gay Billionaire," *Valleywag*, September 30, 2013, http://valleywag.gawker.com/reminder-peter -thiel-is-ted-cruzs-gay-billionaire-all-1427666663.

185 **Paul would spit in 2016:** Ezra Collins, "Ron Paul: Ted Cruz Is No Libertarian," *Politico*, February 5, 2016, https://www.politico.com/story/2016/02/ron-paul-ted-cruz-libertarian -218822.

186 **of the campaign's supporters:** Jesse Walker, "Thomas Massie's Unified Theory of Ron Paul," *Reason*, March 15, 2017, https://reason.com/2017/03/15/thomas-massies-unified -theory-of-ron-pau/.

CHAPTER THIRTEEN: PUBLIC INTELLECTUAL, PRIVATE REACTIONARY

188 **chant onto the stage:** Adrienne Shih, "Protesters Break into Peter Thiel Speaker Event in Wheeler Hall," *Daily Californian*, December 10, 2014, https://www.dailycal.org/2014 /12/10/protestors-break-peter-thiel-speaker-event-wheeler-hall/.

189 **"spinning so much bullshit":** Kevin Montgomery, "Billionaire Peter Thiel Says Technology Isn't Screwing Middle Class," *Valleywag*, November 11, 2014, http://valleywag .gawker.com/billionaire-peter-thiel-says-technology-isnt-screwing-m-1657419404.

189 **"that's somewhat unusual":** Ariana Eunjung Cha, "Peter Thiel's Quest to Find the Key to Eternal Life," *The Washington Post*, April 3, 2015, https://www.washingtonpost.com/busi ness/on-leadership/peter-thiels-life-goal-to-extend-our-time-on-this-earth/2015/04/03 /b7a1779c-4814-11e4-891d-713f052086a0_story.html.

189 **tribune of globalization:** Thomas Friedman, "Welcome to the 'Sharing Economy,'" *The New York Times*, July 20, 2013, https://www.nytimes.com/2013/07/21/opinion/sunday /friedman-welcome-to-the-sharing-economy.html.

189 **"Got Americans to Trust Each Other":** Jason Tanz, "How Airbnb and Lyft Finally Got Americans to Trust Each Other," *Wired*, April 23, 2014, https://www.wired.com/2014 /04/trust-in-the-share-economy/.

190 **Thiel was concerned:** Thiel's 2009 Cato essay refers to the 1920s as the "last decade in American history during which one could be genuinely optimistic about politics," singling out the "vast increase in welfare beneficiaries," in addition to women's suffrage.

190 **back up the shift:** Danielle Sacks, "How Silicon Valley's Obsession with Narrative Changed TaskRabbit," *Fast Company*, July 17, 2013, https://www.fastcompany.com /3012593/taskrabbit-leah-busque.

192 **"America's leading public intellectual":** Roger Parloff, "Peter Thiel Disagrees with You," *Fortune*, September 4, 2014, https://fortune.com/2014/09/04/peter-thiels-contrarian -strategy/.

192 **Thiel laughed this off:** Jennifer Schuessler, "Still No Flying Cars? Debating Technology's Future," *The New York Times*, September 21, 2014, https://www.nytimes.com/2014 /09/22/arts/peter-thiel-and-david-graeber-debate-technologys-future.html?search ResultPosition=1.

193 **"total insider and a total outsider":** For instance, Lillian Cunningham, "Peter Thiel on What Works at Work," *The Washington Post*, October 10, 2014, https://www.washing tonpost.com/news/on-leadership/wp/2014/10/10/peter-thiel-on-what-works-at-work/.

193 **book about Thiel and Gawker:** Holiday's book refers to D'Souza as Mr. A, though D'Souza later acknowledged his role, and told the story of the meeting with Thiel. David Swan, "Gawker's Ruin: 'Mr. A' Revealed," *The Australian*, December 7, 2017.

194 **"which is a big limitation":** Ryan Holiday, *Conspiracy: Peter Thiel, Hulk Hogan, Gawker, and the Anatomy of Intrigue* (New York: Portfolio/Penguin, 2018), 76.

195 **it was winnable:** Holiday, *Conspiracy*, 83.

195 **"even better, sex crime":** Holiday, *Conspiracy*, 76–91; Foster Kramer, "Gawker's March Editorial Review Memo," *The Village Voice*, April 7, 2010, https://www.villagevoice.com /2010/04/07/gawkers-march-editorial-review-memo-essentially-stop-writing-shitty -headlines-also-moar-sex-crimes-plzkthx/.

195 **sue the company:** Holiday, *Conspiracy*, 183.

195 **"a paranoid freakout":** Sam Biddle, "Tinder Confidential: The Hookup App's Founders Can't Swipe Away the Past," *Gawker*, November 23, 2015, https://web.archive.org/web /20151124081258/https://gawker.com/tinder-confidential-the-hookup-apps-founders -cant-swip-1733787036.

196 **"that's not who I am":** "Hulk Hogan on Racial Slurs, His Kids' Reaction to Sex Tape Trial, & More," *The View*, March 23, 2016, https://www.youtube.com/watch?v=xSFsssJKdfM.

199 **closeted to his family:** Tim Murphy, "The Rise and Fall of Twitter's Most Infamous Right-Wing Troll," *Mother Jones*, December 16, 2014, https://www.motherjones.com /politics/2014/12/charles-chuck-johnson-gotnews-rolling-stone/.

199 **a backlash against Michael Brown:** Charles Johnson, "EXCLUSIVE: What We Found on Michael Brown's Instagram Account," *GotNews*, September 5, 2014, https://web .archive.org/web/20140923075236/http://gotnews.com/found-michaelbrowns -instagram-account; Chris Hayes, "Michael Brown's Juvenile Record Had No Serious Criminal Conviction," Fox2Now, September 3, 2014, https://fox2now.com/news/michael -browns-juvenile-record-had-no-serious-criminal-conviction/; Charles Johnson, "What Happened Today at #MichaelBrown Juvenile Court," *GotNews*, September 3, 2014, https:// web.archive.org/web/20140925020517/http://gotnews.com/happened-today -michaelbrown-juvenile-court/.

200 **apologized for the photo:** Charles Johnson, "CORRECTED . . . #JackieCoackley Retweeted Slut Walk 2011," *GotNews*, December 9, 2014, https://web.archive.org/web /20141210054510/http://gotnews.com/breaking-fraud-jackiecoakley-cried-rape-uvahoax/.

200 **connected to Russian intelligence:** Charles Johnson, "Why I Am Suing BuzzFeed's Ryan Mac for Libel Over Peter Thiel Story," Charles Johnson's Thoughts and Adventures, September 12, 2020, https://charlesjohnson.substack.com/p/why-i-am-suing-buzzfeeds-ryan -mac; Mathew Ingram, "Gawker Gets Its First Outside Investment Ever, from a Russian Oligarch," *Fortune*, January 20, 2016, https://fortune.com/2016/01/20/gawker-funding/.

202 **moved on to politics:** Mark Harris, "Disney Should Know the Difference between James Gunn and Roseanne," *Vulture*, July 23, 2018, https://www.vulture.com/2018 /07/james-gunn-is-not-roseanne-and-disney-should-know-it.html; Liam Stack, "Who Is Mike Cernovich? A Guide," *The New York Times*, April 5, 2017, https://www.nytimes .com/2017/04/05/us/politics/mike-cernovich-bio-who.html.

203 **founder of an activist group:** David Holthouse, "'Right-Wing Youth' Group Debuts at CPAC," *Hatewatch*, February 26, 2009, https://www.splcenter.org/hatewatch/2009/02 /26/right-wing-youth-group-debuts-cpac.

203 **according to a court document:** United States v. Marcus Epstein, Superior Court of the District of Columbia, Felony Branch, January 7, 2008, http://www.onepeoplesproject .com/images/Epstein/img072.jpg.

203 **key "ideological architect":** Rosie Gray and Ryan Mac, "Peter Thiel Met with the Racist Fringe as He Went All In on Trump," *BuzzFeed*, September 11, 2020; "Kevin DeAnna" Southern Poverty Law Center Extremist Files, accessed May 15, 2021, https://www .splcenter.org/fighting-hate/extremist-files/individual/kevin-deanna.

204 **"Hail Trump! Hail our people!":** Spencer's gesture, which was filmed by an undercover reporter for *The Atlantic*, was somewhat ambiguous and could have been a rather stiff wave to the crowd. Though dozens of people in the room responded with similar gestures—and Spencer was later filmed doing a Nazi salute at another event.

204 **keep donations secret:** Luke O'Brien, "The Far-Right Helped Create the World's Most Powerful Facial Recognition Technology," *Huffington Post*, April 7, 2020, https://www .huffpost.com/entry/clearview-ai-facial-recognition-alt-right_n_5e7d028bc5b6cb08a 92a5c48.

CHAPTER FOURTEEN: BACKUP PLANS

207 **wearing "assless chaps":** "Peter Thiel's Party Has a Problem: Facebook Investor's Inebri-ated Guests Get Stuck in Elevator," *New York Daily News*, June 22, 2011, https://www .nydailynews.com/entertainment/gossip/peter-thiel-party-problem-facebook-investor -inebriated-guests-stuck-elevator-article-1.128098.

208 **a backup country:** Matt Nippert, "Citizen Thiel," *The New Zealand Herald*, February 1, 2018, https://www.nzherald.co.nz/indepth/national/how-peter-thiel-got-new-zealand -citizenship/.

209 **made a $3 million investment:** Nippert, "Citizen Thiel"; David Streitfeld and Jacque-line Williams, "New Zealand Is 'the Future,' Peter Thiel Said in His Push for Citizen-ship," *The New York Times*, February 1, 2017, https://www.nytimes.com/2017/02/01 /business/peter-thiel-new-zealand-citizenship.html.

209 **showed up to explain:** Pascal-Emmanuel Gobry, "Billionaire Facebook Investor Peter Thiel Pours Money into His 'Utopia,' New Zealand," *Business Insider*, January 14, 2011, https://www.businessinsider.com/peter-thiel-new-zealand-2011-1.

209 **earthquake the previous year:** "Entrepreneur Donates $1 Million to Christchurch," press release from Bell Gully, April 20, 2011, https://www.scoop.co.nz/stories/AK1104 /S00514/entrepreneur-donates-1-million-to-christchurch.htm.

212 **2013 National Review Institute event:** "Peter Thiel at *National Review* Institute Sum-mit," C-SPAN, January 26, 2013, 24, https://www.c-span.org/video/?310618-1/peter-thiel -national-review-institute-summit.

212 **"all the way to the edge":** Fareed Zakaria, interview with Steve Rattner, *Fareed Zakaria GPS*, CNN, July 22, 2012, http://transcripts.cnn.com/TRANSCRIPTS/1207/22/fzgps .01.html. (Disclosure: Rattner manages assets for Mike Bloomberg, my boss's boss's boss.)

212 **pick the right companies:** William Cohan, "What's Really Going on with Mitt Romney's IRA," *The Atlantic*, September 10, 2012, https://www.theatlantic.com/politics/archive /2012/09/whats-really-going-on-with-mitt-romneys-102-million-ira/261500/.

213 **The report noted:** GAO-15-16, "IRS Could Bolster Enforcement on Multimillion Dollar Accounts, but More Direction from Congress Is Needed," October 20, 2014, https:// www.gao.gov/products/GAO-15-16.

216 LETS THE FUR FLY: Meghann Myers, "Odierno Lets the Fur Fly at a House Hearing," *Army Times*, April 26, 2013,http://outsidethewire.armytimes.com/2013/04/26/odierno -lets-the-fur-fly-on-the-house-floor/.

216 **calling Hunter's analysis:** Joe Gould, "McHugh: Rep Was 'Not Correct' in Odierno Kerfuffle," *Army Times*, April 30, 2013, http://outsidethewire.militarytimes.com/2013 /04/30/mchugh-rep-was-not-correct-in-odierno-kerfuffle/.

217 **aired a documentary:** *For the Record*, "Armed & Unaccountable," BlazeTV, April 23, 2014, https://www.youtube.com/watch?v=c1ke9xMBujg.

219 **involved with political work:** Nicholas Confessore and Matthew Rosenberg, "Spy Contractor's Idea Helped Cambridge Analytica Harvest Facebook Data," March 27, 2018, *The New York Times*, https://www.nytimes.com/2018/03/27/us/cambridge-analytica-palantir.html.

220 **on the social media platform:** Connie Loizos, "'When you spend $100 Million on Social Media, It Comes with Help,' Says Trump strategist," *Techcrunch*, November 8, 2017, https://techcrunch.com/2017/11/08/when-you-spend-100-million-on-social-media-it -comes-with-help-says-trump-strategist/.

220 **the Cambridge Analytica offices:** Christopher Wylie, *Mindf*ck: Cambridge Analytica and the Plot to Break America* (New York: Random House, 2019), 83, 112–14.

CHAPTER FIFTEEN: OUT FOR TRUMP

224 **about her appearance:** Paul Solotaroff, "Trump Seriously: On the Trail with the GOP's Tough Guy," *Rolling Stone*, September 9, 2015, https://www.rollingstone.com/politics /politics-news/trump-seriously-on-the-trail-with-the-gops-tough-guy-41447/.

225 **"somewhat lower IQ":** Jamie Weinstein, "Peter Thiel Talks Politics, Living Forever and the Need for the GOP to Get Smarter Reps," *Daily Caller*, September 24, 2014, https:// dailycaller.com/2014/09/24/peter-thiel-talks-politics-living-forever-and-the-need-for -the-gop-to-get-smarter-reps/.

226 **said on *Meet the Press*:** *Meet the Press*, NBC News, August 9, 2015, https://www .nbcnews.com/meet-the-press/meet-press-transcript-august-9-2015-n408516.

227 **to a media circus:** "Trial Judge in Hulk Hogan–Gawker Case Is Most Reversed in Pinellas," *Tampa Bay Times*, March 25, 2016, https://www.tampabay.com/news/courts/trial -judge-in-hulk-hogan-gawker-case-is-most-reversed-in-pinellas/2270818/.

227 **"most humanizing tones":** Sam Thielman, "Nick Denton Grilled in Gawker-Hogan Trial: 'We're Dependent on Leaks,'" *The Guardian*, March 15, 2016, https://www.theguardian .com/media/2016/mar/15/nick-denton-testimony-gawker-hulk-hogan-sex-tape -trial?referrer=justicewire.

228 **"interesting theoretical question":** Kafka, "Why Did Nick Denton Think."

228 **bragging about the length:** Eriq Gardner, "Hulk Hogan Grilled about Sex-Filled TMZ, Howard Stern Interview at Gawker Trial," *Hollywood Reporter*, March 8, 2016, https:// www.hollywoodreporter.com/thr-esq/hulk-hogan-grilled-sex-filled-873435.

229 **published a blog post:** Dan Abrams, "Might a Gawker Hater Be Covering Hulk Hogan's Legal Bills," *Law & Crime*, March 9, 2016, https://lawandcrime.com/high-profile/might -an-anti-gawker-benefactor-be-covering-hulk-hogans-legal-bills/.

230 **a public service:** Andrew Ross Sorkin, "Peter Thiel, Tech Billionaire, Reveals Secret War with Gawker," *The New York Times*, May 25, 2016, https://www.nytimes.com/2016/05/26/business/dealbook/peter-thiel-tech-billionaire-reveals-secret-war-with-gawker.html.

230 **bully media outlets:** Marina Hyde, "Peter Thiel's Mission to Destroy Gawker Isn't 'Philanthropy.' It's a Chilling Taste of Things to Come," *The Guardian*, May 27, 2016, https://www.theguardian.com/commentisfree/2016/may/27/peter-thiel-gawker-philanthropy-paypal-mogul-secret-war-billionaire.

231 **"You can't stop it":** Edmund Lee, "Jeff Bezos on Gawker vs. Peter Thiel," *Recode,* May 31, 2016, https://www.vox.com/2016/5/31/11826118/jeff-bezos-gawker-peter-thiel.

231 **compared him to Batman:** Jonathan Taplin, *Move Fast and Break Things* (New York: Little, Brown, 2017), 155; Milo, "How Peter Thiel Saved Free Speech on the Web," *Breitbart*, May 31, 2016, https://www.breitbart.com/social-justice/2016/05/31/peter-thiel-free-speech/.

231 **used the trending hashtag:** Claire Lehmann, "Thiel vs Gawker: Why a Defensive Media Is the Real Threat to Free Speech," *Quillette*, June 1, 2016, https://quillette.com/2016/06/01/thiel-vs-gawker-why-a-defensive-media-is-the-real-threat-to-free-speech/.

232 **"meeting with him anytime":** Betsy Rothstein, "GotNews' Charles Johnson Has an Indecent Proposal for Nick Denton," *Daily Caller*, June 17, 2016, https://dailycaller.com/2016/06/17/gotnews-charles-johnson-has-an-indecent-proposal-for-nick-denton/.

233 **"sure it's not April 1":** Max Chafkin and Lizette Chapman, "The Strange Politics of Peter Thiel, Trump's Most Unlikely Supporter," *Bloomberg Businessweek*, July 21, 2016, https://www.bloomberg.com/news/articles/2016-07-21/the-strange-politics-of-peter-thiel-trump-s-most-unlikely-supporter?sref=4ZgkJ7cZ.

236 **given to his campaign:** Rebecca Ballhaus and Brody Mullins, "No Fortune 100 CEOs Back Republican Donald Trump," *The Wall Street Journal*, September 23, 2016, https://www.wsj.com/articles/no-fortune-100-ceos-back-republican-donald-trump-1474671842.

236 **news of the event leaked:** Dawn Chmielewski and Ina Fried, "Intel's CEO Planned, Then Scrapped, a Donald Trump Fundraiser," *Recode*, June 1, 2016, https://www.cnbc.com/2016/06/01/intels-ceo-planned-then-scrapped-a-donald-trump-fundraiser.html.

CHAPTER SIXTEEN: THE THIEL THEORY OF GOVERNMENT

241 **conclusion of the convention:** Dowd, "Trump's Tech Pal."

242 **"it's an FEC violation":** Joshua Green and Zachary Mider, "New Super-PAC Launches for Donors Who Won't Back Trump but Loathe Clinton," *Bloomberg News*, June 21, 2016, https://www.bloomberg.com/news/articles/2016-06-22/new-super-pac-launches-for-donors-who-won-t-back-trump-but-loathe-clinton.

243 **"seek out older men":** Glenn Kessler, "The Facts about Hillary Clinton and the Kathy Shelton Rape Case," *The Washington Post*, October 11, 2016, https://www.washingtonpost.com/news/fact-checker/wp/2016/10/11/the-facts-about-hillary-clinton-and-the-kathy-shelton-rape-case/.

244 **the seriously-not-literally line:** Salena Zito, "Taking Trump Seriously, Not Literally," *The Atlantic*, September 23, 2016, https://www.theatlantic.com/politics/archive/2016/09/trump-makes-his-case-in-pittsburgh/501335/.

244 **was the CNBC headline:** Jay Yarrow, "Peter Thiel Perfectly Summed Up Donald Trump in a Few Sentences," CNBC, November 9, 2016, https://www.cnbc.com/2016/11/09/peter-thiel-perfectly-summed-up-donald-trump-in-one-paragraph.html; see also: Dara Lind, "Peter Thiel's Monstrously Naïve Case for Donald Trump," *Vox*, October 31, 2016,

https://www.vox.com/policy-and-politics/2016/10/31/13477236/trump-seriously-literally-thiel.

245 **popular than anything else:** This was a controversial statement in 2016, but it has since been well documented, especially by Kevin Roose at *The New York Times*. See especially: "What If Facebook Is the Real 'Silent Majority,'" August 27, 2020, https://www.nytimes.com/2020/08/27/technology/what-if-facebook-is-the-real-silent-majority.html.

246 **raise $80 million:** Issie Lapowsky, "What Did Cambridge Analytica Really Do for Trump's Campaign," *Wired*, October, 26, 2017, https://www.wired.com/story/what-did-cambridge-analytica-really-do-for-trumps-campaign/.

246 **Facebook engineers embedded:** Deepa Seetharaman, "How a Facebook Employee Helped Trump Win—but Switched Sides for 2020," *The Wall Street Journal*, November 24, 2019, https://www.wsj.com/articles/how-facebooks-embed-in-the-trump-campaign-helped-the-president-win-11574521712.

246 **who were served ads:** Joshua Green and Sasha Issenberg, "Inside the Trump Bunker, With Days to Go," *Bloomberg Businessweek*, October 27, 2016, https://www.bloomberg.com/news/articles/2016-10-27/inside-the-trump-bunker-with-12-days-to-go?sref=4ZgkJ7cZ.

249 **a new moniker:** Eliana Johnson, "Donald Trump's 'Shadow President' in Silicon Valley," *Politico*, February 26, 2017, https://www.politico.com/story/2017/02/donald-trumps-shadow-president-in-silicon-valley-235372.

252 **dangers of climate change:** Scott Walman, "Ex-Trump Adviser: 'Brainwashed' Aides Killed Climate Review," E&E News, December 4, 2019, https://www.eenews.net/stories/1061717133.

252 **presciently pointed out:** Sarah Kaplan, "David Gelernter, Fiercely Anti-intellectual Computer Scientist, Is Being Eyed for Trump's Science Adviser," *The Washington Post*, January 18, 2017, https://www.washingtonpost.com/news/speaking-of-science/wp/2017/01/18/david-gelernter-fiercely-anti-intellectual-computer-scientist-is-being-eyed-for-trumps-science-adviser/.

255 **after just a half hour:** Rosie Gray, "The 'New Right' and the 'Alt-right' Party on a Fractious Night," *The Atlantic*, January 20, 2017, https://www.theatlantic.com/politics/archive/2017/01/the-new-right-and-the-alt-right-party-on-a-fractious-night/514001/.

CHAPTER SEVENTEEN: DEPORTATION FORCE

258 **a "hard look":** Andrew Harris, "Thiel's Palantir Wins Battle over Army Combat Data System," *Bloomberg News*, October 31, 2016, https://www.bloomberg.com/news/articles/2016-10-31/palantir-wins-legal-battle-over-army-combat-data-system.

259 **"and I said yes":** Ryan Mac, "The Trump Administration Has Not Asked Palantir Technologies to Build a Muslim Registry," *Forbes*, January 12, 2017, https://www.forbes.com/sites/ryanmac/2017/01/12/palantir-ceo-has-not-been-asked-to-build-a-muslim-registry-and-would-refuse-anyway/#659f5d667e4c.

260 **millions of undocumented Americans:** Jose A. DelReal, "Trump's Latest Plan Would Target at Least 5 Million Undocumented Immigrants for Deportation," *The Washington Post*, September 1, 2016, https://www.washingtonpost.com/politics/trumps-latest-plan-would-target-at-least-5-million-undocumented-immigrants-for-deportation/2016/09/01/d6f05498-7052-11e6-9705-23e51a2f424d_story.html.

261 **taken out of context:** Stephen Miller, "Tricky Extrapolations," *The Chronicle*, October 26, 2005, https://www.dukechronicle.com/article/2005/10/tricky-extrapolations

263 **More than seven hundred people:** Liz Robbins, "U.S. List of Those Detained for Trump's Travel Ban Is Called Incomplete," *The New York Times*, February 24, 2017, https://www.nytimes.com/2017/02/24/nyregion/travel-ban-trump-detained.html/

263 **"I'm a refugee":** T. C. Sotteck, "Google Co-founder Sergey Brin Joins Protest against Immigration Order at San Francisco Airport," *The Verge*, January 28, 2017, https://www.theverge.com/2017/1/28/14428262/google-sergey-brin.

263 **In an email to staff:** Javier David, "Google, Microsoft Voice Concerns over Trump Immigration Order and Impact on Staff," CNBC, January 28, 2017, https://www.cnbc.com/2017/01/28/google-chief-sundar-pichai-chides-trump-over-immigration-order-affecting-nearly-200-staffers.html.

264 **"the level of criticism":** Casey Newton, "Zuckerberg to Trump: 'Keep Our Doors Open to Refugees,'" *The Verge*, January 27, 2017, https://www.theverge.com/2017/1/27/14420662/zuckerberg-immigration-refugees-trump-executive-orders

264 **"nothing about the dude":** "Here's How a Big Tech CEO Really Feels about Trump," *BuzzFeed*, April 21, 2017, https://www.youtube.com/watch?v=fnh5ImJCfos.

265 **Thiel and Blake Masters:** These documents were disclosed as the result of a freedom of information request by Andrew Granato, a journalist and researcher who'd covered Thiel's influence as a Stanford undergraduate.

266 **he told Maureen Dowd:** Dowd, "Trump's Tech Pal."

266 **such registries had been used:** Jonah Engel Bromwich, "Trump Camp's Talk of Registry and Japanese Internment Raises Muslims' Fears," *The New York Times*, November 18, 2016, https://www.nytimes.com/2016/11/18/us/politics/japanese-internment-muslim-registry.html.

267 **deport anyone charged:** Nicholas Kulish et al., "Trump's Immigration Policies Explained," *The New York Times*, February 2, 2021, https://www.nytimes.com/2017/02/21/us/trump-immigration-policies-deportation.html.

267 **Public records would show:** Spencer Woodman, "Palantir Provides the Engine for Donald Trump's Deportation Machine," *The Intercept*, March 2, 2017, https://theintercept.com/2017/03/02/palantir-provides-the-engine-for-donald-trumps-deportation-machine/.

268 **protestors showed up at Thiel's home:** Jenna Lyons, "Pro-immigrant Demonstrators Rally Outside Peter Thiel's SF Home," *San Francisco Chronicle*, March 14, 2017, https://www.sfgate.com/bayarea/article/Pro-immigrant-demonstrators-rally-outside-Peter-10995442.php; Anna Weiner, "Why Protestors Gathered Outside Peter Thiel's Mansion This Weekend," *The New Yorker*, March 14, 2017, https://www.newyorker.com/news/news-desk/why-protesters-gathered-outside-peter-thiels-mansion-this-weekend.

269 **line about his grandchildren:** Geoff Lewis, "Turn on Reality," *Medium*, November 13, 2016, accessed on May 15, 2012, https://medium.com/@justglew/turn-on-reality-f4331d007f3c; original post accessed via Internet Archive, November 14, 2016, https://web.archive.org/web/20161114060128/https://medium.com/turnonreality/turn-on-reality-f4331d007f3c.

271 **"least contrarian things":** For instance, Peter Thiel, interviewed by Maria Bartiromo, Economic Club of New York, March 15, 2018.

CHAPTER EIGHTEEN: EVIL LIST

274 **restaurants and other businesses:** Julian Guthrie, "Yelp's Jeremy Stoppelman: A profile," *The San Francisco Chronicle*, July 14, 2012, https://www.sfgate.com/news/article/Yelp-s-Jeremy-Stoppelman-a-profile-3707980.php; Erik Schonfeld, "Google Places Stops Stealing Reviews," *Techcrunch*, July 21, 2011, https://techcrunch.com/2011/07/21/google-places-stops-stealing-reviews/.

275 **"In our lifetimes"**: "Transcript: Schmidt and Thiel Smackdown," *Fortune*, July 17, 2012, https://fortune.com/2012/07/17/transcript-schmidt-and-thiel-smackdown/.

276 **negative results about Clinton**: Allana Akhtar, "Google Defends Its Search Engine Against Charges It Favors Clinton," *USA Today*, June 10, 2016, https://www.usatoday.com/story/tech/news/2016/06/10/google-says-search-isnt-biased-toward-hillary-clinton/85725014/.

276 **"rap than it deserves"**: Rubin, "Trump, Gawker, and Leaving Silicon Valley," 1:18.

277 **the Men's Rights movement**: Paul Lewis, "'I See Things Differently': James Damore on His Autism and the Google Memo," *The Guardian*, November 16, 2017, https://www.theguardian.com/technology/2017/nov/16/james-damore-google-memo-interview-autism-regrets.

278 **leaked the memo**: Kate Conger, "Exclusive: Here's the Full 10-Page Anti-Diversity Screed Circulating Internally at Google," *Gizmodo*, August 5, 2017, https://gizmodo.com/exclusive-heres-the-full-10-page-anti-diversity-screed-1797564320.

278 **"They betrayed me"**: Emily Chang, "Fired Engineer James Damore: I Feel Google Betrayed Me," *Bloomberg Technology*, Bloomberg TV, August 9, 2017, https://www.bloomberg.com/news/videos/2017-08-10/fired-engineer-damore-i-feel-google-betrayed-me-video

279 **"individual consumers as Google"**: Daisuke Wakabayashi, "Missouri Opens Antitrust Investigation into Google," *The New York Times*, November 13, 2017, https://www.nytimes.com/2017/11/13/technology/missouri-google-investigation.html.

280 **for an onstage chat**: "Cardinal Conversations: Reid Hoffman and Peter Thiel on 'Technology and Politics,'" interviewed by Niall Ferguson, Hoover Institution, January 31, 2018, https://www.hoover.org/news/stanford-first-cardinal-conversation-spotlights-technology-politics.

282 **connect his move**: Thiel, Economic Club of New York, 2018.

282 **very smart but "brainwashed"**: Rubin, "Trump, Gawker, and Leaving Silicon Valley," 17:58.

284 **critics on the left**: Alex Shephard, "Peter Thiel's Lonely Culture War," *The New Republic*, February 16, 2018, https://newrepublic.com/article/147109/peter-thiels-lonely-culture-war.

283 **"a sort of totalitarian place"**: Maria Bartiromo, "Peter Thiel on Leaving Silicon Valley for Los Angeles," Fox Business, March 16, 2018, https://www.youtube.com/watch?v=v_NhYV63K5E.

283 **senior staff also included**: Jacqueline Klimas and Bryan Bender, "Palantir Goes from Pentagon Outsider to Mattis' Inner Circle," *Politico*, June 11, 2017, https://www.politico.com/story/2017/06/11/palantir-defense-jim-mattis-inner-circle-239373.

286 **government was inflicting on children**: Dara Lind, "'A Recipe for Toxic Stress': An Expert on Why Trump's Family Separation Policy Is So Damaging to Kids," *Vox*, June 20, 2018, https://www.vox.com/policy-and-politics/2018/6/20/17480680/child-separate-parent-trauma-effects.

286 **an eight-minute recording**: Ginger Thompson, "Listen to Children Who've Just Been Separated from Their Parents at the Border," *ProPublica*, June 18, 2018, https://www.propublica.org/article/children-separated-from-parents-border-patrol-cbp-trump-immigration-policy.

286 **in which young children**: Gabrielle Schonder, "The Frontline Interview: Kris Kobach," *Frontline*, PBS, August 20, 2019, https://www.pbs.org/wgbh/frontline/interview/kris-kobach/.

286 **advocacy group Mijente**: "Anduril's New Border Surveillance Contract with the U.S. Marine Corps and CPB," *Mijente*, July 24, 2019, https://mijente.net/2019/07/anduril/; "Palantir Played Key Role in Arresting Families for Deportation, Document Shows," Mijente, May 2, 2019, https://mijente.net/2019/05/palantir-arresting-families/.

286 **advanced artificial intelligence:** Steven Levy, "Inside Anduril, Palmer Luckey's Bid to Build a Border Wall," *Wired*, June 11, 2018, https://www.wired.com/story/palmer-luckey -anduril-border-wall/.

286 **posted the same message:** Kari Paul, "Tech Workers Protest Data Mining Firm Palantir for Role in Immigrant Arrests," *The Guardian*, May 13, 2019, https://www.theguardian .com/us-news/2019/may/13/tech-workers-palantir-immigration-protest-github.

287 **cut ties with it:** Tom McKay, "Dozens Arrested at #JewsAgainstICE Protest at Amazon Store in NYC," *Gizmodo*, August 11, 2019, https://gizmodo.com/dozens-arrested-at-jewsa gainstice-protest-at-amazon-st-1837156701.

288 **The effort, Project Dragonfly:** Mark Bergen, "Google in China: When 'Don't Be Evil' Met the Great Firewall," *Bloomberg Businessweek*, November 8, 2011, https://www .bloomberg.com/news/features/2018-11-08/google-never-stopped-trying-to-go-to -china?sref=4ZgkJ7cZ.

289 **went on CNBC:** "Joe Lonsdale: Google Is Not a Patriotic Company," *Squawk Alley*, CNBC, July 15, 2019, https://www.youtube.com/watch?v=gsmY64N7Y1w.

290 **landing the contract:** Cade Metz et al., "What's a Palantir? The Tech Industry's Next Big I.P.O.," *The New York Times*, August 26, 2020, https://www.nytimes.com/2020/08 /26/technology/palantir-ipo.html.

CHAPTER NINETEEN: TO THE MAT

291 **urged Zuckerberg to consider:** Kirkpatrick, *The Facebook Effect*.

292 **early-morning board meeting:** Steven Levy, *Facebook: The Inside Story* (New York: Blue Rider Press, 2020), 158.

292 **not long after the IPO:** Michael Wolff, "The Facebook Fallacy," *MIT Technology Review*, May 22, 2012, https://www.technologyreview.com/2012/05/22/255726/the-face book-fallacy/.

293 **"we know what we're doing":** Levy, *Facebook*, 293.

293 **"clown car that fell":** Nick Bilton, *Hatching Twitter: A True Story of Money, Power, Friendship, and Betrayal* (New York: Portfolio, 2014).

295 **hadn't bothered mentioning:** Elizabeth Dwoskin, "Facebook Thought It Was More Powerful than a Nation State. Then that Became a Liability," *The Washington Post*, January 22, 2018, https://www.washingtonpost.com/business/economy/inside-facebooks -year-of-reckoning/2018/01/22/cfd7307c-f4c3-11e7-beb6-c8d48830c54d_story.html.

296 **political disputes at Facebook:** Nick Wingfield, "The Culture Wars Have Come to Silicon Valley," *The New York Times*, August 8, 2017, https://www.nytimes.com/2017/08 /08/technology/the-culture-wars-have-come-to-silicon-valley.html.

298 **James O'Keefe, years earlier:** Russell Brandon and Colin Lecher, "Facebook Says It Fired Leaker for Participating in Conservative Bias 'Stunt'," *The Verge*, February 27, 2019, https:// www.theverge.com/2019/2/27/18243097/facebook-leaker-project-veritas-moderation-doc uments; Steven Thrasher, "Conservative Facebook Investor Funded Anti-ACORN Videographer," *The Village Voice*, September 22, 2009, https://www.villagevoice.com/2009 /09/22/conservative-facebook-investor-funded-anti-acorn-videographer/.

298 **unwillingness to stop disinformation:** Jeff Horwitz and Deepa Seetharaman, "Chenault Leaves Facebook Board after Disagreements with Zuckerberg," *The Wall Street Journal*, March 13, 2020, https://www.wsj.com/articles/chenault-leaves-facebook-board-after -disagreements-with-zuckerberg-11584140731.

299 **displayed copies of Xi's book:** Adam Taylor, "Why Would Mark Zuckerberg Want Facebook Employees to Read the Chinese President's Book?" *The Washington Post*,

December 8, 2014, https://www.washingtonpost.com/news/worldviews/wp/2014/12/08/ why-does-mark-zuckerberg-want-facebook-employees-to-read-the-chinese-presidents-book/.

299 **honorary Chinese name:** Emily Smith, "Chinese President Snubs Mark Zuckerberg's Unborn Child," *The New York Post*, October 2, 2015, https://pagesix.com/2015/10/02 /chinese-president-snubs-mark-zuckerbergs-unborn-child/.

299 **disseminated pro-Trump hoaxes:** Sheera Frenkel et al., "Delay, Deny, Deflect: How Facebook's Leaders Fought through Crisis," *The New York Times*, November 14, 2018, https://www.nytimes.com/2018/11/14/technology/facebook-data-russia-election -racism.html.

299 **"This is fun":** Matt Weaver, "Video: Dale Jr. Turns Facebook's Mark Zuckerberg into a NASCAR Fan with Test Drive," *Autoweek*, March 14, 2017, https://www.autoweek.com /racing/nascar/a1816901/video-dale-jr-turns-facebooks-mark-zuckerberg-nascar-fan -test-drive/.

299 **"adviser to the Trump Administration":** Mark Zuckerberg, filmed May 12, 2017, at North Carolina A&T State University, https://www.youtube.com/watch?v=jyuoABPtDzc.

300 **told CNN that Facebook:** Tom McKay, "Kamala Harris Says 'We Have to Seriously Take a Look At' Breaking Up Facebook, *Gizmodo*, May 12, 2019, https://gizmodo.com /kamala-harris-says-we-need-to-seriously-take-a-look-at-1834706259.

300 **"vigorous antitrust legislation":** "Democratic Presidential Candidate Sen. Bernie Sand-ers Talks 2020 Election," Washington Post Live, July 16, 2019, https://www.youtube .com/watch?v=3YYSlyyOXA4.

301 **meeting with employees:** Casey Newton, "Read the Full Transcript of Mark Zuckerberg's Leaked Internal Facebook Meetings," *The Verge*, October 1, 2019, https://www.theverge .com/2019/10/1/20892354/mark-zuckerberg-full-transcript-leaked-facebook-meetings.

301 **proclaim the Trump presidency:** Andrew Ross Sorkin "New York Times Dealbook Conference," November 1, 2018, https://www.youtube.com/watch?v=VanFeyKDJSI.

302 **Gaetz later wrote:** Matt Gaetz, *Firebrand: Dispatches from the Front Lines of the MAGA Revolution* (New York: Post Hill Press, 2020), 148.

303 **CNN refused to air:** Michael Grynbaum and Tiffany Hsu, "CNN Rejects 2 Trump Campaign Ads, Citing Inaccuracies," *The New York Times*, October 3, 2019, https://www .nytimes.com/2019/10/03/business/media/cnn-trump-campaign-ad.html.

304 **allied with the alt-right:** Julia Carrie Wong, "Facebook Includes Breitbart in New 'High Quality' News Tab," *The Guardian*, October 25, 2019, https://www.theguardian.com/us -news/2019/oct/25/facebook-breitbart-news-tab-alt-right.

304 **biggest publishers on the platform:** Judd Legum and Tesnim Zekeria, "The Dirty Secret behind Ben Shapiro's Extraordinary Success on Facebook," *Popular Information*, June 25, 2020, https://popular.info/p/the-dirty-secret-behind-ben-shapiros; Judd Legum and Emily Atkin, "Fact-Check of Viral Climate Misinformation Quietly Removed from Facebook," *Heated*, July 20, 2020, https://heated.world/p/fact-check-of-viral-climate -misinformation.

304 **Zuckerberg denied that:** Mike Allen, "Zuckerberg: No Deal with Trump," *Axios*, July 20, 2020, https://www.axios.com/mark-zuckerberg-trump-facebook-interview-ae28771f -71b9-4df8-bc4b-d9088a99a740.html.

304 **rules against misinformation:** Craig Silverman and Ryan Mac, "Facebook Fired an Employee Who Collected Evidence of Right-Wing Pages Getting Preferential Treat-ment," *BuzzFeed*, August 6, 2020, https://www.buzzfeednews.com/article/craigsilverman /facebook-zuckerberg-what-if-trump-disputes-election-results; Ryan Mac and Craig Sil-verman, "'Mark Changed the Rules': How Facebook Went East on Alex Jones and Other Right-Wing Figures," *BuzzFeed*, February 22, 2021, https://www.buzzfeednews.com

/article/ryanmac/mark-zuckerberg-joel-kaplan-facebook-alex-jones; Sarah Frier and Kurt Wagner, "Facebook Needs Trump Even More Than Trump Needs Facebook," *Bloomberg*, September 17, 2020, https://www.bloomberg.com/news/features/2020-09-17/facebook-and-mark-zuckerberg-need-trump-even-more-than-trump-needs-facebook?sref=4ZgkJ7cZ

CHAPTER TWENTY: BACK TO THE FUTURE

305 **handful of well-known favorites:** Tim Schneider, "How Artist Simon Denny Is Turning Board Games into Hilarious Critiques of Digital Capitalism," *Artnet*, April 2, 2018, https://news.artnet.com/art-world/banksy-guest-stars-sort-of-on-the-latest-episode-of-hbos-silicon-valley-1258157.

306 **Thiel's likeness appeared:** Kristen Brown, "Of Course Peter Thiel Is a Green-Skinned Villain in This Board Game," *Gizmodo*, January 18, 2018, https://gizmodo.com/of-course-peter-thiel-is-a-green-skinned-villain-in-thi-1821514712.

306 **Thiel had remarked to an attendee:** Matt Nippert, "Billionaire Peter Thiel Makes a Rare Visit to New Zealand," *The New Zealand Herald*, December 9, 2017, https://www.nzherald.co.nz/business/billionaire-peter-thiel-makes-rare-visit-to-new-zealand/YS3MSBFDSDRS5QP6KKJXTPCZNU/.

306 **a record price:** "Peter Thiel Buys Maui Home for a Record $27 Million," *The Wall Street Journal*, July 15, 2011, https://www.wsj.com/articles/SB10001424052702304911104576444362936635124.

308 **and ultimately flawed:** Riley Beggin, "Report: The CDC Contaminated Its First Coronavirus Tests, Setting US Back," *Vox*, April, 18, 2020, https://www.vox.com/2020/4/18/21226372/coronavirus-tests-cdc-contaminated-delay-testing.

308 **"Software is eating the world":** Marc Andreessen, "Why Software Is Eating the World," Andreessen Horowitz, August 20, 2011, https://a16z.com/2011/08/20/why-software-is-eating-the-world/.

311 **two more contracts, worth $25 million:** Dave Nyczepir, "HHS Cites Coronavirus 'Urgency' in Speedy Palantir Contract Awards," *FedScoop*, May 8, 2020, https://www.fedscoop.com/hha-covid-funds-palantir/.

311 **former CDC director accused:** Charles Ornstein, "Out of View: After Public Outcry CDC Adds Hospital Data Back to Its Website—for Now," *ProPublica*, July 16, 2020, https://www.propublica.org/article/out-of-view-after-public-outcry-cdc-adds-hospital-data-back-to-its-website-for-now.

312 **the journalist Felix Salmon:** Felix Salmon, "They're Best Friends," *Twitter*, June 23, 2020, https://twitter.com/felixsalmon/status/1275604535709446146.

314 **insufficiently loyal to Trump:** Garret Lewis, "Garret Talks to Blake Masters, COO Thiel Capital," KNST, October 14, 2019, https://knst.iheart.com/featured/garret-lewis/content/2019-10-14-garret-talks-to-blake-masters-coo-thiel-capital/.

314 **opposing gay rights:** "Romney Adviser Kris Kobach Likens Homosexuality to Drug Use and Polygamy," *Queerty*, August 23, 2012, http://www.queerty.com/kris-kobach-homosexuality-drug-use-polygamy-20120823/.

315 **"numbers are being cooked":** Graig Graziosi, "Republican Senate Hopeful Says Coronavirus Numbers Being 'Cooked' to Hurt Trump," *The Independent*, July 28, 2020, https://www.independent.co.uk/news/world/americas/us-politics/coronavirus-deaths-trump-republican-senate-kris-kobach-a9642731.html.

316 **Tesla workers in Fremont:** Neal E. Boudette, "Hundreds of Tesla Workers Tested Positive for the Virus after Elon Musk Reopened a Plant, Data Shows," *The New York Times*,

March 13, 2021, https://www.nytimes.com/2021/03/13/world/tesla-elon-musk-coronavirus-outbreak.html.

316 **virus as the "sniffles":** "Trump Says Son Barron's Covid Illness 'Just Went Away,'" NBC News, October 22, 2020, https://www.nbcnews.com/video/trump-says-son-barron-s-covid-illness-just-went-away-94447173800.

317 **"control the pandemic":** "Mark Meadows: We're Not Going to Control the Pandemic," CNN, October 25, 2020, https://www.youtube.com/watch?v=tN9T73GWam0.

319 **planning on doing immediately:** Danny Crichton, "In Its 5th Filing with the SEC Palantir Finally Admits It Is Not a Democracy," *TechCrunch*, September 21, 2020, https://techcrunch.com/2020/09/21/palantir-is-not-a-democracy/.

320 **stolen the election for Biden:** Curtis Yarvin, "Reflections on the Late Election," *Gray Mirror*, November 8, 2020 https://graymirror.substack.com/p/reflections-on-the-late-election. (The emphasis on "outside" was Yarvin's.)

320 **summed it up succinctly:** Ari Levy, "Peter Thiel's Palantir Is Skyrocketing as Trump's Prospects Grow Dim," CNBC, November 6, 2020, https://www.cnbc.com/2020/11/06/peter-thiels-palantir-is-skyrocketing-as-trumps-prospects-grow-dim.html.

321 **"back to the future":** See for instance, "Back to the Future with Peter Thiel," *National Review*, January 2011, https://www.nationalreview.com/2011/01/back-future-peter-thiel-interview/.

322 **viciously attacked journalists:** Matthew Daly and Michael Balsamo, "Deadly Siege Focuses Attention on Capitol Police," AP, January 8, 2021, https://apnews.com/article/capitol-police-death-brian-sicknick-46933a828d7b12de7e3d5620a8a04583.

323 **"big lie" perpetrated by him:** Alexander Bolton, "Hawley, Cruz Face Rising Anger, Possible Censure," *The Hill*, January 12, 2021, https://thehill.com/homenews/senate/533740-hawley-cruz-face-rising-anger-possible-censure.

323 **a short item:** Dan Primack, "What Peter Thiel Got Wrong about Donald Trump," *Axios*, January 11, 2021, https://www.axios.com/peter-thiel-donald-trump-venture-capitalist-007f70ba-e851-4f6e-af12-a18df6d0612e.html.

EPILOGUE: YOU WILL LIVE FOREVER

325 **2016 study on mice:** Justin Rebo et al., "A Single Heterochronic Blood Exchange Reveals Rapid Inhibition of Multiple Tissues by Old Blood," *Nature*, November 22, 2016, https://www.nature.com/articles/ncomms13363.

326 **interview published that year:** Jeff Bercovici, "Peter Thiel Is Very, Very Interested in Young People's Blood," *Inc.*, August 1, 2016, https://www.inc.com/jeff-bercovici/peter-thiel-young-blood.html.

326 **from an eighteen-year-old:** J. K. Trotter, "Peter Thiel Is Interested in Harvesting the Blood of the Young," *Gawker*, August 1, 2016, https://gawker.com/peter-thiel-is-interested-in-harvesting-the-blood-of-th-1784649830?rev=1470074599426.

327 **was fired the following month** Ron Leuty, "Aging-focused foundation cuts ties with founder amid sexual harassment investigation," San Francisco Business Times, August 23, 2021, https://www.bizjournals.com/sanfrancisco/news/2021/08/23/sexua-harass-ment-aging-aubrey-de-grey-sens.html.

328 **a mental pathology:** Roger Köppel, "Ich unterstütze Trump noch immer," *Die Weltwoch*, August 12, 2020, https://www.weltwoche.ch/ausgaben/2020-33/diese-woche/ich-unterstutze-trump-noch-immer-die-weltwoche-ausgabe-33-2020.html.

331 **"ever made in my life":** Bryan Lowry, "'The Biggest Mistake I've Ever Made.' Danforth Rues Mentoring Hawley, Blames Him for Riot," *The Kansas City Star*, January 7, 2021, https://www.kansascity.com/article248346830.html.

332 **"cancel culture agenda":** Josh Hawley, "It's Time to Stand Up against the Muzzling of America," *The New York Post*, January 24, 2021. https://nypost.com/2021/01/24/its -time-to-stand-up-against-the-muzzling-of-america/.

332 **Mar-a-Lago in the spring:** Alex Isenstadt, "Rise of a Megadonor: Thiel Makes a Play for the Senate," *Politico*, May 17, 2021, https://www.politico.com/news/2021/05/17/peter -thiel-senate-megadonor-488799.

335 **to do with Thiel:** "Peter Thiel's CS183: Startup—Class 18 Notes Essay," Blakemasters .com, June 6, 2012, https://blakemasters.com/post/24578683805/peter-thiels-cs183-start up-class-18-notes.

IMAGE CREDITS

INDEX